Regional Nationalism in Spain

LINGUISTIC DIVERSITY AND LANGUAGE RIGHTS
Series Editor: Dr Tove Skutnabb-Kangas, *Roskilde University, Denmark*

Consulting Advisory Board:
François Grin, *Université de Genève, Switzerland*
Kathleen Heugh, *Human Services Research Council, South Africa*
Miklós Kontra, *Linguistics Institute, Hungarian Academy of Sciences,Budapest*
Masaki Oda, *Tamagawa University, Japan*

The series seeks to promote multilingualism as a resource, the maintenance of
linguistic diversity, and development of and respect for linguistic human rights
worldwide through the dissemination of theoretical and empirical research. The series
encourages interdisciplinary approaches to language policy, drawing on
sociolinguistics, education, sociology, economics, human rights law, political science,
as well as anthropology, psychology, and applied language studies.

Other Books in the Series
Medium or Message? Language and Faith in Ethnic Churches
    Anya Woods
Imagining Multilingual Schools: Language in Education and Glocalization
    Ofelia García, Tove Skutnabb-Kangas and María Torres-Guzmán (eds)
Minority Languages and Cultural Diversity in Europe
    Konstanze Glaser
Global Issues in Language, Education and Development
    Naz Rassool

Other Books of Interest
English in Africa: After the Cold War
    Alamin M. Mazrui
Ideology and Image: Britain and Language
    Dennis Ager
Language and Society in a Changing Italy
    Arturo Tosi
Language Attitudes in Sub-Saharan Africa
    Efurosibina Adegbija
Linguistic Minorities in Central and Eastern Europe
    Christina Bratt Paulston and Donald Peckham (eds)
Multilingualism in Spain
    M. Teresa Turell (ed.)
Negotiating of Identities in Multilingual Contexts
    Aneta Pavlenko and Adrian Blackledge (eds)
The Other Languages of Europe
    Guus Extra and Durk Gorter (eds)
Where East Looks West: Success in English in Goa and on the Konkan Coast
    Dennis Kurzon
Understanding Deaf Culture: In Search of Deafhood
    Paddy Ladd

For more details of these or any other of our publications, please contact:
Multilingual Matters, Frankfurt Lodge, Clevedon Hall,
Victoria Road, Clevedon, BS21 7HH, England
http://www.multilingual-matters.com

LINGUISTIC DIVERSITY AND LANGUAGE RIGHTS 5
Series Editor: Tove Skutnabb-Kangas, *Roskilde University, Denmark*

Regional Nationalism in Spain
Language Use and Ethnic Identity in Galicia

Jaine E. Beswick

MULTILINGUAL MATTERS LTD
Clevedon • Buffalo • Toronto

Library of Congress Cataloging in Publication Data
Beswick, Jaine E.
Regional Nationalism in Spain: Language Use and Ethnic Identity in Galicia/Jaine E. Beswick.
Linguistic Diversity and Lanugage Rights: 5
Includes bibliographical references and index.
1. Sociolinguistics–Spain–Galicia (Region) 2. Ethnicity–Spain–Galicia (Region)
 3. Galician language–History. 4. Nationalism–Spain–Galicia (Region) I. Title.
P40.45.S7B47 2007
305.7'69–dc22   2007000091

British Library Cataloguing in Publication Data
A catalogue entry for this book is available from the British Library.

ISBN-13: 978-1-85359-980-4 (hbk)
ISBN-13: 978-1-85359-979-8 (pbk)

Multilingual Matters Ltd
UK: Frankfurt Lodge, Clevedon Hall, Victoria Road, Clevedon BS21 7HH.
USA: UTP, 2250 Military Road, Tonawanda, NY 14150, USA.
Canada: UTP, 5201 Dufferin Street, North York, Ontario M3H 5T8, Canada.

The policy of Multilingual Matters/Channel View Publications is to use papers that are natural, renewable and recyclable products, made from wood grown in sustainable forests. In the manufacturing process of our books, and to further support our policy, preference is given to printers that have FSC and PEFC Chain of Custody certification. The FSC and/or PEFC logos will appear on those books where full certification has been granted to the printer concerned.

Typeset by Techset Composition Ltd.
Printed and bound in Great Britain by the Cromwell Press Ltd.

Contents

Illustrations

Acknowledgements

First, thanks are due to Clive Willis at the University of Manchester for introducing me to Galicia and its language in the first place, and for his kind agreement to write the foreword to this book. A particular mention must be made of Tove Skutnabb-Kangas, my editor, Rodney Sampson at the University of Bristol, and Xosé Regueira Fernández at the University of Santiago de Compostela, for all their insightful comments and constructive criticisms. I am particularly indebted to Jane Freeland at URACCAN/University of Southampton, for her huge support, camaraderie, and kindness in the final stages of this project. I am also grateful to the various websites detailed in the bibliography for their kind permission to use data, maps, and charts. Special recognition goes to my mother Shirley, my father Fred, and my brother John, for their unwavering faith in me. Most of all, huge thanks are due to Julian for his unquestionable support, without which this book would not have been possible, and to Scarlett, who makes it all worthwhile.

Graciñas!

Foreword

There can be little doubt that there is a close link between ethnic identity and language. The case of the autochthonous language of Galicia merits particular interest, existing, as it does, alongside Spain's national language, Castilian. The sundry, varying, and discrete problems of linguistic dualism, as typified, say, by Belgium or Wales, or even the Basque Country, are not replicated in Galicia. There the issues are of a different order. In this instance, the inhabitants of the autonomous region of Galicia have to confront the challenge of two languages between which there is a strong affinity and much common ancestry as erstwhile Romance dialects.

Superficially, that challenge would appear to resemble the one faced by Catalonia. The respective autochthonous languages, Galician and Catalan, experienced periods of medieval vigour, exemplified by the brilliant florescence of their literatures. However, with effect from the closing years of the 15th century, the ever-increasing political, economic, and cultural hegemony exercised by Castile, abetted by its language, subordinated Galician and Catalan to much lesser and inferior roles. Both cultures saw a partial linguistic and literary resurgence in the 19th century with the Catalan *Renaixença* (from 1833) and the Galician *Rexurdimento* (from 1853). Yet, the 20th century brought periods of attempted suppression, especially, although not exclusively, during the years of the Franco dictatorship (1936–1975). Finally, the creation, after Franco, of the democratic Spain of the autonomous regions brought new vigour, through the 'Laws of Linguistic Normalisation', to the autochthonous languages of both regions (as well as to Basque). These were laws that authorised the co-existence of the national language and the regional languages and encouraged the teaching of the latter, as well as of the former.

Nevertheless, there the similarities end. From the very outset, the Catalan language had higher prestige. Catalonia enjoyed the powerful economic and political thrust of Madrid's great rival, Barcelona, and sunny Costa Brava's booming international holiday industry brought commercial triumphs that rainy Galicia, with less than half Catalonia's population and a much lower economic performance, could not ever hope to emulate. Catalan nationalism, too, was never far beneath the surface. With the enthusiastic support of many in the professional and political classes, the future of Catalan was readily ensured. Moreover, Catalan is a language with both Gallo-Romance and Ibero-Romance characteristics, and is structurally more distinct from Castilian than is Galician.

By contrast, Galician began its recovery with low prestige. Essentially, it was a far from uniform language, largely spoken in rural areas and often by people whose appreciation of the finer differences between Galician and Castilian was so (understandably) confused that a jumble of both tended to emerge. For all that, it was vehemently championed by academics and other men and women of letters, but the professional classes were, on the whole, reluctant to follow. Why learn both, especially as they were apparently so similar, and one an inferior 'dialect'? A further complication rested on the fact that, despite the evident closeness of Galician and Castilian, the former is structurally closer still to Portuguese. The latent political overtones of proceeding down a 'Portuguese' route became only too obvious. There was inevitable feuding on questions of orthography and, to some extent, on pronunciation.

Yet the recovery was bolstered by three events: the publication in 1982 of the *Normas ortográficas e morfolóxicas do idioma galego*, sponsored by the *Real Academia Galega* and the *Instituto da Lingua Galega*, the issuing in 1983 of the *Lei de normalización lingüística* and the triumphant appearance in 1986 of the *Gramática galega* of Álvarez, Regueira and Monteagudo. The citadel of *galego estándar* had been comprehensively seized. These events led to a gradual eclosion of the language. Yet, differences of attitude pervaded through the early years and still persist. Resistance by those who uniquely spoke Castilian, especially in the cities, was the principal but not the only roadblock. Objections also continued to come from minority groups like the *Associaçom da Língua Galega* and the *Irmandades da Fala*, fronted by academics of no little standing and backed by certain publishers and publications. Their wish was to 'reintegrate' Galician within the current of Portuguese, and they resented deeply the orthographic *Normas* of 1982 and what they saw as the 'castilianisation' of Galician.

Three decades after the end of the Franco era, Dr Beswick charts the historical background to the fall and the rise of Galician, examines the particular characteristics that differentiate it and, most importantly, scrutinises objectively and closely the attitudinal, ethnic, and sociolinguistic issues that surround the strategies and procedures of *normalización*.

Clive Willis
Emeritus Professor of Portuguese Studies,
University of Manchester

Introduction

A lingua é o símbolo de identificación colectiva por excelencia e nela se sintetiza a maneira de ser e de pensar dese pobo que contribuíu á súa configuración durante séculos . . . . Nela está sintetizada toda a historia e a personalidade dun pobo, converténdose na verdadeira alma do mesmo.

[A people's language is the most important collective symbol of identification bar none, within which the ethnicity and attitude of this people are united – this people who have contributed for centuries to its elaboration . . . . Within the language all the history and character of a people are unified, which transforms it into the representation of their very essence].[1]

(Freixeiro Mato, 1997: 11)

Galicia is the region of Spain situated in the northwestern corner of the Iberian Peninsula, bordered to the north by the Cantabrian Sea, to the west by the Atlantic Ocean, to the south by the country of Portugal and to the east by the other Spanish regions of Asturias, León, and Zamora. Spain is one of the largest countries in continental Europe, with a total surface area, including the Balearic and Canary Islands, of 505,182 km². Galicia occupies some 29,574 km², that is, nearly 6% of the mainland surface area of just over 493,000 km². Its four provinces are A Coruña, Lugo, Ourense, and Pontevedra. The municipal register of January 2004 puts the official population of Spain at 43,197,684 and that of Galicia at 2,750,985, that is, just less than 6.5% of the total (INE, 2005).

This book arose out of a long-standing desire to bring together research and fieldwork carried out in the 1990s and early 2000s into the relationship between the Galician language and Galician ethnic identity. Since the introduction of the *Normas Ortográficas e Morfolóxicas do Galego* [The Orthographic and Morphological Standards of Galician] in the early 1980s, the aim of which was to standardise the language of Galician, there has been much debate and discussion, primarily within the region itself but also further afield, into their viability and usefulness. This book considers the case of Galician linguistic, ethnic, and cultural revival in a way that underlines its wider implications for the task of reviving, revitalising,

Map 1 Spain and its regions[2]

and maintaining minoritised languages in general. To do this, it adopts an innovative analytical framework, bringing together both linguistic and sociolinguistic analyses of languages in contact.

One of my more original contributions is to consider whether language change phenomena and methodologies can be employed to plot language shift. I appraise the potential for using an apparent time analysis to examine the use of different languages at different life stages, in order to determine whether one language is generally used more at one stage in life than another, or whether a shift in language use is taking place. I also present diachronic and synchronic linguistic analyses of the similarities and differences between Galician, Castilian Spanish, and Portuguese, the three languages in question, as well as a sociolinguistic analysis of their differentiated and overlapping uses in different social contexts. I examine attitudes and loyalties to the Galician language and I evaluate how these complexities relate to the expression of a Galician ethnic identity. In doing so, my intention is to present a comprehensive introduction to the issues surrounding Galician ethnicity and language

Map 2 Galicia[3]

use, in the hope that it will incite the reader to go forth and find out even more.

However, the book both is, and is not, a book about language rights. It plainly is, in that its focus is a particular case study of language revitalisation (of Galician) in a country (Spain) where, following a sustained period of subordination and repression, language rights have been recently conceded, are firmly embedded in national legislation, and are being implemented, upheld, and financed. Yet the primary point of interest is what happens once linguistic rights are won *de jure*: what are the problems and complications of implementing such rights in a particular social, historical, and linguistic context.

Much of the attraction of this case lies in the fact that language rights were granted on the same terms to all the diverse 'nations within the nation' of Spain, terms that derive (as they always have so far) from a nationalist discourse that imagines a clear relationship between nation/ ethnicity, one language/one territory. Yet, in Galicia, none of the constituent parts of this equation is as clear cut as the equation assumes. Because of their history, Galicia and the Galician language are now seen to occupy a social, historical, and linguistic 'transition zone' between Portuguese and Castilian.

This book briefly traces the origins of this situation through the historic interaction of Galicia with both Portugal and Castile. It discusses the inequalities of power this produced for Galicia and examines both the historical and contemporary implications of this situation, especially as these implications affect whether, and how, Galician is to be distinguished from the other two languages and their inherent identities, and what this means for the revitalisation and long-term survival of Galician.

The principal hypothesis of this book is fourfold. First, that the Galician language, whether used or not, may be an intrinsic characteristic of Galician ethnic identity. Secondly, that linguistic policies and planning impact on the behavioural practices of language users, and these practices, in turn, may be reflected in their attitudes towards the language. Thirdly, that although a reversal in traditional perceptions and attitudes is resulting in a reaffirmation of Galician as the autochthonous language, its sociolinguistic relationship with Castilian has not been resolved. Fourthly, that Galicians have to negotiate multiple identities, but these are subject to change and adjustment.

One of the main aims of this book is to evaluate the impact of the Galician written standard and its concomitant linguistic policies and planning strategies, as well as the extent to which such language policies can play a significant part in the general reassertion of loyalty factors towards the use of Galician in contexts where the state language of Castilian was used formerly. In particular, general educational practices, the focus of most attempts at linguistic change, are examined. In this way, it is hoped that the book will also offer a valuable insight into the role of prestige factors concerning the status of a language within an ethnic community and to what extent such a language may determine, reinforce, and situate the idiosyncratic identity of the region in question alongside that of the overarching state system. All societies encompass ethnic communities, and the sense of kinship, group solidarity, and common culture to which the word ethnicity may refer are increasingly gaining paramount importance within contemporary Europe, the United States, and elsewhere. Language status and its role in determining identity have, therefore, far-reaching implications, as such identities are also often associated with national, ethnic, immigration, and sectarian issues.

For many years, Galician was considered a dialect of Castilian. However, recent political and social changes in the region have revived the issue of the status of Galician. In academic circles, there is a broad division between those who advocate autonomous language status, free from the constraints of being associated with either Castilian or Portuguese, and those who claim that Galician is structurally more akin to Portuguese and, therefore, should be allied closely with the Lusophone world. This book evaluates such claims. It examines the hypothesis that even when a community has been assigned to subaltern status for hundreds of years, and retains deep-seated inferiority complexes and negative attitudes, certain sectors of that community may start to demonstrate an upsurge in loyalty to their cultural identity and its symbolic manifestations, as well as to identify positively with their autochthonous language. In doing so, this book also considers contemporary language policies and planning strategies, both within the education system and within social and political institutions, as far as the acceptance and assimilation of a standardised language into a community's linguistic repertoire is concerned.

The following brief overview of the content of each of my chapters demonstrates how they relate to each other and the relevance of their order. As I have pointed out above, this book is about languages in contact, and takes both linguistic and sociolinguistic perspectives. Thus, the very nature of my argument is somewhat complex and multifaceted. In order to be able to fully appreciate this conceptual framework and the implications therein, my initial two chapters present a highly pertinent and contemporary discussion of the sociolinguistic and socio-political agenda, but Chapter 4 examines linguistic concepts as an introduction to the more unfamiliar linguistic discussion in Part 2 of this book.

The second part of this introductory chapter offers readers a short yet illuminating outline of the main sociolinguistic tenets relevant to the context of a multilingual society, such as communicative competence, individual and societal bilingualism and multilingualism, and the notion of diglossic and non-diglossic societies. So that readers can acquaint themselves with the more general implications of multilingualism, issues pertaining to language status are then discussed, such as language contact, competition, conflict and shift scenario. I also compare age- and generation-specific variation within the context of language change in order to establish the validity of the synchronic research that forms a large part of the data evaluated in this book. I finish this chapter by looking at the roles of status and solidarity within the context of language use in order to emphasise their bearing on speaker attitudes and loyalties, discussed in more detail in Chapter 1. These concepts are essential to an understanding of the sociolinguistic situation of Galicia discussed in the rest of the book. However, if the reader is already well acquainted with this terminology, of course, they should feel free to move on rapidly.

In Part 1, I begin to consider the central theme of this book, namely Galician linguistic, ethnic and cultural revival as a case study of minoritised communities. As a starting point, I examine historical and contemporary issues of the Galician language and Galician identity. However, in order to follow my line of reasoning, outlined above, regarding my conceptual framework, as well as the particular circumstances of Galician autonomy, it is essential that the reader be well versed in the socio-political issues surrounding language status, language use, ethnicity and the implications therein for identification strategies.

To this end, I begin Chapter 1 with a short overview of theoretical socio-political factors implicit to the aspirations of ethnic and minoritised societies such as Galicia. In particular, I address the role of language in the manipulation and reinforcement of identity. The social and political constructs of nationalism, nation, state, ethnicity, and ethnic community are highly pertinent to a discussion of devolution in Spain, and are considered therefore, in order to posit their relevance to a community's aspirations for recognition or self-rule. However, as the focus of this book is the role of language, I devote a substantial section of this chapter to issues surrounding the use, or otherwise, of autochthonous languages in individual and collective, single and multiple, symbolic and non-symbolic identification strategies. Once again, in order to clarify the conceptual framework, I concentrate on the most pertinent hypotheses, and in particular, I address the roles of attitude and loyalty factors from a theoretical perspective. In order to provide the reader with an introduction to the Galician situation, my account includes a summary of current approaches to the revitalisation and revival of minoritised languages. Finally, I consider the role that education can play in the survival of minoritised languages, as this is central to the ensuing discussion of language dissemination in Galicia. As above, should the reader already be well informed about such socio-political issues, once again, they may like to focus their attention on subsequent chapters.

An appreciation of the political and historical circumstances of Galicia, its language and its people is essential to an understanding of the modern context. To this end, in Chapter 2 I present the reader with an overview of Galicia and its language from such a perspective. I start by offering an account of the origins of Galician and its historical condition as Galician-Portuguese. I then discuss the demarcation of Galician and Portuguese, and the integration of Galicia into the Kingdom of Castile, for this had far-reaching implications for the development of Galician as a distinct language. Moreover, in my account of both the former and present-day relationship Galician has maintained with Portuguese and Castilian Spanish, I highlight the issue of its changing status as a marker of ethnic identity, for this issue has significant implications for my argument throughout the book. Importantly, of particular relevance to my discussion of identity are the historical attempts to revive a sense of linguistic, political and social consciousness in Galicia, despite linguistic persecution under Franco, as well as recent democratic efforts in language policy and planning and the concomitant promotion of an official orthographic standard. Throughout this chapter, I underline the connection between the loss of prestige status and general attitudes towards the language, for this will be a key issue in my subsequent discussion of more recent events.

Chapter 3 follows on chronologically from Chapter 2, in that it focuses upon the effect the historical context has had upon the more contemporary situation of the Galician language. The main theme here is the political justification for Spanish devolution and regional language use since the 1980s, in order to afford the reader an account of recent attempts to revitalise the Galician language. Through a discussion of the largely academic-based debate surrounding the specific configuration of the official orthographic standards adopted in the 1980s, I offer a brief analysis of their contribution to issues of Galician ethnicity and identity. My concluding section presents a discussion of the general processes pertaining to the integration of a standard language through the procedures of *normalización* in Galicia, together with some of the more specific and pertinent articles of the *Lei de Normalización Lingüística*. In this way, both Chapters 2 and 3 present the reader with a concise but highly pertinent explanation of the background to the contemporary situation.

Part 2 of this book concerns the linguistic differentiation of Galician, taking as a starting point some of its more emblematic features. Given that this book is essentially sociolinguistic in its outlook, I do not presume that the reader will have a detailed knowledge of the more relevant, strictly linguistic terminology surrounding the characterisation of Galician. To this end, readers will find many of the terms used in Chapters 4, 5 and 6 described for reference in a small glossary at the end of the book.

Like this introductory chapter and Chapter 1, Chapter 4 is also intended as a presentation of some of the key concepts relevant to the ensuing discussion. Although I offer a brief overview of microlinguistic issues rather than a comprehensive depiction of some of the more pertinent theories and their application in bilingual and multilingual settings, this section functions as a precursor to my evaluation of potential linguistic homogeneity between Galician, Portuguese and Castilian Spanish.

The main intention of Chapter 5 is to offer a highly comparative account of linguistic differentiation in the western areas of the Iberian Peninsula, taking as its basis a linguistic analysis of the ways in which Galician has evolved in order to complement the more sociolinguistic analysis of historical language change offered in Chapter 2. However, I begin with a discussion of language from a linguistic perspective as a contrast to my examination of the socio-political conceptualisation of language in Chapter 1. I then present a diachronic overview of the evolution of the most salient linguistic characteristics of Galician, offering a comparison, where possible, with their cognates in Portuguese and

Castilian. Given the controversies surrounding the form of the written Galician standard, my focus on contemporary similarities and differences between the three languages is an essential precursor to the detailed discussion that follows. I also examine the creation of an oral Galician standard, for this has far-reaching implications for issues of prestige and identification strategies that are essential to my discussion of ethnicity within Galicia.

In the third chapter of Part 2, Chapter 6, I explore the relevance of linguistic variability to the sociolinguistic setting by evaluating the pronunciation of two of the main characteristic phonetic articulations of Galician, the *gheada* and the velar nasal consonant. These are spoken variables and, as such, would appear to have little relevance to a written Galician standard. However, I point out in the previous chapter that the creation of an oral Galician standard has far-reaching implications for issues of prestige and identification strategies that are essential to my discussion of ethnicity within Galicia. Hence, I am particularly interested in the value of emblematic features to the pronunciation of Galician. To this end, I offer both diachronic and synchronic accounts, and linguistic versus sociolinguistic evaluations are made with the aim of determining the social status (or otherwise) inherent within the variation of each characteristic. Once again, this detailed consideration of issues regarding the potential status values of such characteristics will have bearing on the ensuing discussions in Part 3 of this book regarding loyalty to the use of Galician, as well as on issues regarding identification strategies.

In Part 3, I take my analysis of the Galician situation one step further, by building upon the examination of empirical data carried out in the previous chapter. Here, I am interested in evaluating speaker attitudes towards language use, the role of language status, and its potential application to a distinct Galician ethnic identity. To this end, I compare and contrast recent fieldwork into linguistic practices, with language planning measures initiated from the 1980s onwards in Galicia.

I begin in Chapter 7 by evaluating the impact of linguistic planning strategies and legislation initiated since the 1980s and delineated in earlier chapters, on uses and functions of Galician and Castilian. This is a rather daunting task, for comparative empirical data is not generally forthcoming. However, by examining recent studies and surveys regarding the language of habitual use, mother tongue variation, and language competencies, my intention is to offer an insight into potential linguistic and sociolinguistic changes that have taken place in the last 30 years.

In the second part of this chapter, my particular focus is on the role played by the education system as well as the impact of legislative measures and practices to integrate the standard into the classroom, as this is where the Galician government has concentrated its normalisation activities and where much of the recent controversy lies regarding the future of Galician. Moreover, these policies and directives have also had an impact on the use of Galician by the media, public institutions, and local authorities, hence my brief but pertinent overview of the current situation therein.

In Chapter 8, I continue to examine recent investigations into linguistic practices and choices. However, in this chapter I am more interested in studies that offer intergenerational analyses of behavioural practices and attitudes towards Galician as a viable representation of identity, as outlined in my earlier comments regarding the potential for evaluating language shift based upon language change methodologies. I also reflect on the relationship between mother tongue acquisition and habitual language use, taking into account age, but also geographical and class differentiation factors. In my examination of the functional demarcation of Galician varieties and Castilian, and possible changes over the last few decades, I also consider bilingual communicative competence, particularly in the spoken language. I pose the question as to whether language loyalty is a prerequisite for an increase in linguistic confidence and whether this can influence linguistic behaviour. Again, I adopt an intergenerational analysis to determine whether any differences in attitude and language use can be plotted across different age groups, and whether the latter is indicative of a change in progress or is an age-graded phenomenon. The final section of this chapter offers a detailed comparative discussion of research carried out in the late 1990s in Santiago de Compostela, including my own investigations into these issues.

The final chapter, Chapter 9, synthesises the main arguments and discussions of the book and offers my general conclusions and some predictions as to the future of the Galician language and its people. I start by examining the relationship between attitudinal factors and behavioural practices, particularly in urban settings. In particular, language policy and planning strategies are discussed, taking into account issues pertaining to standardisation practices. I also reassess the policy of *bilingüismo harmónico* and the issue of borrowing and transference phenomena. I then revisit the debates surrounding linguistic differentiation, taking into consideration the notion of an oral standard, and I analyse the ways in which the concept of an idiosyncratic Galician identity may be expressed, either successfully or unsuccessfully. The issue of multiple identities within the context of Galicia, and the role of language as an expression of such identities is considered in order to evaluate the relevance of a reciprocal language/identity relationship to the Galician setting. My conclusions make some tentative suggestions as to how the language may be maintained as a viable means of communication and as a positive ethnic identity marker.

My final comment of this preface concerns my own status as a researcher of Galician. I am not Spanish or Portuguese, but I speak both languages, as

well as Galician, and I have university qualifications in all, including a doctoral thesis in Galician linguistics. Over a period of six years, I lived and
worked (variously) in Spain, Portugal, Brazil, and Mexico. During the
1990s, I spent five glorious summers and two wet winters in Galicia, primarily based in Santiago de Compostela, but regularly travelling throughout the
region, and I made numerous shorter trips there in the course of my work.
However, I am in no way personally involved in the pervading sociolinguistic situation. It may appear therefore that the act of writing about an ethnic
situation other than my own is full of contradictions, for how can I try to
understand the issues from the perspective of a Galician? The answer, of
course, is that I cannot, nor do I claim to. What I can do, however, is offer
an evaluation of these issues from an academic perspective, with 'insider'
experience and information to hand, but acknowledging both the benefits
and drawbacks that this position implies.[4]

In her observations on language and social justice, Monica Heller questions the role of what I term the 'outsider' sociolinguist (2004: 283–286).
She points out the criticisms that have been levelled at research where
'sociolinguistic analysis of linguistic variation, or of ties between language
and identity, meet legal discourses of rights in the framework of a shared
concern for social justice' (2004: 283), and briefly evaluates the problems
therein. She concludes that we cannot consider ourselves to be objective
or even neutral 'experts'; as sociolinguistics, we are active participants
in the many debates regarding language use and we must, therefore,
assume the particular roles and responsibilities that this participation
entails. That is, in bringing our knowledge to the table and sharing it
with others, we acknowledge our role as well-informed experts with our
own analyses and perspectives of a given situation, as well as our responsibility to divulge this information to other participants in the discussion.
Moreover, irrespective of whether our particular approach is accepted or
rejected by other involved parties, since it serves or does not serve their
specific interests, this does not invalidate our position (2000: 286).

This is an important point. Although I fully acknowledge the drawbacks mentioned above of being an outsider to the sociolinguistic
situation in Galicia, I also have privileged access to data, perspectives,
and opinions that more politically or ideologically involved insider
researchers may not have. Even though everyone involved in this particular debate may not accept my specific stance, I believe that my account
offers an extremely clear picture of the situation regarding language use
and ethnic identity in Galicia.

Key Concepts and Issues

This book is about language, identity, and ethnicity. It adopts a
combination of linguistic and sociolinguistic analyses as its conceptual

framework, in order to investigate a particular case study of a minoritised language, that of Galician, within a multilingual society. In the following brief section I will outline some of the basic sociolinguistic issues and key concepts that contribute to the discussion of language and identity, in order to establish their relevance to the Galician ethnic situation and, where necessary, to define from the outset how I intend to use them within the context of this book. To this end, I offer brief descriptions of communicative competence, individual and societal bilingualism and multilingualism, diglossic and non-diglossic societies, and the (often) subjective nature of the terminology used. I then consider what the notion of status implies when a language is in contact, competition, and even conflict with another in a bi- or multilingual scenario. Although I discount the notion that language shift is the outright conclusion of such situations, assimilation and integration questions are briefly described as a way of delineating obligatory and non-obligatory shift. I also compare age- and generation-specific variation as a feature of language change, their association with diachronic and synchronic research, and their relevance to the study of patterns of language use in bi- and multilingual scenarios. This is a particularly important consideration, because synchronic data form a large part of the studies on language use in Galicia evaluated in this book. Finally, I compare status and solidarity processes pertaining to language, as a way of establishing the relevance of prestige, which is, again, extremely pertinent to my later discussion of language use in Galicia. Thus, this section offers the reader the necessary theoretical framework relevant to my subsequent discussion both of the historical and contemporary context of Galicia and its language.

Communicative Competence

No account of Galician identity should discount the importance of the relationship between the languages spoken in the region and their speakers. Within the field of sociolinguistics, language is considered a form of social behaviour, a way of communicating and interacting with others in society according to a set of shared experiences, norms and rules. As part of their specific linguistic behaviour, individuals have to be conscious of and responsive to social factors, such as context, topic, interlocutor, aim of the interaction, and so on (Holmes, 2001: 8). In this way, they acquire the necessary knowledge and experience of societal norms so as to be able to apply the rules to every communicative interaction in which they participate; in this way, they acquire communicative competence.

Dell Hymes established the concept of communicative competence in the 1970s. In essence, it arose out of Chomsky's earlier, formal structural distinction (Chomsky, 1965: 4) between linguistic competence, 'the speaker–hearer's (grammatical) knowledge of his language', and linguistic performance, 'the actual use of language in concrete situations'. The former encompasses the system of rules and principles governing a given language that are internally represented by the speaker, whereas the latter makes explicit use of this knowledge to produce, interpret and understand the language (Chomsky, 1980: 200–205). Bourdieu finds Chomsky's delineation rather abstract, for although linguistic exchanges and interactions are routine, practical encounters, language has to be situated in the socio-historical environment that it both expresses and helps to reproduce (Bourdieu, 1994: 2–7).[5] In other words, the success of an utterance or interaction is bound to the social context and other conditions. With communicative competence, speakers are able to produce, interpret and understand a language, contextualise parts of it, and even pass judgement on what it is appropriate to use in a given context. Thus, communicative competence *is* also culture-specific, in that it has to include information about the social and cultural knowledge speakers are presumed to have, which enables them to use and interpret linguistic forms.

Individual and Societal Bilingualism

The definition of communicative competence outlined above is applicable irrespective of whether the society in question is monolingual, bilingual or multilingual.[6] Indeed, as I will discuss further throughout this book, these issues regarding degrees of competence are important to the sociolinguistic setting of Galicia by dint of the fact that it is considered a bilingual society.

In his early work, Fishman states that societal bilingualism or multilingualism exists when a community as a whole is able to communicate in both (or all) languages (1967: 33). However, a society is often defined as bilingual or multilingual, even though each and every member does not command and display communicative competence in both or all the languages in question. A case in point is Wales. Even though both English and Welsh are officially recognised throughout the country, Welsh speakers in the southern cities at least are uncommon, in contrast to the northern regions, where individual bilingualism is the norm.[7]

Mackey's early definition (1970: 555) defines individual bilingualism as 'the alternate use of two or more languages by the same individual'. However, by not specifying the degree of competence required in different kinds of interaction, such as speaking, reading, writing, and so on, such generic definitions of bilingualism do not take into account the degree to which the speaker is able to communicate fluently in both or all of the languages. Although a community's linguistic repertoire may encompass disparate languages, varieties of language and dialects used in various social situations (Gal, 1987: 286), each and every member of that community will not share each and every resource. In other words, individual linguistic repertoires will differ according to experiences and circumstances. For instance, even when a person is raised from infancy learning to speak and aurally understand two or more languages at the same time, they may not display competence in reading and writing skills in one or more of the languages. Even when a member of a specific community does not know a language well enough to productively speak it, they may still demonstrate receptive competence (Romaine, 2000: 24) and, I would add, be able to write it in some form. It may be more pertinent to define individual bilingualism as a trait of one person's specific linguistic performance and communicative competence. Skutnabb-Kangas offers us a succinct characterisation in this respect:

> A bilingual speaker is someone who is able to function in two (or more) languages, either in monolingual or bilingual communities, in accordance with the sociocultural demands made of an individual's communicative and cognitive competence by these communities or by the individual herself, at the same level as native speakers, and who is able positively to identify with both (or all) language groups (and cultures), or parts of them
>
>   (Skutnabb-Kangas, 1981: 90)[8]

At first glance, this definition may appear rather restrictive, in that its requirements are somewhat demanding compared with other definitions. However, Skutnabb-Kangas clearly points out that such a definition is arbitrary and subject to change (1981: 81); since this particular characterisation was devised primarily as a working objective for teaching (immigrant) minoritised children in school, hence the stringent requisites. Its significance and relevance to the Galician situation is based upon two factors: it stresses the impact both of competence and of positive identity factors. Moreover, Mackey's earlier definition does not take into account the important point of whether the speaker has any sociolinguistic and cultural knowledge of how, when and where a particular linguistic form may or may not be employed.[9] Yet, a community will generally share a set of social and behavioural norms defining language use. Anyone who speaks more than one language chooses between them according to the particular circumstances of the interaction, just as they choose between forms of a given language according to context. In spoken interactions, for example, the initial criterion is which language their interlocutor is capable of understanding. Even when members do not display all the linguistic skills, they still demonstrate a competent knowledge of these norms. All members of a given community will have a well-formed opinion of how and in what context the rest of the community considers it appropriate to employ a given language, will adhere to such societal 'norms' if pertinent, and in this way, will acknowledge their own idiosyncratic relationship with the community.

Contact, Competition and Conflict: Diglossia

One significant concept in sociolinguistic theory and, in particular, bilingualism that has had a direct bearing upon this apportionment of language use is that of diglossia. Ferguson's initial definition of diglossia (1959) pertained to the separate uses and roles, within a given speech community, of similar varieties of one language. However, linguists such as Gumperz (1968: 381–386) and especially Fishman (1971: 74–75), recognised the usefulness of the term to refer to situations where two or more languages exist side by side within a bilingual society, as had Weinreich (1953) early on in his structural–functional hypothesis (the functional differentiation of languages in contact prevents interference phenomena). Fishman's four-way pattern of linguistic alternation, which I delineate as bilingual/diglossic, bilingual/non-diglossic, non-bilingual/diglossic, non-bilingual/non-diglossic (1989: 181–189), is well known and, therefore, I do not propose to offer a lengthy discussion of the general categorisation.[10] However, certain points are outlined here, due to their relevance to the Galician situation.

Fishman points out that diglossia are a 'societal arrangement where individual bilingualism is widespread and institutionally buttressed' (Fishman, 1989: 185). Theoretically, then, languages coexist with clearly marked domains of usage. That is, the selection of these varieties within a community has both social and cultural relevance, with each serving a specialised function. Fishman retains Ferguson's terms H (High) and L (Low) (1959: 336) to characterise the varieties according to their functional demarcation, but alters the definitions slightly to encompass domains more relevant to separate languages that are both used in a spoken form. According to Fishman, popular L varieties are restricted to non-official, informal and private usage; they are generally mother-tongue colloquial forms learnt in the home and used in day-to-day conversations within the immediate community. Conversely, the H variety is used for most written and formal spoken purposes, is related to and supported by educational, governmental, social and religious institutions and is, typically, codified and standardised. Regularly, it is also the language of extragroup functions, of social advancement, the one parents will encourage their children to learn in order to 'get ahead' and be able to move freely outside the confines of the group or local community. Paraguay is a well-known example. In the 1950s, Garvin and Mathiot (1956: 790) concluded that almost the entire population was able to converse in two totally unrelated but official languages, Spanish and Guaraní. Rona (1975: 277–296), however, contradicts this assertion; he avers that although half the nation do maintain a diglossic distinction between the use of Spanish (H) for administrative and educational purposes and Guaraní (L) for informal situations, no true, general bilingualism can exist in Paraguay because the remaining half of the nation neither know nor, therefore, use Spanish in any context. I would add further that not all 'European' descent people know Guaraní. Romaine (2000: 48) states that although Guaraní is spoken at the present time by some 90% of the population, many speakers still regard Spanish as somehow 'superior', because it is a prerequisite for entry to certain professions and formal institutions. Such situations may be relatively stable, long-term arrangements, although this is not always the case, as I discuss below.

In contrast, Fishman contends that when no diglossia exists, rapid societal change may lead to social and cultural norms being forsaken as the languages compete for recognition and use within the same domains. This type of situation is partially in evidence in Sardinia. Sardinian has no standard language in terms of a codified norm, even though grammars and dictionaries exist. Similarly, there is no spoken variety functioning as an interdialectal *lingua franca*, so Sardinian is divided into two principal *koinés*, Logudorese and Campidanese. In the 1950s, Sardinian was considered the autochthonous language of the island. However, by the 1980s, it was gradually being replaced by Italian, and both languages existed side by side with poorly defined domains of usage (Schjerve, 1989). By the turn of the millennium, Schjerve had concluded that Sardinian was a language between maintenance and change. Although it was still used in the rural areas, even by younger generations, it also displayed signs of levelling to Italian in its linguistic structure (Schjerve, 2003: 253–254).[11]

There are inherent problems with Fishman's definition of diglossia, discussed clearly in an early paper of Martin-Jones (1989). She argues that the strict demarcation of language use within Fishman's use of the term does not take account of the fact that diglossic functions are generally not maintained in such a precise fashion. Ferguson's investigations centred on societies where a classical form of the language existed in contrast to local varieties, and where a strict diglossic demarcation was based on clearly defined social and cultural practices.[12] However, it is not common for bilingual individuals, at the very least, to conform in this way to such a closed system of complementary distribution and community norms; more frequently, languages tend to overlap in their uses as individuals choose which language to employ for a given sphere of activity, based upon their own competencies, preferences and allegiances. Moreover, language choices occur in the context of a social network; they are practical instances of language use, rather than abstract constructs, and, as such, subject to influence from factors other than the social setting, such as age, gender, attitude, and so on. Finally, Fishman's model of bilingualism with no diglossia, described above, is considered an almost inevitable phase in the shift to monolingualism, as a deviation from the norm of a static and stable scenario of bilingualism with diglossia. However, Martin-Jones contends that such structural–functional perspectives do not explain the changing social and linguistic processes involved in language retention and shift, such as when one language starts to be used for the functions of the other (1989: 108–112).

Thus, it is apparent that when two or more languages come into contact, the outcome is not always clear. Acts of communication between different groups and individuals imply a degree of contest in the selection of which language predominates. This is implicit in Haugen's statement that whenever languages are in contact, they are in competition for users (1987: 114). This allows even autochthonous languages of well-established monolingual societies to be subject to a certain amount of influence, although contact with other languages may be superficial and at a distance. It may be, for example, that lexical restrictions within their mother tongue oblige even monolingual speakers to utilise another language for certain functions. However, most monolingual communities manage to remain relatively stable, merely borrowing lexis (see p. 99 for a further definition), as an adaptive strategy to enrich certain registers of their own language (Mesthrie *et al.*, 2004: 251). At the micro-level of interaction in bilingual societies (Gumperz, 1982a),[13] constant cross-cultural and social exchange between groups and communities tends to result in habitual, long-lasting, efficient, and effective contact between their languages. Over time, these languages may exert a degree of linguistic influence upon each other – at the very least, lexical items may be borrowed from one language to enrich the other. If such a society does maintain some form of diglossic distinction, intergroup contact may mean that language use itself ultimately becomes variable as both (or all) of the languages are used in some or all of the same contexts. Indeed, as Martin-Jones (1989: 112) has pointed out, rather than promoting a situation of stability, diglossic distinctions may actually promote linguistic change. Although language shift and the loss of one of the languages are not inevitable, a redistribution of languages across domains generally occurs in such circumstances (Appel & Muysken, 1987: 41; Mesthrie *et al.*, 2004: 258).

In many situations, minoritised languages forego functions to the dominant or majoritised language. Gal's groundbreaking study (1979) of language shift among Hungarian speakers in the town of Oberwart in Austria, applied Gumperz's model of language use to demonstrate that issues such as social mobility and language prestige, as well as variables such as age and gender, were impacting on the increased use of German and the decreased use of Hungarian in certain contexts. Such an approximation of uses may be considered confrontational, particularly by the language that is 'losing out'. The ensuing competition for functional domains may result in what has been termed a type of linguistic conflict, as speakers forego any diglossic norms that they may have conformed to and, in many cases, use one of the languages in question in many or all contexts. This is particularly significant when the 'losing' language is spoken by a minoritised group who wield little political power within the society in question.

Indeed, this perspective of conflict in language use and language change among linguistic minorities also relates to issues I raise in the next chapter regarding the influence of political structures on social, economic and linguistic groupings within a given nation or state. As we have seen above, the structural–functional hypothesis of language use in bilingual contexts views the notion of diglossia as a static phenomenon; a 'normal' situation, and the H and L classification a natural form of social and linguistic order. However, the conflict interpretation of diglossic distribution considers why the languages in question were functionally differentiated in the first place, and how this distribution changes over time, as well as what it consists of and how it is articulated (Martin-Jones, 1989: 119). Originally conceived by Catalan linguists such as Ninyoles (1969, 1975) and Vallverdú (1970), this approach has been applied to a far wider context by researchers such as Eckert (1980, 2000) for French, and in particular, Glyn Williams regarding Welsh (Williams, 1979). As Eckert states:

> Diglossia does not arise; it is imposed from above in the form of an administrative, ritual or standard language. By virtue of its political and economic status, this language becomes requisite for access to power and mobility within the society.
>
> (Eckert, 1980: 1056, 2000: 36)

I agree with Martin-Jones' view that the term diglossia is 'both constraining and enabling' (1989: 122). Although a pattern of functional distribution may occur in certain societies, as may be the case in Galicia, individuals use their own linguistic repertoires in a highly complex and variable way, and do not generally adhere to stringently applied categorisations of use. However, it does serve as a way of delineating the *potential* for social determinants of language use, and for this reason, I will continue to use the term in this book. I would also question the use of H and L labels in the context of diglossia. As Glyn Williams has pointed out (Williams, 1992), such terminology is overlaid with far-reaching connotations regarding the balance of power between the speakers of these languages. Domain segregation implies that H varieties are somehow 'better' or 'more valuable' than L varieties. For this reason, I would prefer to categorise these functions in a less subjective manner and according to their inter- or intragroup sociolinguistic demarcation. It may be argued that, in doing so, I negate the important evaluative judgements inherent within their usage. Therefore, I will refer to these judgements when relevant through-out my discussion of language and identity in Galicia.

Implicit to the conflict perspective described about is how political ideologies regarding language use may affect acts of identity within min-oritised communities. Thus, issues of power and solidarity and their role in the social determination of language choice become important as the community in question struggles for its rights.

In her book on linguistic rights, Skutnabb-Kangas presents a thoroughly approachable account of assimilation and integration pro-cesses that may result from such conflict (2000: 123–134). She defines assimilation as the 'enforced subtractive "learning" of another (dominant) culture by a (dominated) group. Assimilation means being transferred to another group'. Integration on the other hand 'is characterised by volun-tary mutual additive "learning" of other cultures. Integration means a choice of inclusive group membership(s)' (2000: 124). Although her defi-nitions do not relate purely to language, this is often an important aspect of the entire assimilation or integration process, as I will discuss further in Chapter 1. For now, what is relevant is that, depending on circumstances, the language in question may or may not be lost, and the speakers may or may not learn the other language(s). This then reiterates my earlier comment that language shift is not always the inevitable outcome of con-flict situations.

Real versus Apparent Time Data

This book considers both shifts in language use from Galician to Castilian and vice versa, as well as changes in the pronunciation of various linguistic features within Galician itself. In contrast to language shift (which, if it does occur, typically does so interlinguistically), language change tends to occur intralinguistically. As such, language change tends to also occur between specific age groups. In the 1950s, Hockett (1950: 423) contended that such change could be predicted purely and simply by taking an agewise cross-section of a group of people and comparing the variation in their pronunciation. However, this concept of 'age-grading' is highly restrictive in the study of language change, because it may simply highlight or capture, for example, forms only used by children and then passed on from one generation of children to another without ever being used by adults. Other linguists have expanded the concept of age-grading to characterise age-specific differ-ences, reflecting language systems, forms and features that tend to be employed more frequently or even exclusively at particular stages of one's life. These are thus associated with specific age groups as a develop-mental stage, such as the two-word utterances of toddlers at around

18 months of age ('Want banana'; 'Daddy cup'), and are thus often termed age-preferential (Cheshire, 1987: 761–762).

Evidence of stable age-graded variation is not always forthcoming, although social dialect research has provided information about patterns of linguistic differentiation between age groups, particularly regarding changes related to childhood and adolescence. Labov's findings (1977: 350) regarding teenage in-group slang in the United States are a good example.[14] Normally, speakers give up the features associated with a particular stage of development as they grow older. Less prestigious forms tend to have a high occurrence in the younger age groups, those of childhood and adolescence, as well as in the older age groups when the speakers have reached retirement age. Conversely, middle-aged speakers tend to favour more prestigious, standardised forms. It is often unclear whether this life-stage differentiation is related to the fact that the middle-aged category tends to be the highest social status group, or whether societal pressures to conform are the greatest within this age category. The important point is that if this pattern of variation is consistent, then it can be considered the normal distribution of stable linguistic forms within a community.

Knowledge of this distributional pattern is essential in research into patterns of language change. Real-time examinations of successive generations of speakers who represent stages in the evolution of a speech community are rarely practical, although some have been carried out.[15] Hence, apparent time studies are commonly used to this end. In order to establish that a pattern of variation does indeed represent a linguistic change in progress, these studies examine what Cheshire has termed 'generation-specific differences', in which discrete mother tongue variations displayed by different members of a single family may be considered synchronic manifestations of a diachronic, (internal) language change (1987: 764–765). Thus, the speech of someone who is now over 70 years old demonstrates the speech of a time earlier to that of someone who is now 40 or 15 years old. Nonetheless, distinguishing between patterns of true varietal change and age-preferential variation in these studies still requires what Milroy and Gordon (2003: 36) term 'some form of baseline against which (their) current results can be interpreted'. Thus, the use of earlier comparative data such as dialectal studies will ensure that cross-sectional data from different age groups at a given point in time does not merely indicate differentiation for life-stage variables, rather than variables indicative of an actual diachronic change in progress. Holmes (2001: 205) states that change is indicated by a steady increase or decline in the frequency of a form by age group, whereas a bell-shaped pattern is more typical of the stable age group variation I have looked at above. She cites in particular Labov's famous example of the use of post-vocalic *r* in New York department stores

(Labov, 1966). Such prestigious changes tend to manifest themselves initially in the more formal styles of the young people in the highest status social group, spreading then to a less formal style for that group and to the most formal styles of older people's speech forms, and other groups, over time. That is, the younger generations tend to adopt these new forms more easily and quickly and employ them more extensively; hence a different pattern of variability emerges (Holmes, 2001: 201–202).

Age-grading pertains to a fairly stable pattern of age-related variation. Milroy and Gordon state (2003: 36–38) that such features may involve a high degree of social awareness and, as a result, are more readily subject to conscious manipulation. However, the basic assumptions outlined above regarding the apparent-time hypothesis are secure *only* if they apply to features that do not attract this type of social awareness. In other words, it seems to be a reasonable hypothesis that the features today's adolescents use now will be what the over 30s will use in 20 years' time, *unless* the feature currently attracts a high degree of attention, in which case it is much harder to predict what will happen.

This raises another important issue. In a recent paper, Milroy considers how socially motivated sound changes may become emblematic characteristics of a given language, by dint of the fact that they are more 'salient' and manipulable (in press). Milroy discusses the interrelationship between psycholinguistic and social constraints on what she terms 'off-the-shelf' and 'under-the-counter' sound changes. The former are more freely available, do not require local support, are more generally accessible to mobile and marginal individuals, and highlight the role of attitude and ideology and the influence of particular identifiable speakers or groups thereof. However, under-the-counter sound changes are due to repeated exposure provided by regular social interaction, and require local support and participation (Milroy, in press: 3–4, 10). Speakers may manifest (unconsciously) or adopt (consciously) such features, and this will have an impact on whether they are age-graded features or not. This point will become relevant in my discussion of emblematic characteristics of Galician in Chapter 6. It is also important to my hypothesis of using an apparent-time analysis to examine the use of different languages at different life stages, in order to determine whether one language is generally used more at one stage in life than another, or whether a shift in language use is taking place.

When standard languages are introduced into situations of dialectal variation, a similar pattern of variability to the above takes place because it is generally the younger members of the community who are the first to be taught and adopt the standard. In many cases, they then avoid learning and using the dialectal variant, or learn and use it rather imperfectly, although I will point out in Chapter 1 that issues of identity may affect this pattern. Moreover, once again, children do not necessarily continue to use these standard forms as adults. That is, they may revert to the dialectal forms of their parents.[16]

Keeping in mind my caveats regarding the viability of apparent-time studies to observe the process of linguistic change, I now return to the issue of language shift, a process that, in certain circumstances, may also be directly observed synchronically. At an individual level, changes in language use, for example, may actually occur very quickly. Thomason and Kaufman state that in certain circumstances, a shift in language use, may even take as little as one generation to present itself (1988: 41, 47–48). I would add that this is particularly the case for those members of the population who are mostly affected by the presence of the language that is taking over in contexts of power. However, overall societal shift in language use involves the adaptation and acculturation of many speakers across different age groups, and, as such, is rarely directly observable.

If a minoritised language is to avoid losing speakers through such processes of language shift to the dominant language, then a situation of linguistic stability must obtain, so that intragroup societal bilingualism prevails and each language variety safeguards functions, domains and contexts. Indeed, both Geerts (1987: 600) and Fishman (1989: 181) have long asserted that linguistic stability within a diglossic/bilingual community has to endure for more than three generations for what they consider to be a 'true' diglossic state to be attained (bearing my earlier discussion in mind).

However, when a minoritised language has lost speakers, revitalisation and revival efforts will also require that speakers display a degree of loyalty to the language and a concomitant desire to use it. In this way, factors such as the attitude and desire of the particular society to advance and implement changes may affect the rate at which the language develops (Thomason & Kaufman, 1988: 47–48).

Integration of the language through revitalisation efforts also needs to be supported by intralinguistic factors such as standardisation. Moreover, if implementation is carried out by formal means, or by extralinguistic factors such as the controlling political, economic and social status of the dominant community, processes of urbanisation and industrialisation, and so on, then the chance that revitalisation of the minoritised language will be rapid will be greatly improved.

Issues of Status and Solidarity

Implicit to any discussion of the role of speaker attitude and loyalty factors in language use are the issues of status and solidarity. Labov's early model of the mechanisms of change (Labov, 1972) seemed to suggest that change tends to be monodirectional, towards forms, and, hence, languages, preferred by the social groups with the highest status.

However, individual speakers' speech behaviour may be influenced by norms of both overt and covert prestige; there is a tension between status and solidarity as forces that motivate the choice of linguistic forms.

Labov was also the first to suggest that the middle-class group of society displays greater fluctuation in stylistic variation, and that its members are extremely sensitive to their own use of what they consider to be stigmatised features. In his widely acknowledged ground-breaking studies of conscious attitudes towards the speech of the lower East Side of New York City (discussed above, pp. 19–20) and Martha's Vineyard (Labov, 1966, 1977), Labov averred that the linguistic insecurity of the lower middle class manifests itself in members' inaccurate perception of their own speech. They consider their own linguistic traits to be stigmatised, non-prestige markers (Labov, 1966: 93–94). Thus, these speakers try to change their speech patterns by adopting prestige forms used by the youngest members of the highest-ranking social class.

Other researchers have since chosen not to employ this classic Labovian approach, but, rather, to focus upon the use of 'vernacular' or non-standard forms and their positive association with a speaker's degree of integration into the social network of their community. Chambers comments that such examples of covert prestige tend to be found in regional working-class varieties of speech in urbanised, industrialised societies, and their continued persistence appears to be a direct consequence of the deep-seated feelings, conscious or not, their speakers have for them (2003: 246). In this way, the dimensions of solidarity and power are in conflict, as we saw above regarding diglossia.

Once again, Bourdieu's comments are eminently valid. Although the practices, perceptions and attitudes that are generated by a given habitus or set of characteristics (dispositions), and that define or motivate a person's actions or reactions, are not consciously co-ordinated, they tend to conform to a fairly regular pattern (Bourdieu, 1994: 12). In this way, the fact that different groups and classes have different accents, intonations and ways of speaking is a manifestation of the socially structured character of the linguistic habitus. Bourdieu stresses that the relative value of a given linguistic utterance is reliant on its particular context, so part of a speaker's practical competence is to know how to produce utterances of high value in a particular context – the overt prestige or status forms discussed above (pp. 21–22). However, different speakers possess different quantities of what he terms 'linguistic capital' – the capacity to produce expression appropriate to the specific context, such as in making a formal speech. Bourdieu relates this capacity to a differentiation based on class and issues of symbolic power, invisible on a daily basis but implicitly accepted as legitimate by all participants. Indeed, for some speakers, typically men with lower-class backgrounds, the adoption of the articulatory styles of the middle or upper classes would be an attempt to conceal their class habitus and increase their symbolic power. By retaining highly euphemistic forms of speech as covert indicators and even positive reinforcers of their social network, as we have seen above (pp. 21–22), they are in point of fact confirming the well-established social hierarchy and their dominated position therein (Bourdieu, 1994: 17–23). In other words, they are contributing to the maintenance of the very characteristics that set them apart from the other classes.[17]

Early studies bear out these assertions. Chambers summarises the findings of one of the very first subjective reaction tests, carried out by Anisfield, Bogo and Lambert in Canada (1962; in Chambers, 2003: 245) regarding status- and solidarity-stressing traits of Montreal and Jewish-accented English. In the matched guise tests they used, the status dimension tends to be associated with intelligence, education, ambition, wealth, success and achievement, whereas the solidarity dimension is associated with kindness, likeability, friendliness, goodness and trust (2003: 245).[18]

In her Reading study (1978), Jenny Cheshire chose to use long-term participant observation to look at the relationship between the use of grammatical variables and observance of peer group culture by groups of boys and girls. She found that there was a conscious use of non-standard linguistic forms influenced by situational constraints; there was a particular way of speaking within the peer group that was required of the members in order to manifest their allegiance and integration.[19] In her Belfast study (1987), Lesley Milroy used the same techniques to focus on three close-knit communities. Like Cheshire, she chose to study the retention of non-standard, non-prestige, and stigmatised linguistic forms and varieties typically employed by working-class speakers. Her results revealed a correlation between the use of particular phonetic variables and their positive association with a speaker's degree of integration into and ties with the social network of the community. She found that this use was typically stratified according to gender, with men predominating.[20]

What is apparent is that social factors can and do affect the selection of particular forms of language. A particularly illustrative example is the use of second-person address forms in French, Latin, Russian, Italian, German, Swedish, and Greek. The use of these forms can also be affected by issues pertaining to solidarity. Hence, in the French example, *tu* and *vous* once had a strictly demarcated relationship based upon issues of power, deference, social status and degrees of intimacy. However, solidarity now appears to be the dominant factor in the selection of T or V forms; mutual *tu* is often found in relationships where asymmetrical usage was formerly found, for example, between a father and son, or between an employer and employee (Wardhaugh, 2002: 259–262).[21]

Concluding Remarks

The main objective of this introductory chapter has been to outline the key sociolinguistic concepts relevant to my conceptual framework detailed in the first part of this introductory chapter and to the general debate surrounding the relationship between language, identity and ethnicity in multilingual societies. This discussion of my use of the pertinent terminology will prove useful to those readers who are not familiar with such issues, and will serve to conceptualise my subsequent analysis of the Galician situation. In particular, I have offered definitions and descriptions of bilingualism and diglossia as I use them within the book, for these will prove fundamental to the reader's understanding of the Galician scenario. I have also considered the inherent problems associated with the existence of two or more languages within a given society, and how their status or prestige affects their survival. Again, the discussion of language contact will prove paramount to an understanding of the Galician situation. My analysis of the viability of synchronic research in both language shift and language change scenario is intended to offer a theoretical basis to the idea of intragroup but intergeneration changes in linguistic forms and shifts in language use, which will be revisited in subsequent chapters. My final comments concern status and solidarity issues regarding the function of different languages, or varieties of language. From a sociolinguistic perspective, these issues are fundamental to my assertion that attitudes towards language impact on the way identities are both manipulated and negotiated. What I do not do in this section is consider the socio-political perspective and its potential impact on language use, nor do I consider the role of identity and ethnicity in language selection. These issues, and others, will now be discussed in Chapter 1.

Part 1

Politics and Privilege: Linguistic Identity and the Role of Standardisation in Galicia

Preamble

As I stated in the Introduction chapter, the principal hypothesis of this book is fourfold. First, that the Galician language, whether used or not, may be an intrinsic characteristic of Galician ethnic identity. Secondly, that linguistic policies and planning impact on the behavioural practices of language users, and these practices, in turn, may be reflected in their attitudes towards the language. Thirdly, that although a reversal in traditional perceptions and attitudes is resulting in a reaffirmation of Galician as the autochthonous language, its sociolinguistic relationship with Castilian has not been resolved. Fourthly, that Galicians have to negotiate multiple identities, but these are subject to change and adjustment.

In order to consider the background to the current situation, Part 1 of this book is concerned with the use and status of the Galician language, from both an historical and a contemporary perspective. It brings together current theories regarding socio-political factors pertaining to language and identity, and addresses the issues of linguistic rights, community status, and power. In my account of the evolution of Galician in Chapter 2, I consider such issues from the perspective of Galicia's relationships with both Portugal and the rest of Spain. These relationships have far-reaching implications for the form and function of the standardised language. To this end, Chapter 3 reviews the main legislative measures to effect language revitalisation, together with the on-going socio-political debates regarding the composition of the orthographic and morphological standard language.

Chapter 1
Language, Culture, Identity

Introductory Remarks

In the introduction to this book, I offered a brief overview of the main sociolinguistic tenets relevant to the study of language use and its relationship with identity. However, in order to offer the reader a coherent and cohesive theoretical framework relevant to a discussion of the historical and contemporary contexts of Galicia and its language, the present chapter examines socio-political influences on the status of languages and concomitant linguistic attitudes and identities within different communities. I begin by delineating issues surrounding nationalism, the nation, and the state from a political and a social perspective, and the role of language in such contexts. In particular, I focus upon the relationship between ethnic communities and their languages from a primarily socio-political perspective, and to this end, I discuss recent theory related to these issues and explain my own measured usage of certain terms within the relevant conceptual framework. I also address the question of individual and collective identities, for these do not necessarily coincide. In particular, the emblematic status of ethnic minoritised languages and other cultural traits and their symbolic role in defining a collective identity distinct from that of the overarching state is examined, as this discussion will prove extremely pertinent to the Galician case study that is the theme of this book.[1] I clarify my conceptual framework by analysing the implications of core value theory and essentialist versus constructivist accounts of identification strategies. Furthermore, I consider single and multiple identification strategies and the role of boundaries in processes of inclusion and exclusion. In this way, attitudinal factors become important concepts to the manipulation of multiple identities. These factors play an important role in the revival of a language, as demonstrated by my subsequent account of revitalisation approaches.

In particular, I examine the socio-political implications of these approaches, and their reliance on community loyalty and support. Although I briefly address issues surrounding linguistic rights, language policies, and planning methodologies, the intention is simply to offer a short overview of these procedures insofar as they are pertinent to the case study of this book, namely that of Galicia. My concluding comments summarise the prevailing situation that minoritised groups may encounter in their attempts to become recognised as autonomous communities, and the implications therein for their languages. This paves the way for the case study examined in ensuing chapters.

Nationalism, the Nation and the State

In this section, I consider the relationship between so-called national languages and their host, and between so-called regional languages, their ethnic community, and the overriding state. Throughout my discussion, I offer definitions of some of the more pertinent terminology.

I firstly consider the concept of nationalism. In his article on the relationship between nationalism and language in Europe, Stephen Barbour (2000: 1–17) defined nationalism as a movement to defend the interests of a nation and its identity; to defend or secure its political independence.[2] In other words, it may comprise the actions of members to secure or maintain the right to self-determination, as well as their desire to be perceived as a nation. Although more explicit terminology is also employed to delineate particular contexts even further, such as the concepts surrounding Indian post-colonialism, post-communist East European nationalism, West European unification, Quebecois separatism, Mohawk autonomy, and neo-Nazi nationalism (Arteaga, 1994: 2), Barbour's definition is still relevant in all cases.

Essentially, Samuel Huntington's 'clash of civilizations' hypothesis (1996) reinforces the notion that a nation has the 'right' to defend and protect its identity and its people, in this case, by legitimising aggressive foreign policies. Huntington maintained that global politics in the modern world would be dominated by cultural differences between nations and different peoples, rather than by ideological or economic considerations. This hypothesis continues to underpin the public face of the Islam-Christianity 'conflict' that has been constructed by western politicians and foreign policy makers, particularly in the current post-September 11th climate. However, there has been much debate and criticism of Huntington's claims, primarily because religious ideology and economic factors *are* inherent to the West-Islam question.[3]

Indeed, ostensibly at least, one of the main motivational factors in attempts to secure the legitimacy of a nation has continuously been that of religious ideology. Popular resistance has often carried a misleading religious banner. For example, despite recent progress on these issues, the unresolved tensions in Northern Ireland are still demarcated, superficially at least, on religious grounds. In this way, the Irish Catholics have claimed autonomy rights from Protestant Britain, but questions of historical family circumstances appear to be just as important. Even more unambiguous is the fact that there was no obvious religious dimension apparent in the sides taken during the two world wars of the 20th century, leading Barbour to comment that 'the defence of one's nation is not always the defence of one's religion' (2000: 3). What appears to be the overriding and constant factor in such situations, in accordance with contemporary portrayals of nationalist ideology, is the very concept of nation. There are two main perspectives on this concept, discussed in more detail later (pp. 43–45) and outlined here by May (2001: 10–11). The essentialist perspective believes that 'nation' implies a common origin and sense of ethnic community, fostered by the apportionment of at least some of the social and cultural characteristics of the collective that unite and bond the populace. The constructivist perspective stresses the contingent nature of national identities, created out of particular socio-historical conditions, variable in salience and subject to change. Thus, following Andersen (1991) and Gellner (1983), the nation (-state) is a product of 18th- and 19th-century nationalisms, industrialisation and modernisation processes.[4]

These two perspectives do not mean that all nations have the right to self-determination, nor that these nations have a relatively easily definable territory and could constitute a sovereign independent entity (Barbour, 2002: 11). Nations may be subsumed within an overarching state, a politically created, sovereign entity that occupies a given territory. By means of territorial expansion, the political and economic interests and aspirations of a dominant power will determine the borders and frontiers of a given state in a somewhat indiscriminate manner.

Implicit to the nationalist perspective has been the concept of nation-state. Skutnabb-Kangas (2000: 425) states that the traditional stereotypical image is that of a high form of social organisation that has evolved from small, tribal societies as a product of evolutionary processes. Barbour's (2000: 4–5) characterisation of the nation-state as the fundamental unit of world political organisation, often identical to the sovereign state, thus depicts this highly developed form. Implicit to this definition was the belief that nation-states are a legally defined entity, created as a political construct and in clear contrast to the nation or nations within, which comprise the actual society, the population, and the people. Yet, the concept of nation-state is often highly ideological, a fictive, artificial construct (Barbour, 2000: 4) based on monocultural and monolingual idealised notions of societal structure. Mar-Molinero (2000b: 11) explains that 19th century nationalist thought did not acknowledge that few, if any, politically marked-out states were naturally monocultural. The use of nation-state simply served to legitimise 'one nation-one language-one state' ideologies, rather than offer an authentic depiction of the overriding situation.[5]

State territorial expansion is invasive and tends to encompass other ethnic groups. In many instances, however, social and cultural traditions and customs, historical background and 'race', as well as factors pertaining to ideology and to religion, are not shared by conqueror and conquered, often resulting in draconian measures by the former to repress those of the latter. Conversely, as Skutnabb-Kangas points out, the existence of unassimilated minoritised groups, having several 'nations' within the framework of the 'larger' one, has been feared because it is seen as leading to a complete or partial disintegration of the nation-state (2000: 426). Moreover, the contrast of the term ethnicity with that of nation-state led to extremely pejorative connotations being afforded to the former by dominant groups.[6] From this period onwards, as May (2001: 19−21) explains, the traditional perspective was that nation-states were all-embracing, cohesive, modern constructs, whereas ethnic groups were viewed as exclusive, divisive and primitive, representing misguided nostalgia and outmoded characteristics. It was determined, therefore, that a homogeneous national identity − reflected in the culture and language of the dominant 'national' group − should supersede and subsume alternative ethnic and or national identities and their associated cultures and languages.

Throughout history, there have been numerous instances of conquest by one group over another that could be considered attempts to impose and enforce a monolingual, monocultural and homogeneous society on ethnic groups under the banner of nationalism. Barbour's examples (2000: 7) of ethnic cleansing policies adopted by Nazi Germany and the former Yugoslavia during the 20th century were attempts to enforce a total correlation between ethnic group and nation in this way.[7] However, although situations where a given ethnic group constitutes the majoritised population of a state are not the exception, many modern states comprise a range of ethnicities, or alternatively, many ethnic groups live in more than one state.[8] For example, Romaine points out that 25 out of 36 European countries are officially monolingual, even though in most of them there are 'minorities' whose languages do not enjoy the same rights and privileges as those granted to the official state language (2000: 34). Two of Barbour's examples illustrate the point.[9] Although Scotland is deemed a nation within the United Kingdom − what Harvie (1994: 1) terms a 'stateless' nation with a devolved bureaucracy − it rejects the overriding national identity promulgated by the state, ostensibly at the very least. Rather than expressing allegiance and a sense of belonging to their host states, many Arabs (be they citizens of Iraq, Morocco, South Yemen, and so forth) feel instead that they are part of a wide-ranging Arab nation (Barbour, 2000: 5−9). This is an ethical question, and once again, it is borne out by recent and not so recent events in the Middle East. In other words, for many communities, their sense of ethnic identity dominates and takes precedence over the state-orientated national identity and is what unites them either against the dominant ethnic group within the nation-state or against a perceived threat to their existence by outside forces.

Nationalism versus Regionalism

Rather than utilise the term nationalism as I have done above, political and unification aspirations of minoritised communities are often subsumed under the term 'regionalism'. Whilst not wanting to open a protracted debate into the subject, I would point out that the application of such terminology largely depends on whose perspective one is employing. Regionalism, rather than nationalism, is commonly closely associated with claims for collective equality that are rooted in grievances over territory, language, culture, and economic disadvantages (Murphy *et al.*, 2002: 77). Colin Williams (1997: 112–138) identifies three main issues that sustain most forms of regionalism:

- Promotion and protection of a unique language and culture.
- Enhanced economic autonomy to further industrial modernisation or to reverse regional industrial decline.
- More democratic forms of political representation.

Harvie (1994) talks at length about European regionalism from a historical-political point of view. He explains (1994: 2–4) that in the 1970s, the upheavals in Ulster, Corsica, and the Basque Country, together with other political agitations elsewhere, started to give the regional issue political salience that intensified during the 1980s. Far from being backward regions of peasants, unemployment, old-fashioned traditions and little political experience, the regions in question were industrialised areas of sophisticated technology, a well-developed, idiosyncratic yet cosmopolitan culture and civil society, and local democracy. Their successes have paved the way for other 'less developed' regions, such as Galicia as I shall show in Chapter 3, to make similar demands.

Other authors, such as Amodia (1998) writing about Spain, and Lane and Ersson (1987) in general, define a region as a sub-national territorial unit. This may be one of the very reasons why, as Lane and Ersson point out, such notions ultimately become the focus for political activity and claims for some form of autonomy, even independence for the region in question.

In her book on the Spanish-speaking world, Mar-Molinero (2000b: 12) prefers to apply the term 'nationalism', for describing the aspirations by sub-state level ethnic communities who have revived a sense of self-consciousness and identity for some economic, political or social end. Moreover, Donnan and Wilson (2001: 2) convincingly employ the term ethnonationalism to describe, for example, the justification behind the conflicts arising from the dissolution of Yugoslavia, mentioned above (p. 30).[10]

My own view is that the aspirations of minoritised groups tend to be labelled as regionalism or even separatism (Holt & Gubbins, 2002: 6) from the state perspective, but as nationalism from the ethnic group perspective. Given that my intention is to represent the minoritised perspective as legitimate and viable, I adopt the terms 'nationalism', 'regional nationalism' and cognates in my own discussions of the politically-charged situation in Galicia throughout this book; but, where relevant, maintain the particular term employed by attributed authors.[11] Inherent to my argument is the notion of identity.

Ethnicity and Identity

How am I going to define identity? According to Le Page *et al.* (1985: 2), the verb 'identify' has at least two meanings:

- To pick out a particular person, category or example by some feature.
- To recognise some entity as part of some larger entity such as a group or cause.

Identity is not just a simple form of inherent self (or other) awareness; it is also a socially constructed phenomenon that is therefore subject to change (Holt & Gubbins 2002: 1). However, there is no conflict between the two meanings because individual, personal identities and group, social identities exist simultaneously. Complex and multiple social identities are the norm and can be assumed or abandoned as required. Many of us simultaneously belong to different social, cultural and even linguistic groups: one group membership does not necessarily preclude another. Thus, identities may be fluid and dynamic; they may change over time and differ in their relative significance and import, as I shall delineate later in this chapter. The following discussion examines these assertions in more detail.

Our perceptions regarding who we are as individuals focus largely upon the recognition and appreciation of our origins; of where we come from and of what we share with the community as a whole. As Karmela Liebkind states 'a person's self-image is comprised of a personal identity and a social identity' the latter embodying an ethnic component (1999: 140–141). Certainly within the western world, demonstrating kinship with other members of one's community or ethnic group has become extremely relevant of late. There is often strong pressure placed upon ethnic groups forming part of larger multiethnic societies to redefine themselves as nations, because the perceived status of a nation (or, more recently 'a people') as opposed to that of ethnic group, accords a form of legitimacy and authenticity that could facilitate any aspirations for self-rule. Yet, the acquisition of an identity designated as 'nation' should not preclude in any way such a people from retaining an ethnic identity. Skutnabb-Kangas points out that both 'ethnic' and 'minority' have often carried negative connotations based on 'race' or 'colour' and from the perspective of the politically dominant group, ethnic groups are powerless, foreign entities. However, 'ethnicity' is not exclusive to small or minoritised communities, despite the fact that many (predominantly) Western authorities do not include themselves in the definition (2000: 165–169). From their perspective, what Skutnabb-Kangas defines as 'exo-definitions' (2000: 172), ethnicity is a highly hierarchical term used to define such groups and to legitimise the overarching, governing role in society of the definer. Conversely, when the rights of such groups come to the fore, self-identification strategies of what constitutes a particular ethnic group, what Skutnabb-Kangas terms 'endo-definitions' (2000: 172–173) become paramount.

As pointed out earlier, complex and multiple identities (that is dynamic, fluid and subject to change) tend to be the norm. From a psychological perspective, Padilla also observes that a person's self-identification strategies are extremely important to overall group membership and, hence, the most important dimension of ethnicity. Thus, for him 'ethnicity refers to an individual's membership in a social group that shares a common ancestral heritage' and is 'multidimensional in nature [. . .] if a person self-identifies as a member of a particular ethnic group, then he or she is willing to be perceived and treated as a member of that group. Thus, self-ascribed and other-ascribed ethnic labels are the overt manifestations of individuals' identification with a particular ethnicity' (1999: 115).[12]

There are no hard and fast rules as to what each member of an ethnic group should demonstrate in order to be considered such a member. As Padilla further notes (1999: 115–116), the notion of a common ancestral heritage may be one criterion of an ethnic group, but specific cultural traits, such as language use and cultural traditions, and some type of formal social organisation at the group level, facilitating inter- and intra-group communications, are also pertinent. Whilst not every member will demonstrate every criterion, Allardt (in Skutnabb-Kangas, 2000: 174) has suggested that all must demonstrate at least one in order to be considered a member.

Nancy Dorian (1999: 25–26) agrees that biological dimensions, such as those of 'race' and 'creed', are not necessarily relevant to a definition of ethnicity. She states that from an ethnographic perspective, ethnicity rests fundamentally on social underpinnings and attitudes therein, which are themselves subject to change. This point is vital to a clear understanding of the nature of ethnic identity.

The key here is attitude, not only to language but, more importantly, to the whole issue of identity. Autochthonous speaker attitudes regarding the value of their own language are related to their relevance within a given context, their prestige value and expressions of their idiosyncratic identity, which, in turn, are related to the speaker's background, upbringing and level of education (Nelde, 1987: 609). Socialisation practices, whereby children acquire a social identity, normally take place through languages of the home and the community, and Liebkind (1999: 144) points out that it is common to find a positive, integrative attitude towards its use and a desire to be associated with it. Thus, the differentiation of such a group from others may be positively expressed through the use of language, and cultural coherence and shared historical memories may be also used to emphasise and even demarcate idiosyncratic identity and, in certain cases, reinforce claims to self-government or total independence. A sense of solidarity between members of a given group or community will emerge if they share the same positive attitudes towards their particular expressions of identity and language. If this is the case, the language becomes fundamental to the group's ethnicity and acquires prestige as an important identifier of the group's dynamism, status and distinctiveness: 'language gives meaning to an ethnic group because it connects the present with the past through its oral traditions, literary forms, music, history, and customs' (Padilla, 1991: 116).[13] Although traditions, cultural artefacts and societal norms are not necessarily crucial to a group's sense of identity, attitudes towards a given language and its function may be tied with regional, social and cultural stereotypes. That is, perceptions regarding the value of such stereotypes held by the speakers of a given language may serve to reinforce aspirations of 'otherness', or may, conversely, serve to negate them. In his examination of British communities, Cohen (1986: 16–17) demonstrates that when local community diversity is subsumed under a type of overarching cultural homogeny, what remains distinctive is their *sense* of difference. Implicit to this are the perceptions and attitudes of the members towards their characterisation and identity. This point is discussed further below.

Boundaries and Identity

Even in the 21st century, many countries are far from recognising the rights of certain ethnic communities and from accepting their demands for some form of political autonomy. In his early work on the relationship between language and nationalism in the 1970s, Fishman (1972) appraised the question as to whether minoritised ethnic groups can exaggerate or understate certain characteristics that constitute their idiosyncratic society. His employment of the terms 'political' and 'cultural' nationalism was an attempt to differentiate between the concept of what he perceived as legitimate nation-building by the state and what he termed emotionally charged claims of a given ethnic community within the confines of such a state. The basis for this distinction appears to be the notion that ethnic communities tend to exploit ideas of a shared history, a shared culture, and a shared memory for their own ends, but that in other circumstances, such characteristics are swallowed up by the majoritised norm. In other words, when the social situation of a given ethnic group alters for the better, members may choose to maintain their identity with that group. However, if this social situation deteriorates, members may choose to redefine and ally themselves with a different ethnic or social grouping. There may be a central core body of people who consistently maintain most or all of a group's ethnic criteria, but there will be members on the periphery who select certain criteria but adopt others from other ethnicities according to their particular identification needs or wants. In this way, identification strategies are reliant upon positive and negative values associated with a given ethnicity.

This notion that identities may be embraced or discarded according to their particular value or otherwise to a given group is considered at some length by the anthropologist Frederik Barth in his pioneering book *Ethnic Groups and Boundaries: The Social Organization of Culture Difference* (1969). Barth states that a particular ethnic group may choose to either emphasise or underplay its cultural identity, or another one, according to which course of action would be the more advantageous in a given context. Padilla emphasises (1999: 118) that, as a direct consequence of inter-group communication and contact, ethnic groups are not necessarily bound entities; instead, they may be fluid and subject to change. This is one of the key concepts of the constructivist perspective of ethnicity, as I discuss below (pp. 44–45).

Barth's early work focussed upon the continual interface, negotiation and above all maintenance of social boundaries between groups and their identities, and the saliency of certain cultural features according to a given situation and in relation to their neighbours (both in a topographical sense and in terms of group awareness, political differences, and so on). Thus, Skutnabb-Kangas comments that Barth's 'way of seeing the boundaries between ethnicities as the focal point of ethnicity makes the very existence of the boundaries, not their content, the essence of ethnicity' (2000: 175). She adds that in this way, it is the binary oppositions used to constitute a boundary, such as language/non-language use, that function as features of a given group, even if they are constantly changing. Barth does not therefore dismiss the content of ethnic groups outright; he simply considers that the actual detail is less important than the boundary maintenance mechanisms that members negotiate and define in different ways in order to create this opposition. Thus, individual experiences and situations determine how people choose to identify with different groups, and ethnic labels are maintained even when members move across boundaries between different groups. Barth writes:

> [...] categorical ethnic distinctions do not depend on an absence of mobility, contact and information, but do entail social processes of exclusion and incorporation whereby discrete categories are mantained *despite* changing participation and membership in the course of individual life histories. (1969: 9)[14]

Thus, the interface and negotiation of boundaries delineates members of ethnic groups from non-members by acting as a contrast or opposition by which each can be identified. In this way, the groups themselves are the outcome of processes of inclusion and exclusion (Donnan & Wilson, 2001: 21–23).

In this respect, Andersen's important concept of an 'imagined community' (1991) has, at least until recently, been considered invaluable to (non-essential) nationalist ideology. Whilst I concede Fishman's point (1999b: 447) that ethnonational groups are no longer generally considered imagined, in that they exist irrespectively of their point of view regarding their ethnicity, Andersen's model does nonetheless reinforce a sense of 'them' and 'us' even when the *impression* of distinctiveness between groups is illusory. So, by employing their idiosyncratic traits to demonstrate the delineation between 'us' the minoritised, and 'them' the dominant group, or, as Padilla (1999: 116) puts it, between the in-group and the out-group, such communities may want to create a form of social boundary that is inclusive towards its members but exclusive towards non-members. Boundaries afford individuals within a community a measuring stick, by which they can evaluate their compatibility with the applicable central identity features (be they social, cultural, racial, historical or linguistic), *and* by which they can recognise their demarcation from some or all of the identity features that lie outside this framework and that are representative of the external community. The perception of boundaries as an interface between 'us' and 'them' may also mean that 'an internal, symbolic group interface occurs within the psyche of its members'. As I stated above (p. 35), community differences and identity issues may exist less in the structures that once served to underpin them, such as traditions, cultural artefacts, and societal norms, than in the minds of the people who express them. If this is indeed a valid hypothesis, then one of the main driving forces behind a community's success or failure to achieve their given autonomy aims is the implicit support, and by analogy, attitude, of its population. These attitudinal and behavioural factors are considered in Giles and Johnson's (1987) theory of ethnolinguistic identity, whereby in interactions with other groups, individuals may adopt strategies of psycholinguistic distinctiveness by switching to their in-group language in order to reinforce their different collective entity and enhance their self-worth.[15]

Skutnabb-Kangas makes a valuable point regarding core value features (pp. 41–43) and their manipulation across boundaries. Although extremely important to the validation of ethnicity, endo- (in-group, 'us') and exo- (out-group, 'them') categorisations of a given ethnic group often do not concur, because what outsiders see as behavioural manifestations of ethnicity, such as the use of a language, may not be what the insiders would use to define their ethnicity themselves. That is, dominant groups have a particular concept of what comprises the important constituents of identity. Typically, they may impose certain features of their own, such as a language, as 'universally' implicit to all members of the dominated group (Skutnabb-Kangas, 2000: 175–177), even though this subordinated group would have chosen to adopt/use a different range of features to characterise their idiosyncratic identity. In doing so, the dominant group overrides the potential for enhanced support and positive attitudinal factors towards such aspirations within the dominated group.

Language and Identity

Language may or may not play an important role in the conceptualisation of group interfaces. In ideologies of nation building, the relationship between a shared language, concepts of nationalism and the construction of a particular national identity appear to be particularly significant. In the 18th century, language and culture started to be viewed as central to the essence or character (Herder's *Volksgeist*) of the nation. Language in particular came to be constructed as the most important distinguishing characteristic of nationhood, thus, as May (2003: 140–141) reports, the continuing existence of a nation was at that time inconceivable without its own language. Moreover, language continues to play an important and influential role in power and control struggles throughout the world. As Romaine (2000: 23) states, 'Languages and nations are continually used to validate one another in (such) acts of identity'. This means that effective communication is often viewed as the key to the survival or demise of a given community. A national language should embrace the communicative needs of the nation as a whole, for as Barbour points out:

> a nation in the modern sense cannot exist without a shared sense of identity, and for people to share an identity a certain minimum level of communication between them must be guaranteed.
>
> (Barbour, 2004: 4)

The existence of a *lingua franca* accessible to members of the group allows the free flow of ideas and may also be an important way of delineating group identity. In other words, language selection is discriminate, and each speech act may manifest a particular identification strategy.[16]

What this implies is that many of the issues surrounding group language choice are not simply linguistic in that they are not related solely to mutual intelligibility or differentiation from other vernaculars.[17] Language is not only a tool of communication. Dorian (1999: 26) and, in particular, Padilla points out that extant languages adopt extralinguistic characteristics that go far beyond a group's or individual's interpersonal communication needs (1999: 115–116). Although nationalist discourse emphasises the conscious use of a shared language as a competent marker of community identity, the viability of the language is also intimately bound up with – indeed, it is the carrier of – inherent societal historical, cultural, and political factors. Societal, because intra- and intergroup speaker interaction and linguistic association may define and delineate a given identity and highlight a particular set of characteristics differentiating the community from others. Historical, because language links a community with its shared past, and in this linking, it can afford legitimacy and authenticity to the meaning of nation. Cultural, because a shared set of cultural norms also offers a background against which the characterisation of a given community can be supported. Finally, political, because without some form of legal standing, the language of a community will not be supported nor promoted.

In many bi- and multilingual situations, where one or more minoritised ethnic groups exist within a state, assimilatory procedures to the majoritised language are often viewed by the state as inclusive, as a way of minimising linguistic, social and cultural differences that would otherwise engender intergroup discord. By advancing the political enforcement of a common language, the intention is to mould and define the characterisation and identity of the state within its territorial limits. Therefore, social and cultural variation will often be regarded as rather perfunctory by the dominant group, a symbol of a bygone era that should be eradicated for the sake of national unity. However, the dominated group may deem such measures highly oppressive, a method of subjugation to the majoritised society that ignores the significance and relevance of the minoritised group's idiosyncratic features, values and norms, or at the very least, ignores the relevance of such features as a foil to those of the majoritised society. It is certainly clear that such ideology appears at times to have inspired a sense of pride and loyalty amongst minoritised communities in those characteristics that do indeed differentiate them from the more dominant group. Consequently, the minoritised ethnic groups themselves may regard language as a viable, politically charged tool. The very existence of this language can foster a sense of solidarity and of inclusiveness, of pride and of identity amongst members; it thus functions as a prominent symbol of the collective identity, even when not all members use it. The role and inclusive nature of a shared language in nationalist doctrine tends to be emphasised more and more by ethnic communities who seek to break away from the authority of states that advocate the global use of a 'mother tongue' not shared by all the population.[18]

The refusal on the part of a given state mechanism to recognise other languages or varieties and ethnic groups within its borders is why their overriding nationalist tendencies may be considered, at least, partially responsible for the emergence of many separatist movements amongst such minoritised groups in the latter part of the 20th century (Mar-Molinero, 2000b: 4–5). This factor may be, in turn, partially responsible for the growing tolerance towards such movements and towards the concept of official bi- or multilingualism within their borders evinced by modern states such as Spain.[19]

Barbour's example (2000: 12) of recent German unification emphasises the influence that ethnic or national identity may command even when the varieties of language in question are related, but mutually incomprehensible. From the perspective of the nation-state ideology, if speakers accept that these constitute dialects of a single language, they may also accept that they share an ethnic or national identity. However, the converse may also be true. Separate ethnic groups who speak related and mutually comprehensible dialects, may consider, nonetheless, that they speak separate languages from a political perspective. In this way, the perception that these groups speak different languages may be cultivated to endorse other kinds of differences, typically for political reasons. In such cases, demarcation occurs along ethnic and/or religious lines.

A valid example once again (see p. 30 above) is that of the former Yugoslavia, where an ostensibly single, common language was redefined in the 1990s as two, based not upon linguistic differentiation, but upon political state-making and ethnic grouping of Serbian and Croatian.[20] In his comparative survey of the language situation in the former Yugoslavia, Bugarski (2001: 69–87) documents the resistance to the maintenance of the once common language Serbo-Croatian by (separatist) nationalist intelligentsia in the new states of Serbia and Croatia. He cites this resistance as 'a particularly telling example of the ultimate inability of a common language to check interethnic tensions when extralinguistic pressure becomes too strong' (2001: 74). The existence of a common language and the concomitant mutual intelligibility between the groups involved has been ignored because it counters their separatist aims. As a result of linguistic nationalism in the new states, three 'splinter idioms' (2001: 84) have emerged: Serbian in the federation of Serbia and Montenegro, Croatian in Croatia, and Bosnian, Serbian and Croatian in Bosnia-Herzegovina. Furthermore, despite the relative linguistic homogeneity of the area, Croatia and Bosnia in particular, have initiated proactive campaigns with the aim of facilitating the rapid differentiation of their languages.[21]

An important point needs to be made here regarding terminology. Skutnabb-Kangas makes an invaluable comment regarding the ideological use of language as the essential linguistic form by which a group can aspire to being a nation:

> an interesting point about language and self-determination is that all definitions of state, nation, or nation-state [...] talk about (a common, unifying, developed, official) language for the entity. None of them use 'dialect', 'vernacular' or 'patois' in their definitions, the implication being that people who form a dialect, vernacular or patois [...] community do not and/or cannot form a nation or a state or a nation-state (and maybe not even a people?).[...] Dialects are not seen as developed enough to fulfil all the linguistic functions of a nation or a state. Having a language (as opposed to a dialect) thus becomes symbolic of a nation and a state (and even a people), in much the same way as a national flag, a national anthem, etc, are or may be symbolic of the state.
>
> (Skutnabb-Kangas, 2000: 426)

Ethnic minorities aspiring to self-determination often contest the criteria of a unifying language employed by official, nation-state ideologies. However, as Freeland and Patrick (2004: 5–6) point out, 'claims are made upon states and granted by states [...] even the international legal instruments by which such rights are recognised depend on agreement among states, and therefore only embody what states are prepared to concede.' Therefore, even linguistic forms that are commonly termed 'dialect' must be redefined if a minoritised group is to succeed with its claims for self-identification and determination, as I discuss below.

Implicit within separatist or ethnonational movements is the idea that the general community demonstrates allegiance to the collective and aspire to its aims. Llobera (1994: 131–2) states that in such contexts, (regional) nationalist feeling has not only to be awakened or even created from scratch, but it has also to 'compete' against the existing state nationalism.[22] Yet, it is not enough for a community to have a strong self-identity or a desire for some form of independence. All successful regional nationalisms, including those involving such minoritised ethnic groups against the overriding state, tend to be linked to a well-developed, dynamic civil society, which utilises its idiosyncratic social and cultural variation to enhance this identity and thus, its political ideology. In this context, Llobera compares the differing fortunes of Scotland and Catalonia in the second half of the 19th century. He concludes that although both enjoyed strong ethno-national potential, only the Catalan civil society was able to develop a sense of regional national identity at the cultural level, through the promotion of the Catalan language and literature, music and the arts during the *Renaixença*. In turn, it was able to turn this sense of identity into a bona fide regional nationalist ideology and, ultimately, into the ideological basis for self-determination.[23]

However, this situation was not paralleled in my earlier example (p. 30) of Scotland, for at the time, their civil society looked more over the border for guidance and inspiration. Hence, there appears not to have been a sense of a strong 'local' identity fostered by tradition, culture, the arts and indeed, a thriving local language, which could countermand the ingrained nation-state culture dictated by London. Appraisals of the more contemporary situation, such as that of Barbour described above (2000: 5), indicate that a renaissance in the strength of feeling as to the notion of a Scottish identity has led to the Scots' rejection of this overriding national identity. To cite a crude example, one has only to attend a Scottish-English football or rugby match to witness the passion the Scots display when pitched against the English. Yet, although there has been a revival of Scottish civil society and of those characteristics it represents, and despite the various linguistic profiles of Scotland, it is English that enjoys the role of national language (Barbour, 2000: 24–5). Scots Gaelic is generally spoken sporadically across all of Scotland, but is concentrated in the Western Highlands and Islands.[24] The lack of an independent linguistic identity with both the support and potential for use by the majority of the people means that the regional nationalist ideology advanced by the Scottish Nationalist Party (SNP) in the 1990s, in order to rally support for an independent Scottish nation, has had to find other ways of appealing to the population. Although there is a deep-seated, historical tradition of conflict between the two peoples, and although differentiating cultural artefacts abound, the principal enabler of such calls for devolution has been arguments of an economic nature.[25] However, very recently, Scots Gaelic has also secured the support of MSPs, and in early 2005, the Scottish Parliament approved the Gaelic Language Bill. This affords the language equal official status in Scotland to English, promotes its use by public bodies and authorities, and guarantees its future by means of a strategic national plan that encompasses educational planning initiatives, such as the new recruitment of Gaelic teachers (Scottish Executive, 2005).

Core Values and Identity

The issue of Scottish identity and its (until now at least) inability to be reliant on linguistic differentiation from England can also be used to demonstrate Jerzy Smolicz's core value theory (1981, 1991, 1997), in which he examines the notion of linguistic and cultural markers as the 'building blocks of the group's cultural identity' (Smolicz, 1997: 67).

Smolicz contends that core values are central to the reputation, creativity, and ultimate cultural survival of ethnic groups, and so their patronage is essential to the maintenance and development of its identity. Core values belong to a given group, and their function is often to emphasise the group's linguistic, social or other, differentiation. Smolicz believes that language is a central and essential core value for most ethnolinguistic groups, without which their ethnic identity cannot survive many generations, but he concedes that this identity can also be based upon other factors such as religion, family or social structure, racial affiliation or descent. In the earlier example of Northern Ireland (pp. 28–29), there may be threats, perceived or otherwise, to a group's characterisation of their ethnicity or even to their continued existence. Members may thus consider the maintenance of cultural core values as the only way of reinforcing ethnic identification and resist pressures from without to assimilate with other groups (1997: 68).[26]

The above example of Northern Ireland is also significant in that it does not totally equate with Smolicz's contentions, for language is not a central core value to these groups. Indeed, many leading authors on multiculturalism and multilingualism subscribe to a conceptualisation of multiculturalism that does not necessarily stress linguistic difference as a cultural core value of a given group, but recognises and defends the creative potential in any society of a wider cultural diversity. This is why the SNP can express in English their allegiances to a definition of 'Scottishness' – even if such a definition has to be enabled by economic factors.

According to this theory, the active retention of community languages in the home need not be central to perceptions of ethnic identity (Watts, 1997: 12–13). May (2001) for example, thinks that language is in most cases a contingent factor, and often not a factor at all in ethnic identity. Whilst he believes that people have the right to maintain their ethnolinguistic identity, he adds that when groups abandon the use of their language, they may also abandon all identification with it (2001: 8–9). This is an important point, for it recognises that language is not necessarily central to the maintenance of ethnic identity. Hence, if second or third generation Galicians speak little or no Galician and attach little importance to this, this does not imply that they have rejected their sense of 'Galicianness', for they may use other core values to construct and demonstrate their 'Galician' identity.

The above discussion makes clear that within a bi- or multilingual nation-state, cultural, social, historical, and linguistic traits that differentiate a minoritised ethnic community from the majoritised host nation may have a dominant role to play in their political aspirations. However, not all need to be exercised, nor do they have to be exercised by all of the population. Although language is often cited as justification for such ambition and is the way in which it can be articulated, it may not necessarily be core in all situations.

The Issue of Symbolism

I now explore further the issue of symbolism and the depiction of ethnicity. As I have pointed out above, language is one of a large number of potential ethnic markers, and despite its importance, at a purely symbolic level, it may be argued that other traits can also serve a role as a marker of ethnic identity. If this is indeed the case, then a given language may not be actively used, and, ultimately, may even be cast aside. Nonetheless, what must be emphasised is that as I have highlighted above, language may still be an underlying and key constituent of ethnic identity. That is, it does not necessarily stop being a core value. Even if it becomes obsolete in practice, its symbolic and emotional values may still serve to reinforce a sense of identity within the community. Conversely, when a community *is* willing and able to maintain its idiosyncratic language as its primary means of communication, then such values will have an even larger role to play.

All core values may carry a heavy symbolic load. The traits outlined above are significant insofar as they function as a boundary between 'them' and 'us', and lend focus to a community's political or social aims. On the surface, it may be that they do not feature in the everyday concerns of the whole community in question, and are not used as typical expressions of its collective identity. Nonetheless, they may exist at a deeper level, and hence, have a purely emblematic or symbolic value, or even be relegated to the level of folkloric artefacts. Once again, the Scottish example is relevant.

Essentialism versus Constructivism

In the above discussion, I have described what are intrinsically essentialist and non-essentialist concepts regarding the ways in which identities are constructed, and I have attempted to consider both equitably. This debate has been raging over the last two decades and is discussed in some detail in Stephen May's recent book *Language and Minority Rights; Ethnicity, Nationalism and the Politics of Language* (2001). I highlight the most salient points below.[27]

According to May, Max Weber's definition of 'ethnic group' as 'those human groups that entertain a subjective belief in their common descent because of similarities of physical type or of customs or of both, or because of memories of colonisation and migration' (1961: 389) summarises the potentially contradictory aspects of ethnicity. Not only does this indicate the implicit association between ethnic groups and ancestral, cultural, and racial traits, it also emphasises that a belief in the shared nature of these characteristics is a consequence rather than a cause of collective political action, and in turn acts as a means of defining group membership (May, 2001: 27). Again, in the case of my earlier Scottish example (pp. 30, 41), economic justification for devolution has enabled historical and cultural features to be adopted as representative of a Scottish identity.

However, this dual perspective of ethnicity has often been polarised to the extent that it is viewed as either the outcome of cultural and linguistic characteristics, termed 'primordial', or the outcome of a dynamic, changeable process of identity construction, termed 'situational'. May examines both perspectives in some detail (2001: 9, 18–19, 27–44). Following Herder, the primordial perspective assigns a fixed and enduring, intrinsic and even predetermined character to ethnicity. This character is linked to and determined by specific cultural traits that demonstrate and are representative of the ethnic group in question. Language is a significant, constitutive factor of this identity, but ancestry and history are also valid. In this way, the primordial perspective is considered an 'essentialist' concept.

Proponents of the situational or constructivist perspective argue instead for the social and political usefulness of ethnicity, its fluidity and malleability between different groups, and its instrumental mobilisation to particular political ends. Ethnicity is thus always considered a social construct, irrespective of whether an 'exo-definition' or 'endo-definition' (Skutnabb-Kangas, 2000: 172–173), is in play.

What is pertinent here is that the groups situationally classify themselves according to their social interactions with others and according to the boundaries erected and then upheld between them as a result, determining who is and is not a member. This then, brings us back to Barth's hypothesis demonstrated earlier regarding ethnic boundary maintenance (pp. 35–36).[28]

In my discussion of ethnicity, identity and language above, I have tried to demonstrate that in essence I agree with May, who states that ethnic identities can both be innate and not (2001: 10). He centres part of his argument around language, as I have highlighted (p. 42) stating that language is not fundamental to the construction of identity. Nevertheless, it can be a significant factor, as evidenced by the increased prominence of language issues and concomitant individual and collective allegiance in many minoritised political conflicts. However although language may well be just one of many markers of identity in theory, in practice, it is often much more than that. Throughout the world, communities continue to define themselves by their autochthonous language, as evidenced by Skutnabb-Kangas' point that in most cases of minoritised language claims she has encountered, language has been a highly significant factor of identity (2003: 7).[29]

May also argues that ethnicity is a valid concept and should be viewed as both constructed and contingent (2001: Chapters 1–2). He suggests that

primordial and situational views do not form mutually exclusive concep-
tualisations of ethnicity but that each represents a limited representation
of the underlying social and cultural movements they seek to describe.
Not only does ethnicity represent deeply rooted perceptions of characterisation, indefinable cultural, and symbolic attributes that groups employ
to define their sense of 'belonging'; it also is a fluid, social, political and
cultural way of life, in which origin, content, and form are subject to
choice and change.

In certain circumstances, groups will emphasise language as part of a
'situational' response, even though it may not be one of their core
values. Freeland's Nicaraguan example (2003) highlights this point: in
the first year of the revolution in 1979, all groups began by making
claims of the Sandinistas for education in their languages, at a time
when the main Sandinista policy was the literacy crusade and education
reform. Although this made sense, each autochthonous and ethnic group
was actually making different kinds of claims, and for some the reasons
behind their claims were highly pragmatic – pertaining to the retention
of land – rather than to do with emphasising their linguistic differences.
This is a clear example of ethnogenesis, the process whereby groups have
to work for their own survival and identity within specific and changing
historical contexts, drawing attention to or away from particular aspects
of their culture according to their requirements.

This perspective mirrors to some extent the constructivist view. May
(2001: 19) states that detractors of the concept of ethnicity consider it a
highly convenient, subjective and situational construction, mobilised
instrumentally by particular groups to achieve social or political ends.
In this way, an ethnic group's _supposed_ distinctiveness may be employed
retrospectively to engender 'ethnic solidarity' as a basis for social and political action. Whilst I find this definition somewhat overcritical, it nonetheless highlights the usefulness of underplaying or overplaying a
group's ethnic differences according to their specific needs at a given time.

Multiple Identities

The above discussion brings me back to the notion of multiple identities. Complex and multiple social identities are the norm, and can be
assumed or abandoned as required.[30] Skutnabb-Kangas describes our
multifaceted general characteristics, such as gender, ethnos, profession,
and so on (2000: 390). Moreover, people simultaneously belong to different social, cultural and even linguistic groups: one group membership
does not necessarily preclude another. Indeed, people may perceive
themselves as belonging more to one particular group than to another
at a given point in time, but may identify more strongly with one
group than with another according to the specific event, situation or

circumstances in which they find themselves. As a result, the ways in which language is used to reinforce differing senses of group membership and, hence, notions of solidarity with that group, may be subject to change as well. This is especially true when I consider bilingual communities. The earlier comments regarding the conscious manipulation of different identities by minoritised ethnic groups could lead us, somewhat erroneously, to presume that such actions are always to be considered highly contentious and Machiavellian. Yet, as Liebkind (1999: 145–147) and Hidalgo (2001: 61–62) both point out, such bilingual, bicultural groups are the general outcome of contact situations between two disparate societies. Despite these claims, one, single ethnic self-identification strategy is extremely unlikely, because inherent identities are not necessarily discarded when others are assumed.[31] Identity, therefore, can be said to be additive (Holt & Gubbins, 2002: 4). I would add that one, single self-identification strategy as far as language is concerned is also unlikely, even if the autochthonous language has been lost as the language of habitual use and any emotional attachment to it is symbolic. Nonetheless, such an identity may still be maintained alongside the national one. To sum up: ethnicity is a social construct, but it is reinforced and enhanced by cultural core values such as language, and it is overtly manifest in the group's idiosyncratic sense of identity.[32]

Revitalisation and Revival

In the above discussion, it is apparent that language can play an important role in the underpinning of identity. As I have commented, this sense of identity and belonging may be highly reinforced if the language also fulfils a communicative function, for in this case, the transmission of such ideologies throughout the group by use of their ethnic language tends to enhance support for the group's aspirations. Thus, it is paramount that all members, not just an intellectual elite, have the means to learn and use the language on a day-to-day basis should they choose to do so. When an ethnic group starts to consider itself a nation, it needs to make a conscious effort to elevate its language to some form of formal, legal status, by taking deliberate steps in order to differentiate it from others with which it comes into contact. Hence, it may become the subject of revitalisation and revival attempts, leading to large-scale language planning and policy making.[33]

Inherent to the whole issue of educational, economic, and political equality of minoritised groups is the issue of linguistic rights. Yet, as I have stated in the Introduction, this book both is, and is not, a book about such rights. It plainly is, in that we can situate the particular case study by focusing on language revitalisation (of Galician) in a country (Spain) where, following a sustained period of subordination and repression, language rights have been recently conceded. Yet, the primary point of interest is what happens afterwards, in other words, what are the problems and complications of implementing such rights in a particular social, historical, and linguistic context. For this reason, I do not propose to address the issue from a theoretical and largely generic, perspective. Should the reader wish to pursue this further, I would direct them to Skutnabb-Kangas' extensive discussion of both linguistic and human rights and the viability and effectiveness of recent legislation (2000, 2003).

Nor do I apologise for omitting from this book extensive accounts of theories and concepts pertaining to language policy making and language planning. Many excellent discussions abound, hence any further detailed exposition would serve little purpose. What follows is a brief and simple outline of language planning and policy issues insofar as they are relevant to the case study of Galician.[34]

Haugen's early definition of language planning (1987), which included every deliberate attempt to change the linguistic behaviour of a speech community, has been expanded over the years. However, it is still considered a form of social planning, and now generally refers to the largely prescriptive, intentional, direct, and observable implementation of the means through which language policies are put into practice.

Through corpus planning, language planning aims to establish a standard, a shared set of linguistic norms pertaining to the grammar, the lexicon and the phonological system, through the codification and elaboration of a particular form (one or more varieties or dialects for example). Through status planning, it attempts to expand the functional demarcation of a particular language and improve its perceived status and in doing so, it may also alter the diglossic framework of a particular community. By affording the language a prestigious image, status planning fosters positive feelings and attitudes towards its use, which in turn, enhances a community's notions of the language's acceptability and appropriateness in hitherto uncharacteristic contexts. Through acquisition planning, language planning attempts to encourage new users through collective and institutional promotion, especially through the identification of ways in which language use and language learning can be expanded and promoted.

The issue of reinforcing the prestige value of a given language is particularly important in the case of minoritised languages. Maintenance of the autochthonous language may be vital to the group for collective linguistic, social and political identification purposes, and one of the ways that it is sustained is through the education system. Its increased learning and application through the medium of education may enhance the status and functional demarcation of the language, and may lead to its formalisation through standardisation practices.

However, education is not necessarily the only, or even the best, option in all circumstances. Fishman's Graded Intergenerational Disruption Scale (GIDS), initially devised in the early 1990s, but still pertinent to present-day studies of multilingual scenario, offers a particularly relevant analysis of the processes through which language shift can be reversed. Fishman terms GIDS a 'sociolinguistic disruption scale' (1991: 87), comprising eight stages that correspond to types of language communities or networks, and ranging from a scenario in which the autochthonous language is severely threatened, to a scenario in which the language is upheld and supported institutionally, but the community at large does not enjoy ethnonational status (1991: 88–109). Significantly, he points out that the revitalisation of endangered languages entirely through formal education is in danger of failure, because before such initiatives can be implemented and before the language itself can be 'reconstructed', there are intragroup stages that should be addressed. As I have delineated in previous sections above (pp. 21–23, 34–35, 37–38), the reconstruction of a positive sense of identity associated with the use of the autochthonous language, particularly among the younger generations, is paramount. Once this is achieved, the re-establishment of the language's oral sociofunction as 'the normal medium or co-medium of communication in home, family, neighbourhood and community intergeneration vernacular activity' (1991: 91) needs to be implemented. Subsequently, the initiation of processes that facilitate the acquisition of literacy skills within the community should be carried out. Only then should more formalised educational programmes come into play. This hypothesis is pertinent to the Galician situation, and will be discussed in Chapter 8.

Both policy and planning procedures can occur at many levels within a given society, implemented both by governmental institutions, such as the education system, and by non-institutional bodies, such as local community pressure groups, corporate bodies, and religious organisations. As stated earlier (p. 46), for a language to undergo processes of language planning and policy making, it must enjoy the support and loyalty of the community as a whole; linguistic rights only become valid from a collective point of view. Thus, if the general population display a positive attitude towards the comprehensive application of the language in as many settings as possible, then it will, in turn, start to acquire prestige value. Of course, the reverse is also true, for if a language belongs to a community that is stigmatised for some reason, its use may convey negative connotations, and be considered representative of a lower social status.

Languages that achieve such status are indicators of some degree of power.[35] Within Western Europe in particular, their survival became a focal point of interest in the 1960s, as the issue of minoritised versus majoritised rights came to the fore. For the individual, language became a potent symbol of social identity; for the community however, it became a symbol of political aspiration, and loyalty to a particular language became associated with national or ethnic identity. Thus, from a political perspective it became necessary to gain control of the state or at least win official state recognition for the language, since struggles to gain independence from autocratic dictators and to gain the right to self-determination are often reflected in a community's resolve to secure the survival of its language. Within a society where two or more languages are in conflict, the minoritised language may have the loyalty of its speakers. If so, the community authorities will endeavour to maintain it in its 'purest' form, that is, as a standard form, and the community as a whole, or at least parts of it, will endeavour to secure the right to use it within their daily lives.

In the Introduction, I offered Wales as a brief example of societal bilingualism (p. 12). The Welsh situation demonstrates, moreover, how allegiance to an ethnic identity is associated with the language for some, but not all of the members of society. By the 19th century, Welsh had managed to survive throughout the country as the language of general, everyday communication. However, the subsequent influx of English-speaking coal miners and their families, together with the exodus of autochthonous communities from the Valleys during the depression of the 1930s, produced an overall shift to the use of English, at the very least in public interactions. In 1840, it is estimated that over two thirds of the population were able to speak Welsh, with over half being monolingual in it (Holmes, 2001: 65–66). By 1921, the Census indicated that 37.1% of the population were able to speak Welsh, and 6.3% spoke only Welsh. By 1981, only 18.9% could speak the language to any degree and less that 1% spoke only Welsh (Williams, 1994: 131). However, this situation is not uniform across the country. In the counties of North Wales for example, there are still substantial numbers of Welsh speakers, as there are in Dyfed in the southwest of the country. However, what is significant is that the vast majority of these speakers are bilingual. Williams in particular, disagrees with the opinion that the significant decrease in monolingual speakers 'tolls the death knell of Welsh as an autonomous language', although he concedes that in functional terms, future Welsh speakers will probably all be bilingual to some extent or other (1994: 131–132). The sustained efforts by the local political party *Plaid Cymru*, what May has termed an ethnonational movement (2001: 20), to secure recognition for the language and its people within a national state of their own, cannot be discounted. Thanks to a deliberate and determined agenda to raise awareness of the autochthonous language as representative of a Welsh ethnic affiliation, Welsh has indeed managed to uphold its status, despite the continued influx of English speakers. Institutional support, such as successful bilingual education programmes initiated by the Welsh Language Board and an enhanced, positive image has meant that in North Wales at least, the language has experienced an upsurge in loyalty and concomitant use. Much of the autochthonous population there actively chooses to employ the Welsh language in their daily transactions. According to the Household Interview survey carried out in 1997, the highest proportion of Welsh speakers are to be found in Gwynedd (74.3%), the Isle of Anglesey (62.6%) and Ceredigion (60.9%) – all in North Wales (The European Charter for Regional or Minority Languages: Initial Periodical Report from the United Kingdom). However, the situation further south continues to be tenuous, with fewer areas where such support has been widespread and fewer communities where the population as a whole feel any loyalty to the minoritised language. The lowest concentrations of Welsh speakers are found in Blaenau, Gwent and Monmouthshire, all in the south, where the proportion of speakers is fewer than 7.5% (The European Charter for Regional or Minority Languages: Initial Periodical Report from the United Kingdom).[36]

My earlier comments regarding Catalonia (pp. 40–41) underline the strong regional nationalist ideology that pervaded throughout the years of Franco's dictatorship, which facilitated both the revitalisation of the autochthonous language and the realisation of many of its ethnonational political and social aspirations. In 1979, as one of the richest, most industrially developed regions of Spain, it was granted self-government status under the auspices of the Spanish government in Madrid. Despite the ever-increasing influx of a non-autochthonous, Castilian speaking workforce, nearly all of the indigenous population are bilingual Catalan/Castilian speakers. Yet, maintenance of this group bilingualism does not conform to the general tenet that high-prestige, national languages tend to displace minoritised languages (Fishman, 1964: 55). Although Castilian continues to be associated with political power, as in the rest of Spain, Catalan is the language associated with economic dominance and control within the autonomous region. Castilian has therefore not displaced Catalan from its high prestige contexts. The Catalan people maintain a tenacious loyalty to their autochthonous language, despite the rigorous imposition of Castilian during the Franco years when the minoritised language was subject to fierce repression. In this case, it is not the topic of conversation but the linguistic identity of the interlocutor that dictates the choice of language employed, for even the most formal of topics are regularly discussed in Catalan.[37]

Colin Williams first employed concepts pertaining to the territorial language principle, the policy under which there is an obligation to use a particular language within a particular territory, thus, rights are granted to the language in that area in order to ensure its maintenance there.[38] Both Catalonia, Wales, and, as I shall discuss later, Galicia are good examples of this policy.

However, the example of Malta is not so promising. Back in the 1970s, Ellul (1978) considered Malta to be a country where ethnic loyalty was successfully helping the revival of a language in crisis. Her claim was that since the island had secured independence, there had been a noticeable reassertion of ethnic pride amongst these communities, evinced largely by a significant shift in language loyalty in favour of the use of Maltese in many of, what she terms, more formal domains. She believed that this was due to proactive institutional support, (principally by the Maltese Language Board and the Maltese Academy), which meant that the entire population was actively encouraged both to speak and write in Maltese. She concluded her study by claiming (1978: 26) that within another decade, a revival of Maltese in situations where English had started to intrude was also highly likely.

Despite the enhanced profile of the language on the international stage, this transformation does not appear to have transpired. On the positive side, Maltese is now an official language of the European Union, it shares co-official status with English, and the Constitution states that the national language of Malta is Maltese.[39] Indeed, it is the first language of 98.6% of the population, even though the majority of the population are bilingual. On the less positive side, Badia I Capdevila's recent research (2004: 4–5) states that some 14% of the population now use English within the context of the family and 29% claim to use it at work. Badia I Capdevila states therefore (2004: 6–8) that the vitality of Maltese is under threat because of its low-prestige profile. English is the language of power, the second language of the middle and upper classes in the towns and cites, and the preferred written language of the well educated. Maltese is generally perceived as only appropriate for intra-group functions, principally within the lower working classes and largely rural communities. Notwithstanding the fact that some 86.23% of the population claim to prefer speaking in Maltese, the author states that the language cannot rely on the loyalty of its speakers and that its survival depends upon a profound change in attitude.[40]

Concluding Remarks

The main aim of this rather theoretical chapter has been to offer working definitions of much of the socio-political terminology that is currently topical within the study of multilingual communities in general, and within the historical and contemporary contexts of Galicia and its language in particular. I make no apologies for the fact that it has taken this somewhat political outlook, for the role of the overarching state government, its policies, practices and attitudes towards its minoritised peoples is inherent to the issues of linguistic and ethnic rights. In subsequent chapters, this will prove to be of paramount importance to discussions of Galicia as an autonomous community of Spain. In particular, the conceptual framework I offer will serve to underline the historical situation and inherent problems faced by the Galician community to achieve self-governing status, which I describe in some detail in Chapters 2 and 3.

One component of my hypothesis concerns the nature of the Galician language as a marker of ethnic identity. To this end, I have delineated the two principal theories of essentialism and constructivism, and I have considered the viability of the core value model, for these will be indispensable to my discussion of identity manipulation in Galicia, and the role therein of language and other traits.

In my hypothesis, I also speculate as to the impact of linguistic policies and planning on behavioural practices and attitudes. The final section of this chapter has considered language revitalisation and revival approaches. However, this section is somewhat brief, for my main concern has been to establish the fundamental principles underlying the actions of the Galician government regarding the autochthonous language since the advent of democracy in Spain, rather than attempt to emulate esteemed works in this field. These points are discussed in some detail in Chapter 3. I now turn to a detailed consideration of the historical significance of Galicia's relationship with Portugal and with the rest of Spain.

Chapter 2

The Origins of Galician

Introductory Remarks

Chapter 1 situated this study within a general conceptual framework relating to issues of language use, language status, and language revival. In particular, I highlighted the potential role of the relationship between language and identity for minoritised communities who harbour aspirations for autonomy from the dominant state. I also made some detailed comments on how the socio-political context can influence attitudes of the community towards the use of their autochthonous language. Yet, an account of the relationship between language and identity within a community such as Galicia cannot be carried out without also establishing the historical framework, for many of the behavioural practices and attitudes towards these issues, discussed in later chapters, are a reflection of what has happened before. Therefore, the present chapter is concerned with the use and status of the Galician language from both an historical and a contemporary perspective in order to offer the reader the necessary background information to understand the context of post-Franco initiatives to revitalise the language. In particular, I address the issue of attitude towards Galician and its value to the community has been especially relevant in Galicia since its scission from Portugal.

In order to understand the motivation behind the various linguistic changes that have occurred over time in Galicia, I now examine the political and social underpinnings, for these have played an important role in the history of Galicia. Throughout the history of Spain, processes of what have been termed centripetal and centrifugal movement have emphasised the influence of the political context on periods of unification and fragmentation of the state.[1] This alternation between centralisation (provoking regional resistance) and decentralisation (provoking further centralisation), often correlates with more or less authoritarian and dictatorial rule, and it is important to linguistic and regional nationalist identity issues, since this process can either repress local identities and languages, or provide spaces within which they can flourish.

I start out by tracing the historical relationship of Galician with Portuguese and Castilian Spanish, for these relationships are fundamental both to its linguistic form and to its prestige (or otherwise) within the community. I offer a brief outline of the Roman and post-Roman period of conquest and domination of the western areas of the Peninsula, and I underline the role the Asturo-Leonese Monarchy played in the integration of what is now Galicia into the Kingdoms of Leon and, ultimately, Castile. This led to the demise of Galician-Portuguese as a linguistic entity and the subsequent emergence of Galician and Portuguese as distinct languages. My analysis of the resultant period of integration with Castile highlights the historical association between Galician and Castilian Spanish by offering a description of the diglossic relationship between them prevalent in Galicia during the Middle Ages, and reiterates the implications that the development of Galician society had for the Galician language and its use.

The emergence and development of a linguistic, political and social consciousness, culminating in the foundation of what was termed a Galician regionalist movement in the 19th century, is fundamental to Galician revival and revitalisation processes.

Throughout this discussion, I emphasise the subsequent struggle for self-governmental status and linguistic unification in Galicia, in the face of social upheaval and unrest and despite the prevailing educational vacuum. The interplay between aspirations for a linguistic standard and the existence of traditional dialectal study during the Franco era is briefly mentioned in order to highlight in particular the role played by the two divergent groups who would ultimately influence the configuration of the official orthographic standards adopted in the 1980s, and discussed in Chapter 3. Finally, I present a brief review of legislation passed in Galicia pertaining to the language once Spain started to undergo the democratic process.

The Emergence of Galician-Portuguese

Invasion and conquest

> A lingoa de .... Galliza & Portugal as quaes ambas erão antigamente quasi hu~a mesma, nas palauras, & nos diphtongos, & pronunciaçaõ que as outras partes de Hespanha naõ tem
>
> [The language(s) of .... Galicia and Portugal, which were both once almost one and the same, both with a vocabulary, diphthongs, and a pronunciation that the other areas of Hispania do not share.]
>
> (Nunes de Leão, 1983: 244) [1606]

From the outset, I must emphasise that the following section is intended simply as a general overview of the ancient history of the western communities of the Iberian Peninsula and their linguistic varieties, rather than any far-reaching analysis or detailed account of events.[2]

Between three and four million people worldwide are estimated to speak the Galician language nowadays.[3] Although Galicia has been part of the Kingdom of Spain for nearly nine hundred years, its autochthonous language shares its origins and early development not with Castilian Spanish but with Portuguese, as the language commonly denoted in English as Galician-Portuguese.

Little is known about the prehistoric societies that lived in Galicia. There were two major migration routes into Galicia at this time (Mariño Paz, 1998: 24). The first, comprising populations and languages that originated all over Europe, came through the Pyrenees in the north east of what is now Spain. The second, principally from North Africa and the Near East, entered Spain on the eastern and southern coasts. Between the 8th and 6th centuries BC, an Iron Age, Indo-European Celtic substratum, the *Gallaeci*, had crossed the Pyrenees and settled in the centre and northwest parts of the Iberian Peninsula. Although there have been many attempts to exaggerate their role in the foundation of Galician culture, society and language (see p. 112, pp. 144–5 and p. 239), they did not limit their migrations to Galician territories.

At the time of the Roman Conquest in the 3rd century BC, the north west of the Peninsula was extremely fragmented politically, linguistically, socially, and culturally. The incorporation of the Iberian Peninsula into the Roman Empire was a gradual process of military domination and cultural and linguistic advance. Roman troops entered north-eastern Spain in 218 BC, and over the course of the next two centuries, armies left their landing sites and began their inexorable advance westwards and northwards, with the northern coastal area (now comprising Galicia, Asturias, Santander and part of the Basque Country) being finally conquered by 19 BC. By the 2nd century AD, the isolated Celtic settlements that formed the basis of the *cultura castrexa* had been abandoned as the Romans unified the diverse communities into larger, more manageable colonies.

Initially, the Peninsula was divided into two administrative provinces, *Hispania Ulterior* and *Hispania Citerior*, based to a large degree on ethnic divisions. In 27 BC, as a consequence of administrative reforms, *Hispania Ulterior* was divided further into *Lusitânia*, what now comprises Galicia and Portugal and which was largely unaffected by the Roman colonisation, and *Baética*, which was by this time much more integrated into Roman culture and society. In 13 BC, the north-western territories of *Lusitânia* were assimilated into the huge province of *Tarraconensis*. More administrative reforms followed, and between 284 and 288 AD, the Roman Emperor Diocleciano further annexed *Hispania*, naming the north-western territories *Gallaecia* after the tribes the Romans had conquered there. These territories comprised what is currently Galicia and Northern Portugal, together with the western parts of what are now Asturias and Cantabria.

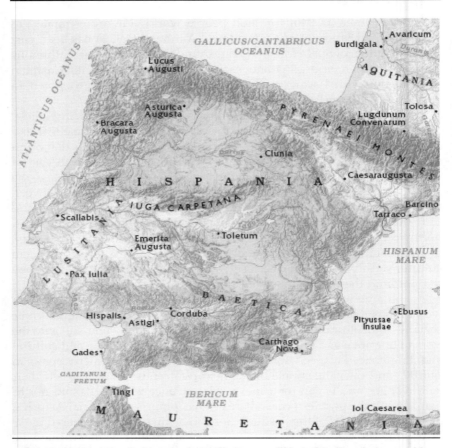

Map 3. The Iberian Peninsula after the Roman conquest

Although the true administrative limits of Gallaecia are not known, Mariño Paz (1998: 43) believes that at this time, the territory was largely homogenous as far as its language and ethnic identity were concerned. Latinisation of the Peninsula occurred more for pragmatic reasons than because of deliberate enforcement, as part of the general centralisation processes of the Roman Empire. In the eastern and southern provinces in particular, the local communities adopted Vulgar Latin, the language of their conquerors, relatively quickly, with the result that by 1st century AD at the very latest, the autochthonous languages had been completely supplanted and all communication, legislation and the school system relied on the use of either Literary or Vulgar Latin. However, this process of acculturation and assimilation appears to have taken place at a much slower pace in the western and northern provinces, isolated to a large degree from the major Roman conurbations elsewhere in the Peninsula, and, as a consequence, from the direct influence of the prestigious standard form of Latin (Cano Aguilar, 1999: 19; Penny, 2002: 8–9). As a result, a state of bilingualism may have persisted at the very least until the end of the Roman period in the 5th century.

Following the collapse of Roman control in the Peninsula in the 3rd century AD, the invasions of the Germanic tribes of Swabians, Alans and Vandals marked the beginning of the Medieval Period of the history of Spain. Most were annihilated, expelled or, in the case of the Swabians, confined to the northwestern territories, including what is now Galicia and northern Portugal, with the invasion in 411 of the Visigoths. The Swabians transformed parts of Roman *Gallaecia* into an independent kingdom. The Visigoths also established an independent kingdom comprising much of the Peninsula as well as southwest Gaul, (which they subsequently lost to the Franks), and finally assimilated the Swabians into the Visigothic kingdom in 585 AD.

The Visigoths were already partly Romanised and bilingual, eventually electing to use Latin over their Eastern German varieties. Despite the Visigoths' political supremacy until the early 8th century, their direct linguistic and cultural influence in the geographically isolated regions of the north and northwest appears to have been minimal, since there was no continual cross-social and cross-cultural contact between conquerors and conquered. In this way, the level of unification and social cohesion of the Peninsula achieved under the Romans, albeit not total, was done away with.

The Islamic conquest of 711 had huge linguistic consequences for most of the Peninsula, including what is now southern and central Portugal. However, the linguistic varieties of the northwestern regions were virtually directly unaffected by Arabic varieties. These areas were conquered and overrun in 713 but the Moors, content to leave the area in the command of small garrisons of men, virtually abandoned the zone. During the Reconquest, the Christian focus of resistance against the Moors was centred round the Pyrenees and the Cordillera Cantábrica in the north of Spain, the areas that had tenaciously resisted Moorish invasion. Thus, Galicia remained fairly well protected in its remoteness by the strategic desert of the Meseta to the north of the Douro after the Asturian Monarchy led the people of the area to the inaccessible, and more defensible mountainous regions. However, this did not prevent the Moors from striking back at insurgencies within the region, with several devastating campaigns during the 9th century. Indeed, they were only routed fully by the end of the 10th century.

Scission and integration

The isolationist policies of the 8th and early 9th centuries engendered language fragmentation throughout the Asturian Monarchy, so that once again, the northwestern regions were effectively cut off from the linguistic influences of the centres of power. Hence, the linguistic varieties of the regions retained highly archaic, conservative forms. It was only with the repopulation of the Meseta area as part of the Asturoleonese Monarchy, together with Galicia's newly found status as an important Christian pilgrimage centre after the discovery of the supposed tomb of the Apostle James in what is now Santiago de Compostela, that this region in particular began to experience more than minimal contact with the outside world.

Early attempts to gain Galicia's autonomy from the Asturo-Leonese Monarchy by means of royal wills and internal dissensions had no effect. However, after the fall of the Caliphate of Córdoba in the first half of the 11th century, a period of political and territorial instability began. Between 1093 and 1097, Alfonso VI of Leon formally divided the reconquered regions to the north and south of the River Minho. He gave the land to the north to his daughter Urraca and her husband Raymond of Burgundy, and the land to the south down to the River Douro to another son-in-law, Henri, who was the brother of Raymond. Henri's son, Afonso Henriques, continued his father's policies to secure control over territories further south. In 1128, after defeating his mother Teresa's armies in the battle of São Mamede, he became Count of Portugal and subsequently proclaimed himself the first King, despite the fact that he had only gained control of the region of Portucale between the rivers Minho and Douro. Until her death in 1130, Teresa continued to rule south of the river Douro, after which Afonso Henriques moved his court from Guimarães to Coimbra.

Despite constant rebellion against his cousin Alfonso VII of Leon, and in particular their clash in the Battle of Ourique in 1139, by 1143 Afonso Henriques appears to have gained a stable peace settlement with, and some form of independent status from, the Crown of Leon. By 1179, formal autonomy was achieved when the Pope officially recognised the independent Kingdom of Portugal and conceded the title of King Afonso I to Afonso. By the end of the 12th century, the scission and isolation of Portugal from the rest of the Peninsula was complete. Henceforth, the history of Galicia would be inextricably bound up not with that of the independent Kingdom of Portugal, but with that of the other dominant kingdoms of the Peninsula.

Galicia remained part of the Kingdom of Leon until the death of its king, Alfonso IX, in 1230, and the subsequent accession of his son Fernando III, which definitively united Leon, and therefore Galicia, with the Kingdom of Castile. This was a major turning point in the history of the western regions, and the linguistic consequences of this division of the areas where varieties of Galician-Portuguese were spoken would prove to be considerable, as I will clarify further in Chapter 5.

As occurred elsewhere in the period, beginning in the 11th century, Galicia had undergone a degree of internal transformation. Its population grew substantially, an urban network was established, and agricultural practices were enhanced, leading to a general economic revitalisation and in some rural areas, to the consolidation of isolated and numerically small groups of people into larger communities (Mariño Paz, 1998: 56). However, Galicia remained a peripheral territory, largely isolated from outside influences and maintaining a highly traditional and religious socio-cultural way of life.

Integration into the Kingdom of Castile marked the beginning of the end of Galicia's cultural and linguistic isolation. According to Freixeiro Mato (1997: 26–31), during the 13th century Galician was still the language of general use within the region, assuming many functions without distinction of social class or rural/urban setting. Moreover, with the exception of the eastern regions, Galician started to assume a cultural and literary role in the Peninsula, becoming the vehicle of the majority of Hispanic love lyrics and poetry, the *cancioneiros*, such as the *cantiga de amigo, cantiga de amor, cantiga de escarnio* and *cantiga de maldizer* (González López, 1980: 107), and the language of official documents. However, the events of the 14th century profoundly affected the region's chances of economic, social, political and, ultimately, linguistic stability.

The civil war between the son of Alfonso XI of Castile, Enrique Trastamara, and his half-brother Pedro the Cruel lasted for decades, but was finally decided in 1369. Enrique became Enrique II of Castile and quickly established a new ruling aristocracy in the region. The Galician nobility were a warring faction, indiscriminate in their attacks on the social groups of the region. By the 15th century, bad harvests, severe famine and plague had led to a period marked by social conflict and unrest. The second *Guerra Irmandiña* in particular, was a rebellion, an authentic civil war provoked by popular revolt. The enemy was the nobility and aristrocracy who defeated the uprising but who were aided and abetted by the Monarchs of Castile and Portugal.

This era marks the beginning of a progressively centralising period in Spanish history. The region had enjoyed a degree of political autonomy until the unification of Castile and Aragon in 1479 by the *Reyes Católicos* [Catholic Monarchs], Ferdinand and Isabella. Castile now had a strong foothold in Galicia, instigated a period of relative peace and order on the serious social unrest that had pervaded the region. One of the ways to achieve this was to severely limit the power of the Galician aristocracy;

to undermine or even expel the nobility by dispossessing their lands. Hence, the new upper echelons of society were Castilian in the main. They appear to have had no desire to understand the cultural and linguistic configuration of the region, or to learn its language. As the foreign, dominant class, they attempted to establish Castilian, the language of social prestige and power, as the official language, the tool of colonisation, with the seat of the Asturo-Leonese-Castilian monarchy within the territory based primarily in Santiago de Compostela. The subsequent creation of the *Real Audiencia*, a judicial district that functioned as an appeals court, enabled the Castilian nobility in Galicia to reinforce by legislative means the use of Castilian as the official court language and that of the clergy, a process they had started during the reign of Fernando IV.

The Dark Ages

This period also marks an important sociolinguistic turning point in the history of the Galician language, for the social inequalities and class differences that prevailed in the region were no longer simply between the Galician nobility and the Galician peasantry. This contrast had been based upon urban and rural division, but the arrival of a Castilian nobility paved the way for further discrimination based on a language-power divide. Galician had started to fulfil nearly all the roles and functions of a normalised national language, but in the 14th and 15th centuries, it was devalued by the existence of a centralising, socio-political situation that demanded the use of Castilian in official documents and institutions. The Galician lyric had fallen into decline, and by the end of the 15th century, the region was totally integrated into the Crown of Castile, which thwarted any attempts at establishing Galician as the national language (Mariño Paz, 1998: 180–186). Galician continued to be used in private papers until what Galician philologists and historians commonly term the *Séculos Oscuros*, [the Dark Ages] of the 16th and 17th centuries, when it finally lost all its status as the language of public administration and official documentation to the state language, Castilian.

The diglossic scenario between the predominantly urban monolingual Galician-speaking nobility on the one hand, and the monolingual Castilian-speaking nobility on the other, was counterbalanced by the large, monolingual Galician-speaking community located primarily in the rural areas. Language discrimination based on class was largely irrelevant to the autochthonous people at the time, for they were mostly isolated from the cultural influence of Santiago and the linguistic influence of Castilian. However, the Church continued to play an important role in their day-to-day lives, and when the Galician clergy was ousted from the region in the 15th and 16th centuries, their replacement by Castilian-speaking priests and abbots served to enhance the subaltern status of Galician, for the people could no longer communicate with them. The remaining Galician nobility also began to view the issue of Galician ethnicity as a negative social trait. The Castilian language was a prerequisite for social progression: the new ruling elite of Galicia was predominantly Castilian-speaking, and the Galician nobility increasingly learnt Castilian out of necessity and also out of a desire to use what was perceived as a noble and courtesan language.

Other wealthy town and city dwellers followed suit. By the 17th century, Castilian was used for certain intergroup functions, but to varying degrees, Galician continued to be employed for intragroup purposes within families and immediate communities. In the Introduction to this book (p. 21), I intimated that this kind of continuous exchange between ethnic groups and societies could result in regular, prolonged, and systematic contact between their speech forms, and could sometimes lead, as it did here, to a certain degree of acculturation on the part of the less prestigious group. In this case, Castilian, as the dominant language, began to exert substantial linguistic influence on the less prestigious Galician varieties of the urban, but not the rural, areas. This is what has led certain linguists to argue a situation of diglossia with bilingualism, based upon classic informal/formal domains was evident at this time in the use of language by the upper echelons of the urban population (Freixeiro Mato, 1997: 40, 53–59; Mariño Paz, 1998: 217; Penny, 2002: 21–22).[4] However, the rest of the autochthonous population did not use Castilian, for they were isolated both geographically and socially from its influence and benefits. The foreign elite on the other hand, did not use Galician, since any communication with the autochthonous elites was conducted in Castilian. This scenario served to enhance the elite/ rural divide and emphasise the need for Castilian as an aid to social progress over the next few hundred years.

In 1700, the installation of the Royal House of Borbón in Spain brought with it important changes, for the monarchy strived to create a united, homogenised Spain. In contrast to the somewhat tactic use of Castilian in the previous century, the imposition of Castilian was now unequivocal: decrees were passed calling for the exclusive use of Castilian as the official and public language of the State, and in education, the *Ley Moyano* of 1857 forbade the use of any language other than Castilian:

La Gramática y Ortografía de la Academia Española serán texto obligatorio y único para estas materias en la enseñanza pública.

[The official grammar and written forms of the Royal Spanish Academy will be used exclusively and compulsorily in teaching within the public education system.]

(García Negro, 1991: 216)

These measures greatly facilitated its dissemination throughout the middle and upper classes, and one of the primary reasons why this could be achieved was its internal linguistic homogeneity. Arguably, the standardisation of Castilian Spanish goes back to the endeavours of Alfonso X in the 13th century. He promoted a variety of Castilian that was probably based on the speech of the educated speakers of Toledo, raising its prestige by using it exclusively for affairs of state and extending its functions of use by developing its grammar and increasing its vocabulary by borrowing from Latin and Arabic and through word formation (Penny, 2000: 20–21). In order to facilitate the dissemination of Castilian, the *Real Academia Española* was set up in 1713 in the service of the Crown and State. Its main objective was to *fijar las voces y vocablos de la lengua castellana en su mayor propiedad, elegancia y pureza* [to purify and preserve the Castilian language and its component parts]: in the words of the Academy's crest: *limpia, fija, y da esplendor* [cleanse, establish and make splendid]. It also aimed to reform the spelling of Castilian, to provide a grammar and to produce and regularly update a dictionary.[5]

Regueira Fernández (2006: 62) states that the processes of centralisation and subsequent administrative homogenisation initiated by the Borbóns were based upon a belief in the ideological, cultural and linguistic assimilation of the territories and communities that did not comply with the model of an imagined Spain (see Andersen, 1991 and also p. 36). In Galicia as elsewhere, the hegemony of Spanish society by the imposition of a Castilian linguistic identity was to continue virtually unabated for the next two hundred years.

Towards the end of the Dark Ages, as we saw above (p. 60), Galician lost the vestiges of its former status and prestige as the language of public administration. This had a concomitant effect on perceptions of the language held by the region's neighbours. As far as the Portuguese from the central and southern regions were concerned, Galician started to appear somewhat antiquated, rustic and comical (Cano Aguilar, 1999: 202), with its linguistic forms overlaid by a strongly northern Portuguese accent (Teyssier, 1990: 39–40), itself the bearer of many pejorative connotations. Many jokes surfaced based on the 'country bumpkin' image of the *galego*, the traditional figure of fun in the popular theatre.

In Galicia itself, much of the population began to view their language as lacking in prestige and worth. There arose the idea, primarily fostered by the rich and culturally advanced regions of Spain but adopted rapidly by the rest of the country and in particular, by Galicia, that Galician was simply a corrupt and degraded variety of Castilian, lacking a formal, standardised written form and thus, not a language in its own right. Its use began to be considered merely shameful and contemptible evidence of the community's own low social status within Spain. The rest of Spain regarded Galicia as a poor, backward cousin, tolerated and even supported economically, which mean that it contributed little to the rest of the country. As Rodríguez Rodríguez comments:

> Desde o século XV até o XIX non existiu praticamente literatura escrita na língua galega [...] Surxe en Portugal un desprezo polo galego e pola língua, imaxe demasiado aproximada da portuguesa para poder ser tolerada, e en Castela un anti-galeguismo no que vai implícita unha constatación da excesiva proximidade lingüística do noso povo co portugués. Desta maneira, abre-se paso a crenza de que a forma que teñen de falar os galegos é unha corrupción do castelán [...]

> [From the 15th until the 19th centuries, practically no literature was written in Galician [...] in Portugal a contempt for the Galician people and their language arose, their stereotype being too similar to that of the Portuguese to be tolerated, whilst in the rest of Spain an anti-Galician attitude arose, implicit in which was the conviction that our people were too closely connected linguistically to Portuguese. In this way, the belief was fostered that the variety of language spoken by Galicians is a corrupt form of Castilian [...]]
>
> (Rodríguez Rodríguez, 1991: 63–64)

As a consequence, although Galician continued to be used in the region, it had lost credence both in the eyes of its speakers and of others, and any overt loyalty to the language was quashed. Such negative attitudes towards the use of Galician continued well into the 20th century: as recently as 1987, Vilariño lamented the fact that it was not afforded any type of prestige or status:

> A la identitad gallega le sucede lo mismo que a su lengua: aunque es hablada por la casi totalidad de la población, nadie la reconoce, porque no tiene otra carta de ciudadanía que los estigmas de la pobreza, la incultura y el atraso.

> [The Galician identity is undergoing the same process as the language: although almost everyone speaks it, nobody acknowledges it, because it carries with it no other credentials of citizenship but the stigma of poverty, lack of culture and backwardness.]
>
> (Vilariño, 1987: 268)

Galeguismo and the *Rexurdimento*

This period of Galician history was marked profoundly by much social, political and economic upheaval. Despite the somewhat denigrated reputation of Galicia at this time, by the 18th century, the region had experienced a degree of economic development, with agrarian reform and the growth of small textile, fish salting and pottery industries. However, its history was inextricably linked to that of the overriding

State. In the 19th century, Spain initiated far-reaching political, economic, social and cultural reforms; its transformation from an absolute monarchy towards a liberal and constitutional state led to a new society being forged, linked to the capitalist means of production and constitutional parliamentary political structures. However, these transformations did not generally occur in Galicia, for the region maintained the structures of the ancient regime, and demonstrated a strong incapacity to modernise and integrate into the highly developed State economic and political system (Mariño Paz, 1998: 331).

Even the somewhat draconian policies regarding language use were not fully implemented. By the end of the 18th century, the pervading situation in Galicia had appeared to be leading inexorably to the assimilation of Galician by Castilian. Despite the official line regarding the use of Castilian, the reality was not so clear-cut. In the countryside and in the face of persecution, the clergy continued to use Galician with their congregations. Landowners too, had to communicate with their workers in Galician, and to an extent, the State ignored this use. However, in urban areas, castilianisation of the middle and upper classes continued unabated, exacerbated to a degree by the development of industry and the presence of military bases and soldiers from other parts of Spain in coastal cities such as A Coruña and Ferrol.

It is debatable whether the castilianisation of the regional language was curtailed to an extent by the emergence of *galeguismo*, although it is often considered one of the most important social phenomena to affect the region in the last three centuries. Freixeiro Mato (1997: 72) for example, maintains that the pioneering studies undertaken by Martín Sarmiento in the 18th century on Galician and its lexis, its etymology and its toponymy as a means of defending its claim to language status, were the prelude to the literary renaissance of the 19th century, of which the *galeguista* movement was the first step.

In many areas around the globe, language had become one of the foremost ways by which a community could articulate its political aspirations. Its use became emblematic of the idiosyncratic characteristics that set the community apart from the rest of the nation. Although a small group predominantly from the upper echelons of Galician urban society, the intellectual proponents of *galeguismo* were established by the intelligentsia as what was termed a regionalist movement, under the banner of the *Rexurdimento*. They attempted to demonstrate their strong ethnic ties and close identification with their region, its history, culture and language through innovative works ostensibly written in Galician, such as the literary compositions of Rosalía de Castro, Enrique Curros and Eduardo Pondal, and the historical writings of Manuel Martínez Murguía (Pensado, 1982: 72). Rosalía's book of poetry *Os Cantares Gallegos* [Galician Songs], published in 1863, was the first modern work written entirely in the language and marked the beginning of this literary renaissance.[6] *Galeguismo* was linked to the Romantic Movement prevalent in Europe in this century and which shaped the *Renaixença* in Catalonia, amongst others. The *Rexurdimento* was an attempt to lend credence to the use of Galician as a literary language among the cultural elite. It tried to induce a sense of historical conscience, to highlight the use of Galician as the Medieval literary language, as well as its links with Latin and Portuguese. Although its proposals regarding the basis of the written form were somewhat impractical and ideological (Mariño Paz, 1998: 447), in reviving such interest, it led to the conclusion that the use of Galician was not a signal of illiteracy, but of progress. Thus, there appeared for the first time a collective voice preoccupied with the establishment of a cultured and unified variety of the language.

This course of action was made possible by the pervading situation in Spain as a whole, since under the First Republic, there was at least a tacit recognition of regional nationalisms in the peripheral areas. The regionalist movement was ostensibly a literary and cultural movement. However, the subsequent 'reawakening' of political consciousness and attempts to have Galician officially recognised as the regional language led to the *galeguista* movement becoming synonymous with attempts to identify and demonstrate the idiosyncratic traits possessed by the region, traits that set it apart from the rest of Spain. In other words, the *galeguista* movement was the precursor to the rise of regionalism as a political doctrine, in order to highlight the increasing influence of the State mechanism and to underline and defend the interrelationship between ethnic and linguistic identity. As a regionalist movement, the ultimate aim of *galeguismo* was to achieve total autonomy from Spain's governing bodies in Madrid, harking back to calls for the right to self-determination which had continued to be sought, albeit by no means entirely proactively, since the 12th century. Consequently, the movement organised its own political party, the *Asociación Regionalista Gallega* [Galician Regional Association], based on Murguía's ideology that Galicia needed to modernise socio-politically whilst retaining its ethnic identity and roots in order to survive.

The movement faced opposition both within Galicia and without. Some detractors understood the recuperation of the Galician language as an attack against the dominance of Castilian and as a threat to the political unity of Spain. Others claimed that it would lead to the stagnation of Galicia, for its use meant that the region would not be able to communicate with the rest of the State. Moreover, *galeguismo* was primarily an urban-based movement and, as such, did not characterise the Galician population as a whole. Although its greatest achievement was to bring the debate regarding language to the public attention, Galician society was not ready to accept its aims and the consequent implications (Mariño Paz, 1998: 400).

The rural exodus

At this time, the countryside was still the one evident refuge of the Galician language. Vilariño (1987: 266) has stated that *no puede sorprender que la lengua constituya – junto con la tierra – el símbolo y el lazo más sólido de identificación con Galicia* [it is no surprise that the language – together with the land – symbolises the strongest link of identification with Galicia]. This may well be true, but largely due to poor communication methods, rural communities were generally isolated from the aims and objectives of the *galeguista* movement, and from calls for closer integration between the autochthonous language and a collective sense of Galician identity. Thus, they continued to maintain a sense of inferiority that was linked intimately with their use of the language.

However, this situation was largely untenable. An important contributing factor to changes in the overall linguistic composition of Galicia during the 19th and 20th centuries was internal migration. At the beginning of the 19th century, Galician was habitually spoken by over 95% of the population, mostly in tiny rural areas (Mariño Paz, 1998: 229–230). However, as a direct result of the worsening economic crisis within the agricultural and fishing industries, a substantial percentage of the rural workforce staged an exodus *en masse* from the countryside. This economic migration led to the growth of towns and cities in Galicia. These migrants aspired to improve themselves, and their desire for social mobility meant that they started to increasingly use Castilian (Regueira Fernández, 2006: 64–65). Social groups are bound by a series of characteristics such as language, and a change in social group may lead, as here, to a change in language use.

Many people also emigrated from Galicia to other parts of the world: in 1752, the region's population comprised 14% of the national total, but by 1993, this percentage had been reduced to three million inhabitants, that is, just 7.4% of the population (Monteagudo and Santamarina, 1993: 117, 124). In the 19th century, the major reception areas outside Galicia were other parts of Spain and the Americas; indeed, in the second half of the 19th century, immigration to Cuba from Asturias, the Canary Islands and, in particular, Galicia, was so intense that Cubans began to call all Spaniards from the Peninsula *gallegos* [Galicians] (Lipski, 1994: 228).[7] Important migrant communities sprang up in Buenos Aires in Argentina, Havana in Cuba, and Bahia in Brazil, where *Centros Galegos* [Galician Centres] were established to promote the maintenance and use of the Galician language and cultural practices.[8]

By the 20th century, other parts of Europe had become the main destination, and it is estimated that between 1911 and 1964 some 1,140,926 Galicians emigrated overseas, constituting a third of all Spanish emigrants during this period (Iribarne, 1991: 60). Even recently, this tradition of emigration has continued, with 603,000 people leaving Galicia between 1961 and 1975 (Regueira Fernández, 2006: 65).

Twentieth Century Reform

The history of Spain in the Restoration period of the late 19th and early 20th centuries is characterised once again by the centralising and unifying policies of the state government. Although linguistic unification was perceived as the only way in which the identity of the region could be preserved and its autonomy objectives demonstrated, the linguistic practices of certain *galeguistas* were not commensurate with their ideologies, which meant that the movement itself lost credibility.[9]

The revival of the language was affected badly by the education system, which had been centralised throughout Spain in the 19th century, and which prescribed the use of Castilian. Although many primary school teachers refused to abandon the use of Galician, very few people knew how to read or write in Galician, particularly in the rural areas. Moreover, Galician had as yet no standardised, authoritative orthography and the only written form of Galician until now had been that used by the elites in the cities. Hence, any texts that were written in Galician, including articles that started to appear in the press, were subject to the strong influence of Castilian and its official norms.

The economic situation too, continued to affect the social stratification of the region. By the 20th century, Galicia started to abandon some of its traditional practices and started to modernise. Within a few decades, this led to a predominantly urban culture and a growing middle class, and allied to this, a greater awareness of their rights and entitlements.

The struggle for social reform was consolidated after 1916 with the creation of the *Irmandades da Fala* (IF) [The Brotherhood of the Spoken Word] in A Coruña (Monteagudo and Santamarina, 1993: 126). It generally comprised intellectuals and liberal professionals who, ironically, belonged to the social group that did not use Galician. The main aim of the IF was to defend the Galician language, and initially, it was extremely proactive in its attempts to disseminate both a spoken and written form of the language, and other brotherhoods were set up elsewhere.

It is no coincidence that the concept of Galician nationalism was also initiated in 1916, although the true birth of modern Galician nationalism is considered 1918, the year in which the *Irmandades da Fala* held their first assembly in Lugo. From this meeting emerged the IF *Manifesto*, which adopted the term nationalism instead of regionalism (see pp. 31–32 for the earlier discussion of these terms), marking a distinct contrast with the regionalist doctrines of the *Rexurdimento*. It also proposed the co-officiality of Galician and Castilian, thus resolving the contradictions between ideological discourse and linguistic practice that had been apparent in the earlier regionalist doctrines (Mariño Paz, 1998: 266).[10]

Their focus was the language itself and their objective was to 'dignify' Galician. They encouraged its use in literature, education and other areas of public use, they put on plays and set up publishing houses, the most important of which was *Nós*, founded in 1927 by Anxel Casal. *Nós* published the magazine of the same name in order to disseminate the work of the intellectual-based group *Xeración Nós* [Our Generation], an alliance that included the Galician authors Alfonso Castelao, Ramón Otero Pedrayo, Antón Villar Ponte, and Vicente Risco. It also published the work of the subsequent *Seminario de Estudos Galegos* [The Seminary for Galician Studies] founded in the early 1920s, and took over the publication of the newspaper *A Nosa Terra* [Our Land], written entirely in Galician and the mouthpiece of the IF.

The *Xeración Nós* identified the Galician spoken in the rural areas as the truly authentic language, since these varieties had not generally been subject to castilianisation influences. However, although they claimed an intimate and fundamental link between the maintenance of the *lingua do pobo*, that is, the community language, and the recuperation of a (primarily) cultural identity, they also echoed the need voiced by earlier *galeguistas* to release Galician from its traditional characterisation as a vulgar and uncultured language. For this, they advocated the establishment of a written standard, which could be applied to academic disciplines other than literature, for example, in scientific, historic and geographic papers and studies. Although their general objectives accorded with those of the *Irmandades da Fala*, their methodologies differed. The *Irmandades da Fala* believed that the way to achieve their nationalist aims and, hence, the recuperation of the language was through the Spanish political system. The *Xeración Nós* wanted to undermine such a system by stimulating a sense of national consciousness within Galicia itself, by defending the rights of the people to use Galician as a means of expressing their ethnic identity.

In the late 19th century, some effort was made to catalogue the lexis and grammar of Galician. In 1864, Mirás' grammar *Compendio de gramática gallego-castelana* [Compendium of Galician-Castilian Grammar] was published, followed by the highly acclaimed *Gramática Gallega* [Galician Grammar] by Saco Arce in 1868, and the less acclaimed *Elementos de gramática gallega* [Elements of Galician Grammar] (Valladares Nuñez, 1892), which was not edited until 1970. Valladares Nuñez also published the best Galician-Castilian dictionary of the period in 1884. The publication of books on the Galician language continued, albeit slowly, into the 20th century. In 1918, the book *Filología de la lengua gallega* [Philology of the Galician Language] by Santiago y Gómez appeared, closely followed in 1933 by a provisional proposal for a standard form entitled *Algunhas normas pra a unificazón do idioma galego* [Some Norms for the Unification of the Galician Language] by the *Seminario de Estudos Galegos*.

The Franco Dictatorship and Linguistic Persecution

The alternation of centralising and decentralising processes continued to characterise the period of Spanish history from 1923 to the present day. The dictatorship of Primo de Rivera lasted from 1923 to 1930, in which he drafted a series of measures to combat what he considered to be the harmful separatist movements that prevailed in the peripheral territories. However, despite his opposition to the notions of regional nationalism and the use of languages other than Castilian, he did not significantly encumber the progress of Galician literature.

During the brief era of the Second Spanish Republic, the loose federalism and decentralisation of the State allowed regional nationalisms to become politically organised. In contrast to the earlier *galeguista* movement, the IF nationalists offered a viable political alternative in the form of the *Partido Galeguista* [Pro-Galician Party], which sought and partially achieved legal recognition for the language. This also succeeded in awakening a sense of national consciousness in a minority of the population. The culmination of *Partido Galeguista* actions was the ratification of the *Estatuto de Automonia* [The Statute of Autonomy] in 1936, thus establishing the co-officiality of Galician and Castilian in the region.

However, Franco's rise to power in 1939 put paid to all hopes for regional autonomy and linguistic unification.[11] Franco's dictatorship was nationalistic and authoritarian in the extreme, and highly intolerant of aspirations for regional autonomy. The ensuing repression of the regional nationalist movement in Galicia prevented any further development of the written form of the language at the very least. Franco's regime was also characterised by its total defence of Castilian as the only language of the State, with the view that Spain should be culturally and linguistically homogeneous and by the consequent linguistic persecution of other languages spoken in Spain, even though in fact, no legal text was ever written to this effect (Portas, 1999: 197).

Under Franco, the rural exodus continued and, in the urban areas, this had concomitant effect on the growing number of bilinguals. Although monolingualism in Galician was still widespread in the rural areas, a bilingual, diglossic scenario was starting to characterise the towns and cities. In the rural areas, the private use of Galician was largely ignored, since Franco's intransigence towards Basque and Catalan was not as severe in his homeland. However, once again, both the people and the language suffered a further loss of dignity, for the State vehemently stated that there was only one viable and worthwhile language.

By maintaining a stringent control of both the mass media and the state education system, the dictatorship ensured that only Castilian was broadcast and taught throughout Spain. This repression paralysed the *galeguista* movement to a large extent, with many of its leading academics and supporters being jailed or even executed, for example Alexandre Bóveda and Anxel Casal, and with the language itself going underground. The subsequent diversion of activity to the communities abroad, largely to Brazil, Venezuela, Mexico, Cuba and, in particular, to Buenos Aires in Argentina, allowed the movement to continue its cultural campaign at the very least, free to a large extent of the fear of persecution (Pensado, 1982: 89–90). Here, exiles encouraged the retention of Galician cultural activities within the diasporic communities by setting up societies such as the *Instituto argentino de cultura gallega* [Argentinian Institute of Galician Culture] and the *Patronato de cultura gallega de México* [Society for the Support of Galician Culture in Mexico], broadcasting radio programmes in Galician and encouraging language courses. Moreover, publishing houses such as *Citania* were established, hence the appearance of magazines such as *Galicia emigrante* [Emigrant Galicia] and *Vieiros*, and in 1944, the groundbreaking *Sempre en Galiza* [Always in Galicia] by Castelao, which traced the political and historical development of Galician and which is considered by many to be the unofficial 'bible' of the *galeguista* movement (1961 [1944]).[12]

The advent of the 1950s coincided with a small degree of permissiveness displayed towards the regional languages by the Spanish Regime. In 1949, the academic Otero Pedrayo had employed Galician publicly for the first time since 1936 during a conference in Ourense, and in the early 1950s, the publishing house *Editorial Galaxia* was founded in Spain by Ramón Piñeiro. This was a turning point in the cultural recuperation of a written form of the language, and one of the first works to be published was the poetry of Benito Soto, written entirely in Galician. Works of narrative followed, such as *Merlín e familia* [Merlin and Family] by Alvaro Cunqueiro. Thus, the *pro-galeguista* stance of *Galaxia*, prevalent until the present day, allowed both the language and culture to become the main focus of the autonomy movement.

By the 1960s, cultural institutions were being set up to serve as the focus for ideological resistance to Franco, as were two more political parties (albeit clandestine), the Marxist-Leninist *Unión do Pobo Galego* (UPG) [Union of the Galician People] and the Socialist *Partido Socialista Galego* (PSdeG) [Galician Socialist Party]. Despite their differing left-wing perspectives, they both considered the defence of Galician as the official language of the region as the way to enhance and reaffirm a Galician cultural identity. Civil protest poetry became prevalent, such as the famous *Longa noite de pedra* [The Long Night of Stone] by Celso Emilio Ferreiro, whilst emigration dominated other spheres, such as in the poem *Viaxe ao país dos ananos* [Voyage to the Country of Dwarves] also by Ferreiro. By the 1970s, the demand for language rights was firmly established within cultural circles, with both singers and poets proclaiming their allegiance to the *lingua materna* [mother tongue] in order to underpin their notion of regional identity. A good example is the poem

Terra Cha [Your Land] by Manuel María and the novel *O camiño de abaixo* [The Low Road] by Juan Casal.

Notwithstanding the renewed interest in a revival of the language, the teaching of Galician was still prohibited, and to a large extent, the difficulties of establishing a written standard were put on hold in favour of dialectal study, an area of traditional philological research still sanctioned by the dictatorship. This type of dialectal study chronicles linguistic variation. Consequently, it greatly reinforced the earlier perceived necessity for a unification process such as standardisation in Galicia.[13]

In the official sphere, in the later years of the dictatorship both the language and its concomitant scholarly output started to be tolerated. Consequently, the first history of Galician literature appeared, entitled the *Historia da literatura galega contemporánea* [History of Contemporary Galician Literature] by Carballo Calero in 1963. In 1965, *Galaxia* published what was to be the first edition of many of Carballo Calero's groundbreaking *Gramatica elemental del gallego común* [A Basic Grammar of Common Galician]. This was the same year as he was appointed Professor of *Lingua e Literatura Galegas* [Galician Language and Literature] and modules in the study of the language and its literature were introduced at the University of Santiago de Compostela. The success of the courses in Galician philology quickly led to the creation of the research foundation *Instituto da Lingua Galega* (ILG) [The Galician Language Institute], which was to play an extremely important role in the standardisation of Galician, to some extent because of its role in encouraging the dialectal surveys discussed above. Moreover, *galeguista* demands started to increase. Road sign place names began to appear in Galician and it began to be used, albeit with limitations, by the regional press and broadcast institutions. Finally, in 1975, and just before Franco's death, a decree regulating the use of regional languages was published, with the aim of *incorporar las peculiaridades regionales al patrimonio cultural español* [integrating regional peculiarities into the Spanish cultural heritage] (Pensado, 1982: 92–96).

Democracy and Devolution

By the 1960s, there was a general upsurge in activity. The political indolence in Galicia under Franco was seen as detrimental to the social, linguistic and cultural aspirations of the region, and the first true nationalist parties were created: the *Partido Socialista Galego* (PSG) [the Galician Socialist Party] and the *Unión do Pobo Galego* (UPG) [Union of the Galician People]. In the 1970s, the first texts legally written in Galician were published, and in 1974, a fifteen-minute news programme entitled *Panorama de Galicia* [A Panorama of Galicia] appeared on local television. However, only after Franco's demise was it ultimately possible for Galicia to attempt to create a role for itself and its language and to attempt to divest itself once and for all of its perceived identity as a backward, under-developed region of Spain.

Once again, the transition to a parliamentary monarchy initiated a process of decentralisation to the peripheral regions. One of its first achievements was the revival of basic and fundamental human rights, hitherto suppressed by the dictatorship. Skutnabb Kangas' (2000: 123, 481–563) states that an inherent, non-discriminatory and self-evident quality of the human rights of minoritised groups should be that they guarantee the right to exist and reproduce themselves as separate groups, and closely related to this right is the idea that learning the auto-chthonous language is considered either a duty or right. The *Constitución Española* [Spanish Constitution] of 1978 declared Castilian to be the official language of the State, but it also allowed for Catalan, Basque and Galician to be co-official within their respective regions. Accordingly, once the *Constitución de Galicia* [Constitution of Galicia] was ratified in 1978, the Statute of Autonomy and the creation of the autonomous government, the *Xunta*, quickly followed. Henceforth, Galician would become the language employed in the political discourse of the region.

Article 5 of the preamble to the *Estatuto de Autonomía de Galicia* [the Statute of Autonomy of Galicia], clearly defines the linguistic aspirations of the region:

Título Preliminar do Estatuto de Autonomía para Galicia – Lei orgánica 1/1981

Art 5.

a. A lingua propia de Galicia é o galego.
b. Os idiomas galego e castelán son oficiais en Galicia e todos teñen o dereito de os coñecer e de os usar.
c. Os poderes públicos de Galicia garantirán o uso normal e oficial dos dous idiomas e potenciarán o emprego do galego en tódolos planos da vida pública, cultural e informativa, e disporán os medios necesarios para facilita-lo seu coñecemento.
d. Ninguén poderá ser discriminado por causa da lingua.

a. [Galician is the autochthonous language of Galicia.
b. Galician and Castilian are the official languages of Galicia and all have the right to learn and use them.
c. The public authorities of Galicia will guarantee the normal and official use of both languages and will promote the use of Galician in all walks of public life, through culture and the arts and infor-mation systems, and will provide the necessary means to facilitate its learning.
d. Nobody can be discriminated against because of language.]

(Xunta de Galicia, 1989)

The subsequent linguistic normalisation laws (see pp. 76–77 for a definition) ratified in 1983 reinforce the sociolinguistic status of Galician as the autochthonous language of the region, as well as the role it has to play, alongside Castilian, as a viable language of administration. As well as highlighting every citizen's right to use Galician without prejudice, these laws also state that they have a duty to be acquainted with the language at the very least:

Lei de normalización lingüística
TÍTULO I
Dos dereitos lingüísticos en Galicia
Artigo 1°
O galego é a lingua propia de Galicia.
Tódolos galegos teñen o deber de coñecelo e o dereito de usalo.
Artigo 2°
Os poderes públicos de Galicia garantirán o uso normal do galego e do castelán, linguas oficiais da Comunidade Autónoma.
Artigo 3°
Os poderes públicos de Galicia adoptarán as medidas oportunas para que ninguén sexa discriminado por razón de lingua.
Os cidadáns poderán dirixirse ós xuíces e tribunais para obte-la protección xudicial do dereito a empregala súa lingua.

[Title 1
Concerning linguistic rights in Galicia
Article 1
Galician is the autochthonous language of Galicia.
Everyone has the duty to know it and the right to use it.
Article 2
The public authorities of Galicia will guarantee the normal use of Galician and of Castilian, as official languages of the self-governing region.
Article 3
The public authorities of Galicia will adopt the necessary measures to ensure that no one is discriminated against because of their language. As far as the right to employ their own language is concerned, citizens will have recourse to the law courts and tribunals in order to obtain legal protection.]

(*Lei de normalización lingüística*, 1983)

Concluding Remarks

As I stated at the beginning, the main role of this chapter has been to determine the historical framework of the relationship between language and identity in Galicia. In particular, the deeply rooted relationship Galicia has with Portugal, together with its integration into the Kingdom of Spain, have both had an enormous impact on the vitality of the autochthonous language and its status within the region. These factors are especially pertinent to my discussion of standardisation in Chapter 3, and to issues surrounding linguistic differentiation, considered in Chapter 5.

My hypothesis suggests that the Galician language, whether used or not, is an authentic characteristic of Galician ethnic identity, but that its relationship with Castilian at the very least, is still unresolved. I have also examined the status/solidarity distinction regarding the role of language in Galician ethnicity, bearing in mind political and social considerations and in particular, revitalisation efforts, and once again, the issue of education and the advancement of viable legislation has been seen to be imperative to such efforts. The political and legal clarification of the linguistic dynamics of Galicia offered clear justification for the compilation of an official set of orthographic standards, to which I now turn in Chapter 3.

Chapter 3
Contemporary Galicia: The Evolution of a Standard

Introductory Remarks

In the previous chapter, I established the historical framework of the evolution of Galician and its correlated linguistic association with Portuguese and Castilian Spanish. I suggested that a political and social collective consciousness regarding the relationship between the Galician language and Galician ethnic identity started to emerge, culminating in recent legislative measures aimed at the revitalisation of the language.

As I emphasised in the Introduction, an appraisal of the particular circumstances surrounding ongoing revitalisation procedures in Galician cannot be carried out without a more general analysis of the pervading linguistic landscape in Spain as a whole. To this end, the present chapter starts by offering a brief examination of the political reasoning behind the recent devolution in Spain and the role of ethnic and linguistic identity therein. Following on from my analysis of language planning in Chapter 1, I begin this chapter with an overview of standardisation practices and procedures in general compared with those pertaining specifically to the *Comunidades Autónomas* of Spain, as well as the processes of *normalización* and *normativación*. I consider the political and social successes pertaining to language legislation and use in Catalonia and Galicia. In particular, I address the ongoing debates and diverse opinions regarding the status of the Galician language and its relationship with both Portuguese and Castilian. The somewhat controversial creation of the standard written form of Galician, the *Normas Ortográficas e Morfolóxicas do Galego*, is discussed from the perspective of its major proponents and detractors, whose largely intellectual-based struggle to assert and establish differing linguistic forms onto the Galician language and thus, to influence the notion of Galician identity and ethnicity is considered at some length. Finally, I offer a brief discussion of the processes pertaining to the integration of a standard language through the *normalización* procedures in Galicia, together with some of the more pertinent articles of the *Lei de Normalización Lingüística*.

The Creation of a Norm

One of the most important elements of corpus planning relevant to the notion of identity is that of the standardisation of (typically) the written language, the process by which, through direct and deliberate intervention of society (Hudson, 2001: 32), the 'linguistic code becomes subject to deliberate regulation leading to a canon of good usage' (Coulmas, 2005: 131). Haugen's first model of language standardisation appeared in 1959. His classic matrix (1966a) of social versus linguistic processes has since been adapted and elaborated; however the following stages are still considered the schema of the prescribed model, implemented through the three categories of language planning I have described in Chapter 1. These stages can, but do not need to be, sequential.[1]

- Selection or determination of the status norm. Initially, a particular, dominant, social or regional dialect, or a combination of more than one, are selected as the formal official or national medium with which to facilitate communication within a community of users. As a consequence, the other dialects will then be viewed as dialects of the standard. An example of the former is that of modern French, where the standard is based upon the prestigious dialect spoken in the region around Paris called the *Île-de-France*; of the latter, the recent amalgamation of the four main Basque dialects to create the standard (Mesthrie *et al.*, 2000: 389). Mar Molinero (2000b: 78) points out that this stage includes what I have called language policy selection, whereas subsequent stages are more to do with the implementation process.[2]
- Codification of form. Standard languages tend to be highly codified varieties, in that legislation prescribes, fixes and regulates the grammatical and lexical standard forms, and the resultant written form is implemented through official publications such as orthographies, grammar books and dictionaries. In the absence of suitable varieties for such, a model for imitation may have to be artificially created. Closely linked to corpus planning, codification is commonly divided into the three stages of graphisation (writing system development), grammatication (grammatical rule establishment) and lexicalisation (vocabulary enhancement).[3]
- Functional implementation. Implementation practices include the production of books, textbooks and so forth, that are written in the newly codified standard form. The state authorities must also seek to introduce the standard into the education system, the media, local institutions and so forth. Whether this implementation is legally enforced or not, the state must encourage the use of the standard in order to hasten its acceptance by the community as well as its subsequent stabilisation. As I have discussed, simply

prescribing a form does not constitute standardisation. It must also be accepted and utilised across regional and social variation as the norm of the community, both internally as a unifying force, and externally as a symbol of independence.

- Elaboration of function. The variety of language chosen must develop the linguistic tools needed for use across a broad range of new functions implicit within modern life, such as technical terminology and new writing styles. This has huge implications for lexical enrichment in particular. Once the written form has been fully implemented through the formal education system and modes of communication, it may start to influence certain elements of pronunciation, and so become accepted for interactions between speakers from different regions.[4]

Many present-day standard languages of Europe have emerged from the linguistic hierarchies established by the integration as the standard of the usually capital-based dominant language. Regarded as a means of social and political advancement and mobility, such standards were adopted readily in some quarters, resulting in a newly literate middle class in countries such as France and Denmark.[5]

Normalización and Normativación

No account of linguistic standardisation with respect to Spain would be complete without a discussion of *normalización*, typically translated as normalisation. Mar-Molinero (1997: 132) makes the point that all present language legislation in Spain, and indeed, within the self-governing regions, refers to linguistic normalisation. Linguistic normalisation implies a concerted attempt to make a language and its use a 'normal', everyday occurrence for formal and informal use, and primarily through educational practices. Stemming from its by Catalan sociolinguists in the 1970s, such as Valverdú, who termed it an *extensión social da lingua* [social extension of the language] (Santamarina, 1995: 53), it signifies far more than the establishment of a supradialectal variety through standardisation processes as part of corpus planning. Cobarrubias claims that it is

a general language planning objective that will bring about a desirable level of linguistic equality [..] specifically aimed at changing the status of 'minority' languages

(Cobarrubias, 1987: 59–60)

Thus, standardisation practices tend to accompany those associated with normalisation, the latter also comprising functional, social, demographic, and geographical dissemination and spread of the language within a political framework (Regueira Fernández, 2006: 61). Closely linked to both status and acquisition planning aims, normalisation processes are aimed at affording a minoritised language an alternative to its subordinate status through positive self-image practices in order to allow it to acquire new users, to enhance existing communicative competence, and to expand its range across a given territory or region (Mar-Molinero, 2000b: 80–81).

Another term relevant to Galician is *normativización* [normativisation]. Valverdú once again defines it as the *escolla e formulación da norma* [the selection and creation of a norm or standard] (Santamarina, 1995: 53), what Haugen (1987: 59–64) terms 'language planning' and which refers to the codification and elaboration of the language. That is, *normativización* refers to the conscious manipulation of the linguistic corpus in order to create reform or restructure a particular language.

This idea of consigning or restoring a language to what is considered it 'normal' level, where it will be on an equal footing with other languages, is linked closely to the political aspirations and ideologies of a given community. The perpetuation of an idiosyncratic identity by the use of a particular language requires at the very least that the community enjoy self-government status, as I have commented previously in Chapter 1 (pp. 48–49). Below I will examine Galicia in this context.

Political Change: The *Comunidades Autónomas*

Today, democratic Spain is an excellent example of 'internal nationalism', in that it exhibits linguistic diversity within its internal space and even across its internal regional borders, which underlines its reputation as a 'nation of nations'. In contrast, Franco's dictatorship was a clear-cut example of 'state nationalism', strongly characterised by his defence of Castilian as the only language of the State. As I started exploring in Chapter 2, this type of emphasis on the role of particular traits, such as a group language, by state-nationalist discourse, serves to define both it inclusiveness and differentiation from others, even if these observations are purely imaginary. Thus, such an ideology embodies the notion of a collective mother tongue as a symbol of popular solidarity and of community identity (Andersen, 1991).

Andersen's imagined community, which here is Spain itself, requires that the population as a whole be both culturally and linguistically homogeneous. Thus, the use of Galician, Basque and Catalan as regional languages was prohibited in all areas; the communities in question had no right to a language-related social and cultural identity nor to an official language of their own that would be in direct competition with Castilian Spanish for speakers, functions and domains. There were aggressive attempts to enforce language shift towards Castilian; for example, access to formal primary education in the autochthonous languages was denied. In this way, the dictatorship violated every individual right regarding language use. Moreover, the collective rights of these linguistic minorities were also denied: the very existence of these minorities was not legally recognised and thus, their right to maintain their idiosyncratic languages and cultures was not upheld.

In the case of Galicia, and cited by Freixeiro Mato (1997: 90), a directive from a pamphlet that appeared in *A Coruña* in 1942, is an early but extremely pertinent examination of the way that state-nationalistic tendencies were endorsed under Franco:

> Hable bien.
> Sea patriota. No sea bárbaro.
> Es de cumplido caballero que Vd. hable nuestro idioma oficial, o sea, el castellano.
> Es ser patriota.
> Viva España y la Disciplina y Nuestro Idioma Cervantino.
> ¡Arriba España!

> [Speak correctly.
> Be patriotic. Do not be coarse.
> It is the patriotic duty of every true gentleman to speak our official language, Castilian.
> Long live Spain, Authority and the Language of Cervantes.
> Spain forever!]

> (Freixeiro Mato, 1997: 90)

Even during the latter part of the dictatorship in Spain, the Regime continued to view the existence of local languages as an obstacle to the consolidation of a centralising Spanish national identity. Despite the entry of Spain into UNESCO in the early 1950s, political, social and linguistic repression in Catalonia, Galicia and the Basque regions continued.

However, with the political upheaval of the 1970s came democracy and freedom of speech and the issue of (regional) nationalism began to set the political agenda. Devolution came as a direct result of the transition to a parliamentary monarchy, as I highlighted in Chapter 3, and afforded at least these regions the legitimate opportunity to seek some form of political self-determination and, consequently, have their languages recognised and established as official markers of their distinctive identities.[6] Article 3 of the 1978 Spanish Constitution thus recognises their official status:

> 3:1 El castellano es la lengua española oficial del Estado. Todos los españoles tienen el deber de conocerla y el derecho a usarla.
> [Castilian is the official Spanish language of the State. All Spaniards have a duty to know it and the right to use it.]

3:2 Las demás lenguas españolas serán también oficiales en las respec-
tivas Comunidades Autónomas de acuerdo con sus Estatutos.
[The other languages of Spain will also be official in their respective
self-governing communities, in accordance with their statutes.]

3:3 La riqueza de las distintas modalidades lingüísticas de España es un
patrimonio cultural que será objeto de especial respeto y protección.
[The linguistic wealth of the various linguistic varieties of Spain is a
cultural patrimony that will be the object of particular respect and
protection.]

Constitución Española (1978)
                    http://www.constitucion.es/constitucion/index.html

As a point of comparison for my examination of Galician, I will first
look at the implications of self-government and autonomy for Catalonia.

Catalonia

In contemporary democratic Spain, language legislation has prescribed
the language rights of linguistic minorities. As I commented in Chapter 2,
official acknowledgment of these rights in the *Comunidad Autónoma* of
Catalonia, on behalf of an autochthonous population who had maintained
a tenacious loyalty to it during the years of the dictatorship, has been
extremely important to the development of a sense of Catalan national
identity at a social and cultural level. Charlotte Hoffmann points out
(2000: 428) that Catalonia's claim to autonomous status is based largely
upon the ethnicity principle, and Strubell i Trueta reinforces this assertion
when he highlights the 'belief that, among other things, Catalan gained an
inner strength by being illegitimately suppressed. The suppression of
democracy and Catalan culture and language gave them strong links in
the public mind' (1998: 156). Moreover, demands for official acknowledgment of the language ultimately became important to the development of
Catalan nationalist ideology at a political level.[7]

The most active and successful language planning and promotion programmes in Spain examined to date have taken place in Catalonia. The
transition from dictatorship to democracy meant a reversion to the
former scenario of linguistic pluralism. Hoffmann (2000: 428–429)
points out that the legal basis for recent language planning was established within the Spanish Constitution, discussed above, *L'Estatut
d'Autonomia* [Catalan Statute of Autonomy] and the *Llei de Normalització
Lingüística* [Linguistic Normalisation Act]. The latter was passed in 1983
as a direct response to Article 3 of the Statute of Autonomy, which constitutes the basis for Catalan language policy. Catalan and Castilian Spanish
have co-official status and the regional government, the *Generalitat*,
undertakes to ensure adequate knowledge of both languages and their

normal and official use (Hoffmann, 2000: 429). A Directorate was set up in the 1980s to coordinate language promotion programmes, including the encouragement of the teaching of and through the medium of Catalan, the development of modern terminologies in Catalan, and its use in all government, administration, and official public services as well as in the media. In 1998, the second major piece of legislation on language was ratified, entitled *Llei de Política Lingüística* [The Linguistic Policy Act], also known as the 'Law of Catalan'.[8] Its main aim was to guarantee the presence of Catalan in the legal system and several social and cultural contexts previously not included in the legislation (Hoffmann, 2000: 429).

Over the last three decades, the Catalan authorities have managed to instigate a generally dynamic, successful and thriving normalisation processes in Spain.[9] Catalan has gained status, prestige, support and users. Hoffmann points out that this has been achieved by the compulsory teaching of Catalan in schools and for social and economic purposes, which has meant that Catalan is used increasingly as a second language both by children and adults with a non-Catalan family background (2000: 439).

These successes have been helped by the increasing impact of the European framework. Spain signed the European Charter for Lesser-Used Languages in 1992, although it was only ratified in 2001. However, the increasing political power wielded by European Union supranational bodies has taken over the traditional influence of the Spanish State over regional centres such as Catalonia. In recent years, the European Union directive regarding minoritised and regional or 'lesser used' languages, together with the initiatives of the European Bureau for Lesser-Used Languages and the Mercator Project, which supplies regional aid and subsidises teaching and learning programmes, have contributed substantially to local language policies.[10] Many minoritised communities consider this 'Europe of the Regions' as a way of strengthening their particular cultures and languages, and hence, as a way of reinforcing their political aspirations (Mar-Molinero, 1997: 127).[11]

Galicia

Much of the attraction of the case study of Galicia lies in the fact that language rights were granted on the same terms to all the diverse 'nations within the nation' of Spain, terms that derive (as they always have so far) from a nationalist discourse that imagines a clear relationship between nation/ethnicity, one language/one territory. Yet, in Galicia, the situation is not as clear-cut as this equation assumes. As a result of their history, Galicia and the Galician language are now seen to occupy a social, historical and linguistic 'transition zone' between Portuguese and Castilian, and these perceptions have had a significant influence on the processes of language revival and revitalisation in the region.

After Galicia achieved the right to self-government in the late 1970s, the *Xunta* initiated a policy of institutional support and promotion of the language, as I outlined in Chapter 2. The aim of the normalisation processes was to re-establish Galician as a foremost symbol of ethnic identity, at the very least from a socio-political and socio-linguistic perspective, in line with the earlier attempts at linguistic revival during the *Rexurdimento* of the 19th century, as I discuss below. This type of (regional) nationalist concept tends to be based upon democratic principles. The defining characteristics consciously selected and promoted as part of the regional national identity, such as the autochthonous language, are already deeply embedded in at least part of the population's perceptions of their ethnic characterisation. Yet, although the Galician language may confer a sense of 'belonging' to its speakers, its embodiment as a significant core value of Galician ethnicity is also a deliberate attempt to differentiate the region from the rest of Spain. Thus, in accordance with May's earlier comments (pp. 44–45), Galician ethnicity in this sense is indeed both constructed and contingent (May, 2001: Chapters 1–2). If the population in general does start to attach positive values to its use, then they may start to renegotiate their perceptions of who they are in terms of being 'Spanish' or 'Galician' or both. This contrasts strongly with the situation found in Catalonia, which has not experienced this problem of differentiation, as we have already seen (pp. 80–81).

From an essentialist perspective, cultural characterisations of Galician ethnicity are also valid. Indeed, cultural nationalism is associated with such a community, rooted – as it tends to be – in somewhat tenuous recollections of a potentially glorious past, or perceptions and constructed memories surrounding anecdotal narratives and oral histories.

Rather than being artefacts and relics of a distant past, some of the region's cultural celebrations are very much alive in Galicia and attended by many people to this day. Religion still plays a hugely important role in the lives of many Galicians. Each province has its own *romería*, processions to a holy shrine in honour of a particular saint, some other religious icon or important day in the Christian calendar, such as the *Virxe da Barca* [the Virgin of the Boat] in Muxía, A Coruña, and the procession to celebrate the battle between the Moors and the Christians in A Saínza, Ourense. Similarly, every parish has its own saint's day *fiesta*, the 25th July being an extremely important date in the calendar of Santiago de Compostela, when Saint James the Apostle is fêted. There are also secular festivities that stem from the traditions and stories steeped in Galician folklore, such as the bonfires of San Juan and the floral carpets found in many areas. A unique celebration is that of the *curros* [horse corrals], also known as the *rapa das bestas* [the capture of the beasts]. These run between May and August, when the animals are led down from the mountains to the corrals to be branded and their manes and tails cut. Although this is a necessary chore of stockbreeders, in fact it has become a highly popular festival, principally in Pontevedra but also in A Coruña and Lugo.[12]

Both Galicia and Catalonia experienced a renaissance in their cultural and literary profile during the 19th century, as I discussed in Chapter 2. The industrialised, cosmopolitan and economic wealthy nature of Catalonia greatly facilitated the promotion of a strong sense of identity and hence, an ideological basis for self-determination by Catalan civil society. On the other hand, Galicia was experiencing huge emigration, motivated by crises within the agricultural sector. Although urban centres such as Santiago de Compostela did exist, Galicia at this time was still largely an industrially underdeveloped, predominately rural and financially poor region. Within the cities, the perception was that Castilian was the language of sophistication, of advancement, and success, and that Galician was a local spoken form used primarily by the poor and by rural populations.

The largely unsophisticated character of the political and social structure of the region, and its lack of infrastructure, meant that even after the *Rexurdimento*, few people in the outlying areas were affected or even knew about the so-called 'recuperation' of the autochthonous language, and dialectal diversity and variation continued to grow. However, some degree of (regional) national awareness and sense of identity in certain circles did start to occur, albeit slowly. Yet, aspirations for self-determination were based not on issues of economic power, as in Catalonia, but on cultural sentimentality and desires to end linguistic discrimination (Regueira Fernández, 2006: 62). As we saw in Chapter 2, the *Rexurdimento* and the positive efforts of the authors of the time paved the way for 9th and 20th century intellectuals, such as Otero Pedrayo, Cunqueiro, Castelao, and Risco, to employ Galician in both fictional and factual writing, as well as in the media. Thus, at least in the towns and cities, a sense that a revival of the language and its status was underway started to prevail. In recent years, their efforts have not only inspired contemporary writers of many genres, such as Ramón Piñeiro, Torres Queiruga, Manuel María, María Xosé Queizán, and Manuel Rivas to employ Galician, but they have also managed to raise the general common profile of the language in more outlying areas, too.

Despite these advancements, the perception remains that there is a need for linguistic homogeneity throughout the region. Although diverse communities can be cohesive, the Galician authorities have disparaged the dialectal variation prevalent in the region and as a way of avoiding it, they have promoted the dissemination of a standardised, written form of the language in the belief that this is the only way for the language to survive. The political, social and even cultural furore surrounding the issue of standardisation in Galicia has continued until the present day, and I now elucidate some of the main issues.

Politics and the Orthography Debate

> O importante é propoñer o castelán como norma de perfeición.
> [The important thing is to recommend Castilian as the standard for perfection.]
> (Rodríguez, 1991: 63–64)

Earlier in this Chapter (pp. 78–84), I contended that the autonomous Spanish regions discussed here do perceive and utilise their languages as unifying symbols of ethnic identity, albeit to different degrees. By the end of the Franco era, newly acquired rights such as freedom of speech, together with a hitherto unfamiliar recognition of regional self-rule and its significance, was promoting widespread debate in Galicia regarding the status of Galician and its intimate role as an identity marker. Standard-isation does not only produce a shared set of linguistic forms to facilitate communication between linguistically diverse internal groups. As a potential and potent symbol of regional national and ethnic identity, one of the main objectives of the written standard in Galicia, the *Normas Ortográficas*, is also to improve and then consolidate the prestige value of Galician among both its first-language (L^1) and second-language (L^2) speakers. This, in turn, should enhance its status to the outside world.

In her account of Galician standardisation (1996: 206), Henderson avers that the use of a print language in newspapers, journals, books, and so on, should thus serve to confirm the role of the language in the process of (regional) nation building. However, the use of the spoken language in the political sphere can also reinforce the aspirations of the region. Until the mid-1970s only Galician nationalist or *independentista* political parties, such as that which would later become the *Bloque Nacionalista Galego* (BNG) [Galician Nationalist Party] used Galician in their public dis-course, their main aim being political independence from Spain. However, by the late 1970s, there was a strong sense that every politician in Galicia, irrespective of political affiliation, should strive to defend the language. Other left-wing groups such as the Marxist-Leninist *Unión do Pobo Galego* (UPG) [Union of the Galician People] recognised the significance of Galician to their political manifestos, but only the francoist right contin-ued to use Spanish as the language of political communication in Galicia. By the early 1980s, even the *Alianza Popular* (AP) [Popular Alliance], for-merly a staunch supporter of Spanish nationalism, conducted its success-ful election campaign in Galician (Regueira Fernández, 2006: 66–69).

The political significance of the language to the validation of the region's rights to self-determination, discussed throughout Chapter 1, also drew attention to the long-standing academic and scholarly contro-versies regarding the construction of the Galician official written standard.

Control of the form and structure of the standard has become as important in contemporary Galicia as it was in the early days of democracy, and it is to the intellectual debates surrounding this form and structure that I now turn.

In the 1970s, two main groups had emerged as the vying proponents of the Galician standard. The so-called *independentistas* and *reintegracionistas* can both trace their roots back to the various erudite movements that arose in 18th and 19th century academic circles as part of the overall process of nation building in Galicia, and both have tended to utilise historical linguistic evidence as a way of justifying their differing views regarding form and structure.

These groups' ideologies regarding normalisation policies in Galicia are undoubtedly relevant to the general socio-political arena. Galician nationalism is clearly opposed to the notion of Castilian nationalism advocated by some political parties (Regueira Fernández, 2006: 90–91), and the formation of an official Galician standard would enhance the nationalists' cause, since they celebrate the language as a key component of Galician ethnicity. Disagreements regarding form and structure have pervaded political issues pertaining to Galician nationalism for nearly two decades. The two groups involved in these debates regarding the standard language are primarily intellectual movements, and their perspectives are not directly allied with the political doctrines of *independentismo* and *reintegracionismo*. However, as I discuss below, there have been various attempts to demonstrate that the issue of language standardisation is firmly embedded in the political ideologies of Galicia, and thus, the more radical perspectives of language *reintegracionismo* in particular, have acquired a political inference.

Language *independentistas* believe that the only way for the Galician language to recuperate and then survive as a viable form is as an independent language, as far as possible uninhibited by much influence from other languages, including Castilian Spanish and Portuguese. Their main defence is that political division between Galicia and Portugal was accompanied by concomitant linguistic division, and that two separate languages emerged as a result. They also claim that the majority of the Galician population view Portuguese as a very different language to Galician. As far as Castilian is concerned, they believe that Galician has to differentiate as much as possible from Castilian in order to survive. For such reasons, *Independentistas* advocate autonomous language status for Galician and their claims are subsumed thus under the terms *autonomismo* [autonomism] or *diferencialismo* [differentialism] (Herreiro-Valeiro, 2003: 293). I prefer to use the first term, since it distinguishes the academic group from the political, and because it is the group that has been involved the most with the creation of the *Normas* since the establishment of Galicia as a *Comunidad Autónoma*.

Independentistas are also often called *isolacionistas* [isolationists], by detractors such as *reintegracionistas*.

In general terms, *reintegración* holds fast to the earlier doctrines of the *Xeneración Nós*, who advocated the need for Galician to align itself more closely to Portuguese. Their common claim has been that diachronically, Galician is a variant of Portuguese, split from its 'natural' progression by Castilian linguistic and political dominance, and that from a purely linguistic perspective, Galician should conform to the Portuguese orthographic standard drafted in the *Acordo Ortográfico* of 1986.

As will be demonstrated to some extent in Chapter 5, it is undeniable that diachronically, Galician and Portuguese share the same linguistic roots; *son formas da mesma matéria, variantes de idéntico sistema lingüístico* [they are cut from the same cloth, alternative forms of the same linguistic system] (García Negro, 2000: 94). García Negro and other radical advocates of the *reintegración* movement utilise this historical characteristic in order to protest that if Galician had been allowed to flourish and develop after the scission of Portugal, then it would have evolved free from what they consider to be the stultifying influence of Castilian on the writing system. Thus, a general claim of *reintegración* is that Castilian has encumbered the growth and development of Galician, and from a purely linguistic perspective, Galician does indeed experience a high degree of overlap with Castilian forms due principally to its proximity to Castilian and to the long-standing sociolinguistic situation of the region.

This movement can be split into two main groups, designated *mínimos* [minimalists] and *máximos* [maximalists] according to the degree of *reintegración* they advocate within the Portuguese-speaking world. The *mínimos* stance uses Standard Galician with some minor graphic differences and a few Portuguese structural and lexical items (see p. 127 for a comparative account of the proposals for standard Galician). This is a rather more moderate view than the somewhat uncompromising positions held by advocates of *reintegración de máximos*, comprising cultural and linguistic agitation groups such as the *Associaçom Galega da Língua Associaçom Galega da Língua* (AGAL) [the Galician Language Association] and the *Movimento Defesa da Língua* (MDL) [the Movement for the Defence of the Language]. The more radical contention is that Galician only achieved its cultural zenith from a sociolinguistic perspective when it was associated with Portuguese within the medieval Galician-Portuguese linguistic family. In line with groups such as the *Primeira Linha-Movimento de Libertaçom Nacional* (MLN) [the First Line Movement of National Liberty], they reject what they consider as the 'contamination' of Galician by Castilian and advocate instead monolingualism in Galician-Portuguese or even Portuguese, discussed in more detail in Chapter 5.[13]

Other language *reintegracionistas* share the general political objectives of *independentismo*, and some political *independentistas* aspire to *reintegracionista* views as far as the language is concerned. For example, we have seen above (p. 84) that orthodox regional nationalist or *independentista* ideology, such as that advocated by the *Bloque Nacionalista Galego* (BNG) [Galician Nationalist Party] (comprising the former UPG and other national-socialist parties), tends to place the language central to the definition of a Galician nation. They believe that Galician society should be monolingual, based on the 'one nation-one people-one language' principle, and have in the past advocated linguistic reintegration with Portugal. However, like the majority of *reintegración* intellectuals nowadays, the BNG believe that links with Castilian cannot be completely ignored, and at least until the recent elections, employed a *mínimos* perspective regarding the structure of the Galician standard.

Certain groups who advocate full independence for Galicia, comprising young people with middle class, urban backgrounds, are also language *reintegracionistas*. However, nationalist political parties such as the *Fronte Popular Galega* (FPG) [Galician Popular Front] do not accept the linguistic policies of *reintegración* as a viable political solution to the issue of Galician independence, given that this would situate the linguistic power base outside Galicia itself and within the Portuguese-speaking world (Regueira Fernández, 2006: 92–93).

The disputes regarding the construction of a Galician standard that is both authentic and workable mask intrinsic concepts of what a Galician ethnicity should entail. Moreover, the political *reintegracionista* perspective does not take into consideration the purely pragmatic but highly important point that Galicia is a region of Spain, not of Portugal, and to dismiss this as irrelevant to the whole standardisation issue would, I believe, be somewhat imprudent. If Galician became part of the Portuguese linguistic family, then ultimately, the region itself might not remain part of the Spanish nation. Although this is highly improbable considering that prominent present-day *reintegración* supporters of such total integration are in the minority, political *independentistas* at the very least have taken it as a serious threat, debating as to whether, in fact, a concomitant form of economic and perhaps even political reintegration might follow, irrespective of the desires of the community as a whole. To a large extent, it is for this reason that the majority of *independentistas* view even language *reintegración* demands as purely political, in that to them, they are simply an attempt by adherents to infiltrate Galicia and, ultimately, to impose integration of either the northern territories or the entire Portuguese nation on the region. In his early work, Herreiro-Valeiro (1993) rather vehemently terms this conflict 'a virulent confrontation of elites around the control of the graphic construction of Galician and its symbolic value as (a) national or ethnic identity marker'. In a later paper, he states that the *reintegracionista* view may not always recognise the political and the linguistic-cultural borders of Galicia with Portugal.

He also believes that whilst the *autonomista* perspective upholds the 'linguistic-cultural individualisation' of the region, there *is* a political stance embedded therein.

Despite these assertions, there have been various attempts at demonstrating that language *reintegracionismo* at least is a social and cultural movement rather than an economic or political one. One of AGAL's main aims is to create a favourable public opinion towards the notion of *reintegración* with Northern Portugal, and in this sense, they are strongly allied to the political *reintegración* perspective. However, the more radical, separatist claims of the *máximos* are not upheld by any major political players, since to do so would not be popular with the general public. Henderson (1996: 162–163) has also found that many language *reintegracionistas* demonstrate no obvious institutional affiliation to a particular political party, without which any political aspirations regarding assimilation with Portugal are entirely unfeasible. It is not even clear whether this is the ultimate goal of many adherents. Certainly, protests against the *Xunta*, and what are perceived by some as its large concessions to the overreaching influence of Madrid regarding standardisation, tend to be carried out by students and academics affiliated to the *máximos*; but they are in the minority, and the general public do not appear aware of the dissent. In sharp contrast to events in some other parts of Spain, demonstration is largely non-violent and limited, publicly at least, to the daubing of separatist graffiti on the walls of the main cities, the distribution of flyers around some of the universities, rallies around July 25th, the Festival of the Apostle, and Galicia's National Day. In academic circles, articles are still published and conferences occasionally held, but even here, support for the more radical view is not immediately apparent.

The general thrust of the *reintegracionista* argument does not mention the economic advantage of being allied more closely with the Portuguese-speaking world. Notwithstanding my earlier comments, the majority of adherents who *do* believe that integration is the best option for Galicia, state that it would gain access for Galician literature and culture to a wider audience and hence, the standing of the language would be improved. This then, would allow Galicians themselves to finally accept and be proud of the fact that their language enjoys the status and prestige value of the global language of Portuguese. Henderson's (1996: 204–205) *reintegracionista* respondents go so far as to claim that to present Galician as an independent language is tantamount to restricting its status to that of a regional, minoritised language with little or no prestige or status. However, on the other hand, *autonomistas* argue that full reintegration with the Portuguese language would severely disadvantage Galician as far as its status is concerned. That is, the use of Portuguese as the norm to be adhered to in the written form would simply exacerbate the problem of low prestige, because the population would have to contend with a form that is, ostensibly, alien to them, unlike the Castilian orthography they use or at least read everyday. Monteagudo (1995: 9–10) adds that in such a situation, standard Portuguese could become the high language within a Galician diglossia, with the Galician varieties as low-prestige, dialectal varieties of Portuguese – in much the same way as Galician varieties have, historically, been considered dialectal varieties of Castilian. This view squares favourably with the idea that as part of the Spanish nation, the maintenance of an independent orthographic system by Galicia would afford the community as a whole a heightened sense of their own, idiosyncratic identity within the greater framework of the Spanish state.

Moreover, in the previous section, I posited the idea that if linguistic reintegration with Portuguese did occur, albeit highly improbable, could we also expect to witness some form of economic and even political reintegration with Portugal? Indeed, would Portugal itself embrace the incorporation of Galicia into its borders?

The general Spanish perception regarding the relationship between Galicia and Portugal is that the Portuguese are not interested in Galicia. From a purely economic perspective, Galicia is a poor region and integration into Portuguese territories would do little to enhance the latter's economic clout, despite the recent depiction of this area as coherent and cohesive, enhanced by the inauguration in 1992 of the *Eje Atlántico del Noroeste Peninsular* [The Atlantic Axis of the Northwest Peninsula]. Now comprising the 18 principal cities of Galicia and Northern Portugal, its aim is to promote *la cohesión económica social y cultural a través de la estructuración de un territorio común* [economic, social and cultural unity through the creation of a common territory].[14]

Yet, the maintenance of cross-border alliances and commercial trading between communities on both sides of the River Minho has not done away with the deep-seated mistrust between many Portuguese and Galicians, who still trade *gallego* and *portugués* as respective insults. This is a feature shared with many people across political borders. Centuries of military and political disagreement and, more recently, actions such as the imposition of strict border controls and guards after World War II, intensified general feelings of aversion and suspicion between the two communities. Portugal considers Galicia as part of a united Spanish nation and the Portuguese state does not manifest any desire to interfere in Spain's political configuration or machinations. For example, during the 1970s and 1980s, Portugal displayed little or no solidarity with Galicia during its protracted negotiations for self-government status with the Madrid government. Although the traditional impression that the Spanish and the Portuguese view each other with mistrust and like to keep each other at a distance is still widespread, in recent times, both countries have appeared rather eager to recognise each other's viability as states and to increase their mutual commercial transactions. Indeed, since the entry of Spain and Portugal into the European Union in 1986 and the introduction of the Schengen Agreement also in the mid-1980s, which did away in effect with the border between the two countries and its duty restrictions, commercial contact and collaboration have also increased between the countries as a whole.

Integration of the Standard

In an earlier section of this chapter (pp. 76–77), I discussed issues pertaining to language standardisation, and I stated that the promotion and integration of a standard language often implied the following stages: codification of form, functional implementation and elaboration of function. As is the case for many standards, the Galician recommended model is an artificially created form, an amalgamation of dialectal traits still undergoing adjustment and amendment, but by necessity, put into place by legislative measures.

This is an important point. When majority linguistic communities within a given state hold the main political power, the use of their language does not necessarily have to be sanctioned by legal directives. This is clear in the case of Spain. As the overarching state, Spain does not necessarily need the rights of its main language guaranteed by stringent legislation, even where other languages are spoken, because Spanish is the official language of the state and as such, is present throughout the country. Galicia on the other hand, is a minoritised linguistic community, whose language requires legal backing not just at regional level, but also, and perhaps more importantly, at state level. Consequently, the Spanish government is obliged by law to promote an all-encompassing language policy within its borders, resulting in the declarations I highlighted above (p. 80), whereby Catalan, Galician and Basque are cited within state legislation as being official linguistic entities within their respective territories.

The authorities in Madrid are responsible for defining basic educational parameters. As a result, there is a curriculum model common to the state as a whole, entitled the *Diseño Curricular Base* (DCB) [Base Curriculum Design]. The aim of the DCB is to determine basic educational parameters, such as system design, duration and segmentation of compulsory education, basic subject options, most of the curriculum including the minimum teaching of the Spanish language, basic rights and functions of state school teachers, confirmation of studies, and so on (Mercator Education, 2001: 11). However, the Madrid authorities are not legally required to carry out any form of language planning programme on behalf of the linguistic minorities. Although such a programme is essential to the diffusion and promotion of each of the minoritised languages within the *comunidades autónomas*, it receives little support or funding from Madrid. Hence, language planning initiatives are the sole responsibility of each of the local governments and their institutions.

The focus of such initiatives, which includes the social promotion and functional elaboration of the language, tends to be centred upon the education system. In theory, these measures should disseminate the concept of good practice regarding the use of the written form, not only within educational establishments but also within the media, town councils and other local government representatives. These measures should also enable the authorities in Galicia to plan for a more advantageous delineation of the autochthonous language, once the population as a whole has accepted the viability of the standard language and new users have been acquired – what I have referred to earlier (p. 77) as *normalización*. As was stated above, this implies that the Galician standard, not its regional and social variants, is accepted on a day-to-day basis as the language of normal use. The expectation is that in this way, the standard language will start to function internally as a unifying force, thus strengthening the notion of a positive idiosyncratic identity amongst the Galician population. At the same time, the hope of the nationalist political parties is that, externally, the language will start to function as a symbol of autochthony, allowing Galician to regain an equal footing with Castilian Spanish and with other languages, and reinforcing the political aspirations of the region.

Normalización in Galicia

In order to evaluate how far the current legislation has been successful in altering general linguistic practices and perceptions regarding the autochthonous language, I now consider further the issue of *normalización* in Galicia. The main regulation governing the use of the Galician language in Education is the *Lei de Normalización Lingüística de Galicia* [Linguistic Normalisation Law of Galicia] ratified in 1983, a year after the *Decreto 173 sobre a normativización da lingua galega* [Decree 173 on the Normativisation of the Galician Language] (17/11/82) was passed by the *Xunta*. The purpose of this law was to develop the idea of co-official language status by encouraging the population to accept Galician as a valid language choice for various functions formerly reserved for the use of Castilian, such as in administrative sectors, education and the media. To this end, it both sanctions and largely decrees the implementation and use of the *Normas* within the education system and the media, as well as within political and public institutions. Certain articles of the *Lei de Normalización Lingüística* that pertain to education and the media reinforce this message. For example, the aim of Title III, Article 12:1 was to begin integration processes pertaining to the compulsory teaching of Galician throughout the region, and to make Galician the main language of teaching and learning in schools. Interestingly, immersion programmes were employed even though typically, as Skutnabb-Kangas points out:

> An immersion programme is a programme where linguistic majority children with a high-status mother tongue voluntarily choose [...] to be instructed through the medium of a foreign (minority) language, in classes with majority children with the same mother tongue only [...] where the teacher is bilingual so that the children can at the beginning use their own language, and where their mother tongue is in no danger of not developing or of being replaced by the language of instruction – an additive language learning situation
>
> (Skutnabb-Kangas, 2000: 612–614)

Initially pioneered by Wallace Lambert in Canada, the majority of immersion programmes are still in French, but other programmes have been initiated in other languages: Spanish is used frequently in the United States, and Catalonia has also adopted the same techniques as has the Basque Country as was discussed above (pp. 80–81). Typically, as here, two languages are used as medium of instruction. However, unlike Catalonia where legislation requires all children, whether mother tongue Castilian-speaking or mother tongue Catalan-speaking, to learn Catalan (and engenders a degree of resistance for this reason), in Galicia the goal has been to reintroduce the language to those who have stopped using it, or to only use it in very restricted contexts. The principle behind these immersion techniques, that is that mother tongue majority language children learn a minoritised language, is certainly not the case in Galicia.

The main objective of the legislation envisaged a situation in which pupils would become competent in their autochthonous language so that within schools, the status of Castilian would ultimately be limited to that of a subject of study:

Título III
Do Uso Do Galego No Ensino
Artigo 12:1 O galego, como lingua propia de Galicia, é tamén lingua oficial no ensino en tódolos níveis educativos.

[Title III.
Pertaining to the Use of Galician in the Education System.
 Article 12:1 Galician, as the autochthonous language of Galicia, is also the official language of the education system at all levels.]

(Lei de Normalización Lingüística de Galicia, 1983)
http://galego.org/lexislacion/xbasica/lei3-83.html

Yet, in some ways, the Galician model is indeed an 'additive language learning situation', for the authorities did not envisage the functional replacement of Castilian in all contexts. I will return to this issue in Chapter 7.

Article 13 of the same Title also assured the right of all children to be taught through the medium of their mother tongue – Galician or Castilian – at pre-school and primary level:

Artigo 13 Os nenos teñen direito a recibir o primeiro ensino na sua língua maternal.
O Goberno Galego arbitrará as medidas necesarias para facer efectivo este dereito..

[Article 13 Children have the right to receive their pre-school and primary education in their mother tongue. The Galician Government will decide upon the measures needed in order to affect this right.]

Article 14: 1 made the study of the Galician language mandatory at all compulsory education levels:[15]

Artigo 14: 1 A lingua galega é materia de estudio obrigatorio en tódolos niveis educativos non universitarios. Garantirá-se o uso efectivo deste direito en todos os centros públicos e privados.

[Article 14: 1 The study of the Galician language is compulsory at all non-university levels of education. The effective use of this right will be guaranteed in all public and private institutions.]

As far as the media was concerned, the aim of Title 4, Article 18 was to encourage the use of Galician on the local television and radio channels, and in the local newspapers:

Título IV
O Uso Do Galego Nos Medios De Comunicación
Artigo 18 O galego será a lingua usual nas emisoras de radio e televisión e nos demais medios de comunicación social sometidos a xestión ou competencia das institucións da Comunidade Autónoma.

[Title IV.
Pertaining to the Use of Galician by the Media.
Article 18 Galician will be the customary language used on radio and television and in other means of public communication liable to administration by or competition from business concerns of the Self-governing Community.]

Finally, Title II stipulates legislation relating to language use by governmental institutions in communications with the general public:

Título II
Do Uso Oficial Do Galego
Artigo 6:1 Os cidadáns teñen dereito ó uso do galego, oralmente e por escrito, nas súas relacións coa Administración Pública no ámbito territorial da Comunidade Autónoma.

[Title II
Pertaining to the Official Use of Galician.
Article 6:1 Citizens have the right to demand the use of Galician, both in spoken and written communications with Public Service Authorities within the confines of the self-governing Community.]

The content of this particular legislation implies that, if required, all inhabitants can expect a public service official to be able to communicate with them in Galician.

Concluding Remarks

The main thrust of this chapter has been a delineation and appraisal of the political perspective of regional autonomy in Spain and in particular, its implications for the autochthonous language of Galicia. In this sense, I have established the contemporary relevance of linguistic issues and, in particular, the debates and controversies surrounding the standard form of Galician. When read in conjunction with Chapter 2, the present chapter offers a clear appreciation of the issues surrounding the use of Galician in contemporary settings and their historical origins. Thus, this chapter serves to clarify the significance and importance of such issues to the underlying hypothesis of this book regarding language contact scenario, the standard Galician language and its concomitant linguistic policies and planning strategies. These issues are addressed further in Parts 2 and 3, where I assess the potential impact on the behavioural practices and attitudes of Galician speakers. In doing so, I reinforce my earlier delineation of language policy and language planning in Chapter 1, as well as the diachronic overview of Galician-Portuguese-Castilian relationships described in Chapter 2.

In this chapter, I have considered the *reintegración/autonomismo* debate to be largely intellectual-based, but linked to political aims. However, I have taken great pains not to elaborate upon the nature of the linguistic differentiation inherent to each proposal, for such issues will constitute a substantial part of Chapter 5. Instead, my discussion has focussed upon the interplay between language and identity inherent in the standardisation debate, once again based upon my initial hypothesis that language may be an important characteristic of ethnic identity in Galicia.

I now consider the linguistic basis of the standardisation debate. I begin in Chapter 4 by offering an explanation of the concepts pertinent to my essentially linguistic description of Galician, should the reader require such clarification.

Part 2

Forms and Features: Galician Linguistic Conventions and Characteristics

Preamble

Part 1 was, essentially, an introduction to the Galician situation and the significance of its historical and more contemporary relationships with Portugal and the rest of Spain. I considered the implications therein for the Galician language and its role as an identity factor, and I ended the section by examining the debates and discussions surrounding the linguistic composition of the official orthographic standard of the Galician language since the advent of democracy and the resurgence of revitalisation processes.

The form of the orthographic standard continues to be a somewhat divisive issue in Galicia, based once again on the deeply-rooted relationships that Galicia maintains with Portugal and the rest of Spain highlighted in Part 1. In order to explain the polemic, I now focus specifically on the linguistic evolution of Galician, its similarities to and differences from Portuguese and Castilian, and the role played by some of its more salient characteristics in self-identification practices. This section thus offers a backdrop to my final discussion of the standard and its implications for language use and language prestige in Part 3. This section of the book also constitutes an essential component of my innovative and original approach of utilising a combination of historical and contemporary sociolinguistic and linguistic analyses to address issues of languages in contact.

Part 2 is divided into three chapters. Due to the rather linguistic focus I take in these sections, I have presented a brief glossary at the end of this book for those readers unfamiliar with the terminology I employ to discuss the theoretical concepts and issues relevant to an examination of phonetic characteristics, which is not explained in the body of the text.

I begin Chapter 4 by presenting a brief discussion of microlinguistic issues, considering in particular positive and negative transference and borrowing phenomena, under-differentiation and over-differentiation, and external and internal change, focusing in particular on their role in language contact situations. Chapter 5 is a comparative summary of the most salient diachronic and synchronic linguistic characteristics of Galician, together with its similarities to, and differences from, Portuguese and Castilian, bearing in mind issues of linguistic equivalence and linguistic homogeneity. Finally, I revisit the standardisation question and consider the issue of an oral standard. In Chapter 6, I explore the relevance of linguistic variability to the sociolinguistic setting, discussed in more detail in Part 3. Issues of prestige and identification are essential to my discussion of ethnicity within Galicia, and the reason why it is necessary to consider the potential socio-symbolic role of phonological variation. Therefore, I examine what I have termed two 'emblematic' characteristics of Galician, the *gheada* and the velar nasal consonant. I examine how these two pronunciation traits in particular may be used to distinguish a speaker's identity and the reasons therein, in order to highlight the importance of pronunciation to the issue of Galician, its standard forms, and ethnic identification strategies.

Chapter 4
Microlinguistic Issues: Theoretical Concepts

Introductory Remarks

This Chapter offers a brief overview of the terminology relevant to my discussion about the linguistic differentiation of Galician. As such, it is intended as reference for those readers who may not be entirely familiar with the conceptual issues implicit within the microlinguistic study of language variation, rather than an exhaustive account of linguistic theory. I begin by delineating the relevance of allophonic variation to sociolinguistic variationist studies, for this will prove important to my discussion of emblematic characteristics. I outline the notion of transference phenomena and look at the issue of language production errors regarding under- and over-differentiation. In particular, I consider the influence of the standard form of a language on dialectal variation. This has specific resonances in Galicia, due to the loss of much dialectal variation in the last century. My discussion of the notion of code-switching as a communication device, bearing in mind its potential role in contact phenomena, is followed by a brief comparison of externally and internally motivated linguistic change and, finally, a short analysis of the theoretical constructs therein.

The Allophone in Sociolinguistic Variationist Studies

The aim of variationist linguistics is to try and pinpoint linguistic features within a speech community that manifest variability in their occurrence, and then to offer an explanation of the motivations behind their selection in a given setting or situation. In this, variationist linguistics study the relationship between linguistic and social patterns, and the functions and values of different languages within speech communities.

Most commonly, the variables that have been studied in this way are phonological. Phonological variables tend to be associated with a particular group of words in which phonemic or allophonic variation has already been observed. For each variable, a list of discrete variants or alternative forms is identified, such as the alternate pronunciation of English *either* starting with [iː] or [ai]. Speakers can be grouped based on their use of these variants. A potential correlation may then be established between the variable and influences of the sociolinguistic environment, although this may only be justified if the outcome of the choice process is normally unpredictable from the given linguistic contextual information (Sankoff, 1988: 984). That is, allophonic variation is generally predicted from the linguistic environment, but some types of variation have little to do with the characteristics of adjacent sounds, and more to do with factors that are external to the linguistic configuration. In such cases, the socio-linguistic setting becomes highly relevant.

This type of variation may be influenced by the syntax and the discursive function, topic or style of the utterance, such as age, gender, social background, class and cultural factors. However, again, an unambiguous association between a given variable and a particular stylistic or social category does not always occur.[1] Such variation appears to be an integral characteristic of language itself: Trudgill points out (1983: 45–46) that linguistic varieties in urban areas tend to display such inherent variability as a rule rather than as an exception.

This phonological variation has been described as occurring either above or below the level of conscious awareness in accordance with the speaker's position in the social hierarchy (Mesthrie *et al.*, 2000: 118). Thus, a 'change from above' is described as the conscious and sporadic introduction of a new sound into a language; a type of correction or modelling of the form already present within the recipient variety, generally towards the prestige form prevalent within that of the highest status group or dominant social class. A classic example is that of postvocalic *r* in New York City department stores (Labov, 1966) examined in the Introduction (pp. 19–20, 22). In contrast, a 'change from below' is described as sound that was originally part of the speech patterns of working-class groups, which speakers (may) adopt unconsciously. Typically, these intermittent changes manifest themselves as phonetic processes that simplify the articulation of a particular word (Mesthrie *et al.*, 2000: 118). Examples from English include the deletion of /t/ in consonant clusters in casual speech forms, for example *bes' be off.*[2]

Transference Phenomena

In the Introduction to this book, I briefly discussed the concepts of language contact and language shift from the perspective of diglossic societies (pp. 14–18). I now examine the linguistic outcomes of such contact situations.

In his early work on bilingualism, Weinreich (1966: 1–3) employed the now largely outmoded term 'interference'. He defined (externally motivated) interference phenomena as a 'rearrangement of patterns' leading to 'the deviation from the norms of either language occurring in the speech of bilinguals as a result of their familiarity with more than one language, that is, as a result of language contact'. Put rather more dispassionately, the introduction, transfer and incorporation of foreign linguistic elements into a recipient language may produce a readjustment of the linguistic configuration of one or all of the highly structured fields of language, such as the phonological, morphological and syntactic systems. Throughout this discussion, I adopt Clyne's widely accepted proposal that instead of interference, the term transference should be used to delineate such language contact phenomena (2003: 70–76). Fasold (1984: 54) has propounded a two-stage process: a) leakage in function and b) mixing in form. Thus, the two languages in question start to 'overlap' in their usage, and some form of linguistic mixing of the relevant forms has to occur before the transference can be totally integrated into the structure of the recipient language, and so not appear as a foreign element.

Again, of particular importance to this hypothesis is the Thomason and Kaufman framework of language change (1988), which states that there are two overriding major contact-induced phenomena that differentiate between shift and maintenance situations: borrowing and transference through shift, sometimes rather imprecisely referred to as substratum interference (1988: 4, 20, 37).[3] They define borrowing as 'the incorporation of foreign features into a group's native language by speakers of that language' (1988: 21). Typically, the first elements a speaker borrows from another language (L^2) are lexical items.[4] However, any lexical item that undergoes some form of transfer from one language (L^2) to another (L^1) becomes open to influence from both the grammatical and phonetic systems of the L^1, especially if the loanword is ultimately adopted by a group's monolingual speakers through more intense cultural contact. This implies, then, that the syntactic and phonological items of the L^2 are not permanently borrowed. However, in transference through shift scenario, it may be that the focus of shift are the syntactic and phonological systems themselves, as I discuss below (p. 100).

Second-language acquisition scenarios offer a good example of borrowing phenomena. Speakers who become bilingual as adults firstly introduce phonetic adaptations of L^2 loanwords and L^2 norms into their L^1 repertoires – just as speakers of the Low language in a traditional diglossic, bilingual setting initially speak the inter-group language with a certain degree of (typically) phonetic transference from their primary intra-group language (see p. 14 regarding the use of these terms in a diglossic scenario). With continual use and repetition, however, new language learners identify L^2 phonemes with either the same or similar ones in their L^1, and reproduce them according to the phonetic rules of their L^1. Thus, elements of the L^1 phonetic repertoire may replace those of the L^2. If L^1 monolingual speakers then adopt the loanword, a complete or almost complete substitution occurs within the sound structure, and it is in this form that the loanword will be adopted and integrated into the L^1 grammar (Lehiste, 1988: 5). Weinreich (1966: 18) has termed this 'phonic substitution'. Examples of such borrowings include the pronunciation of the following words in English: from the languages of India, *bungalow, polo* and *chutney;* from the Pacific Islands, *kiwi, sarong* and *koala,* and from Amerindian sources, *chipmunk, kayak* and *tomato.*[5]

There is a well-established assumption within studies of linguistic repertoires and linguistic variation that transference can take place at all levels of linguistic structure and not just within the lexis. Indeed, unlike borrowing, transference tends to start within the phonetic and syntactic systems rather than within the lexis, as I have highlighted above (p. 99). The English spoken in the Indian subcontinent is a valid example. Indian-influenced characteristics such as the use of a progressive tense form instead of the simple present tense may result in statements such as *I am understanding it now,* and the distinctive Indian accent with its retroflex pronunciations of *t* and *d* is widely heard in English utterances (Crystal, 1988: 258). Transferences depend on how the contact takes place, on its intensity, and notably on whether it is speakers of the source or target language who are the agents.[6] However, once the transference phenomenon is frequently applied, it may be a simple step for it to become totally integrated and established as part of the repertoire of the language (Thomason and Kaufman, 1988: 37–41, 47). In this way, its existence becomes no longer reliant upon the bilingual status of the speaker (Weinreich, 1966: 11).

Underdifferentiation and Overdifferentiation

I now examine some examples of transfer phenomena involving language production errors. In certain instances of contact-induced language shift, the influence of the L^1 phonetic system on an adult bilingual's L^2 may lead to the loss of phonemic contrast or of certain allomorphs. Similarly, second language acquisition sound substitution may involve under-differentiation (Weinreich, 1966: 18; Lehiste, 1988: 4–5). This occurs when the L^1 lacks a phonemic contrast that is present in the L^2, meaning that sounds that are allophones in the L^1 are separate phonemes in the L^2, and thus, the autochthonous L^1 speaker displays an inability to produce the L^2 phonemic distinction. For example, English final nasal consonants are generally considered phonemically distinct /m, n, ŋ/, whereas in Standard Castilian Spanish there is only one nasal phoneme in the same position /n/. Until the specific phonemic rules for the pronunciation of English word-final nasals are learnt, autochthonous Castilian Spanish speakers may under-differentiate. Thus, the final consonant of the L^2 English words *ham, sang* and *can* will be consistently pronounced as /n/, as in the Castilian Spanish speaker's L^1.

In contrast, the term over-differentiation describes the imposition of L^1 phonemic distinctions onto the sounds of L^2, with the result that L^2 allophones are treated as phonemes (Weinreich, 1966: 18). In English, /d/ and /ð/ are in phonemic contrast, for example *dough* /d/ and *though* /ð/. In Castilian Spanish however, they are positional allophones. [ð] occurs between vowels (*poder* [to be able to]), after any consonant except /l/ or /n/ (*perdón* [sorry, excuse me]), and word-finally (*usted* [you (polite singular)]); [d] occurs elsewhere (*donde* [where]). Thus, English L^1 speakers have to learn the rules that dictate this occurrence, otherwise distinctions made in the L^1 will be carried over to the L^2 (Lehiste, 1988: 5–6).

Phonological dialectal distinctions arise diachronically. They do not normally affect inter-communicative functions and often evolve into an excellent method of divulging a specific geographical identity. However, they are often subject to assimilation processes, sometimes due to the introduction of a standardised language, as I mentioned in Chapter 3. The classic example of phonemic assimilation between a standard and a dialect has been described by Blom and Gumperz (1972) and by Gumperz (1975: 33–40). These works examined the impact on the dialect of Rana of Bokmål, one of the two officially recognised standard languages of Norway. Continual pressure to accept and implement this standard and the strong similarities in form between the two resulted in the assimilation of dialectal grammar forms and a gradual reduction in the major phonetic differences between the standard and the dialect. Elements that already existed in the L^1 dialect but with different distributional rules, such as certain L^2 phonemes, were adopted first. Phonemes that did not normally occur in the L^1 were then introduced, followed by distinctive phonemic features. There would have been a period of under-differentiation, in which such phonemic distinctions were not totally applied. However, variations that appear in the dialect but not in the standard were ultimately abandoned and the phonemic system was simplified. Gumperz (1975: 33) concluded that individuals were gradually using the same phonetic system whether they were talking Bokmål or Rana.

Another example of phonemic assimilation described by Hamp (1989: 204), concerns transference in bilingual contact situations. In the late 1980s, Mandritsa, a variety of Albanian spoken in South Eastern Bulgaria, was surviving quite healthily in a state of stable bilingualism, yet it displayed marked characteristics of acculturation in its phonology to neighbouring languages. For example, it had simplified its vowel diphthongs to monophthongs, in accordance with those found in the Bulgarian, Turkish and Greek phonotactic systems surrounding it.[7]

Code-Switching

Unlike the phenomenon of structural transference, code-switching is generally considered a short-term effect of language contact. Gumperz (1982a: 59) offers an early but workable definition: 'the juxtaposition within the same speech exchange of passages of speech belonging to different grammatical systems or subsystems'.

The field of code-switching has developed rapidly in the last few decades, with constant refinement of analytical frameworks based upon the findings of wide-ranging ethnographic fieldwork. Early approaches generally held that speakers 'mixed' languages because they were 'semi-lingual', that is, not 'fully competent' in both (or all) of their codes. However, the latter is a somewhat prejudiced assumption: Milroy and Muysken (1995: 3) for example, point out that 'bilingual speakers characteristically use each of their languages in different social contexts and would not be expected to use either of them in all contexts'. Nonetheless, this supposition still features in the language policies of many multilingual societies, and will be important in my subsequent discussion regarding Galicia.

Later research took one of two directions. In the 1980s, Shana Poplack attempted to discover a 'grammar' of code-switching. Poplack was concerned with discovering the linguistic constraints on switching-points, and she concluded that intersentential code-switching, whereby speakers move between languages without violating the syntax of either, was symptomatic of a superior knowledge of both languages (1980, 1984).

Subsequent research has questioned this hypothesis, but the general premise regarding the maintenance of syntactic distinction remains: code-switching is a strategic communicative device in that it involves the selection and use of more than one language by speakers within a particular speech event, in order to convey some particular extralinguistic meaning. As such, no transfer, substitution of form, or system readjustment is necessary and the phonetic, syntactic, or morphological characteristics of the host language are not generally adopted.[8]

Equally important to the focus of this book is the second direction of later research, for it examines the function of code-switching as a resource of meaning in oral interactions, the focus being pragmatic inference and its use as a tool of identity. That is, it postulates that code-switching follows certain identifiable patterns rather than being entirely spontaneous or idiosyncratic. Fishman's early approach (1971) emphasised situational language choice and was strongly influenced by his analysis of diglossia, and Gumperz (1982a, 1982b) saw such code alternation as one of an array of 'contextualisation cues/conventions' of the communicative practices of speech communities. Gumperz developed a typology of conversational points in which switching is highly frequent and signals specific changes of function. This has since been extended and modified (see also Auer, 1995) and I offer two pertinent examples.

The rhetorical use of code-switching for the amusement of the interlocutors or to create some form of dramatic effect is typically from the intergroup to the intragroup language. Switches from the intra to the intergroup languages however, are more likely to express disapproval or as an attempt to superimpose authority on a particular situation. Thus, it is the motivation behind the switch itself rather than the specific meaning of the communication that is relevant. Metaphorical switching, on the other hand, tends to be employed only by skilled bilinguals and draws on specific associations that are inherent within each of the codes in question in order to create a particular effect, which normally embraces elements related to the use of both codes in other contexts. Of particular interest are situations in which inserted switched items from the L^2 into the L^1 appear as foreign elements in order to provoke a particular reaction by the interlocutor.[9]

Importantly, Gumperz (1982a) also began to interpret some switches in terms of group identities. Often, there appears to be a symbolic distinction between 'I' (or 'we' as discussed below) and 'they' embodied in the choice of varieties. Thus, in certain contexts the 'we' code (typically, the intragroup variety or varieties signifying informal, personalised activities), is selected in order to overtly mark or demonstrate solidarity or shared ethnicity with the in-group. Moreover, the emblematic use of tags, interjections or sentence fillers may also signal a collective group membership motivated by the identity of and relationship between participants (Romaine, 2000: 60). In contrast, selection of the 'they' code evokes the values of the 'outsider' or out-group, potentially for reasons of enhanced status. Thus, in the case of a formal relationship such as that of doctor-patient, where the intergroup code would generally be used, there may be a switch to the intragroup code if the two participants know each other well and are discussing a topic of a more informal nature. Alternatively, the typically informal scenario between friends or members of the same family may be altered by a change from intra to intergroup code due to the introduction of a more formal type of topic necessitating such a change. Although Gumperz's hypothesis is still highly influential, it does have some drawbacks, not least regarding the definition of marked and unmarked choices of language in a given community (see pp. 105–106 below).[10]

Of particular relevance to this study is the notion of stability. We have seen above that within a stable, well-established bilingual setting, code-switching may occur but the structures of the two languages may still maintain their autonomy. This is situational code-switching – the individual or interpersonal correlate of diglossia as a social phenomenon. However, in her article on the non-discreteness of codes, Gardner-Chloros (1995) questions the relevance of such approaches, particularly to communities where codes are similar from a linguistic point of view. Some of her comments reinforce to a large extent Le Page and Tabouret-Keller's discussion (1985) of 'acts of identity'. Le Page and Tabouret-Keller suggest that people move, or 'focus', their speech towards one or another language for all kinds of metaphorical and identity-negotiating purposes. When speakers are not formally educated in one, either, or both of the languages in question, they may not have a clear idea of the linguistic boundaries they are crossing when they code-switch, although they will generally be clear about its social effects. This is particularly evident in bilingual situations where codes are linguistically similar. More educated speakers tend to have a much clearer sense of these boundaries, probably due to their reading and writing skills. Thus, they will be more conscious of crossing them.

Gardner Chloros (1995) emphasises that there is, in reality, no 'hard-edged' binary code choice available in that switches are fluid and can occur at different levels. Importantly, certain communities may now only use code-switched varieties, hence new identities and languages are being constructed. In subsequent chapters, I will suggest that this particular hypothesis is extremely relevant to the Galician situation, where switches exist between dialectal and standard Galician, and between Castilian and Galician.[11]

External versus Internal Change

So far, I have largely discussed examples of externally motivated linguistic change since this is the type of change that occurs in contact scenario and forms the basis of the variationist model. However, I should also establish what constitutes an internal linguistic, or internally motivated, change, since this will be pertinent to my discussion of linguistic features in Galician and their evolution. Internal changes are often described as 'natural changes', in that they are considered regular in occurrence, not contact-induced but occurring independently of the particular sociolinguistic situation of a given language.

Hajek (1992), Labov (1994), and McMahon (1994) have all considered the regularity or non-randomness of diachronic sound change. In particular, the theory of Lexical Diffusion has been well documented and is considered extremely credible, as it focuses on the processes underlying linguistic change rather than the end result. Moreover, unlike other hypotheses, it proposes the word as the basic unit of change, not the sound.[12] Thus, the change is the result of the perceptible substitution of one phoneme for another in words containing that phoneme: see pp. 153–155 regarding nasal attrition in Galician for example. The fact that this change gradually occurs through the relevant lexis means that older and newer forms of the word will usually differ by several phonetic

features. This process is most characteristic of the late stages of an internally motivated linguistic change, which may also have developed a high
degree of social awareness by its speakers (Hajek, 1992: 21).[13]

This reiterates once again an important point regarding the change processes, discussed in this chapter. In a recent paper, Milroy (in press) highlights the problem of trying to differentiate between internal and external
determinants of language change, since these determinants are not
mutually exclusive in every instance. Although the internal direction of
spread of a change process could be motivated by purely linguistic
phenomena, the process itself may be triggered by external, sociolinguistic, contact-induced phenomena. In other words, when no internal motivation can be found, external factors are examined in the search for
an explanation.

External, sociolinguistic contact-induced phenomena may also
reinforce and accelerate an internally motivated change that is already
in progress (Clyne, 2003: 93).[14] In this way, language contact situations
may simply illustrate the (external) strengthening of (internal) tendencies
of evolution that exist independently in the languages involved in the
contact scenario. To this end, Campbell and Muntzel (1989: 190) and
Thomason and Kaufman (1988: 57), amongst others, adopt the term
multiple causation, which assumes that a combination of both social
and linguistic pressures may determine sound change.

The Social Implications of Marked/Unmarked Features

My final comments concern the issue of what constitutes marked and
unmarked forms and their social implications. In the 20th century, the
original notion of markedness was coined in the early Prague school of
linguistic theory by linguists such as Jakobson and Trubetzkoy, who, in
the most formal and narrowest of senses, applied the term 'marked' to
phonological forms characterised by the presence of a feature absent in
corresponding 'unmarked' forms (Andrews, 1990: 1–2). Chomsky and
Halle (1968) integrated the Praguian notion into their rule-based
account of Standard English pronunciation (SPE) and redefined phonological markedness features for English based on distributional criteria in
the form of general rules. For example, English vowels are normally
voiced and they would have to be marked for voicelessness. According
to Hooper's definition (1976: 135: 16), this would make the unmarked
voiced state of vowel phonemes a more natural phenomenon: more
expected, more easily learnt and interpreted, and generally more commonly found, whereas the marked term, that of voicelessness, would
demonstrate opposing characteristics. Other examples include the
nasal/non-nasal vowel phoneme opposition in French, and the long/
short vowel phoneme opposition in Czech, Japanese and Thai.

If the term is expanded to encompass other linguistic usage, then following Coulmas (2005: 90–92), every society or community has linguistic features, styles, behaviours, and so forth, that are considered unmarked normal usage and to which speakers generally conform. Speakers have a strong sense of what constitutes a marked form and the implications therein of its usage in a particular context. Thus, the unmarked/marked contrast refers to the relative expectedness or normality of a linguistic choice, in contrast to the conspicuous or unusual use of such a choice. In the example above of internal/external change, external factors may be marked changes if they are dependent upon unpredictable societal forces.

In a linguistic sense, marked forms carry neither positive nor negative connotations in their usage, but the contrast can have, at the very least, social implications in conversational analysis. For example, markedness theory is particularly relevant to the study of politeness; Coulmas states that 'every unmarked choice functions as an affirmation of the existing social order, and every marked choice is a potential threat to it' (2005: 91). In this way, the unmarked form is considered societally more appropriate. The pertinence of this theory to the Galician situation will be discussed briefly in Chapter 6 (pp. 148, 152, 159–160).

Concluding Remarks

I do not offer far-reaching implications for the content of this chapter, for it is intended primarily as a background to Chapters 5 and 6 and the issues of linguistic differentiation. As such, the discussion of microlinguistic theory and terminology is somewhat succinct. Nonetheless, some interesting points have been raised regarding the limiting factors inherent to linguistic variation, such as age and social background, and these will prove important not only to the ensuing discussion in Chapters 5 and 6, but also to the later discussions in Part 3 of this book.

In Chapter 6, my deliberations regarding the use of the *gheada* and the velar nasal consider the notion of conscious versus unconscious phonological variation discussed above, alongside status and solidarity issues that were highlighted in the Introduction Chapter. Although I avoid discussing the most negative linguistic outcomes of contact situations (language death) in my delineation of transference phenomena, I look at issues pertaining to code-switching, for these are particularly relevant to standardisation issues as well as to the findings of my own investigations, discussed in Chapters 5, 8 and 9. Of particular importance to my hypothesis regarding the Galician/Castilian contact situation is the issue of the direction of potential changes, and why. In other words, is a bilingual's Galician repertoire strongly influenced by Castilian transference phenomena?

Finally, my comparison of externally and internally motivated linguistic change is important for my later discussion of the relevance of the social milieu to the Galician situation. In Chapter 6, I will demonstrate that some instances of variation tend to be preferred socially, whereas others are slightly less prestigious, and others have eminently negative stigma attached to them. Chapter 5 will now offer a diachronic linguistic perspective of language contact in Galicia.

Chapter 5
The Linguistic Differentiation
of Galician

As víctimas do bilingoismo – os que calaron i enmudeceron para producir un silenzo literario de tres séculos – foron as camadas inteleituaes, que non estimaban as verbas vivas do seu falar e admiraban as verbas mortas do seu escrebir.

[The victims of bilingualism – those who became silent and who remained voiceless through three centuries of a literary vacuum, were the intellectual classes, who did not hold in high regard the living words of their speech forms and who instead, revered the lifeless words of their written forms.]
(Castelao, 1961: 104 [1944])

Introductory Remarks

In Chapter 2, I traced the history of Galicia and its language until the advent of democracy. In my examination of the sociolinguistic relationship between Galician, Castilian and Portuguese societies, I emphasised the implications and consequences of this relationship for the language of Galicia, its status, role in ethnic identity strategies, and use by its autochthonous speakers. This discussion was continued in Chapter 3, where I presented more contemporary, socio-political concerns surrounding devolution and linguistic, ethnic and cultural revival in Galicia. Just as issues of language usage and attitudes towards language use continue to be associated with notions of identity, so have issues regarding the structure of the standard language become ingrained into the political framework of the region.

In order to examine the various opinions regarding Galician language configuration, I now revisit the debate on language contact. However, this time, my approach starts out from a more diachronic linguistic perspective. As I outlined in the Introduction, one of the more original contributions of this book is the use of an analytical framework bringing together both linguistic and sociolinguistic analyses of languages in contact. The aim is to focus on Galician linguistic, ethnic, and cultural revival in a manner that underlines its wider implications for the task of reviving, revitalising, and maintaining minoritised languages. To do this, I review the most significant linguistic occurrences that were determining factors in the evolution of Galician as the autochthonous language of the region of Galicia. I begin by looking at the issues surrounding the linguistic definition of Galician as a language, rather than a dialect of Castilian or of Portuguese, just as I examined the political issues surrounding the concept of 'language' in Chapter 1 (see in particular pp. 37–41). I offer a brief overview of the major post-Roman diachronic changes, including issues surrounding the point at which Galician and Portuguese became linguistically differentiated and Castilian began to exert linguistic influence on Galician. Central to my discussion of the revival of certain Galician forms as a precursor to the development of a written standard, is the contrast of these processes with the linguistic fragmentation that permeated Galician speech forms, since this juxtaposition highlights the issue of purism and attempts to 'cleanse' the language of both Castilian and Portuguese forms. Moreover, the problems the authorities faced regarding the issue of form are still in evidence, hence this discussion emphasises the relevance of historical features to present day standardisation efforts.

In order to examine the various contentions regarding the approximation of Galician to Portuguese and Castilian, the second part of this chapter considers the pertinence of linguistic equivalence and linguistic homogeneity by looking briefly at the similarities between the transitional dialects of Southern Galician and Northern Portuguese. My comparison of some of the linguistic characteristics of Galician with Portuguese and Castilian is relevant to the ensuing discussion of linguistic form in the Galician standard, whereby I reconsider the initial debates regarding the form of the written standard, their social, political and linguistic implications, and the ways in which these debates have been resolved of late. Finally, I focus my attention on recent discussions regarding the need for some form of oral standard, by firstly considering the differences between standard and dialectal Galician and the ways in which the written form has attempted to integrate speech forms.

Language from a Linguistic Perspective

No discussion of linguistic differentiation in Galicia can be carried out without at least a cursory examination of issues and definitions surrounding linguistic definitions of language and dialect.

In the Introduction, Footnote 6 (p. 253), I cited recent Ethnologue data regarding the number of languages in the world today. However, the definition of a language based upon linguistic criteria alone is untenable. In her discussion of language identification, Skutnabb-Kangas considers the viability of a language/dialect distinction based upon the concepts of structural similarity or dissimilarity and mutual intelligibility or unintelligibility (2000: 6–16). She makes the important point (2000: 7) that structural claims are only valid when the languages in question are highly differentiated from each other, as is the case for example of English and Chinese. In many other cases varieties are termed languages even though, structurally, they differ minimally from others. Skutnabb-Kangas cites the cases of Swedish, Danish and Norwegian, of Serbian and Croatian, and of Hindi, Urdu and Punjabi (2000: 8; 13). I would add that Castilian Spanish and Portuguese, and to a lesser extent, French and Italian, all display degrees of structural and lexical similarity, despite their well-established political language status in each of their respective countries.

In a similar way, Skutnabb-Kangas points out that mutual intelligibility/unintelligibility as a criterion only discriminates well in comparisons of structurally unrelated languages (2000: 12). So in certain cases, such a demarcation would appear to be satisfactory. For example, I would consider that the linguistic differentiation and concomitant unintelligibility of my earlier English and Chinese comparison is sufficient enough for us to be able to classify them as distinct languages, but that the similarities between dialectal varieties of British English allow speakers to (more or less) understand each other, and thus, allow us to state that they are mutually intelligible dialects of the same language.

However, in many other cases, such a criterion is inadequate, as Skutnabb-Kangas points out. Wardhaugh (2002: 26) also cites the example of Hindi and Urdu. In India, both are recognised as separate languages from a political and religious perspective, but they display many similarities and even some identical linguistic forms at grammar level, which offer them a degree of intelligibility. To this, I may add Skutnabb-Kangas' earlier example of Punjabi and the same can also be said of Castilian Spanish and Portuguese.

Degrees of mutual intelligibility are scalar and tend to exist along a linguistic continuum. Both Chambers and Trudgill (1998) and Hudson (2001: 34) cite examples of European continua based upon intelligibility. Thus, Castilian Spanish and Portuguese are part of a Western Romance continuum stretching from Northern France to Southern Italy and encompassing several politically defined languages. However, this does not imply that the varieties spoken at the furthest ends of the continuum chain are mutually intelligible. As I have intimated in my example of British English, inherent to the term mutual intelligibility/unintelligibility is a degree of ambiguity regarding the level of comprehension/incomprehensible required for a variety to be defined in this way. Thus, I could state that structurally different languages are incomprehensible to any community but that of their own mothertongue speakers (or, by analogy, to second language learners), but as Haugen stated long ago (1966b: 102) and Skutnabb-Kangas confirms (2000: 9), how can we determine what is 'complete' or 'incomplete' understanding? Villages and towns on the peripheries of a given state, and occupying adjacent positions across state borders, may be able to communicate with each other because they share isogloss traits, vocabulary (Romaine, 2000: 11) and other linguistic features. However, speakers of the concomitant standard forms, who tend to be geographically isolated from such border areas, may not share such features and hence, find such localised varieties to a certain extent unintelligible. Thus, although regionally defined dialects of one particular language may display degrees of mutual intelligibility, geographically distanced dialects may not. This issue is particularly relevant in the context of my ensuing discussion in Chapter 6, where I contend that mutual intelligibility is also subject to the personal and political will of the speakers. Hence, it depends upon relationships of many kinds.

So, can I suggest a workable definition of the differentiation between the Galician, the Castilian and the Portuguese languages based upon linguistic criteria? The simple answer is no. What should be apparent is that in many cases, the criteria of structural similarity or dissimilarity and mutual intelligibility or unintelligibility are not really tenable. They offer little in the way of a clear-cut distinction between the two terms 'language' and 'dialect'. In the latter case, the premise that size can be considered a viable gauge – that dialects tend to enjoy fewer speakers than overarching language counterparts – is also an arbitrary and non-technical concept, one that implies that such a status can be quantified. Hudson (2001: 34) illustrates this with British English. The variety containing all the items used in Britain – designated the English language – is large compared to Standard English or Cockney, for example. However, it is small when compared with the variety consisting of all the items present in English-speaking countries – designated dialects of English.

Even the criterion that languages are standardised varieties, as espoused by Trudgill's old definition (1983: 16) is untenable, for, as Skutnabb-Kangas points out, it drastically reduces the number of varieties that could potentially be considered a language and does not necessarily aid communication between speakers (2000: 13–16). Even though standardisation practices are inherent to the language policies and planning of Galicia, as I will demonstrate further on, they are not always a viable way of reinforcing language status among the speakers themselves.

What emerge as more relevant to the definition of language are the political considerations outlined in Chapter 1 (pp. 37–41). Thus, the primary criterion for determining whether a variety is a dialect or a separate language is the relative political power of the speakers. Hence, the cut-off points between various languages are arbitrarily decided (Skutnabb-Kangas, 2000: 13) and this is why mutual intelligibility can override state boundaries. A language refers to a variety that is the overarching, and politically defined state language, whereas a dialect is a variety that is subsidiary to the said language in terms of its regional and geographical range.[1]

For the reasons cited above, the concepts of structural similarity or dissimilarity and mutual intelligibility or unintelligibility are somewhat irrelevant to the earlier claims to Galician language status. Moreover, the actual form of the language will not necessarily enhance its status, and hence, significance in terms of identity, among the Galician people. I would contend that the ongoing arguments surrounding the standard language are more to do with deep-seated historical, social and cultural issues, and that the question of form is used as a way of articulating these issues in the public arena. For this reason, the following sections focus upon the linguistic differentiation of Galician as a way of gaining a better understanding of why it should be so important to the current debates on language in the region.

The Diachronic Evolution of Galician

Little is known about the Indo European period of Galicia's history, as we saw in Chapter 2 (p. 55). Therefore, it is somewhat difficult to postulate whether many pre-Roman, Indo-European linguistic features were retained after the introduction of Latin to the region. Although there may be vestiges of lexical items originating in the Stone Age, the Celtic impact on the language appears to be limited to the adoption into Latin of idiosyncratic lexical items for indigenous fruits, plants, animals, geographical locations, and so on (Mariño Paz, 1998: 18–19).

The reputation of linguistic conservatism afforded to both Portuguese and Galician, whether merited or not, owes much to the long and drawn out process of linguistic substitution during the Roman period, and to the political, social, economic and administrative isolation of the provinces, ably illustrated by Mariño Paz (1998: 45). Once the Romans had established Vulgar Latin varieties throughout the Peninsula, the only veritable direct linguistic influence exercised on the linguistic configuration of the western regions until the 8th century were a few lexical items and a vestige of levelling processes by the Visigoths (Mariño Paz, 1998: 63; Cano Aguilar, 1999: 41–42; Penny, 2002: 14–16). The language group denoted Galician-Portuguese remained in relative isolation and retained highly archaic, conservative forms until the arrival of the Moors in 711 to the regions now comprising southern and central Portugal. Galicia was not under Moorish power for very long, and any lexical items that occur in the language are also found in Portuguese, in Castilian, or in both, for example *alcalde* [mayor] (Mariño Paz, 1998).

As I discussed in Chapter 2, this period heralded the start of the scission of the northern varieties from their more southern counterparts. This continued through the creation and attendant isolation of the Kingdom of Portugal from the rest of the Iberian Peninsula in the 12th century to the assimilation of the northern territories and the creation of the Kingdom of Spain in the 15th century.

The consequences of this separation on Galician-Portuguese varieties were considerable. The process had been accelerated by spatial considerations: Portugal may have cut itself off from the rest of the Iberian Peninsula for political reasons, but these were upheld by the geography of the area. Initially, the intersection of the River Tejo divided the Northern provinces and their linguistic varieties from their counterparts in the South, where the influence of Mozarabic forms on the phonetic, morphological, syntactic, and lexical systems was considerable. By the time the seat of power had shifted from Guimarães, in the extreme north, to Lisbon in the southern half of the country in the mid 13th century, the River Minho had become the definitive state frontier between Galicia in Spain and the northern regions of Portugal, quite effectively severing almost all intercultural contact and collaboration between these communities. Consequently, the linguistic varieties in the Kingdom of Portugal began to diversify progressively, influenced particularly in the later Middle Ages by the imposition of forms not only prevalent in Lisbon, but also in Coimbra, the exalted Portuguese seat of learning.[2]

In contrast, and due to the inaccessibility of many of the inland areas at this time, there was little linguistic innovation or development of the language until Galicia was fully integrated into the Kingdom of Castile in the 13th century, when Galician became the language of lyric and public administration.

In my earlier discussion (pp. 109–112), language demarcation in linguistic terms is a difficult task. Indeed, there is still an element of debate and disagreement as to when the definitive break between the written forms of what are now designated Galician and Portuguese was achieved, and when Latin forms became less apparent. Mariño Paz (1998: 82) states that the first non-literary texts written in Galician but still containing much Latin, appeared in the 13th century. He concludes that this demarcation was consolidated in the 14th and 15th centuries (1998: 152).[3] The Portuguese linguist Azevedo Maia concurs (1986: 885–890, 906), stating that there is some evidence in the 13th century of a written form being employed in both regions to supplant the use of Latin in official texts and documents. Azevedo Maia claims that Galician notary texts from around 1250 are the most ancient documents written entirely in Galician-Portuguese, and that the will and testament of Afonso II of Portugal was written in the same form. Yet, he also recognises that other texts from this period demonstrate evidence of the onset of linguistic differentiation. Many of the linguistic characteristics that distinguish the varieties of Galician-Portuguese – which, to a large extent, have survived into contemporary Galician and Portuguese – can be found, albeit extremely sporadically, in texts from this period, with those employing a more archaic, conservative language (at times more akin to Latin forms) being considered Galician rather than Portuguese. However, Azevedo Maia adds that despite the evidence, there are still many problems in typifying texts from the 13th to as late as the beginning of the 15th centuries as being of either Galician or Portuguese origin. He states that it was only truly from the 15th and 16th centuries onwards that the differences between written Galician and Portuguese became highly accentuated. This is exemplified in texts such as wills and testaments, bills of sales and other legal documents.[4]

The linguistic influence of Castilian Spanish on Galician intensified after the unification of Castile and Aragon in 1479. It is generally unclear whether changes witnessed in texts from the 15th century onwards were motivated internally or externally. However, it is worth noting that Galician had already started to lose its prestigious status as the language of public administration and documentation, and Castilian had already started to predominate in such areas. The establishment of Castilian as the high prestige language of the region resulted in an increasing degree of structural, phonological, and in particular, lexical transference from Castilian – indeed, the latter has been prevalent both from a political and linguistic perspective, until the present day.

Of course, there was no sudden handover of written function. Rather, it would seem that as the linguistic conflict between Galician and Castilian intensified, many of the texts from the late Middle Ages in particular, started to exhibit a heavy Castilian influence on Galician linguistic structures. Whereas Castilianisms appear to be sporadic in notary texts dating from the 13th and 14th centuries, those from the 15th and 16th centuries contain frequent Castilian lexical and structural items and forms. Azevedo Maia has gone so far as to state that an entire text may be affected to such a degree, that the mother tongue of the writer becomes largely unclear (1986: 900–902). By the time the Galician language underwent its literary revival in the 19th century, its linguistic relationship with Portuguese had been superseded by the influence of Castilian and the concomitant association that this engendered.

Therefore, fundamental to these issues of linguistic differentiation and convergence in Galicia is the consequent decline in status and prestige of the autochthonous language, not least because of the debates regarding the form and structure of the standard, as discussed below (pp. 125–131). As we saw in Chapter 2, in Portugal, the rest of Spain, and in Galicia itself, Galician acquired a reputation as an old-fashioned and bucolic language, reliant on an outmoded lexis and a risible pronunciation. Certainly, such defamatory comments are not exclusive to Galician, but they are generally associated with specific dialectal and accentual variation. In Galicia however, no variety was excluded from this general downgrading and the effect such opinions had on the Galician population should not be underestimated. The perception that Galician was merely a bastardised variety of Castilian reinforced the need for a formal written form, but until its revival, it was not considered 'worthy' of standardising.

The Recuperation of the Galician Language

The increase in bilingualism during the 19th century resulted in hitherto unseen interference between Galician and Castilian, with Castilian lexical items from everyday life, such as the days of week, colours, body parts, and so on predominating. Their integration was to such an extent that speakers quickly lost the ability to determine the provenance of many words, such as *abuelo* and *avó* [grandfather], the former transferred from Castilian. Many forms such as these continued to exist side by side, fulfilling at times different functions. For example, the Castilian transfer *lágrima* was used in more informal contexts than the literary form *bágoa* [tear] (noun) (Mariño Paz, 1998: 444–445).[5] The result of this transference was that by the 20th century, even dialectal Galician was influenced by Castilian.

Early attempts to cite historical links with Portuguese as a way of enhancing the language's status and differentiation from Castilian came to nothing, since they were based on somewhat ideological notions of integration and assimilation. To a large extent, they were also undermined by general aphorisms regarding Spanish/Portuguese relationships, such as the rather derogatory Portuguese saying *De Espanha, nem bom vento nem bom casamento* (literally 'neither good wind nor good marriage comes out of Spain', hence [nothing good will ever come of it]). More significantly, however, it was Castilian Spanish that continued to exert a strong influence on the literary, written form of Galician recuperated in the 19th century, because this was the predominant mother tongue of authors, academics and intellectuals from the elite classes, and, therefore, was generally used as the orthographic basis for standard Galician proposals from this period onwards. In an interesting account of the problems associated with linguistic structure, Fernández Salgado and Monteagudo (1993: 207–210) term this period of recuperation Popular Galician. Although not always successful, these proposals were an attempt to reproduce a faithful representation of spoken Galician by using interdialectal forms that embodied a degree of differentiation from Castilian. As Saco Arce stated:

> Una lengua que apenas puede llamarse escrita, no puede tenerse por pura, sino tal como la hablan las únicas personas que no se han dejado aun contagiar del castellano, esto es, los rústicos

> [A language that is only has a written form cannot be considered pure, unless it is just like the language spoken by the only people who have still not been contaminated by Castilian, that is the peasants]

> (Saco Arce, 1868: VIII; in Mariño Paz, 1998: 449)

This use of interdialectal forms was vehemently opposed by a group calling themselves the *cultistas*, who considered such forms linguistic defects and not worthy of inclusion in a literary standard form (Mariño Paz, 1998: 449–453).[6] Regueira Fernández (2004: 79–80) points out that these groups were creating a written standard not for the rural *pobo*, the poor and rural population, but for the use of the urban elite. Hence, the standard was constructed largely with elements of the popular language on a schema of standard Castilian Spanish, whose orthography was familiar to these elites since Castilian was the language of education at this time. Moreover, the linguistic fragmentation of the region meant that the prevailing characteristic forms of Galician integrated were from somewhat diverse sources. In this sense, Regueira Fernández contends (2004: 80) that the written standard of this time was neither 'popular' nor 'dialectal' Galician, for importantly, this period marks the beginning of the diversification of the written form of the language from traditional speech forms, as I will discuss in more length below (see pp. 117, 134–137).

The proponents of the written standard based on Castilian forms instead of rural dialectal forms were well aware that they were susceptible to the introduction of Castilianisms because these were the forms with which they had grown up. The famous author Rosalía de Castro, for example, tended to employ Castilian forms such as *suelo*, *nudo* and *cuna* instead of their traditional Galician cognates *chan*, *nó*, and *berce* for [floor], [knot], and [cot], and words now considered vulgarisms were also numerous. It is thus apparent that, during this period, no strong tendency is evident towards the purification of the language of Castilian lexis in order to distance the two languages in linguistic terms. However, Fernández Salgado and Monteagudo also maintain that there was rare use of hyperpurisms, archaic forms or words derived from Portuguese (1993: 210), probably due to the negative connotations therein.

Notwithstanding the intrinsic structural problems and dilemmas regarding form, from the end of the 19th century onwards and largely as a consequence of the increased use of Galician in literary and non-literary genres, many new terms started to be introduced into the language. Fernández Salgado and Monteagudo (1993: 211) term this period Puristic Galician. Eminent writers such as Otero Pedrayo, Pintos, Murguía and Curros recognised the inherent shortcomings of earlier attempts to avoid the use of Castilianisms, and believed that the establishment of a standard written orthography was the only way to avoid the definitive lexical Castilianisation of Galician. Tendencies towards purism, what was termed *enxebrismo* [pure, unmixed], were rife, hence popular words shared with Castilian were either rejected in favour of Galician synonyms or phonetically or morphologically altered through a process of hyperpurism.[7] The efforts of such authors led to the creation of the *Real Academia Galega* [The Royal Galician Academy] (RAG) in 1906, an official institution whose main objective was the promotion of the preservation and diffusion of the Galician language.

The principle agenda of the *Irmandades da Fala* and the alliances of the intellectual elite grouped within *Xeración Nós* was, as I pointed out in Chapter 2 (pp. 67–68), to release Galician from its traditional characterisation as the language of the *pobo*. This is the period Fernández Salgado and Monteagudo (1993: 212–213) term Proto-Standard Galician. In contrast to the earlier periods, Castilianisms were purged from the lexis, whilst lexical items both from foreign sources and created internally within Galician were introduced. Subsequently, they saw the advantages of linking the language with Portuguese and supplanted certain Galician forms to this effect.

In the final period, the spelling system was simplified, heralding the start of what Fernández Salgado and Monteagudo (1993: 213) term Standard Galician (the evolution and form of which is discussed in some detail below, pp. 125–134). By the 1950s, *Galaxia* had started to influence written, published text, since they began to impose their own set of orthographic norms on writers. This simplified to a certain degree the problem of variability of the written form highlighted by the authors of the late 19th century (Pensado, 1982: 120). It also rid the language of many hyper-purisms and ancient Galician forms. For example, the Galician form *sombra* [shade], supplanted by *soma* in the Puristic Galician Period, was reintroduced. However, the written language was still subject to a large degree of variability depending on author; even though Celso Emilio Ferreiro, for example, claimed that his version was *o galego que falaban o meu pobo* [the Galician that my people spoke], in general, this form dissociated even further the written language from the spoken one.[8]

This was the general situation that prevailed when the orthographic debates regarding an official standard were fully initiated in 1970s democratic Spain. Irrespective of whichever methodology was initiated, and whether Castilian, Portuguese or even dialectal forms were omitted from the standard, the overall objective appears to be rather more linguistic than social or political. However, in earlier discussions of standardisation ideologies (pp. 84–87), we saw that socio-political allegiances did play an important role in each groups' specific claims regarding orthographic form. In the next sections, I consider whether these claims can be upheld by linguistic data, and to this end, I start by evaluating the degree of linguistic homogeneity between Castilian Spanish and Galician, and Galician and Portuguese.

Linguistic Homogeneity in the (Western) Iberian Peninsula

What distinguishes Portugal from Spain as a nation today is its relative linguistic homogeneity. Spain is 'a nation of nations', comprising communities who aspire to, and in some cases have achieved, some form of self-government and autonomy from Madrid, and who have auto-chthonous languages supporting their status, as we have seen. Portugal on the other hand is one nation, with one official language and no highly differentiated autochthonous communities. The degree of linguistic hom-ogeneity within mainland European Portuguese itself is significant. There are no highly distinguishable dialects; Mirandese, confined to an extremely small administrative division in the northeast corner of Portugal along the border with Spain and sharing many linguistic forms with Portuguese, is recognised as a separate language by the Portuguese authorities. However, the northern Portuguese regions of Tras-os-Montes, the areas surrounding the Rivers Minho and Douro, parts of Beira-Baixa, the Alto-Alentejo and the Algarve (Estremenho) in the central-southern zone are relatively isolated from the influence of the more southern Portuguese cities. As a consequence, they display certain idiosyncratic phonetic characteristics that differentiate them to an extent from the standard language. Both geographical and political factors are responsible for the high degree of mutual intelligibility between the Portuguese and Galicians living around the Minho. Many of the features of northern Portuguese are still shared with southern Galician, harking back to the orthographic characteristics of the region in both Galician and northwestern Portuguese texts of the Middle Ages (Azevedo Maia, 1986: 924–928). The eminent Galician linguist Fernández Rei (1988: 100; 1990: 17) claims that from a strictly linguistic point of view, the dialectal varieties of southern Galicia are simply a con-tinuation of the Minho and Tras-os-Montes dialects. Southern Galicia is a transition zone and, thus, mutual comprehension between the varieties spoken on either side of the river is extremely high.

My recent research in the towns of Tuy in southern Galicia and Valença in northern Portugal (Beswick, 2005a) both confirmed and contradicted many of the long-standing assertions regarding the approximation of certain phonological features in the borderland regions. The overriding conclusion was that the degree of linguistic homogeneity and structural similarity between the two dialects in question was high. From a purely linguistic perspective, I can therefore state that a well-established transi-tional dialect between southern Galician and northern Portuguese, facili-tating communication between the two communities and overriding the existence of a clearly defined geographical border between the two, is indeed in evidence.

Hence, I can confirm my earlier general assertions and those of Fernández Rei concerning Galicia (1988: 100) that delimitations with respect to the political demarcation of regional and national bound-ary lines are not easy to establish on purely linguistic grounds. Although this approximation of the two languages may lend some credence to the *reintegracionista* contentions regarding a linguistic alliance (see pp. 86–89), it could be conversely argued that this high degree of homogeneity with Portuguese underlines the *independentista* claim for the need for a linguistically independent standard language in order for Galician not to be 'swallowed up' by Portuguese.

Despite the somewhat tenuous intergroup relationships between Portuguese and Galician (pp. 89–90), and despite the prevailing linguistic influence of Castilian on Galician, a substantial degree of equivalence still prevails between Galician and Portuguese, as I now demonstrate. I will then return to the standardisation debate and the overarching form of the *Normas* proposed by the diverse factions, as well as the issue of variation in speech forms.

The Differentiation of Galician

The following account is based on syntheses of Galician or Portuguese features presented by various authors, although the examples and comparative summaries are generally my own.[9] It comprises a list of the most salient characteristics that have distinguished Galician and Portuguese from the Middle Ages until the present day. In it, I attempt to summarise some of the most important changes that took place. I also take into consideration a few more contemporary and predominantly morphological and syntactical features. Although certain dialectal features are discussed, the intention of this comparative account is more to highlight the most pertinent phonemic and structural similarities and differences between the standard and other varieties of Galician, Portuguese, and Castilian, in order to give a general indication of these to readers who are not familiar with one or more of the languages. Therefore, this is in no way intended to be an exhaustive list.[10] Pertinent phonetic features and orthographic representations are described for vowels, consonants, morphological and syntactic features, and a few verb paradigms; linguistic terminology is described briefly in the glossary once again. In Appendix 1 (p. 274), I also offer a summary of some of the orthographic differences between standard Galician, Portuguese, and Castilian.

Vowels

The Galician vowel system is poorer and more archaic than its Portuguese counterpart. In general, Galician retains the 16th century pronunciations of syllable-final atonic *o* > [o] and syllable-final atonic *e* > [e], as does Castilian and varieties of Brazilian Portuguese:

Gal/Br. Port. chamo	Cast. llamo [o]	'I call'
arte	arte	'art'

European Portuguese raises syllable-final *o* > [u] and the Portuguese derivation of *e* > [ə] may be pronounced extremely weakly or, at the end of a word, may disappear completely:

Eur. Port. chamo[u]   arte [ə]

Although most issues regarding vowel dialectal variation are discussed below, (pp. 131–134) it is pertinent here to mention that Galician pretonic *o* > [u] is still a dialectal characteristic of Galician but is also found in Portuguese; elsewhere [o] as in Castilian is to be found:

Dial.Gal./Port. coser [u]   Gal./Cast coser [o] 'to sew'

Atonic *a* retains its timbre in Galician, as in Castilian, but in Portuguese it is [ɐ]:

Gal. falar [a]   Port. falar [ɐ]   Cast. hablar [a] 'to speak'

Both Galician and Portuguese retain Latin stressed short *e* and *o*, whereas Castilian has diphthongised both vowels:

Gal./Port. terra [ɛ]   Cast. tierra [je]   'land'
Gal./Port. nove [ɔ]   Cast. nueve [we]   'nine'

The Galician-Portuguese diphthongs [ow] and [ej] were retained in both Portuguese and Galician. In Castilian, they are monophthongised:

Gal./Port. pouco [ow]   Cast. poco [o] 'little'
Gal./Port. madeira [ej]   Cast. madera [e] 'wood'

There is evidence however, that the Galician [ow] resolution is currently being replaced by [o] (see p. 140).

Latin-ULT-and-UCT-were generally resolved orthographically as *oi* + /t/, in standard Galician, whereas the Portuguese resolution is primarily *ui* + /t/. In Castilian, orthographic *ch* represents the medieval palatal affricate /tʃ/:

Gal. moito [oj]   Port. muito [wi]   Cast. mucho /tʃ/ 'much'[11]

Consonants

In the 13th century, the *Provençal* orthographic forms *lh* and *nh* were imposed on written Portuguese by Afonso III to replace the archaic forms that were retained, however, in Galician: *l/ll/li, n/nn/ni/nni*. The latter was ultimately resolved as *ñ*, an orthographic form prevalent already in Castilian, but, the pronunciation remained the same in all languages as [ɲ]:

Gal./Cast. señor   Port. senhor /ɲ/ 'Mr., sir'

Orthographic *l*/*ll*/*li* tends to be retained as *ll* in Galician, with the same pronunciation as in Portuguese /ʎ/ or even /j/. Castilian developed the *jota* /x/, also as a consequence of palatalisation:

Gal. ollo /ʎ/   Port. olho /ʎ/   Cast. ojo /x/   'eye'

The confusion in the use of orthographic *b*/*v* was rife in texts considered to have a Galician provenance. Galician adopted the Castilian allophonic distinction based on place of articulation: [β] in intervocalic position and [b] elsewhere, whereas standard Portuguese maintained a phonemic distinction between the two graphemes. Thus:

Gal. baca 'roof rack'
Cast. boca 'mouth' } homogeneous in /b/
Gal./Cast. vaca 'cow'

but

Port. baga 'berry' /b/
Port. vaga 'wave' /v/

Confusion also occurred with orthographic *s*/*ss* and *z*/*ç* in Galician texts, due in no small part to the loss of the phonological opposition of the Middle Age sibilants, the apico-alveolar /ś/ and /ź/ (*passo*, *coser*) and the predental /s/ and /z/ (*paço*, *cozer*). Orthographic *s*- -*ss*- *c*/*e*, *i* and -*ç*- were ultimately resolved as /s/ in Portuguese, as in the following examples:

Port. sem 'without'
 passo 'step'
 cem 'one hundred'
 paço 'palace'

Orthographic -*z*- and -*s*- were retained as the voiced counterpart /z/, hence the following have homogeneous phonetic forms:

Port. cozer 'to cook'
 coser 'to sew'

In Galicia however, the modern opposition is between /ś/ and the interdental fricative /θ/, just as in Castilian:

Gal. paso 'step'   /ś/
 coser 'to sew'
Gal. pazo 'palace'   /θ/
 cocer 'to cook'

Until the 18th century, a distinction between the use of orthographic *g*, *j*, *x* was maintained to a large degree, however nowadays Galician tends to use orthographic *x*, which is pronounced as a voiceless palatal fricative

/ʃ/, whereas Portuguese uses orthographic *j, g*, the voiced palatal fricative /ʒ/. The Castilian counterpart varies:

Gal. xaneiro /ʃ/	Port. janeiro /ʒ/	Cast. enero /ø/ 'January'
Gal. xema /ʃ/	Port. gema /ʒ/	Cast. yema /j/ 'egg yolk'

The retention of /ʃ/ for Portuguese syllable-final *s* is not a characteristic of Galician or Castilian, which both use /s/:

Gal./Cast. casas /s/   Port. casas /ʃ/   'houses'

Latin initial F is generally retained in both Galician and Portuguese, but has been replaced in Castilian by orthographic *h*, which is no longer pronounced except dialectally:

Gal./Port. fabla /f/   Cast. /Ø/ habla 'speech'

Confusion between *l* and *r* used to be common, especially when either occurred as the second part of a consonant cluster. Both Galician and Portuguese now tend to resolve the confusion according to the provenance of the word in question. Thus, learned words and recent borrowings tend to retain *l*, for example Gal./Port. *claro* [clear]; *explicar* [to explain], whereas semi-learned and old loanwords have adopted *r*, for example Gal./Port. *branco* [white], *cumprir* [to fulfil]. However, in reality, the division between learned and semi-learned words is unclear and there is, therefore, still some dialectal variation in evidence, for example Gal. *craro* for *claro* [clear]. Castilian generally uses *l* in all cases: Cast. *claro, explicar, blanco, cumplir.*

The *gheada*, the Galician pronunciation of word-initial and intervocalic orthographic *g*, may vary substantially and is discussed in more detail in Chapter 6 (pp. 141–152). However, it does not occur in either Portuguese or Castilian:

Gal. gato [x], [h] etc.   Port. gato /g/   Cast. gato /g/   'cat'

Morphological and syntactic features

Portuguese has phonological nasal vowels and diphthongs. Galician and Castilian retain a vowel plus nasal consonant:

Gal./Cast. ladrón /Vn/	Port. ladrão [ãw̃] 'thief'
emoción /Vn/	emoção 'emotion'[12]

The standard resolution of the Galician cognate is an oral vowel plus velar nasal consonant, [Vŋ]. As I discuss below (p. 134), Fernández Rei (1990: 28–29, 161) employs this as one of three isoglosses that establish a linguistic frontier between Galician and Portuguese. However, in morphological terms, dialectal variation is in evidence. Compare for example the following:

Gal.   irmán [aŋ] (Std. West)
        irmao [aw] (Centre, East)
        irmá [a] (Northwest)   } 'brother'
Port.   irmão [ãw̃]
Cast.   hermano [ano]

The plural of polysyllabic words in *-l* is an important feature of Portuguese and Galician. Portuguese generally resolves such words with a diphthong, which also occurs generally in Galician and is the standard resolution. However, there is also substantial evidence of dialectal variation, the most prevalent form being the addition of the plural morpheme *-es*, as in Castilian:

Gal./Port./Cast. animal 'animal' > pl.   animais [ajs] (Port.)
                                           animais [ajs]
                                               (Std. Gal./eastern form)
                                           animales (western/
                                               central form)
                                           animás (sporadic form)
                                           animales (Cast.)[13]

In Portuguese, the plural of words resulting from Latin intervocalic *n* is resolved in one of three ways:

Port.   mão 'hand' > mãos [ɐw̃]
        cão 'dog' > cães [ɐj]
        oração 'prayer' > orações [oj]

In Galician all three forms are resolved as /ns/. Once again, any variation to this standard resolution tends to be considered dialectal but is also accepted. In Castilian, where cognate forms occur, the plural morpheme is *-s*. Thus:

Gal. can 'dog'   pl. >   cans [kans] (Std. Gal./western form)
                                cás [kas] (central form)
                                cais [kajs] (eastern form)
Port. cão 'dog'   >   cães [kɐjʃ]
Gal. man 'hand'   pl. >   mans [mɐns] (Std Gal./western form)
                                más [kɐs] (central form)
                                manos [mɐnos] (eastern form)
Port. mão 'hand'   >   mãos [mɐw̃ʃ]
Cast. mano 'hand'   >   manos [mɐnos]

In Galician and European Portuguese, object pronoun contraction is common, but it does not occur in Castilian:

Gal. ela déullelo
       deu + lles + o
Port. ela deulhos
       deu + lhes + o
Cast. ella se lo dio
     les + lo + dio
[he/she gave it to them]

In Galician, object pronoun order is variable, rule-determined in a similar way to European Portuguese; however, in Castilian, object pronoun order is generally fixed:

Gal.   A muller comproume un libro
Port.   A mulher comproume um livro
Cast.   La mujer me compró un libro
    [The woman bought me a book]

Gal.   O home non che deu o premio
Port.   O homem não te deu o premio
Cast.   El hombre no te dio el premio
    [The man did not give the prize to you]

As can be seen in the above example, the Portuguese second person pronoun *te* 'to you' is resolved as *che/chi* in Galician, unlike Castilian where *te* is also found. Only in Galician is it syntactically optional, as what is termed a solidarity dative:

Gal. dóecheme o dedo 'my finger aches'

Verb paradigms

The following are selected examples intended to highlight comparisons between the languages in question, rather than to offer a comprehensive account of all forms.

The Galician range of tenses approximates that of Portuguese. For example, compound tense forms are not common and a personal infinitive form is in evidence. In Castilian, compound tense forms are common and there is no personal infinitive.

Gal.   Compraran o coche cando eu os atoparei
Port.   Compraram o carro quando eu os encontrei
Cast.   Habían comprado el coche cuando yo los encontré
    [They had bought the car when I found them]

Gal. Para faceres o traballo, precisas chamarme cedo
Port. Para fazeres o trabalho, precisas chamar-me cedo
Cast. Para hacer el trabajo, necesitas llamarme temprano
[In order to do the work, you will have to call me early]

The Portuguese verb second person singular preterite ending -*ste* [st] was resolved as -*sche* and then -*che* [tʃ] in Galician, and there has also been some divergence of other verb paradigms.[14]

As I have stated, in no way is the above comparison of some of the similarities and differences between the languages of Galician, Portuguese and Castilian intended to be exhaustive. In particular, the issue of vowel resolution and timbre in contemporary Galician is rather contentious, as I will discuss later (pp. 139–141). Nonetheless, this section demonstrates that Galician does retain certain phonetic, morphological and syntactic traits cognate with Portuguese, whilst a degree of levelling of certain traits with cognates in Castilian is also witnessed. Bearing this in mind, I now turn to the issue of form inherent within the orthographic debates of recent years.

The Issue of Form in the *Normas Ortográficas*

Castilian versus Portuguese

The first point to be made regarding form is that a categorical, clear-cut delineation on orthographic grounds between the two main opposing movements is not entirely possible. Significantly, as Regueira Fernández points out (2004: 80), all the various proposals (except that of the *máximos*) accept literary Galician as the basis of the standard, so the differences between them – which I delineate below – are more to do with issues of internal codification. Moreover, there has also been a general consensus that the standard is needed to avoid the use of morphological and lexical forms that coincide with Castilian.

As I have commented previously (p. 86), the *reintegración* language movement can be split into two main groups, designated the *mínimos* and the *máximos* in accordance with the degree of reintegration they advocate with Portuguese. In the early years of debate, the main social, cultural, and didactic association that advocated the *mínimos* orthographic standard was the *Asociación Sócio-Pedagóxica Galega* (AS-PG) [the Galician Socio-Pedagogic Association]. Although they considered Galician to be a variety of Portuguese, this standard, delineated in the *Orientacións para a escrita do noso idioma* (1980) [Guidelines Regarding the Written Form of our Language] and used regularly in their correspondence, did not differ much from that established by the *Xunta*. Indeed, the AS-PG have recently abandoned their claims to such a standard form, since they are generally happy that the latest edition of the *Normas*

(2003) has integrated minor changes in order to take into account certain similarities with Portuguese that they felt had been overlooked in previous versions. These changes are discussed further below.

Groups comprising the *máximos* have always manifested radical ideologies. Their initial fundamental position was that Galicia should be a monolingual society and that the orthographic standard should be based either on Galician-Portuguese or on a standard that was, essentially, identical to Portuguese except for some particular phonological and lexical items (Regueira Fernández, 2006: 92–93).

One of the main proponents of the *Associaçom Galega da Língua* (AGAL) [the Galician Language Association] was the Portuguese philologist Rodrigues Lapa, who considered Galician a rustic, antiquated dialect of Portuguese (1973). However, other adherents were less scathing and more aware of the sociolinguistic implications of treating Galician as a 'poor man's Portuguese'. AGAL's standard proposal is contained in the *Prontuário ortográfico galego* (Rabade Castinheira & Alonso Estravis, 1985). Ostensibly based primarily on Portuguese forms, this proposal does attempt to maintain certain forms exclusive to Galician, such as some of the verb and noun endings and prepositional forms. Although this group is somewhat minoritised in society, they are still extremely active and continue to employ this standard in their publications.[15]

The most extreme group in terms of their orthographic proposal was the collaboration between the *Irmandades da Fala* (IF) and the *Associação Sociopedagógica Galaicoportuguesa* (ASPGP). Often rather pejoratively termed *Lusistas* or 'Portuguese-lovers', the proposal of this group was that the simplified Portuguese orthographic standard drafted in *Acordo Ortográfico* of 1990, should become the standard for Galician as well, thus integrating Galician totally within the Portuguese linguistic sphere.[16]

Although some of these proposals are no longer in existence, as I discuss below, their general tenets are summarised in Figure 5.1. In

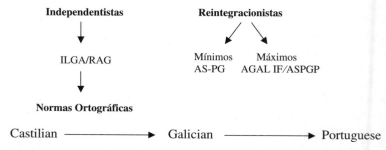

Figure 5.1 Standardisation proposals in the 1980s

Table 5.1 Some linguistic differences between Standard Castilian, Standard Portuguese and the proposals for Standard Galician[17]

Proposal/Controversial form	Standard Castilian	ILGA/RAG	AS-PG	AGAL	IF/ASPGP	Standard Portuguese
a 'to, at' + masculine definite article	a el	ó/ao	ao	ao	ao	ao
a 'to, at' + feminine definite article	a la	â	â	a	à	à
Masculine indefinite article	un/unos	un/uns	un/uns	um/uns	um/uns	um/uns
Feminine indefinite article	una/unas	unha/unhas	unha/unhas	umha/umhas	uma/umas	uma/umas
/ʎ/	ll	ll	ll	lh	lh	lh
/ɲ/	ñ	ñ¹	ñ	nh	nh	nh
/ʃ/	–	x	x	g (+e, i) j x	g (+e, i) j x	g (+e, i) j x
-ble bel vel	amable	amable	amable	amabel	amável	amável
ç or ss	estación/sessión	estació/sessión	estació/sessión	estaçom/scssom	estação/sessão	estação/sessão

Tables 5.1, I also offer a brief evaluation of the most salient differences between the various movements and Castilian and Portuguese.

So, to what extent have these disputes over the construction of the present Galician orthographic standard been resolved over the last 30 years? In the early 1970s, two proposals for standardisation of the Galician language were put forward by the *Real Academia Galega* (RAG), both of which took into account some of *Editorial Galaxia*'s earlier reco-mmendations to its authors, as discussed in Chapter 3. For example, features such as the use of the plural noun ending - *ns*, the adjectival suffix - *bel* and the contraction of the preposition *a* plus the masculine defi-nite article *o* as *ao* were recommended. However, the suggestions of these proposals were not entirely comprehensive, and one of the main problems was that they relied heavily on Castilian when a particular problem in resolving an orthographic rule presented itself (Mariño Paz, 1998: 482−483).

Other, more thorough proposals followed, largely initiated by ILG. In the late 1970s, the *Real Academia Galega* approved an initial set of ortho-graphic and morphological norms, the *Bases prá unificación das normas lingüísticas do galego* [Basis for the unification of the Galician linguistic standard] (Regueira Fernández, 2004: 80). However, it was not until 1980, when Professor Carballo Calero was asked to preside over the lin-guistic commission created by the *Consellaría de Educacion e Cultura* [the Council for Education and Culture] that the aim of creating an official and cohesive standard that could be used for all written functions, started to become a reality. Carballo Calero was considered one of the forerunners of the minimalist *reintegracionista* movement, his book *Grama-tica elemental del gallego común* [A Basic Grammar of Common Galician] often being cited as one of the main constituents of their orthographic norm proposals. As the commission also included members of RAG and ILG, it was hoped that the *Normas ortográficas do idioma galego* [Ortho-graphic Standards of the Galician Language], published the same year in the Xunta's Bulletin, the *Boletin Oficial da Xunta*, would go some way to resolving at least the more generic opposing viewpoints. To this end, these standards attempted to integrate both the orthography rec-ommended by the *mínimos* and that used by *autonomistas*.

Despite the hype, the tacit understanding throughout procedures was that this particular set of standards was purely provisional, as they were conceived for the Xunta's internal use and for official publications. More-over, the attempt to integrate the issue of traditional historical links and allegiances with more synchronic and pragmatic evidence for modernis-ation implicit within this integration of two different orthographic models was somewhat unfeasible.

Indeed, in academic and educational circles, these standards were strongly criticised and general distribution of the leaflets detailing the standard (published by the *Consellería de Educación e Cultura*) was not thoroughly carried out.

Over the next two years, the debate and discussion continued to gain momentum. On 17 November 1982, Decree 173/1982 was approved. Article One states:

> Artigo 1 – O Acordo da Real Academia Galega e do Instituto da Lingua Galega, aprobado na sesión conxunta de ambas Institucións celebrada o día tres de xullo de mil novecentos oitenta e dous, que nas súas grandes liñas é recollido no Anexo do presente Decreto, queda aprobado como norma básica para a unidade ortográfica e morfolóxica da Lingua Galega

> [Article 1 – The agreement made between the Royal Galician Academy and the Institute of the Galician Language, approved in a joint session of both Institutions on the third of July, 1982, and the framework of which is to be found in the Annex to the present Decree, has been approved as the standard form of the orthographic and morphological unification of the Galician Language]

> (Decree 173/1982).

The revised standard, published for the first time in 1982 was entitled the *Normas ortográficas e morfolóxicas do idioma galego* [Orthographic and Morphological Standards of the Galician Language]. Articles 2 and 3 also afforded the planners the authority to make any future amendments to the orthographic standard, and to assemble the tools necessary for its dissemination, such as vocabulary inventories, orthographies, grammar books and dictionaries.

This time, the *Xunta* adopted the standards for official use. However, *reintegracionista* representatives were not invited to contribute to the drafting processes of this version. Their non-involvement, together with their perception that the form adopted contains many traits that have deliberately been aligned closely to analogous Castilian features, has proven to be one of the more contentious characteristics of the official standards for, once again, differing political viewpoints entered the arena. Many *reintegracionistas* felt that they were deliberately excluded from these (and other) standardisation processes for political reasons (Santamarina Conde, 1985: 145; Henderson 1996: 182–183). Indeed, in the 1990s, one of the most vociferous critics of the *Normas*, the *reintegracionista* academic Celso Alvarez-Cáccamo, commented informally that all versions of the standards related more to issues of social and political power and control than to the issue of linguistic homogeneity based on the predominance of a particular language. His belief was that official attempts to impose a system heavily based on the Castilian Spanish model simply served to underline an unofficial programme of pure, unjustified differentiation from standard Portuguese.[18] Alvarez-Cáccamo's comments echo to an extent those made in the 1980s by Carballo Calero, another key adherent of the *reintegracionista* language cause, who also averred that the Galician written form was based primarily upon the Castilian orthographic system and also considered this an issue of political and social control (1981: 88). His claim was that the direct intervention of the Madrid authorities in the standardisation processes was also a deliberate attempt to move away from linguistic elements shared with Portuguese and hence, to move away from, and hopefully quash, the issue of Galician identity and independent status.

It is certainly true that the *Partido Popular* (PP), the political party that governed Galicia until recently, has been keenly opposed to the total independence of Galicia, as well as to any linguistic measures that have brought Galician linguistic forms more in line with Portuguese cognates. Indeed, they even boycotted the recently approved amendments to the official standard, achieved in 2003, with an important agreement signed between the *autonomistas* RAG and ILG, and the BNG as representatives of the *mínimos*, published in the 19th edition of the *Normas Ortográficas e Morfolóxicas do Idioma Galego* (2004). Several significant changes were made, carried out in line with the more reasonable *reintegracionista* demands, to which the PP was totally opposed.

I would contend that the validity of allegations regarding the 'bully-boy' tactics of the Spanish government are somewhat more contentious. Nonetheless, these comments highlight once again the importance to Galician of its linguistic status and sociolinguistic credibility. Bearing in mind my earlier comments regarding the definition of languages and the limitations of Trudgill's old definition of language (1983: 16), (p. 111), it is clear that, as with many of the world's major languages, Castilian and Portuguese are considered both *Ausbau* and *Abstand* languages (Kloss, 1967: 29–41).[19] That is, they are 'languages by elaboration': they have been recreated in a literary sense and indeed, are still undergoing a process of adjustment and standardisation, but they are also considered languages 'in their own right', by linguistic distance or internal differentiation from others (Kloss & Mc'Connell, 1974: 32–33). In the case of Portuguese and Castilian, as I intimated earlier (p. 110), this linguistic distance is not unequivocal. That is, both of the languages in question have political language status in their respective countries but, for historical reasons, they display a degree of structural and lexical similarity and a degree of mutual intelligibility, even though the majority of common linguistic continua are found in the borderland communities.

This issue of linguistic distance or internal differentiation is clearly manifest in the case of Galician. In accordance with Kloss's definition and Muljačić's later observations regarding Galician (1986; 1993), the implementation of the standardised form contained within the early editions of the *Normas* prompted Williamson and Williamson (1984: 403), Fernández Rei (1988: 88, 1990: 18), and Monteagudo and Santamarina

(1993: 126), among others, to define Galician as an _Ausbau_ language. This definition, it would seem, is not contentious in any way: the Galician standard has been created artificially and is still subject to adjustment and modification, even if the reasons behind the selection of its form are still subject to debate. However, Galician can also be considered 'minimum _Abstand'_ in that it developed from the _Abstand_ language Galician-Portuguese (Muljačić, 1986: 56). That is, despite its official political and social status as a regional language, linguistically Galician appears to suffer from 'maximum overlapping' with linguistic forms of both Portuguese and Castilian. Thus, the degree of structural similarity and mutual intelligibility with both languages may be high, reinforcing once again the argument that such criteria cannot be used in the definition of a language but also prejudicing the _autonomismo_ argument I have examined above regarding linguistic autonomy. In quarters other than _reintegración_ factions, it is accepted that Galician _is_ a variety of Portuguese or, at the very least, of Galician-Portuguese. Yet once again, this does not necessarily reinforce the more radical _reintegración_ claim that Galician structural components should be reconstructed in line with the Portuguese norm, for we cannot dismiss the present situation and pervading influences. More relevant to the development of a workable standard in the present day than the origins of the language, has been the perception of the Galicians themselves – based no doubt on the political and social situation of the region – that Galician is also a sociolinguistic variety of Castilian. This is undoubtedly a somewhat pejorative claim, as from the perspective of the society, the description of Galician as a _lingua minoritaria_ [minority language] implies its subordination to the overarching politically defined state language of Castilian. Nonetheless, it does go some way to explaining why the use of Castilian as the main _external_ authority and influence on the written standard is, in principal, to be expected.

Standard Galician versus dialectal Galician

In Chapter 2, I stated that an official standard is usually an attempt to codify the spelling system and to produce a set of shared linguistic forms with which to facilitate communication between the linguistically diverse groups within a given region or nation. However, it is not necessarily the 'purest' or linguistically the most 'correct' variety (Zamora Munné & Guitart, 1982: 17) of a language – in the sense that it conforms most closely to a diachronic patterning – which is chosen to be the status norm. More frequently, as we saw in Chapter 1, and typically for social and political reasons, the language policy of a given region or nation dictates that a specific, dominant dialect or conglomeration of dialects is ascribed this position of cultural and official medium. Subsequently, language planning and implementation precepts determine its superimposition on the other dialects of the region or nation, by some means of social reform (Mar Molinero, 2000b: 78).

All editions of the *Normas* state that the aim of the standard is to create *unha lingua común asentada na fala, mais depurada de castelanismos, supradialectal, enraizada na tradición, coherente e harmónica coas demais linguas de cultura* [a common language based on speech but purged of Castilianisms; encompassing many dialects, rooted in tradition, coherent and in harmony with other cultural languages]. They also state that their intention is to *valorar a contribución do portugués peninsular e brasileiro, mais excluír solucións que (...) sexan contrarias á estrutura lingüística do galego* [value the contribution of European and Brazilian Portuguese, but exclude solutions that (...) are contrary to the Galician linguistic structure]. Interestingly, and no doubt due to the recent concessions to some of the demands of *reintegración*, the following line has been omitted from the latest version: *que non debe sacrifice-las súas características propias e relevantes en beneficio das dunha lingua irmá, pero diferente* [which must not sacrifice its own pertinent characteristics in favour of those from a language which is related, but different].

In a recent paper, Regueira Fernández (2004) contends that when the issue of an orthographic standard was first raised, the ideological stance adopted did not so much uphold the use of Castilian as the base form for political reasons, but more significantly, sought to distance the standard from all dialectal forms of Galician for reasons of class differentiation. In the 19th century, Galicia was not a homogenous society and the proposed written form was the language of, and for, the educated urban elite; not of, or for, the uneducated rural community (2004: 79–80). This then, as I have already discussed in Chapter 2 and earlier in this chapter (pp. 113–117), is why it was based to a large extent on Castilian, for it was the L^1 of this sector of society.

Moreover, dialectal study at this time was somewhat limited, and when it was carried out, it often simplified the true situation to such an extent that as a result, much of the variation was never documented. Fernández Rei (1990: 31–32) offers a succinct compendium of some of the more prominent dialectal surveys carried out before 1975. Many linguists failed to acknowledge the predicament of the region or the relevance of their studies to the restoration of Galician as a regional language. For example, like García de Diego some 40 years later, Saco Arce's 1868 book *Gramática Gallega*, the first to recognise that dialectal variation even existed within Galicia, dismissed the notion of major linguistic fragmentation, for Saco Arce also divided the region into two dialectal zones, north and south. In the 1950s, Zamora Vicente distinguished two major east/west dialectal zones based on the derivations from the Latin ending–ANUM, subsequently subdivided into four by Carballo Calero (1968: 38–43), this time based on nine Latin derivations. Although more work followed, it was based primarily upon a detailed study of one particular dialect rather than a comparative analysis of linguistic diversity in Galicia as a whole, and as such, did not serve to underline the dialectal complexity of the region and the problems therein for standardisation procedures.[20]

However, more recently the *Instituto da Lingua Galega* [The Galician Language Institute] (ILG), established at the University of Santiago de Compostela, has carried out detailed field research throughout the region, published in the five volumes of the *Atlas Lingüístico Galego* [The Galician Linguistic Atlas] (ILG 1990, 1995, 1999, 2003, 2005). Based on their early work in the 1970s, they also produced a series of proposal entitled *Galegos* 1, 2 and 3, when the controversy regarding the inclusion of dialectal variation in the standard language was first brought to the general attention of the Galician public. However, the model, which took into account such forms, was censored severely by RAG and others.

Back in the 1990s, Santamarina (1995: 80) stated that in the *Normas* published since 1982 there had been a general attempt to be descriptive rather than prescriptive in the written standard, particularly regarding syntactical and morphological forms. The prescribed morphological standards were loosely based upon the dialects of what was termed *galego iriense*, spoken in the Ira Flavia and Tui western regions, with the prescribed phonological standards being based loosely upon the dialects of what was termed *galego lucense*, spoken in the areas of Lugo, Mondonhedo and Ourense. However, there are some substantial anomalies in that certain traits were chosen irrespectively of their provenance. One of the examples proffered by Regueira Fernández (2004: 81) concerns noun morphology. Although the standard masculine plural morpheme of *leons* [lions] is indeed from the western zone, the morpheme of *animais* [animals] is from the eastern zone. Similarly, the masculine singular morpheme of *irmán* [brother] is from the western zone, whereas the feminine singular morpheme of *irmá* [sister] is from the central zone. Galician can therefore be considered to some extent as a type of koine. Such combinatory processes result in a highly artificial form being created, which is very different from any traditional spoken dialectal form.[21]

Regueira Fernández offers other examples to underline his hypothesis that Galician dialectal forms were supplanted in favour of Castilian or Portuguese cognates for ideological reasons. For example, he questions the selection of *sexa* over its cognate *estea* [I, you, he, she, it, is] (first, second and third person present subjunctive), since the former is identical in Portuguese, yet it is not widely found in Galician, whereas *estea* is a 'true' Galician form, coinciding neither with Portuguese nor with Castilian forms (2004: 81). In the lexical example of *dios/deus* [god], Regueira Fernández points out once again that the purist criteria of suppressing Castilians from the lexis simply serves to distance the written form of the language from that commonly found in speech. Here, *dios*, which is identical to the Castilian form, prevailed throughout Galicia until the Spanish Civil War, when the form *deus* (cognate with Portuguese) was adopted instead. This is also the contemporary standard form (2004: 81).

It is clear that certain forms selected as the standard were not necessarily the most common dialectal forms from the perspective of geographical extension. Indeed, in some cases, they were not even the traditional forms found in any dialectal variety, but were, in contrast, forms that coincided with either Portuguese or with Castilian cognates. As we have seen, many of the initial arguments regarding the form of the official standard have centred on whether it would inevitably bring Galician closer to Portuguese, or whether Castilian loanwords would be integrated. Although the *Normas* and its adherents recognise the usefulness of Portuguese, their aim has been to avoid relying upon cognate Portuguese forms whenever possible. However, they also state that Castilianisms should also be generally avoided. I would contend that *reintegración* comments regarding the deliberate inclusion of Castilian structures and forms in the Galician standard to the detriment of Portuguese cognates are, indeed, somewhat ideologically based. In terms of the recent standardisation reforms, once again, the inclusion of pertinent dialectal variation has not been appropriately addressed.

The oral standard

Let us now return to the ideas expressed in Regueira Fernández's recent paper (2004) regarding the development of an oral standard and the implications therein for dialectal forms.

The data published in the first two volumes of the *Atlas Lingüístico Galego* (ILG, 1990, 1995), was also utilised by Fernández Rei (1990) to produce his detailed and widely accepted study of a general three-way split of the spoken variations present within the whole of the Galician-speaking area; namely, a western coastal zone, a central zone, and an eastern zone. The demarcation is demonstrated in Map 4.

Hence, for *cans* [dogs] (masculine plural morpheme):

cans - Northwest Coastal area of A Coruña, selected
as the norm [kans]

Lat. CANES   >   cas - most areas, particularly Central [kas]
cais - all Eastern Galician varieties [kajs]

(Fernández Rei, 1990: 33, 67)

The written standard has, to a large extent, attempted to take such forms into consideration, but the result has been somewhat of a koine, as we have seen above. By the 20th century, the written standard was fairly well defined and used by the elite classes in literary works and other formal documents. However, dialectal variation was still widespread, as I discussed earlier (pp. 115–117). The rural communities used Galician

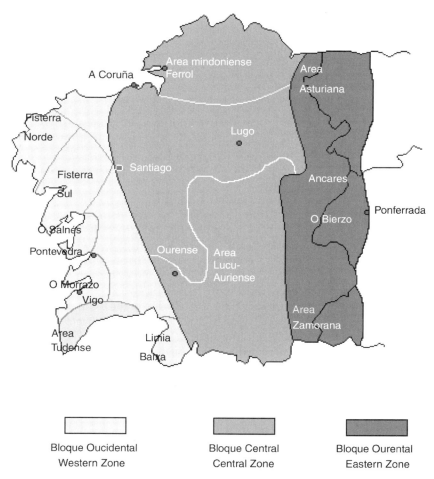

Map 4 The linguistic zones of Galicia[22]

oral varieties, and with the written form being centred predominately in the towns and cities, the disparities between the written and spoken forms of the language became even more diverse. It was only truly from the 1960s onwards that Galician started to be used in urban areas as a formal oral language as an alternative to Castilian. What is highly significant is the pronunciation of this spoken form, for the new, largely urban speakers had learnt Galician as an L^2 and the only pronunciation model available for comparison was that of their L^1, Castilian Spanish, mirroring to a large extent the problems the planners themselves have encountered since standardisation attempts have been made in

Galicia. As a result, they superimposed certain phonetic and phonological aspects of Castilian on their Galician (Regueira Fernández, 2004: 83–84), meaning that much Galician phonetic variation was omitted, such as the more wide-ranging system of vowel timbre, prosodic features, and potentially, other phonetic characteristics, such as the velar nasal, the *gheada* and so on.[23]

Even in official spheres, the use of a Castilian Spanish phonetic system was upheld as the spoken form that would encourage new speakers to adopt Galician. In schools and on the radio and television, the Galician community have become accustomed to learning and hearing a castilianised pronunciation of the Galician written standard, as I will detail further in Chapter 7 (p. 180).[24]

The prescription of an oral standard has implications for social status and prestige, for its diffusion may lead to linguistic discrimination (Mey, 1989) against those who use phonetic and prosodic traits that are not integrated in the standard, and, hence, socially acceptable in certain contexts. In Galicia, Regueira contends that the disparities between oral forms used in urban and rural communities serve as a form of discrimination, once again more in line with issues of social power than with that of linguistic form per se (2004: 85). Indeed, the empiral research into language attitudes carried out by the *Seminario de Sociolingüística da Real Academia Galega* [the Sociolinguistic Institute of the Royal Galician Academy] (SSRAG) demonstrates that the younger population at the very least are well aware of the implications regarding such pronunciation traits (2003: 185–186). So, in other words, it is one thing to speak Galician, but quite another to use a Galician accent.

With some reservations, Regueira Fernández believes that the general purist criteria applied to the formation of the written language could and should also be employed in the oral language (2004: 89–90). Although its inherent ideologies would have to be resolved, he believes that a purist approach would ensure that 'real' Galician forms were used; that is, he advocates the use of regional dialectal forms. Where necessary, the oral language could also borrow forms from Portuguese, for the important point is that a prescribed Galician pronunciation should enhance the language's differentiation from Castilian. In this way for example, the seven tonic and pretonic vowels would be maintained, as would the timbre of atonic final vowels I discuss in Chapter 6, the distinction between /ʃ/ and /s/, the velar nasal and prosodic features.

There are once again two issues at play in the Galician situation. In general, states do not legislate on pronunciation as they do with orthography, since variation in speech is generally tolerated more than in the written form of a language (2004: 83–84). The general tenet is that the prescription of an oral standard is somewhat divisive, in that it discourages people who speak different varieties of a language, with different accents. A case in point was the debate some years ago in British schools regarding the dialectal speech forms of pupils and the requirement, now defunct, that they should learn to speak English with a standard pronunciation, termed Received Pronunciation. The overriding implication is that different interactions and communicative acts are realised in speech and writing and when a language is revised, then this needs to be taken into consideration.

In fact, Regueira Fernández is not advocating a rigid, oral standard to the detriment of dialectal variation, even though he uses the term quite freely. Indeed, he underlines the point that speakers cannot be expected to use such a form in their oral interactions, and its use would only apply to certain formal contexts. In all other contexts, variation in speech is to be encouraged, but it should be based on Galician and not Castilian dialectal variation. What form the standard should take, and to what degree traits that are inherently non-prestigious should be sanctioned, is still very contentious, and at this stage, no far-reaching decisions have been made.

The second issue in play in the Galician situation concerns the bilingual situation itself. The problem of pronunciation at the present time has more to do with the overriding Castilian model than with the choice of dialectal variant, since its implementation negates many Galician dialectal traits, irrespective of their status. In this context, I would contend that Regueira Fernández's line of reasoning is eminently valid, although persuading the urban populations concerned to adopt a more 'Galician' style of pronunciation is inherently problematical. In no small part this is due to pervading negative connotations associated with certain traits, evidenced clearly in SSRAG's results (2003: 185–189). Nonetheless, in academic circles there appears to be very little opposition to the suggestion that some form of model is needed, and this is one of SSRAG's main conclusions. These concerns are revisited in later chapters, where I examine recent research into the effect the prevalent pronunciation of Galician is having on issues of status and prestige.

Concluding Remarks

This chapter is important to the overall hypothesis of this book, because it considers the issue of language revitalisation in areas such as Galicia, considered a social, historical and linguistic 'transition zone' between Portugal and the rest of Spain. In order to do so, I have taken a more linguistic approach to the evolution of the Galician language, since I consider it extremely important to present a multifaceted account of languages in contact. Thus, the linguistic argument is centred around the form and structure of Galician, and in particular, its standard. It serves as a direct comparison to the socio-political and ideological notions of power associated with a language such as Galician, discussed in Chapter 2, manifest in the deliberations of *autonomista* and *reintegracionista* debates surrounding linguistic form in the latter part of the present chapter.

Throughout my assessment of the diachronic development of Galician, I have tended to emphasise these debates surrounding externally motivated influence on the language from Portuguese and Castilian. However, the issue of internally motivated dialectal variation is, I believe, just as important to the intellectual and political debate regarding the development of a written standard. Moreover, I wholeheartedly agree with the need for some form of model of imitation for Galician speech forms. In Chapter 6 and beyond, I will examine in some detail the issue of linguistic fragmentation still present in speech forms, and I will consider speakers' attitudes towards the pronunciation of Galician heard in the media and taught through the education system. The Galician language exists; it is upheld by institutional support, but the issue of form and structure is still subject to some debate.

Chapter 6

The Idiosyncratic Characteristics
of Galician

Introductory Remarks

In the previous chapter, I highlighted some of the more salient linguistic similarities and differences between Galician, Castilian and Portuguese. I also considered some of the more vociferous concerns regarding the construction of the Galician standard, particularly those pertaining to external/internal influences. Pertinent to the discussion carried out in this chapter is the contention that a Castilian pronunciation model has been superimposed onto Galician, eliminating many elements of the Galician phonetic and phonological system present in dialectal forms. As an introductory section to the chapter therefore, I offer a brief example of Galician vowel timbre and the influence of Castilian speech forms on its appearance in contemporary speech forms.

Of prime importance to my discussion of ethnicity in Galicia is the presence, or otherwise, and socio-symbolic or emblematic role of linguistic features that are not found elsewhere, together with their intrinsic value as potential tokens of prestige. To this end, this Chapter focuses on two idiosyncratic phonetic characteristics of Galician, the *gheada* and the velar nasal consonant. I am particularly interested in their impact on language status and identification strategies, indispensable to my discussion of ethnicity within Galicia. I analyse their function and relevance to the sociolinguistic setting as well as their form and structure. Diachronic and synchronic accounts are given, and linguistic versus sociolinguistic evaluations are made with the aim of determining in my concluding paragraphs, which instances of variation tend to be preferred socially, which others are slightly less prestigious, and which others have eminently negative stigma attached to them.

Galician Vowel Timbre

In Chapter 5 (pp. 132–137), I highlighted Regueira Fernández's concerns regarding the use of phonetic and phonological aspects of Castilian in Galician speech forms (2004: 83–84). This has far-reaching implications for some of the more idiosyncratic pronunciation traits of Galician. We saw in Chapter 4 that phonological dialectal distinctions do not normally affect inter-communicative functions and often evolve into an excellent method of divulging a specific geographical identity. Hence, speech forms are not generally subject to institutional standardisation procedures. However, when a written standard is introduced, such speech forms are often subject to assimilation or acculturation processes, as we saw in Chapter 3. In Galicia, it is not so much that the implementation of the standard form of the language has led to the assimilation of dialectal phonetic traits. Rather, acculturation processes have been facilitated by the pervading bilingual contact situation, by similarities between the Galician and Castilian phonetic systems and by the tactic acceptance of a Castilian pronunciation for the Galician standard. As a result, L^1 dialectal speech forms are generally only found in rural varieties, and often carry low prestige value, whilst the urban elite at the very least are gradually using the same phonetic system for Galician and Castilian. Thus, in line with SSRAG (2003: 186), Regueira Fernández contends that the creation of a standard form of oral Galician, based on certain dialectal features, would enhance the language's differentiation from Castilian and retain such intrinsic forms (2004: 87). The feature of dialectal Galician speech forms that I will use as a brief example is that of vowel timbre.

Even the latest edition of the *Normas* (2004) does not generally make detailed reference to the pronunciation of vowels in Galician, primarily because their position within a word has no effect on their orthographic resolution. However, the influential grammar of Alvarez Blanco *et al.* (1986) states that the traditional Galician vowel system comprises seven oral vowel phonemes in tonic and pretonic position: /u/, /o/, /ɔ/, /a/, /ɛ/, /e/, /i/, and five atonic oral vowel phonemes /u/, /o/, /a/, /e/, /i/. As far as timbre is concerned, the open and close vowel opposition of /o/ and /e/ appear to have been neutralised, particularly evident in words that are homogeneous in Castilian and Galician (Alvarez Blanco *et al.*, 1986: 17–19; Kabatek, 1991: 41). In his empiral research, Kabatek (2000: 117–122) found many instances of this neutralisation. Thus, the open [ɛ] of *especie* [type, kind] in Galician is being substituted by a close [e] and the open [ɔ] of *aborto* [abortion] is being replaced by a close [o], both by analogy with the more simple and non-distinctive Castilian forms. Similarly, although Galician pretonic *o* > [u] is still a dialectal characteristic of Galician, there is evidence that it too, is being supplanted by the [o] found in other dialects and in Castilian. There is also strong evidence that Galician orthographic *ou* in words such as *pouco* [little] is generally pronounced as [o], in line with the Castilian cognate *poco*, rather than as the Galician resolution of [ow].

These brief examples closely echo Hamp's findings (Hamps, 1989: 204) regarding the simplification of vowel diphthongs to monophthongs in Mandritsa due to language contact (see p. 101). The levelling processes outlined above for Galician are examples of transference that has already taken place. Unless the issue of Galician pronunciation is addressed, such a marked acculturation of certain characteristics of Galician phonology to the Castilian system may well continue.

The *gheada*

In contrast to the phenomena of open and close vowels, the presence or absence of the *gheada* is still one of the most prominent phonetic features of present-day Galician. The term denotes a lack of the standard (non-*gheada* zone) Galician voiced velar plosive /g/ and its positional allophones [g] and the approximant [ɰ], and its replacement by a (predominantly) voiceless continuant pronunciation. The realisation of this may range from a rather weakly articulated voiceless velar fricative [x] or its aspirated counterpart [xʰ], through a voiced glottal fricative [h] or a murmured voiceless glottal fricative [ɦ], to a voiceless pharyngeal fricative [ħ] or its voiced counterpart [ʕ], to a voiceless [χ] or voiced uvular fricative [ʁ]. So, in initial position of isolate forms of orthographic *g* or the grapheme *gu*, such as in the words *gato* [cat] and *guerra* [war], the non-*gheada* Galician pronunciation is [g]ato and [g]uerra, and intervocalically, [ɰ] obtains, for example *pagar* [to pay] > pa[ɰ]ar. Potentially, all may be pronounced in the following ways in the *gheada* areas:

Gal. *gato*	*guerra*	*pagar*
[x]ato	[x]uerra	pa[x]ar
[xʰ]ato	[xʰ]uerra	pa[xʰ]ar
[h]ato	[h]uerra	pa[h]ar
[ɦ]ato	[ɦ]uerra	pa[ɦ]ar
[ħ]ato	[ħ]uerra	pa[ħ]ar
[ʕ]ato	[ʕ]uerra	pa[ʕ]ar
[χ]ato	[χ]uerra	pa[χ]ar
[ʁ]ato	[ʁ]uerra	pa[ʁ]ar

In the course of investigations carried out over the last few decades, many Galician linguists have found examples of some, but not all, the allophonic variation I have outlined above, and most agree that there has been a levelling of some of the *gheada* realisations.[1] Generally, it is also believed that the high degree of variation in articulation of the *gheada* is not found in all geographical and social dialects. However, in their recent acoustic and perceptual analyses of recordings made in the *gheada* zone, Labraña-Barrero and van Oosterzee (2003) did note a degree of regularity in the geographical distribution of some of the variants, although their findings regarding distribution according to the type of adjacent vowel are rather more tenuous. On the coast, these researchers found voiceless pharyngeal and velar articulations, and, inland, found voiced (intervocalically) and voiceless uvular and glottal articulations. No far-reaching conclusions can be made on the basis of such a small-scale study, but it does offer an instrumental confirmation of earlier perceptual findings regarding the predominance of the voiceless pharyngeal fricative.[2] Thus, in the course of the following discussion, I adopt a simplified schema in order to illustrate overriding tendencies rather than possible variants. In line with Recalde (2003: 44–5) in her article on the origin of the *gheada*, I group potential articulations under that of the voiceless pharyngeal fricative, /ħ/, but I highlight the voiceless glottal fricative articulation [h] and the voiceless velar fricative [x] as those that may be most commonly found nowadays.

In principle, the *gheada* is primarily a marker of regional pronunciation of a speech variety denoted *galego de gheada*, although the situation has been complicated somewhat over the centuries with stylistic considerations also playing a part, as I will discuss further below. Nonetheless, dialectal variation in the realisation of orthographic *g* has been put forward routinely as evidence for the two (or three) major linguistic divisions within Galicia, which was outlined in Chapter 5 (pp. 132–133).[3] In this respect, the *gheada* appears to be a feature of all western and much of the central areas of Galicia, although there is evidence that it used to be more widely found (see Mariño Paz, 1998). Its demarcation line runs north to south through the province of Lugo, excluding the capital but then sweeping down to include Ourense, as well as the western cities of A Coruña, Santiago de Compostela, Pontevedra, and Vigo, as demonstrated in Map 5.[4]

The ILG grammar book *Gramática Galega* (Alvarez Blanco *et al.*, 1986: 27) confirms that the *gheada* is incorporated into the standard form como *pronuncia alternativa ó sistema de non gheada* [as an alternative pronunciation to the non-*gheada* system]. However, the authors only make specific reference to the voiceless pharyngeal fricative pronunciation [ħ] of /h/ in this context:

> [..] en grande parte do noso territorio lingüístico o sistema fonolóxico non presenta /g/, xa que evolucionou a /h/, fonema aspirado, normalmente farínxeo xordo
>
> [In much of our linguistic territory the phonological system does not display a /g/, since an aspirate phoneme /h/ has evolved, normally pronounced as a voiceless pharyngeal fricative.]
>
> (Alvarez Blanco *et al.*, 1986: 27)

Map 5 Isogloss indicating the Eastern limit of the *gheada* in Galicia

However, the second edition (Alvarez Blanco & Xove, 2002) refers to voiced and voiceless velar through to glottal fricative and approximant articulations.

The 19th edition of the *Normas Ortográficas e Morfolóxicas do Idioma Galego* (2004: 15–16) makes a tacit allusion to the *gheada*. As well as non-*gheada* pronunciations of orthographic *g*, the *Normas* also list the voiceless glottal fricative [h] and the voiceless pharyngeal fricative [ħ] as dialectal variants, but not as alternatives to the standard form. They offer a way of demonstrating a *gheada* pronunciation by stating that:

> Para explicita-la pronunciación con gheada utilízase o dígrafo gh (ghato, ghicho, amigho)

> [To make it clear that a word should be pronounced with the *gheada*, use the digraph *gh* (*ghato* [cat], *ghicho* [a small item], *amigho* [friend])][5]

> (Real Academia Galega (RAG) and Instituto de Língua Galega (ILG),
> 2004: 19)

None of the prestigious varieties of Galician has the *gheada*, so its non-standard status is unsurprising. Alonso Montero (1990: 149) has contended that the elitism present in the standardisation of Galicia excluded such a form because its use continues to imply a strong degree of stigma and ignorance. Indeed, only a few academics involved in potential reformulations of the Galician language endorse its use as a standard variant, and Recalde (2003: 47) believes that the acceptance or rejection of *gheada* pronunciations as alternatives to /g/ is closely linked to considerations and beliefs concerning its etymological origins.

The use of the *gheada* has long been linked intimately to rustic, working-class speech forms of farming and fishing, and over the years, its use acquired connotations of low prestige, stigma, and marginalisation in certain sectors of Galician society. Even in more recent times, most Galician grammars, linguistic treatises, and newspaper articles on the subject have adopted negative value judgements regarding the use of the *gheada*. At the beginning of the 20th century, García de Diego suggested that its pronunciation could even be considered in some way defective:

> [...] esta pronunciación, reputada como defectuosa, recibe el nombre de 'geadas'

> [[...] this pronunciation, with the reputation of being defective, is given the name '*geadas*']
>
> (García de Diego, 1984: 11 [1909])

Likewise, Cotarelo Valledor makes clear his aversion to the use of the *gheada*:

> sin embargo, cuando las gentes *incultas* de la zona costera occidental hablan castellano *incurren en el vicio de* pronunciar como gutural explosiva fortísima la *g* suave (jato [...]), y lo que es más raro todavía, como g suave la j (garro [...]). Claro que *tan grosero hábito* solo se usa entre el *vulgo*, pero a veces induce a confusión a personas algo ilustradas.

> [yet when *uneducated* people of the western coastal areas speak Castilian they *commit the gross error of* pronouncing a *g* as a strong guttural sound (*jato* for 'cat' [...]), and, what is even more strange, they pronounce a *j* as a g (*garro* for 'jar' [...]). Of course, such *a coarse practice* is only employed by the *masses*, but it sometimes leads to confusion even amongst more learned people.] (my emphasis)
>
> (Cotarolo Valledor, 1927: 90–91)

Even the eminent linguist Carballo Calero (1968: 38–43) dismissed the *gheada* as a 'mere' dialectal phenomenon. He regarded it as not part of 'cultured' or 'refined' – implicitly, formal – language.

In an attempt to explain the diachronic evolution of the *gheada*, three theories have been put forward, with varying degrees of success. These are: a substratal hypothesis, one pertaining to internal evolution, and another citing a process of external, superstratal transference phenomena. I shall briefly consider each in turn.

Although upheld by eminent linguists such as Zamora Vicente (1986: 23–24), the suggestion that the *gheada* has its roots in a Celtic substratum, or even earlier substrata, based upon the contention that geographically it coincides with the area of Galician formerly occupied by these settlements, has largely been discounted. One of the main arguments against this theory is that written evidence can only be attested from possibly the 17th and 18th centuries onwards (Recalde, 2003: 46, 48).[6]

The second hypothesis is that the *gheada* has arisen due to language-internal evolutionary processes within the Galician phonetic-phonological system. Despite slight differences of theoretical opinion, Schroten (1980: 209–221), Prieto Alonso (1980: 223–241), and Santamarina (1980: 243–249) have all concluded that the *gheada* evolved as a predictable internally motivated phonetic change (pp. 104–105). As such, they claim that its existence is not dependent upon any significant contact-induced change. This contention appears to influence their attitudes towards its potential inclusion within the standard form: by and large, proponents of this theory tend to accept the *gheada* as a potential standard variant of the pronunciation of orthographic *g* and, consequently, endorse its use. This issue is discussed in further detail in the following, where I discuss the notion of linguistic ideology.

The third hypothesis concerns external transference phenomena. According to this superstratal hypothesis, the evolution of the *gheada* has been motivated entirely by language external factors, in that it arose due to the influence of the Castilian *jota* /x/ on the Galician phonetic system by means of transference phenomena within diglossic, bilingual contact situations.[7] The claim is that since no /x/ was present in Galician, an interim pronunciation /g/ was obtained from Castilian words such as *jarra* [jug] when spoken by L[1] Galician speakers. In this way, a process of underdifferentiation affected the Castilian phonological distinction between /x/ and /g/ for such speakers (Recalde, 2003: 50). Over time, this articulation of /g/ underwent a process of correction back to /x/ in Castilian tokens uttered by those who became competent in both languages. However, for some speakers this process appears to have been overgeneralised, resulting in the incorporation of /x/ into their Galician phonemic inventory, and its employment in both Castilian and Galician tokens as a substitute for /g/ (and, by analogy, /h/ and its derivations) wherever syllable initial *g* was found:[8]

Gal. gato 'cat' ['xato]/['hato]

One of the main criticisms of this theory by detractors such as Fernández Rei (1990: 186–187) is that it does not account for the restriction in geographic distribution of the *gheada* to western and central linguistic zones. There have been attempts to align this distribution with the notion of urban regeneration and consequent contact with Castilian in the west, versus rural degeneration and a lack of contact with Castilian in the east. However, a clear-cut demarcation on these lines is not borne out by historical fact. Moreover, it is somewhat difficult to uphold the notion that in the 18th century, the period in which this theory is based, a diglossic, bilingual situation truly existed even in the towns and cities (see for example, p. 114), paving the way for the transference phenomena I have outlined above. I tend to agree with Recalde. In her thorough critique of the Castilianist theory, (Recalde, 2003: 43–74), she recognises the social nature of much linguistic change. However, Recalde points out that the *gheada* is *not* necessarily a product of the presence of Castilian Spanish within Galicia as the prestige language of power since the 15th century, for the percentage of inhabitants who sufficiently dominated both languages in 18th-century Galician society and beyond was minor. Consequently, it would have been difficult for phonetic transference phenomena to take place from Castilian to Galician.

Recalde bases her argument partially on the idea that there is a clear-cut demarcation between the theories of internally and externally motivated change in terms of a politically inspired ideological basis that has much to do with the issues of identity and autonomy I outline in this book. She contends that: 'those who accept the *gheada* base their opinion on its endogenous origin, its popular nature, and its presence in the rural environment [. . .] it is a trait that separates Galician from the dominant language and reinforces ethnolinguistic borders'. On the other hand, 'Those who reject the *gheada* usually point to its exogenous origin, its low prestige, and its absence in the literary tradition [. . .] the *gheada* is absolutely unacceptable, because its acceptance would bring standard Galician closer to Spanish [. . .]' (Recalde, 2003: 47). In other words, she believes that those who sanction the potential inclusion of the *gheada* as a standard variable tend to endorse the internal change hypothesis, whereas those who reject its use outright within the standard tend to endorse the external, Castilian-based hypothesis.

I agree with Recalde that this demarcation would appear to be based upon a politically motivated ideology. To an extent, this demarcation between supporters of the language internal change hypothesis and the tacit acceptance of the *gheada* in the standard, versus supporters of the Castilianist hypothesis and the exclusion of the *gheada* from the standard, echoes some of the more general debates and disagreements I outlined in Chapter 5 regarding the overall composition of a standard Galician. The *Normas Ortográficas* have been constructed largely by devotees of *autonomismo*. It would be unsurprising if they adhered to a theory concerning the origins of the *gheada* that emphasises its autonomy from Castilian and its inherent nature within the Galician language, principally within that of the social and cultural heartland of the countryside, but nowadays also within the standard forms taught throughout the region. If this were the case, then the *gheada* could potentially function as an emblematic characteristic for this group. However, the Normas do not consider the *gheada* a standard variant but a dialectal one that is simply included for reference, as I have pointed out above (p. 143). Again, this is probably to do with issues of prestige rather than considerations pertaining to form and structure.

On the other hand, it is certainly true that *reintegracionistas* have been keen to voice their objections to what they consider the Castilianising of the Galician language, as we saw earlier (for example, p. 86). Indeed, one of their most ardent supporters, Freixeiro Mato, upholds the externally motivated theory and vehemently attacks the use of the *gheada* (Freixeiro Mato, 1998: 142–159, 162–175).

However, despite Recalde's assertions, it is unlikely that the *Normas* will ever recognise the *gheada* as a standard variant, given that they have not done so until now. Moreover, even though only less radical proponents of the *reintegracionista* perspective were included in the decision-making processes regarding form, to them, the inclusion of the *gheada* may well be ideologically unacceptable, given that if they *do* uphold the external motivation hypothesis, it would imply a tacit acceptance of the linguistic influence of Castilian on Galician.

Of course, I am not suggesting that this demarcation is clear-cut or totally adhered to by both those in academia and government alike. In particular, I have problems in justifying the claims regarding the *reintegracionista* perspective, but as there is no /x/ in Portuguese, the language internal hypothesis of origin cannot satisfy the *reintegracionista's* need to enhance the diachronic, and, implicitly, the synchronic relationship between Portuguese and Galician.[9]

At this juncture, we are less concerned with assertions made regarding potential misinterpretations of the sociolinguistic situation prevalent over 200 years ago, than with issues about its contemporary value and possible relevance in the process of forging some form of Galician identity. Although I fully recognise the important role historical factors play in present-day attitudes, I do not intend to postulate further as to the provenance of the *gheada*. Irrespective of where such opinions stem from, they are widely disseminated throughout Galicia nowadays, even if they are not necessarily agreed or complied with.

Rather than treat the *gheada* exclusively as a regional variant, I now contend that it would be more appropriate to also consider it as an indicator of social differentiation originally based upon accent and dialect, but currently influenced largely by attitude and opinion. What the above arguments and comments do suggest is that the *gheada* may be an indicator of regional pronunciation, but that political and ideological considerations also dictate whether it is accepted or not as a viable speech form. Hence, following Recalde (2003: 45) I hypothesise that the use of the *gheada* has become stratified by extralinguistic variables such as age and speech style, and as such, is a sociolinguistic marker with the underlying sociolinguistic variable being represented as (gh).

In order to examine contemporary attitudes and uses of the *gheada*, I consider the findings of recent investigations, such as Alvarez-Cáccamo's paper on conversational code-switching in Galicia (Alvarez-Cáccamo, 1990), which examines interactional manoeuvres between members of the board of directors of a museum during their meetings. The point of interest is raised when the members start to digress into a conversation about an impeding football match. One of the participants employs *galego de gheada*. Interestingly, he himself describes this as a non-standard form, not to invoke his social background, his class affiliation, or consciousness, but rather as a metaphorical device. The author claims (Alvarez-Cáccamo, 1990: 6–7) that although educated speakers appear to be restricting the use of their vernacular language varieties to intimate, in-group functions, primarily through the influence of exposure to standard Spanish, and recently, also to standard Galician within the education system, there *has* been a marked change in the way the *gheada* is employed in certain contexts. That is, even educated urban dwellers who did not acquire its use through their L^1 speech forms *or* their acquisition of such L^2 forms appear to be acutely informed about its socio-stylistic meanings for local identification and informality with their daily lives. As a result, the author concludes that they are choosing to employ the *gheada* strategically. In accordance with Coulmas (2005: 90–92) discussed earlier (p. 106), in such a context the *gheada* is a feature of marked usage, in that users are aware of the potential implications non-conformity to the unmarked feature will have on social interactions.

I would add that such strategic devices function as solidarity mechanisms, and that in this case, the participant is attempting to convey a particular allegiance with a given community or social group that is *not* necessarily his own. This situation echoes the examples of solidarity-processes discussed at the end of the Introduction (pp. 22–23), where we saw that social relationships may be determined, negotiated, and articulated in different ways and for different reasons. My results confirm that solidarity practices are not restricted to working-class males. Rather, even speakers of the elite language, such as the standard language, may choose to employ in their speech a non-standard or regional form inherent to a non-elite community or social group as a solidarity mechanism. Their choice is not generally determined by concepts of hierarchy and power, but rather, by loyalty factors. Thus, such forms acquire a positive association with a speaker's degree of integration into the social network and as such, can be considered examples of covert prestige.

Kabatek's empirical research (2000: 152–155) confirms that there is still much stigma attached to the use of the *gheada*. However, some of his younger informants manifest a desire to use the *gheada* in certain contexts. One offered the example of an interview on Radio Galega to emphasise the difference in her speech to that of the interviewers; another confirmed that they use the *gheada* in order to integrate with people from their local area. The consensus regarding its authenticity was manifest by a mother tongue Castilian speaker who also tried to use it as often as possible. Again, these results are somewhat tentative, but they do suggest that the use of the *gheada* is linked intimately to issue of solidarity.

Bearing these comments in mind, I now discuss a pilot survey I carried out in Santiago de Compostela in the mid 1990s, during the course of my investigations into uses of and attitudes towards Galician (discussed in Chapters 8 and 9), which produced similar results. The aim of this supplementary study, the results of which have not been reported until now, was to analyse my respondents' behavioural practices regarding the *gheada*, and to examine their statements regarding such practices. A summary of the results can be found in Appendix 2.

Firstly, every respondent without exception and irrespective of age, gender, profession, educational background, and other social factors, states that they employ the *gheada* in general, everyday conversation. Moreover, the responses elicited by the respondents in the 10 to 21 age group imply that most (80%) are fully aware of doing so. Similarly, most (70%) do not consider the use of the *gheada* to be a problem, and would not try to avoid its use even if they were able to. Indeed, no issues of low prestige or inferiority are mentioned explicitly. Rather, for this age group, the *gheada* seems to be indicative of informal or intragroup speech, the latter exemplified by the comments of one particular respondent: '*non vexo problemas en manexá-la gheada dentro da miña comunidade, porque forma parte da nosa maneira de falar; é unha indicación da nosa identidade colectiva*' [I see no problem in using the *gheada* within my community, because it is part of our way of speaking; it is a marker of our collective identity].

In the 21 to 40 and 40 to 70 age groups, all those respondents who claimed to use dialectal or non-standard forms of Galician in the other questionnaire that was distributed (Appendix 5, p. 282), consider the *gheada* to be either a dialectal form or a part of an inferior speech pattern. All who consider it indicative of an inferior speech pattern also stipulated earlier that Castilian was their language of preference. In the 21 to 40 age group, nearly everyone is aware of using the *gheada* on a regular basis. 50% consider it indicative of informal speech patterns, and 66% of those state that if they could, they would avoid its use either at work or with their children or with strangers. Those who attach inferior connotations to its use (25%) would like to be able to avoid it in all contexts. However, even these respondents state that this is difficult to achieve, given that the *gheada* is well embedded in their speech forms. The responses of the 40 to 70 age group reinforce those of the 21 to 40 age group, in that 70% of the respondents would try to avoid using the *gheada* in some or all contexts if they could, but state that this is unfeasible.

In a similar way to Alvarez-Cáccamo above, my results, albeit some-what tentative given the small-scale nature of the investigation, indicate that the younger respondents in particular view their use of the *gheada* as a solidarity mechanism. In this case, however, they are simply reinfor-cing their allegiances with their own, and not another, community. There-fore, although behavioural practices have not changed, given that all respondents use the *gheada*, attitudes towards the significance of the *gheada* within social networks may be starting to do so. As yet, however, the reasons behind this remain unclear and are worthy of future investigation.

Even more recently, and as a general precursor to her 2003 article dis-cussed above, Recalde (1995) carried out a study of four schools within the *gheada* zone, in order to determine the extent to which the respondents agreed or disagreed with subjective notions of prestige and status associ-ated with the use of the *gheada*. Her overall conclusion was that there was a clear tendency within her participants to prefer spoken Galician that did not contain the *gheada* (1995: 16). More specifically, she found that as far as attitudes towards the use of the *gheada* and the social stereotypes associ-ated therein were concerned, opinion was divided according to whether the respondents themselves used it in their speech forms. Negative preju-dices surrounding the notion that its speakers are from a low cultural background were rejected progressively as a respondent's level of famili-arity with the phenomenon increased (1995: 27). Thus, a lack of familiarity with the *gheada* led to speakers overgeneralising its more negative traits, whilst those who did employ it simply renounced any negative connota-tions attached to its use.

As I have already discussed earlier in this chapter, stigma attached to the use of the *gheada* tends to be embedded within historical, socio-econ-omic and cultural issues, as well as within associated attitudes. However, Recalde's findings demonstrate that her group of respondents at least, displayed a need to avoid being considered prejudical against those who did employ it on a regular basis. Therefore, although some of them believed that the *gheada* did devalue spoken Galician, they were at pains to stress that it did not imply that they considered its devotees socially inferior to those who did not use it (Recalde, 1995: 28). Although we should be somewhat cautious about the significance of such com-ments, they do nonetheless display a slight shift from outright exclusion of the phenomenon to its tacit acceptance in certain circumstances.

During the 1990s, Dubert García carried out detailed research into the morphological, phonetic and phonological features of Santiago de Compostela speech forms (1995, 1996, 1999). His early studies indicated that although the western city lies within the *gheada* limits, nearly all his respondents meticulously avoided using it wherever possible, but that it was normally uttered in more informal interactions. Dubert García concludes from this that within Santiago de Compostela, the *gheada* is not found in formal and careful registers, but that it is still common in other contexts and registers. In a later paper (Dubert García, 1999: 134), he concedes that his earlier respondent sample was too limited for his general assumptions to be totally valid. Nonetheless, his later findings do confirm that within the confines of the city, the *gheada* has little prestige value.

Dubert García also found that he heard the *gheada* more and more as he travelled away from the capital, and upon investigation, he concluded that either speakers demonstrated little competence in controlling or avoiding its use, or they were simply not interested in modifying their linguistic practices in order to do so.

The realisation of orthographic *g* also depended to some extent on location. Within the more formal styles and registers employed in the city of Santiago de Compostela itself, there appeared to be a phonological distinction between /g/ and /x/. Both [g] and [ɰ] occur, apparently in complementary distribution: [g]*ustar* [to like]; lo[ɰ]o [then], whereas [x] and [h] were in evidence in free variation in more colloquial speech forms (Dubert García, 1999: 49).[10] In the surrounding suburbs, he found that the occurrence of [h] increased, and there was also evidence of some free variation with [g/ɰ]: hence the pronunciation of *chegar* [to arrive] with [h], [x] and [ɰ]. Finally, in the most outlying areas around Santiago, the *gheada* was always pronounced as [h] (or as [g] in *ng* clusters for example un#ghato [a cat]).

Dubert García claims that this variation is symptomatic of ongoing linguistic change, leading to the loss or near loss of the *gheada* in certain city contexts and its replacement with what are considered more prestigious forms. However, he is somewhat circumspect in his later paper regarding the motivation for such change. His hypothesis considers the linguistic influence of Castilian, but he does not necessarily believe that this is the sole motivating factor behind the ongoing loss of the [h] articulation, although he does concede that it may have a bearing on its spread and consolidation. The author avers that the only reason Castilian could affect the phonological system of Galician would be because the speakers are 'perfectly bilingual'.

This brings me back once again to the issue of Galician speech forms in urban areas. Earlier (p. 146), I discounted the Castilianist hypothesis that in the 18th century, a bilingual/diglossic situation truly existed in the towns and cities, facilitating transference phenomena between the two languages in question and resulting in this [h] pronunciation of the *gheada*. However, this may not be so far away from the truth nowadays. Castilian is both the state-sponsored language and the model for imitation in urban areas – particularly in education – for despite the recent revival of Galician, as we have seen (pp. 134–137) a Castilian pronunciation and its idiosyncratic phonetic traits are often overlaid onto Galician forms.[11] In the media, not only do Galicians regularly listen to Castilian speakers, but the form of spoken Galician heard on the local television and radio stations, particularly in news broadcasts, is strongly Castilian-influenced. Many of the broadcasters and reporters employed are L[1] Castilian speakers, and learn a form of Galician overlaid by a phonetic system full of Castilianisms and Castilian features (see p. 185 for further detail).

This is what Alvarez-Cáccamo (1990), above, and Valcárcel Riveiro (2002: 224) mean when they refer to the influence of standard Galician as a significant factor in the loss of the *gheada*. It is not that the written standard has resulted in a levelling of *gheada* variation, but more that the spoken form, based on Castilian, does not contain such phonetic variation. Dubert García's tacit querying of these authors' claims is largely understandable, since he found that the *gheada* can still be differentiated along the lines of urban/rural geographical variation. Yet it would also appear that certain stylistic considerations are functioning simultaneously, and that these changes are occurring because within certain urban communities, attitudinal factors are consciously determining its use in certain contexts, thus overriding other considerations. In this way, a given speaker's perceptions regarding the use of the *gheada* appear, at least partially, to determine its viability. For some, as in Alvarez-Cáccamo's paper (1990) and for the youngest respondents of my own study, it may be starting to be viewed as a intragroup solidarity mechanism, associated with local, Galician, identification strategies. However, for the majority of respondents, there is still a great deal of stigma attached to its use despite the fact that they themselves may not be able to avoid it in all but the most formal of speech. Consider for example, Dubert García's finding that within the city of Santiago de Compostela, the *gheada* enjoys little or even no prestige value. I would claim that this conclusion is unsurprising. Santiago may be the seat of (national) regional government and the focus of recent language standardisation activity, but this does not necessarily imply that its inhabitants all can be expected to have modified long-standing and widespread perceptions that using the *gheada* in formal contexts is careless or even disrespectful to the interlocutor.[12] Although the results of my study may imply the contrary as far as the younger age groups are concerned, given the small-scale nature of the investigations, these are only tentative. Marked use of the *gheada* is dictated by contextual cues regarding social mores; it is also a stylistic variable, occurring in colloquial, informal styles but not in more formal and careful ones, at least within the confines of the city; and its overarching geographical distribution, although not as clear-cut as before, is still in evidence. Before considering the emblematic status of the *gheada*, I should now examine the use of the velar nasal, as well as attitudes towards this use.

The Velar Nasal

Unlike the *gheada*, there is no variation in the pronunciation of ortho-graphic word-final nasal segments (/VN/ sequences) for the velar nasal [Vŋ] in final position occurs throughout Galicia. Its use does not therefore correlate with a linguistic zone theory. Although the *Normas Ortográficas* do not offer much information regarding pronunciation norms in Galician, they do counsel the use of the velar nasal not only in many cases where a nasal consonant occurs in word-final position, but more significantly, as the standard pronunciation for intervocalic orthographic *nh* (*Normas Ortográficas*, 2004: 20). It is in this position that the velar nasal can be considered a somewhat idiosyncratic feature of Galician, at least as far as Romance languages are concerned.[13]

As I pointed out in Chapter 5 (p. 118), in order to establish a linguistic frontier between Southern Galician and Northern Portuguese, Fernández Rei (for example) considers three isoglosses, one of which is the almost universal occurrence of [aŋ] where Portuguese has [ãw̃]:

Gal. can 'dog'   [kaŋ]
Port. cão 'dog'   [kãw̃]

(Fernández Rei, 1990: 28–29, 161)

Asturian and Leonese varieties, Andalusian and, for well-documented historical reasons, some South American dialects of Spanish, may all also employ the velar nasal in word-final position.[14] Except in cases of antici-patory assimilation to /k,g/, such as in the example *ha*[ŋ] [k]*reado* [they, you (pl.) have created], no such articulation occurs in these positions for standard Castilian.

As I shall now outline, it has been claimed that the velarisation of Latin N segments was the first stage of a diachronic process of weakening and, as such, a necessary precondition for subsequent nasal consonant del-etion, thus:

Vn   >   Vŋ   >   VØ

However, such nasal consonant erosion procedures and the role of the velar nasal therein are somewhat debatable. I will take vowel nasalisation as a first point of examination. In accordance with the historical develop-ment of other Romance languages, it is generally agreed that vowel nasa-lisation evolved in Galician-Portuguese as a result of regressive assimilation to a conditioning nasal consonant of the Latin base word (Sampson, 1999: 179). This corresponds with the traditional generative phonology view, which regards this as a universal process:

Rule (1) V   →   [+nasal] / NV
Rule (2) N   →   Ø / V–V[15]

Durand (1990: 45) adds that in such circumstances, even Castilian may exhibit allophonic nasalisation of the preceding vowel:

Cast.   hablaron [õ]   'they spoke'

In order to account for the presence of the velar nasal in Galician, Brandão de Carvalho's thesis (1988: 249) maintains that such vowel nasalisation was accompanied by velarisation of the nasal consonant in Galician-Portuguese. This would conform to the diachronic weakening processes I have exemplified above, whereby nasal consonant place shift would lead to velarisation as the necessary precondition for nasal consonant deletion (Chen, 1973: 162). For example in Portuguese, the nasal consonant would finally drop and the nasal vowel would be retained, whereas in Galician, the nasal consonant would be retained as the velar and the vowel would have denasalised:

Lat. MĀNU 'hand'   >   GP [manu   >   mano   >   mãŋo]   >
                          Port. [mão]
                          Gal. [maŋ][16]

However, Hajek (1992) rejects such a model. In his study of North Italian dialects, he avers that phonetic weakening is not a necessary precondition for nasal consonant (N)-deletion (Hajek, 1992: 232–266). Sampson (1999: 184) concurs and proposes an alternative derivation, where [ⁿ] indicates some form of attenuated nasal:

[n   >   ⁿ   >   Ø]

In this way, nasal vowels would have been restructured to nasal vowel plus nasal consonant, the latter either as the default nasal [ŋ] or as a nasal homorganic with the following consonant. The vowel would then have denasalised (Sampson, 1999: 207–210):[17]

Lat. FĪNE 'end'   >   G.P. fĩ⁽ⁿ⁾   >   fĩ   >   fĩŋ   >   Std. Gal. fĩŋ
Lat. VIGĬNTI 'twenty'   >   G.P bĩnte   >   bĩ⁽ⁿ⁾te   >   Std. Gal.
bĩnte/bĩŋte

According to this theory, the restructuring of the nasal consonant as an anti-hiatic device in my earlier example would have resulted in the loss of vowel nasality:

Lat. MĀNU 'hand'   >   G.P. manu   >   mano   >   mã-o   >
maŋo   >   Std. Gal. maŋ

The changes that preceded the emergence of the velar nasal in intervocalic position for the small set of grammatical forms consisting of Latin ŪNA and its derivatives ALIC-ŪNA [some] (fem.sing.) and

NEC-ŪNA [no-one] (fem.sing.), would have been similarly complex. Sampson's brief account (1999: 209) claims that when the nasal consonant transferred its nasal resonance to the preceding vowel, this resulted in hiatus between the two (now) adjacent vowels. These forms appear to have then reinstated the nasal segment as an anti-hiatic device, in the form of [ŋ]:[18]

Lat. ŪNA 'one' (fem.sing.) > una > G.P. ũ-a/hũ-a > Std. Gal. uŋa

Interestingly, eastern Galician also retains the form *úa* in non-standard forms, where the vowels remain in hiatus (González & González, 1994: 17).

Synchronic patterns

Standard Castilian Spanish has three nasal consonant phonemes: /m, n, ɲ/, with the velar nasal only occurring as a positional allophone before /k, g, x/. However, Alvarez Blanco *et al.* (1986) assert that there are four nasal consonant phonemes in Galician: /m, n, ɲ, ŋ/, although the velar and palatal nasals cannot occur in word-initial position. Other linguists believe that the palatal nasal *can* occur word-initially, albeit with a somewhat restricted distribution, but the velar nasal does not occur in such a position.[19] Thus, it is claimed that the velar nasal cannot be considered a phoneme, since consonant phonemes tend to display a maximum capacity for meaningful distinction (Veiga Arias, 1976: 121). In other words, meaningful oppositions should be found for phonemes in every syllable position they are able to occupy. Word-finally, there appears to be no controversy; neutralisation to the archiphoneme /N/ occurs, which is frequently realised as [ŋ] before either a pause or vowel:[20]

Gal.　　pan [ŋ] e auga　　'bread and water'

The first two volumes of the *Atlas Lingüístico Galego* (ILG, 1990, 1995) contain examples of [ŋ] found throughout Galicia, even where other morphological variation is found:

Gal.　　cantaron　　cantar [oŋ]　　'they, you (pl.) sang' (1990: 67)
　　　　irmán　　　irm ['ãŋ]　　　'brother' (1995: 49)[21]

Moreover, before another consonant and most often within rapid, casual speech styles, although the most common resolution in all instances is still the velar nasal, nasal consonants may assimilate to the place of articulation of a following plosive, both within the confines of a word and across a word boundary:

Gal.   [m] before /b,p/; un peixe 'a fish'   [umpejʃe]

                [ɱ] before /f/; en fin 'at last'   [emfiŋ]

/N/ > {   [n̪] before /d,t/; un dedo 'a finger' [un̪deðo]

                [n̪] before /θ/; un cinto 'a belt'   [un̪θinto]

                [ɲ] before palatals; enxame 'exam' [eɲʃame]

                [ŋ] before /k,g/, áncora 'anchor' [aŋkɔra]

(Adapted from Alvarez Blanco *et al.*, 1986: 34)

Rather more contentious is the articulation of nasal segments before the definite article and direct object pronouns. There are two forms of the definite article for each singular, plural and gender morpheme, and three forms of the third person singular and plural direct object pronoun, which occur in complementary distribution, being phonologically conditioned by the final phoneme of the preceding word:[22]

Gal. masc. sing. o, lo   masc. pl. os, los   'the'
    fem. sing. a, la   fem. pl. as, las
Gal. masc. sing. o, lo, no masc. pl. os, los, nos 'this, her, your'
    fem. sing. a, la, na   fem. pl. as, las, nas

In both systems the *o* form may be considered the default form, used if the criteria do not dictate use of the others.[23] The *no* variable of the direct object pronoun is limited to clitic use after verbal diphthongs:

Gal.   cantei a canción 'I sang the song'
       canteina 'I sang it'
       sacou os libros 'he/she/you took the books out'
       sacounos 'he/she/you took them out'

Alvarez Blanco *et al.* (1986: 34) and the *Normas* (RAG/ILG, 2004: 84) claim that the default form *o/a/os/as* is employed and that the nasal consonant is resolved as [n] after the following:

verb forms in *-n*
adverbs *non*, [no, not] *ben* [good] and *tamén* [also]
pronouns *alguén* [someone] and *ninguén* [noone]
conjunction *nin* [not even]
prepositions *con* [with] and *sen* [without]: *se*[n] *a súa axuda* 'without your help'[24]

The *Normas* (RAG/ILG, 2004: 41) also advocates that a [ŋn] pronunciation is required in cases of a third person plural verb form in *-n* plus the first person plural atonic object pronoun *nos*, for example, *chámannos* [they call us]. The orthographic resolution *nn* also occurs in compound words such as *connosco* [with us]. However, other linguists such as Alvarez Blanco

(1983: 179) maintain that assimilation to the alveolar nasal takes place in such circumstances.

The velar nasal is also found in words in *in-*, in learned words, where it forms a tautosyllabic cluster with /s/ before another consonant, and before /m/ and /n/:

Gal.   inhalar 'to inhale'   inhóspito 'inhospitable'
          inherente 'inherent'   inhumar 'to bury'
          inhibir 'to prevent'   inhabilidade 'inability'

(RAG/ILG, 2004: 18; RAG/ILG, 2004: 81–87)

Gal.   inspirar [iŋspirar] 'to inhale, to inspire'
          ensinar [eŋsinar] 'to teach'

(Alvarez Blanco *et al.*, 1986: 34)

Gal.   inmerecido [iŋmereθiðo] 'unwarranted'
          alumno [aluŋno] 'pupil'

(Alvarez Blanco *et al.*, 1986: 34)

There is some dissent as far as plurals in /n/ are concerned. Alvarez Blanco *et al.* and ILG state that the velar nasal is retained, data from the latter revealing that it is prevalent more in the western than in the eastern provinces (ILG, 1995: 81–87). However, Veiga Arias tends to favour an alveolar nasal articulation throughout the region:

Gal. bens [bɛŋs] 'goods'   (Alvarez Blanco *et al.*, 1986: 35;
                                ILG, 1995: 82)
     [bɛns]   (Veiga Arias, 1976: 123)

In the context of the Latin prefix IN > Gal. *en*, the nasal consonant is articulated as [ŋ]. Latin IN > Gal. *en-* may also give rise in certain dialectal varieties of spoken Galician to an epenthetic voiced velar occlusive *g*, in which case, the velar nasal consonant will be predictable in accordance with nasal assimilation rules highlighted earlier. It may also occur before paragogic /e/:

Lat. IN-ORDINE   >   Gal. engorde /eŋgɔrde/ 'slow'
                        (González & González, 1994: 16)[25]

                Gal. corazonhe /koraθoŋe/ 'heart'
                (Carballo Calero, 1968: 63; Alvarez Blanco
                                et al., 1986: 105)

Finally, as far as intervocalic position within a word is concerned, the general consensus is that [ŋ] *does* occur, albeit somewhat restrictively, and that a phonological opposition may arise with /n/ and /ɲ/:

Gal.   unha [uŋa] 'one' (fem. sing)
        que una [una] (pres.subj.) 'that he/she/you (sing.form.) unite'
                                              (Carballo Calero, 1968: 89)
        uña [uɲa] 'fingernail'   (González & González, 1994: 4)

In the mid 1990s, using the same respondents as in my earlier research into the *gheada* (see pp. 149–150), I carried out a study into the syllabification of Galician words containing nasal consonant segments by perceptual, auditory and acoustic experimentation (Beswick, 1999b). Although most of the study is extraneous to my present considerations, the perceptual study, aimed to compare written and spoken tokens, did reveal interesting data, which I shall now discuss.

The Galician target set of words included VNV patterns within a word and those over word boundaries, such as verbal diphthongs plus enclitic pronouns, verb forms in -*n* plus enclitic pronouns and the definite article, and orthographic *nn* sequences, as discussed earlier. VCV patterns were used also as a control. The respondents were required to state how they would divide them at the end of a line and to read them out loud in a slow and careful speech style. A series of Castilian phrases also was presented, containing VNV patterns within a word and over word boundaries. Once again, the aim was to establish both the syllabification and the pronunciation of the nasal consonants in context. All the tokens are found in Appendix 3.[26]

My results demonstrate that [ŋ] is generally retained for the pronunciation of Galician intervocalic and syllable-final nasal segments. However, they do not substantiate the theory that there is a correlation between a casual/formal style interpretation and ŋ/n variation in Galician. Despite the morphological rule by which the *o/a* allomorph of the definite article or atonic personal pronoun causes the phonological modification of a preceding *n* in verb forms and particles, there is a clear tendency to retain the velar nasal, even in slow, careful speech styles.[27]

Moreover, unlike the *gheada*, no conscious, overtly social constraints appear to be generally influencing the pronunciation of /N/ and hence, I would posit that no conscious sociolinguistic stigma appears to be attached to the use of the velar nasal in Galician.

Yet, it may very well be that nasal segment distribution is not totally random. For example, the percentage of respondents proffering [n] for certain Galician tokens where [ŋ] would be predicted, is proportionally higher in the younger age group. I cannot categorically claim that these are examples of underdifferentiation due to a process of degalicianisation, or that it is due to the presence of the Castilian pronunciation in urban areas, because in other instances, and with many Castilian tokens, this age group overdifferentiates the velar nasal, as is potentially the case with definite articles and personal pronouns above.[28] Nonetheless, as I have already pointed out, the lexical and structural influence of Castilian on written Galician has been well documented, so in a similar way, some form of phonetic and phonological transference phenomena, resulting in the use of [n] where [ŋ] is expected in spoken Galician, *is* theoretically possible.[29] Despite this, it is also somewhat difficult to substantiate instances where transference phenomena occur in the direction Castilian to Galician through the use of sociolinguistic criteria, given that in certain contexts, [n] is in actual fact predictable by phonetic rule. My results pertaining to the Castilian tokens are also somewhat problematical, for they indicate that due to transference phenomena, [ŋ] may be manifest as a superimposed phonetic form and, hence, supplant [n] in syllable-final nasal segments, meaning that Galician and not Castilian forms would appear to dominate in both languages. The claim that normalisation efforts have exerted an influence on the way in which such nasal tokens are articulated would be somewhat premature, as would the claim (based upon such a small sample) that a process of regalicianisation in spoken forms may be occurring as far as the younger respondents are concerned. More pertinent is the fact that when I compare this data with that pertaining to issues of status and prestige discussed later in Chapter 8, it becomes apparent that, irrespective of age group, a correlation does exist between the possibly *unconscious* use of final [ŋ] in both languages, loyalty and preference for Galician over Castilian, confidence in its use, and positive attitudes towards its future. Similarly, although the findings were more restricted, where [n] was employed in both languages, the respondents evinced a preference for Castilian over Galician, a lack of confidence in speaking Galician and total ambivalence towards its future.

Concluding Remarks

Traditionally, the *gheada* has been considered a dialectal variant found primarily in the western areas, whereas the velar nasal is found throughout the region. In certain urban scenario discussed in this chapter, the *gheada* appears to be subject to stylistic considerations, which are in turn embedded within societal attitudinal factors. Based upon the results of the majority of studies discussed above, I can justify stating that the *gheada* has no (overt) prestigious symbolic status. In other words, the marked use of the *gheada* does not appear to be emblematic as far as a *positive* Galician ethnicity is concerned. Indeed, for most of the cited studies, it would appear that the opposite may be true: its use is generally associated with a degree of subjective negativity, intimately linked to notions of how the Galician people address the issue of language status as well as their own ethnicity, a point that will be revisited in Chapter 8. However, I should introduce a note of caution here. Alvarez-Cáccamo's (1990), Kabatek's (2000) and my own studies reveal some form of association between the use of the *gheada* and local identity reinforcement strategies, functioning as solidarity mechanisms. Use of the *gheada* may not be viewed as overtly prestigious in such contexts, but neither is it disparaged, and in certain contexts, it may even be starting to symbolise a desire to convey an allegiance with non-elite communities or social groups – a covert prestige marker.

The case of the velar nasal is more complicated. Despite the fact that the Galician learnt and heard in many urban areas may be overlaid with a strongly Castilian pronunciation (Regueira Fernández, 2004), the velar nasal appears to be generally well integrated into the phonetic repertoire used by the respondents of the studies discussed in this chapter, and may also be found in the pronunciation of certain Castilian tokens. The latter could indicate a degree of overdifferentiation of the velar nasal, however, [n] also occurs in certain Galician tokens, and not always where phonetic evidence would predict its use.

Although I cannot claim that the velar nasal enjoys prestigious status since it does not appear to be utilised in this way, nonetheless, its significance as a linguistic trait of Galician does appear to be recognised. If we were to discount the more sociolinguistic data pertaining to status and prestige, then it may appear that in certain contexts, a degree of free variation between [ŋ] and [n] is in evidence. Although I do not believe that this is the case here, as the majority of respondents do not manifest the velar nasal as a salient or manipulable feature as Milroy suggests (in press) (see p. 20). However it may be that for some, the velar nasal *does* function as a socially motivated emblematic characteristic of spoken Galician, one which, given the fact that it does not typically occur in final nasal segments in Castilian, serves to differentiate Galician pronunciation from that of its larger neighbour. If this can be demonstrated, then its use would be significant, as it would reinforce the notion of a Galician linguistic identity distinct from that of the overarching Spanish one.[30]

I must stress that these conclusions are rather tentative, given the limited breadth of data available, but they may encourage further study. Nonetheless, these examples also offer some justification for my hypothesis that Galician/Castilian and Standard Galician/Dialectal Galician contact phenomena also influence issues of language status and identification strategies. This hypothesis is indispensable to my discussion of ethnic identity within Galicia in Chapters 8 and 9, where I analyse their function and relevance to the sociolinguistic setting as well as their form and structure. Before such considerations however, I turn to the impact of language planning strategies.

Part 3

Prestige and Practice: Language and Identity in Galicia

Preamble

In Part 1, I described the historical and contemporary issues regarding the evolution of Galicia, its language, its society, culture and ethnic identity, bearing in mind its close associations with both Portugal and the language of Portuguese, as well the rest of Spain and the language of Castilian Spanish. I then turned to the issue of language standardisation and policy-making. It was seen that although socio-political considerations play an important part in the ongoing debates regarding the *Normas Ortográficas e Morfolóxicas do Galego* [The Orthographic and Morphological Standards of Galician], inherent to such discussions is the issue of linguistic differentiation. To this end, Part 2 considered the linguistic homogeneity and demarcation of the western Iberian Peninsula, together with some examples of how the latter is reflected in the *Normas*. I also investigated the role of two of the more characteristic features of Galician as markers of identity.

However, no account of the use and role of the Galician language in contemporary settings would be complete without a detailed analysis of the impact on Galician society, of normalisation and normativisation methods carried out since the early 1980s. To this end, Part 3 of this book brings together the issues discussed in previous chapters in order to determine how much, if at all, recent language revitalisation and revival practices have influenced the community's perceptions regarding the roles and uses of both Galician and Castilian. I consider fieldwork carried out since the establishment of a standard language in Galicia, and I examine a wide range of data regarding general and institutional linguistic practices, as well as societal and individual uses of both the written and the spoken language. I also discuss findings pertaining to attitude towards the use of Galician and Castilian in particular contexts, as well as perceptions regarding status and prestige.

I conclude that although language use and opinions therein appear to be in a state of flux, it is nonetheless apparent that changes in the status value of Galician and an attendant modification in its application within certain contexts, may be taking place.

The final chapter reviews the main issues of the book. Pertinent issues such as the relationship between behavioural practices, attitudinal factors and issues of identity are discussed and an overview of the issues surrounding normalisation policies and planning is made, focussing in particular on the role of the written standard and the policy of *bilingüísmo harmónico*. Social and cultural implications of linguistic differentiation on ethnic identities are addressed in the context of multiple identities and, finally, I make some tentative proposals regarding the future. In doing so, I am not trying to dismiss the efforts already made since devolution. Rather, I suggest that the underlying aims and objectives of the policy and planning strategies adopted by the *Xunta* do indeed take into account the contemporary issues that minoritised communities have to deal with regarding language and ethnic identity, but, perhaps they do not go far enough.

Chapter 7

Language Planning and Language Use in Galicia

Introductory Remarks

One of the main hypotheses of this book is that linguistic policies and planning impact on the behavioural practices of language users, and that these practices are in turn a reflection of their attitudes towards the language. Accordingly, in Chapter 3, I looked at linguistic policy-making in Galicia, and in the present chapter, I outline Galician planning strategies delineated by local government legislation since the 1980s as part of the general revitalisation and revival processes that have taken place in the region. In order to evaluate the potential impact of such strategies on both use and attitude, I examine the findings of governmental and non-governmental contemporary investigations and fieldwork into L^1 variation and language competencies, and I take a brief look at generic language choice patterns. I also consider the ways in which many of the laws and decrees pertaining to language use have been integrated into the daily procedures and practices of institutions and organisations such as the education system, local authorities, and the media. I discuss the impact that an increased perception of the standard, as well as the standard itself, may have on general attitudes and opinions towards its status and general use. My particular interest here concerns the issue of whether a model of pronunciation is warranted, and if so, what impact it may have on language use. By necessity, my conclusions will be rather tentative, but I am generally optimistic that the efforts that have been made so far are a step, albeit a small one, in the right direction.

Dialectal Variation in the Spoken Language

In a bilingual setting, the revival of the intragroup, autochthonous language and the standardisation of its written form should, in theory, reinforce its status as a viable linguistic form, and in doing so, incentivise the community to employ it on a day-to-day basis. However, when the spoken form is still fragmented, and when the model for pronunciation is the intergroup language, then normalisation processes may, ultimately,

lead to the levelling of much of the existing spoken linguistic variation, paralleling to an extent the effects of transference phenomena I have commented
upon in previous chapters. Many of the characteristic traits of Galician witnessed as recently as the 1970s may now be in decline, such as the differentiation of vowel timbre and the use of the *gheada*, discussed in Chapter 6. As a
result, the contemporary language may have started to display a relatively
limited amount of internal, dialectal variation, which may account for the
tendency outlined in Chapter 5 to delineate the region into linguistic
zones rather than into dialects per se. In order to chronicle and document
some of the more important aspects of linguistic diversity still in evidence;
in the last couple of decades a dedicated team of researchers from ILG
have carried out highly meticulous language surveys throughout Galicia,
as I highlighted earlier (pp. 132–133). Their exhaustive results are detailed
within the five volumes of the *Atlas Lingüístico Galego* [The Galician Linguistic Atlas], each focussing upon a different theme: verb morphology (ILG,
1990), nonverbal morphology (1995), phonetic variation (1999), lexicon of
time and weather (2003), and lexicon of the human being (2005). As well
as contributing to the general gamut of data available to the study of the
form and structure of the Galician language, this research has also led to
the production of glossaries, dictionaries of synonyms and antonyms, and
technical and administrative word lists, all of which document in some
detail the lexical variation that is still in evidence.[1]

However, what these Linguistic Atlases cannot claim to contribute is
any worthwhile data on the impact of written standardisation practices
within the region, primarily because they generally detail spoken linguistic variation. Although the *Normas* do propose certain pronunciation
recommendations, it is doubtful whether it is the cause of any loss of
allophonic variation. Indeed, certain varieties of Galician have been
subject to a degree of linguistic transference from Castilian for over 800
years. Hence, it is more likely that any levelling is simply indicative of
further transference and, I as have already pointed out, the lack of a formalised oral form that does not rely on Castilian as its model. Even if we were
to accept that the *Normas* could have had much effect on dialectal variation,
they were only implemented to any degree in the mid 1980s, and even then,
their introduction was not consistent throughout the region. As I shall
discuss further below, the *Xunta* has a fair way to go before it is able to integrate fully the teaching and use of the standard throughout the region, so it
will be some time before any far-reaching empirical investigation into its
impact on linguistic forms, however small, can be made.

Linguistic Normalisation

Initial studies

Instead, the majority of the studies carried out since the mid-1980s have
tended to focus upon other issues, such as the role of legislative measures

in the overall distribution of Galician. It has been, and generally still is, largely unclear whether such measures have succeeded in shaping the public's attitudes to the use of Galician in contexts that, hitherto, tended to be reserved for the sole use of Castilian. Wardhaugh's unflattering observations (1987: 26–27) regarding the Galician situation during the mid to late 1980s are somewhat open to discussion given that they appear to be rather anecdotal and not based on any solid research findings. Moreover, they do not concur with the findings of ethnolinguistic studies carried out at the time.[2] Several of these studies, such as the work carried out by Rodríguez Neira (1988), demonstrate that within certain sectors of the community, changes with respect to the use of Galician were already occurring by the mid-1980s. This investigation evaluated comparative data from five studies dealing with language use by housewives, *Educación Xeral Básica* (EXB) [Basic State Education] teachers, and schoolchildren up to the age of 16.[3] His general findings, albeit somewhat indeterminate, were quietly optimistic with respect to the re-emergence of Galician in certain spheres of activity. He also concluded that overall group attitude to the use and to the promotion of Galician as the (regional) national language was generally positive as well.[4] Nonetheless, the impetus for this remains unclear, although it probably has little to do with any influence of the incipient normalisation processes themselves, and more to do with the new self-government status and a general revival of interest in the Galician language manifest in the media at this time.

Rodríguez Neira was also involved in the coordination of a highly detailed investigation of language use and attitudes towards such use in Galicia that was carried out in the 1990s (Fernández Rodríguez & Rodríguez Neira, 1994). The regional-wide survey was supported by two local government institutions, SSRAG in collaboration with the *Dirección Xeral de Política Lingüística* [the General Directorate of Linguistic Policy]. By means of a questionnaire and interview methodology, the initial large-scale study was carried out in 1992 on 38,897 Galicians, that is, on nearly 2% of the total population over the age of 16 at the time. The first volume of the *Mapa Sociolingüística de Galicia* [Sociolinguistic Map of Galicia] (1994) details the findings pertaining to the mother tongue (L^1) and language of use in the home. Some 62.4% of the people interviewed claimed Galician as their L^1, compared with 25.6% for Castilian and 11.4% who claimed to have been bilingual from childhood (1994: 39). However, when age factors were then taken into consideration, Galician was the L^1 of 81.8% of the over 65's, but only of 34.4% of the 16 to 20 year olds. Indeed, the data in Figure 7.1 indicates that some 43.35% of the younger age group (16 to 25 years old) were learning Castilian in the home as the L^1, compared to only 11.3% of the 65+ age bracket that had similar experiences in childhood (see Figure 7.1).

Despite the finding that only 63.7% of Galician L^1 speakers claimed to employ it as their primary means of communication and of a loss of

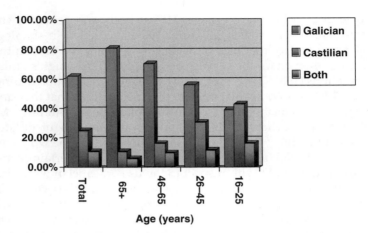

Figure 7.1 L^1 variation, by age group (Source: Fernández Rodríguez and Rodríguez Neira, 1994: 39–41)

transmission of Galician between the generations, the authors' conclusions offer a note of optimism. They counter that of the 25.6% whose L^1 was Castilian, 14.9% claimed that Galician had started to take over in their day-to-day communications (1994: 49–50). This is a small percentage and, once again, the main motivation behind such a change is rather unclear. However, this research did coincide with the period of initial enthusiasm for the language and with its institutional introduction on a wider scale, carried out through *normativización* processes.

If these figures are compared with more recent data collected by the *Instituto Galego de Estatística* (IGE) [Galician Institute of Statistics] (discussed at p. 169), it becomes clear that the situation has not vastly improved in the last decade. In particular, only 34.05% of the younger age group, born between 1974 and 1998, claimed Galician as their L^1. What is interesting, however, is that there is a slight increase in the proportion of this age group claiming to be bilingual from childhood – from 16.05% to 23.35%.

The education system

As far as the use of language in education, there is a substantial amount of literature available on issues surrounding the recuperation of Galician within the classroom. Although initial investigations were cautiously optimistic about the success of legislative measures, recent studies are at times highly critical of the local government's attempts to implement these measures and to ensure that they are carried out throughout the region. In the following account, I offer a succinct evaluation of the main issues surrounding the process of _normativización_ [normativisation], defined in Chapter 3 as 'the conscious manipulation of the linguistic corpus in order to create, reform, or restructure a language' (p. 78) to make its use 'normal' through, in this case, the education system.[5]

In accordance with Title III, Article 12:1 of the _Lei de Normalización Lingüística de Galicia_ (1983) discussed earlier, the compulsory teaching of Galician was introduced to the EXB curriculum in the 1980s. Once again, Fernández Rodríguez and Rodríguez Neira's study (1994), summarised in Figure 7.2 below, offers by far the most comprehensive data on the dominance of specific language competencies by a given sample of the population at that time.

At first glance, the findings in Figure 7.2 appear rather disappointing, for although over 90% of the total respondents claimed to understand Galician and over 80% claimed to be able to converse in it, under half claimed to be able to read it and under a third claimed to be able to write it. However, the authors point out that of those claiming to be able to read Galician, 75% were less than 26-years-old, and of those claiming to be able to write it, 90% were less than 30-years-old. This latter figure should come as no surprise, given that before the _Normas_ were implemented, the general population did not employ Galician as a written medium, one of the reasons being that it was rarely, if ever, taught as a subject in its own right (Fernández Salgado & Monteagudo, 1993: 200). What is important to highlight is that just over half of the younger age group asserted that their Galician language skills had been acquired primarily at school (Fernández Rodríguez and Rodríguez Neira, 1994: 175–178). Therefore, although this study was carried out less than a decade after the implementation of legislative measures, the

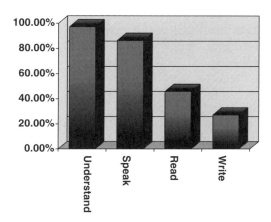

Figure 7.2 Galician language competency, by discipline (Source: Fernández Rodríguez and Rodríguez Neira, 1994: 82)

data in Figure 7.2 appear to indicate that attempts to integrate the teaching of Galician into schools did have some success. Initially at the very least, educational agendas on *Lingua e Literatura Galegas* [Galician Language and Literature] introduced in the 1980s may have encouraged some EXB teachers to begin to employ Galician within the classroom. Indeed, Rubal and Rodriguez report (in Portas, 1999: 164) that as early as 1985, some 13.9% of EXB teachers interviewed claimed to have started to use Galician in their lessons, and that, as a consequence, more younger people were learning both to read and to write in Galician.[6]

The 1991 census also offered conclusive evidence that, at least during the 1990s, Galician predominated as the L^1 in the region. In this respect, it concurs with Fernández Rodríguez and Rodríguez Neira's (1994: 39) findings even though its own figures offer substantially higher percentages: overall, some 91% of the 2,753,000 inhabitants claimed to understand Galician, and 84% claimed to use it as a spoken language.[7] The census also demonstrated that Castilian still predominated as the language of reading and writing in the early 1990s. Even in the major cities such as Santiago de Compostela, where initiatives to integrate the Galician standard into the education system were well established, the census found that less that 50% of the population (49.24%) claimed to be able to read Galician, whilst only a third (33.37%) claimed to be able to write in it. On the face of it, such findings may appear somewhat disappointing, but as I have already pointed out, before the implementation of the standard few people would habitually read in Galician, and even fewer would know how to employ a written form of the language. Given that these figures encompass the overall population and, so, do not take into account any variation according to age group, these percentages may not be as pessimistic as they first appear, although I concede that it is somewhat difficult to offer any concrete conclusions regarding their significance as far as educational agendas are concerned.

Fernández Rodríguez and Rodríguez Neira's (1994) findings at the very least reflect the overall sense of expectation regarding the recuperation of Galician that prevailed throughout the political sphere of the region in the mid to late 1980s and early 1990s. This sense of optimism may well be what led one member of the government-sponsored council, the *Conselleria da Presidencia e Administración Pública* [Council of the Public Administration] to state in 1991, that since the *Lei da Normalización Lingüística* had been established eight years previously, Galician had been able to recuperate a sense of pride and of dignity (Rodríguez Rodríguez, 1991: 7–8). Further, he added that Galician and Castilian appeared to be living in harmony, with no discrimination being suffered against either language.[8] He concluded that the recuperation of Galician was, therefore, irrefutable, and that this was all down to the establishment of a standard language.

However, such positive assertions may have been somewhat prema-ture, for other research has not tended to be as optimistic regarding the future of Galician. Further investigations carried out into the situation of the Galician language within the education system in the late 1980s, such as those made by the *Grupo de Normalización Lingüística* [The Linguistic Normalisation Group] in 1988, implied that both linguistic policy and linguistic planning procedures were rather inadequate at the time. In response to their rather pessimistic findings, the group initiated their own two proposals for action, culminating in the late 1980s in the *Modelo de Normalización Lingüística para o Sistema Educativo Galego* [The Linguistic Normalisation Model for the Galician Education System] and the *Modelo de Normalización Lingüística para o Ensino* [the Linguistic Normalisation Model for Teaching].[9] Both Models made further substantial recommendations regarding the compulsory teaching of and teaching in Galician.

Contemporary research also questions the validity of linguistic policy and planning practices, as even recently, many initiatives appear not to have been entirely successful. The most comprehensive and up-to-date data regarding the use of Galician and Castilian within the general community has been compiled by the *Instituto Galego de Estatística* (IGE) [Galician Institute of Statistics] seen above (p. 166). A local government organisation set up in the late 1990s, its function is to gather statistical information pertaining to the state of the region regarding economic, social and demographic issues. Based upon extensive interviews carried out across the region, the Institute has collated almost 3,400 reference tables on the use of both official languages in many different social, cultural and educational settings.[10] An examination of all of their data is beyond the scope of this book, but some of their most interesting findings published in 2004 pertain to the education system. The overriding general tendency appears to be that, at the turn of the century, despite the introduction of further educational initiatives to establish a standard written form of Galician in the classroom, as we shall see in continuation, Castilian still predominated. Nearly half the students stated that they received most of their classes in Castilian, as evidenced in Figure 7.3.

Figure 7.3 also demonstrates that only just over a third of schoolchildren (38%) were taught primarily in Galician. I do not want to claim that this is a discouraging percentage, but given that its use was decreed as law in the 1980s, it is clear that at least until recently, the relevant legislation has been largely being ignored in many schools throughout the region.

However, on a more positive note, further IGE data also suggests that when these educational initiatives are put into place and acted upon, the use of Galician as the primary medium of instruction has an attendant effect upon children's linguistic practices. A comparison of language use in the 5 to 16 year old age group of students taught in Galician with

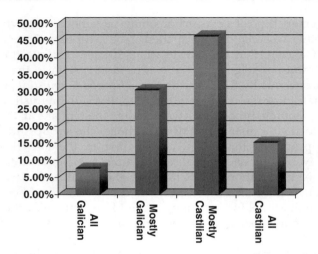

Figure 7.3 Language of classroom studies (Source: IGE, 2004)

that in the over 17 age group, illustrated in Figures 7.4 and 7.5, indicates an increasing tendency in the former group to use Galician instead of Castilian in conversations with both teachers and other pupils. Although this is in no way conclusive, it confirms that at least until the turn of the century, there was an increase in the use of Galician in the classroom, and it suggests some form of tentative correlation between the language of instruction and at the very least spoken language use at school by the pupils themselves.

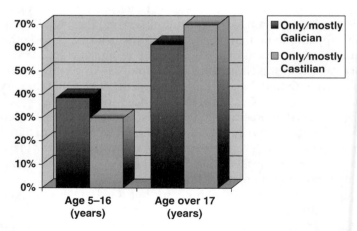

Figure 7.4 Pupils taught in Galician: Language used with classmates (Source: IGE, 2004)

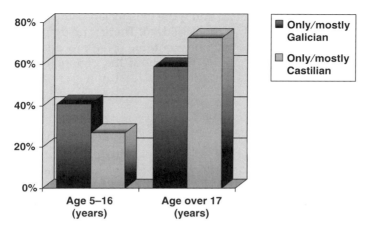

Figure 7.5 Pupils taught in Galician: Language used with teachers (Source: IGE, 2004)

Other _Xunta_-supported research offers seemingly optimistic data regarding the improvement of reading and writing language skills in the classroom during the 1990s. Mercator Education: European Network for Regional or Minority Languages and Education (2001: 3–4) compared the results of a government-funded study carried out by the _Centro de Investigaciones Sociológicas_ [Centre for Sociological Investigations] (1998) with the earlier results of the _Mapa Sociolingüística de Galicia_ [Sociolinguistic Map of Galicia] (Fernández Rodríguez _et al._, 1994).[11] The results are summarised in Table 7.1.

Once again, the data in Table 7.1 would appear to indicate that during the 1990s there was a substantial increase in Galician reading and writing skills. However, it must be borne in mind that the respondent sample in each of the years in question was different, which may have influenced the results. Mercator Education: European Network for Regional or Minority Languages and Education (2001) attributed the overall increase

Table 7.1 Comparison of Galician linguistic skills: 1991 and 1998

Year	_Understand Galician_	_Speak Galician_	_Read Galician_	_Write Galician_
1991	97.1%	86.4%	45.9%	27.1%
1998	98.4%	89.2%	68.4%	52.9%

Source: Mercator Education: European Network for Regional or Minority Languages and Education, 2001: 3–4.

in respondents who could read and write in Galician to the acquisition of reading and writing skills by schoolchildren. There is no doubt that this is an encouraging sign, but it will only continue if the process of linguistic normalisation progresses rapidly throughout the region. The IGE data in Figure 7.3 (p. 170) demonstrates that at least until very recently, this was patently not the case.

Political debate and the PNL

Political opposition has claimed, perhaps unsurprisingly, that failures in the implementation and reinforcement of current legislation are due to a lack of leadership and direction within the *Partido Popular de Galicia* (PP) [Galician Popular Party], the political party in power until June 2005. Certain institutional organisations, such as the *Consello da Cultura Galega* [the Council for Galician Culture], a legislative body established to promote the cultural aspects of Galician life, also recognises the potential shortcomings of recent legislation. In a meeting on linguistic policy in 1999, they concluded that the few advances made to bring the issue of language into the public arena were more than offset by many failures regarding the progress of linguistic normalisation.

Observers who ostensibly have no direct connection with the political machinations of the region also claim that there are inherent weaknesses within the normalisation process. In the late 1990s, Domínguez Salgado *et al.* (1999) recommended the creation of an organisation responsible for the design and execution of normalisation programmes throughout Galicia so that local councils and other community institutions could get involved.[12] Other criticisms have been more vehement. Oliveira's 2004 article in the online newspaper *Galicia Hoxe* states that the *Xunta* has failed to produce a set of workable and feasible linguistic education policies.[13] The basis for Oliveira's assertions lies in his examination of *Decreto* 247/1995 (modified by *Decreto* 66/1997) as a precursor to the *Plano Xeral de Normalización Lingüística* (PNL; also known as the PXNL) [General Plan for the Linguistic Normalisation of the Galician Language], ratified in September 2004 and made public on the 22 of January 2005.[14] I will now look at each of these in turn.

The culmination of other decrees of the early 1990s, *Decreto* 247/1995 was intended to clarify and enhance recommendations set out by *Lei* 3/1983 regarding the curriculum of infant and pre-school, primary, secondary and *bachillerato* (pre-university) education. For example, Article 4, Point 1 expands upon the 1983 legislation by prescribing the use of the L^1 of the majority of children in the class as the teaching medium at nursery and infant (pre-school) school. It also prescribes the same in initial primary school stages, whilst at the same time, ensuring that pupils receive oral and written knowledge of the 'other' official language, whichever that may be:

Artigo 4°

1. - Na etapa de educación infantil e no primeiro ciclo de educación primaria os profesores e profesoras usarán na clase a lingua materna predominante entre alumnos e alumnas, terán en conta a lingua ambiental e coidarán que adquiran de forma oral e escrita o coñecemento da outra lingua oficial de Galiza, dentro dos límites proprios da correspondente etapa ou ciclo.

Decreto 247/95

[Article 4

1. - At pre-school level and in the first years of primary school, teachers will use in class the mother tongue that prevails among the pupils, taking into account the language that is predominant in their local environment and making sure that they acquire oral and written skills in the other official language of Galicia, within the appropriate limits of the stage or course].

Decree 247/95
http://www.cig-ensino.com/descargas/00455.pdf

Despite the rewording, Oliveira believes that Article 4 does little to clarify the earlier legislation. His argument centres on the fact that the use of Galician as the language of instruction is never mentioned explicitly, and he claims that the wording is deliberately vague. Based on this legislation, it would appear that if the L^1 of the majority of pupils is Castilian, then at this level, they could only come into contact with Galician as a subject, rather than as the language of instruction for other subjects.

Oliveira is also concerned with Article 5:

Artigo 5°

1. Na educación secundaria obrigatoria impartirase en galego a área de ciencias sociais (xeografía e historia) e a área de ciencias da natureza.
2. Das materias optativas impartiranse en galego as de ciencias medio ambientais e da saúde e, se é o caso, a optativa ofertada polo centro.[15]

Decreto 247/95

[Article 5

1. In secondary education, the social science subjects (geography and history) and natural science subjects will be taught in Galician.
2. Of the optional subjects, environmental studies and health sciences will be taught in Galician, as will other optional subjects offered by each individual School.]

Decree 247/95[16]

Article 5 clearly stipulates that for older primary school and secondary school pupils, the language of instruction should be Galician for at least some subjects. However, Oliveira believes that it has been possible to ignore such directives because they are not enforced strongly enough by the legal system. Whether or not this is due to some form of ideological or political resistance against what the *reintegracionista* Freixeiro Mato (1997: 142–143) has termed 'the imposition' of the language in the education system is difficult to quantify, but once again, it is clear that it is somewhat difficult to keep politics out of the frame.

In a similar way, when the Partido Popular [Popular Party] were in power, the academic María Pilar García Negro was extremely vociferous regarding what she perceived as government ineffectuality regarding *Decreto* 247/95. In her recent book on linguistic rights (García Negro, 2000), she levels a tirade of criticisms at the authorities who were in power at the time, citing 'unacceptable delays' in the enforcement of the decree (2000: 45–48). Her criticism of the *Xunta's* competence extends to what she considers a failure to implement fully and competently this legislation (2000: 67–69). Viewed by García Negro as more declarative than prescriptive, her claim is that legislation has had little impact on its status and standing, even though it may have succeeded in conceding language rights. Official public and political institutions still view Galician as a regional language, and legislation has not been able to determine how such institutions apply legal considerations regarding its official use in their own organisations.

Undoubtedly, García Negro's more emotive comments are politically charged, due in no small part to her long-standing links with the opposition party to the PP government (at least until the elections of 2005), the *Bloque Nacionalista Galego* (BNG) [Galician Nationalist Party].[17] Nonetheless, she does make a valuable point: if the education authorities do not thoroughly enforce linguistic normalisation, supported by investment and promotion programmes of the *Xunta*, then Galician will not be integrated fully into schools as the language of instruction.

Recent legislation, such as that of the *Plano Xeral de Normalización Lingüística* (PNL), has made a tacit attempt to disengage from the political deliberations surrounding linguistic normalisation processes, although such issues can never be viewed from a purely impartial perspective. Nonetheless, in his preamble, the former President of the *Xunta de Galicia*, Manuel Fraga Iribarne, outlines its general objectives thus:

[...] este Plan de Normalización está orientado, no seu conxunto, a informar e a poñer en práctica unha serie de medidas que permitan a recuperación de falantes, unha maior dignificación da lingua, e a súa asunción con naturalidade, sen ningún tipo de imposicións. O galego, lingua propia de Galicia, como establecen a Constitución e mailo Estatuto, non pode ser utilizado como un instrumento político nin como arma partidaria. A nosa fala constitúe o cerne central da nosa identidade, o alento e a alma do pobo galego, e como tal, debemos traballar todos moi unidos e na mesma dirección. A defensa do galego é algo moi serio e debe levarse a cabo sen falsidades nin demagoxias baratas.

(2005: 9)

[...] [In its entirety, the intention of this Normalisation Plan is to communicate and implement a series of measures that will provide for a recovery in the number of Galician speakers, will generate more respect for the language, and will encourage speakers to use the language naturally, without any restrictions. Galician, the autochthonous language of Galicia, as established by the Constitution and the Statute of Autonomy, should be used neither as a political tool nor as an instrument to support political bias. Our language is the mainstay of our identity, the heart and soul of the Galician people, and as such, we must all work together towards the same goals. The defence of the Galician language is an extremely serious undertaking and must be carried out without deceit or shameful attempts at demagogy].

Moreover, and perhaps unsurprisingly given his political allegiances, the former Minister for Education, Celso Currás, has welcomed the Plan as *unha ferramenta básica para a supervivencia do idioma* [an essential tool for the survival of the language] (Eiré & Valverde, 2005: 1). In principle, it is the first time since the *Lei* of 1983 that such a plan has received tentative support from certain political parties of both the left and right. The result of some years of investigation, the final version of the PNL incorporates many of the suggestions proposed by the *Consello da Cultura Galega* [Council for Galician Culture] and its main objective appears to be the implementation of a thorough and concerted promotion of the Galician language in order to overturn what is perceived as the age-old inferiority complex. This is to be achieved by introducing changes in the social behaviour of speakers, such as encouraging people to use Galician outside their intragroup environment, in other and more influential sectors of society, and persuading parents to pass on their use of spoken Galician to their children. In its preliminaries, the PNL offers a comprehensive diagnosis of the Galician education system to date, and offers suggestions as to how improvements could be made. For example, one of its main suggestions has been that pupils in compulsory education should receive at least 50% of their instruction in Galician.

The general implementation of the Plan was due mid-2005, although this also coincided with a change of local government. Despite the initial enthusiasm, criticism was quick to follow its publication in January 2005. Regueira Fernández (2006: 70) has pointed out the limitations of the Plan, in that its aims are far too modest and it has not been afforded the necessary resources it needs in order to carry out even these objectives. Moreover, he agrees with Eiré and Valverde (2005: 3) that it does little to clarify how it will achieve its aims (2005: 3). However, the general consensus is still cautiously optimistic, although any far-reaching implications or results will not be apparent for some time.

Bilingüísmo limpo e harmónico

One of the more contentious issues vociferously opposed by García Negro (2000: 66) and members of other regional nationalist political parties has been that of *bilingüísmo limpo e harmónico* [clean, harmonious bilingualism], generally referred to as *bilingüísmo harmónico*. This vision was initially promoted and advocated by Manuel Regueiro Tenreiro, the former Director General of *Política Lingüística* within the *Xunta*, and constituted the main thrust of linguistic policy of the right-wing *Partido Popular* (PP) [Popular Party] from the early 1980s until their defeat in the June 2005 governmental elections. Despite opposition to its aims, the present coalition, comprising the PP, *Partido Socialista de Galicia* (PSdeG-PSOE) [Galician Socialist Party] and *Bloque Nacionalista Galego* (BNG) [Galician Nationalist Bloc], continues to endorse this linguistic policy, hence its importance to a contemporary analysis of revitalisation processes in Galicia.

As I have already highlighted (pp. 84–90), the role of language as a clear expression of Galician identity has been a fundamental component of regional nationalist political rhetoric since the early 1980s. Even legislation passed by the PP government when the *Lei de Normalización Lingüística de Galicia* [Linguistic Normalisation Law of Galicia] was ratified in 1983 (see p. 73), appears to endorse this agenda. The preamble makes it clear that the Galician language is the *núcleo vital da nosa identitade [. . .]: é a maior e máis orixinal creación colectiva dos galegos, é a verdadeira forza espiritual que lle dá unidade interna á nosa comunidade* [vital nucleus of our identity [. . .] it is the most important and most original collective creation of the Galician people; (it is) the true spiritual force that gives internal unity to our community] (On www at http://galego.org/lexislacion/ xbasica/lei3-83.html).

However, whether this declaration is truly borne out by the objectives of *bilingüísmo harmónico* is somewhat unclear. Regueiro Tenreiro views the linguistic situation in Galicia as unique, in that he considers *both* Galician and Castilian as community languages and as such, equally representative of the collective identity (Regueiro Tenreiro, 1999: 56). He contends that social bilingualism should prevail in Galicia, where speakers are freely able to choose which language they wish to use, and where both languages can coexist harmoniously within society. In structure, it is reminiscent to an extent to Fishman's definition of bilingualism with no diglossia (see p. 15), for it does not imply the maintenance and preservation of a general diglossic framework of Galician and Castilian, although see my further comments below. Yet, to the frustration of regional nationalists, nor does it imply the promotion of Galician as the language of common use for all functions. Rather, *bilingüísmo harmónico* appears to have been devised in order to avoid any type of linguistic or social conflict that may arise from competition for contextual functions.

This is particularly apparent in PNL doctrine. *Bilingüísmo harmónico* is an intrinsic feature of the PNL, and its vision was summed up by Celso Currás as *manter unha lingua viva nunha situación de igualdade entre ambos os dous idiomas (galego e castelán) sen que se estabeleza unha competencia entre eles* [the maintenance of a living language in a situation of equality between both languages (Galician and Castilian) without any competition between them being established] (Eiré & Valverde, 2005). Although this stipulation of *bilingüísmo harmónico* does not fully equate with the typical wording of revitalisation policies normally initiated by minority language communities within multilingual societies, its sentiments regarding the potential outcome are similar. However, when a minoritised language undergoes revitalisation, any increased use will have some impact on the other language, particularly if the minoritised language starts to acquire new contexts. In this way, linguistic competition is generally considered a plausible outcome.[18]

So the general aims of *bilingüísmo harmónico* appear to be to attempt to develop and promote Galician, and when potential conflictual situations arise, to simply do nothing and let 'nature take its course'. This is how the PP, and others, have justified its implementation. It is not entirely clear however, how this is to be achieved. One possible interpretation generally espoused by detractors of the policy, is that despite its stated aims, language use and survival in Galicia will ultimately be determined by 'the survival of the fittest'. Thus, this is somewhat in line with Fishman's earlier contentions (1989) that a lack of diglossic demarcation is not a stable scenario and as such, will lead to the dominance of one of the languages. Eiré and Valverde (2005: 3) contend that the main implication of *bilingüísmo harmónico* is that Galician and Castilian are by definition in conflict, since they compete for contextual use within the same community precisely because they are *not* assigned rigid functions. In other words, their interpretation is that the implementation of this policy has meant that a degree of competition may well be occurring between these languages, *despite* the fact that either can be used in any context. Thus, the harmonious maintenance of functions implicit to *bilingüísmo harmónico* may not be adhered to.

Despite the many reservations levelled at the policy, I would contend that at the moment, no viable alternatives to *bilingüísmo harmónico* have been proffered. The claim that monolingualism in Galician is the only viable outcome of the Galician situation does not take into account the ongoing pressure on the social and linguistic processes of Galicia since devolution, leading to a concomitant shift in language requirements. It is also rather idealistic when this claim is rooted in political bias. As we have seen, the desire to achieve a monolingual nation is at the heart of the vitriolic and vociferous opposition to the policy in Galicia itself, primarily by left-wing political entities such as the *Fronte Popular Galega* (FPG) [Galician Popular Front]. Their assertion that the only way for Galicia to survive is for the region to become monolingual does not take into account the pervading social and political situation, nor the historical context (see my earlier comments, pp. 87–90). Irrespective of the more far-reaching political implications of total independence from Spain, any linguistic policy in Galicia should take into account the growing number of bilingual speakers, so a claim to monolingual status in favour of Galician is untenable.

Moreover, as Romaine has pointed out (1995: 37), the strict compartmentalisation of language through domain segregation can affect a society's perceptions regarding the value and prestige of that language, for it implies that certain languages are somehow better or more valuable than others. By sidestepping this, *bilingüísmo harmónico* is a valiant, if somewhat idealistic, attempt to rid the sociolinguistic milieu in Galicia of prejudices regarding the use of Galician in certain contexts. I will return to these points in my concluding chapters.

The data I have presented so far in this chapter tends to uphold the contention that the local government has deliberately adopted a somewhat 'softly softly' approach to the implementation of planning processes – or what Regueira Fernández terms a *laisser faire* attitude (2006: 85) – simply because it wants to prevent competition between the two languages in question.[19] Furthermore, there is evidence that when in power, the PP did not deliver what they promised regarding the diffusion of Galician through normalisation processes. At the very least, our earlier positive observations regarding the number of EXB teachers starting to use Galician may *not* have been entirely borne out over the last two decades, for the following reasons: knowledge of and linguistic competence in Galician is, in theory, a pre-requisite for all primary and secondary school teachers, but in practice, it appears to be more of a bonus or advantage than an unequivocal requirement. The *Dirección Xeral de Política Lingüística* (DXPL) [General Directorate of Linguistic Policy], as I have already discussed, is responsible for the promotion of Galician language courses throughout the region, and by 2001, about 23,000 teachers had already attended these courses. Moreover, 80% of these teachers felt that they were competent enough to teach other subjects in Galician (Mercator Education: European Network for Regional or Minority Languages and Education, 2001: 19–20).

However, there has been a certain amount of resistance in some quarters to what has been perceived as the bureaucratic machinations of the *Xunta*. Freixeiro Mato's comment (1997: 142–143) that some teachers view the introduction of teaching in and of Galician as an imposition seems highly subjective. It is, nonetheless, the case that some have been put off starting or even completing the language courses by the theoretical requirement that they pass the course exam before being formally allowed to utilise the language in the classroom, despite the fact that in practice this is not enforced to any degree. Even so, this does not really explain why there has been a decline in the number of teachers attending such language courses over the last few years.

I suggest that whereas in the 1980s, the large numbers of attendees were from Galicia itself, teachers recently attending these courses have mainly been from outside the region – hence the (theoretical) mandatory exam success. Therefore, and given the somewhat haphazard enforcement practices that have been documented, it may well be that young teachers from the region itself feel that they have no need of such courses, they themselves being mother tongue speakers of Galician or having successfully studied the language at school. If the latter case is valid, then it marks at least a degree of success in the institutionalisation of Galician over the last two decades. It may even be commensurate with a slight increase in the number of classes being taught in Galician, but I must emphasise that this is indeed very slight. The wide-ranging investigation into the use of Galician in compulsory and non-compulsory education carried out at the turn of the century by the AS-PG *Asocioción Sócio-Pedagóxica Galega* [the Galician Socio-Pedagogic Association] and the CIG-Ensino *Confederación Intersidical Galega do Ensino* [The Galician Inter-Union Confederation – Educational Branch] has not produced encouraging results, at least for certain sectors. The aim of this survey – a huge undertaking involving 100,000 students – was to evaluate the degree to which linguistic normalisation and the requirements of *Decreto* 247/95 had been initiated in state education. As far as the compulsory sectors are concerned, although nearly 80% of the latter stages of primary education do meet the legal requirements for teaching in Galician, some 91.5% of pre-school and initial stage primary education schools and 77.1% of secondary schools do not (Villar, 2001).[20]

There seems to be a general and pervading lack of commitment to the use of Galician by much of the teaching profession, irrespective of whether or not they have completed the requisite course and language proficiency test. I would hazard that this has been allowed to occur because implementation measures intended to secure the instructional role of Galician in compulsory education have not been effective. This means that the teaching of the majority of subjects other than the Galician language is still carried out in Castilian. Moreover, as I pointed out earlier (pp. 135–136), there are important issues to resolve regarding the model of pronunciation that these teachers acquire themselves and ultimately, pass on to their pupils. Even when they teach or use Galician as the language of instruction, teachers who are from regions other than Galicia will have had little, if any, exposure to the Galician spoken outside of institutional practices. Even teachers from Galicia itself may have been raised in Castilian, or been taught Galician at school with a model of pronunciation based largely on that of Castilian.

As far as post-compulsory education is concerned, the situation is somewhat similar. Oliveira (2004) examines the success of present legislation regarding use of the Galician language in the region's three universities. Although all three institutions stipulate that Galician has official status alongside Castilian within their malls, and although the entrance examinations have included a Galician language test equally weighted with Castilian since 1988, regional legislation does not require that Galician be employed as the language of instruction. At the University of Santiago de Compostela, for example, for many years a vociferous supporter of and even contributor in the restoration of the Galician language in all walks of life, around 80% of lecturers do not regularly employ Galician in their courses (Rodríguez Neira & López, 1998). However, more recently the education authorities have recognised this shortfall and have stipulated that an average of 50% of university courses are to start employing Galician over the next 10 years (Oliveira, 2004), so the situation may start to improve.

In order to conclude this section, I return to the issues surrounding the teaching of Galician as a subject in compulsory education. Nowadays, nearly all primary and secondary schools teach Galician as a subject, and studies carried out since the late 1990s appear to demonstrate a correlation between the increase in Galician language classes and the acquisition of reading and writing skills. For example, in Table 7.1 above we saw that when Mercator Education: European Network for Regional or Minority Languages and Education (2001: 3–4) compared the results of two studies on Galician reading and writing skills, they concluded that there had been an improvement in the acquisition of both skills in the 1990s. Further and more recent IGE data, as illustrated in Figure 7.6, appears to concur. Although Castilian still predominates as the habitual written language, there appears to be a noteworthy increase commensurate with age, in the number of respondents employing Galician in this way – from less than 14% of the 30 to 49 year age group to nearly 25% of the 5 to 29 year age group.

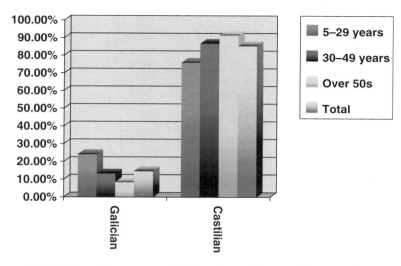

Figure 7.6 Written language of habitual use, by age (Source: IGE, 2004)

However, the ultimate objective of Decreto 247/95 has been that all students should leave school with an equal knowledge of both languages. Therefore, whilst an increase in reading and writing skills is laudable, it does not equal linguistic competence. Back in the late 1990s, the University of Vigo carried out a study into the potential correlation between language competences and mother tongue variability, the results of which are illustrated in Table 7.2.

The conclusion was that whilst children with Castilian as their mother tongue tended to acquire the receptive linguistic skills of reading and writing more competently than their Galician mother tongue peers, their acquisition of oral skills was hampered somewhat. More recent

Table 7.2 Galician language competence in schoolchildren, by mother tongue variability (Study carried out by the University of Vigo (1997–1999)

Linguistic Skill	Mother tongue Galician: Competence in Galician	Mother tongue Spanish: Competence in Galician
Understand	99.3%	83.5%
Speak	97.9%	30.3%
Read	40.1%	45.1%
Write	22.2%	24.3%

Source: Mercator Education: European Network for Regional or Minority Languages and Education, 2001: 11–13).

data are not yet available, and it must be remembered that this situation may have already changed. Nonetheless, these data imply the general tenet that even when the teaching of Galician advances reading and writing skills, it does not necessarily do the same for oral skills. In this, I wholeheartedly endorse the research of the Mercator Project. They make the point that language classes cannot contribute sufficiently to what is considered a 'normal' use of the Galician language (in line with the aims of *bilingüísmo harmónico*) when more wide-ranging normalisation efforts are totally insufficient (2001: 10); and, I would add, when Galician is not employed as the language of instruction: recall the earlier Figure 7.4 (p. 170) data, where I suggested that there was a correlation between the language of instruction and the pupils' spoken language use at school. Indeed, the only children who can truly be considered productive bilinguals are those who have Galician as their L^1 and who have been initially educated either with Galician as the language of instruction or with both languages as such. If this use of the spoken language is to be expanded, then normalisation practices must be also, and the issue of pronunciation must also be addressed. Educational institutions may often be a valuable tool in achieving short-term aims, but that is not always the case. Moreover, as I have already pointed out, in Galicia they have generally not been enforced thoroughly and quickly enough.

Moreover, there has to be some form of long-term attitudinal shift outside the school gates regarding the prestige value of speaking in Galician. Only then may the language gain any ground where it needs to – within the daily lives of Galician families. Before I consider such uses in Chapter 8, I will now take a brief look at language use by other Galician institutional organisations.

The communications industry

As I have already highlighted (see p. 91 and in particular, my comments on p. 152), another important outlet for the widespread promotion of the Galician language is the communications industry. *Radio Popular de Vigo* and *Radio Popular de Lugo* have been broadcasting sporadically in Galician since the 1950s, with regular broadcasts in Galician since the 1970s. There are also some 30 or so local radio stations broadcasting many, if not all of their programmes, in Galician although their audience numbers are somewhat limited. However, in the 1980s a public radio station, *Radio Galega*, was introduced broadcasting 24 hours a day exclusively in Galician to an audience of some 152,000 listeners. Furthermore, the regional centre of *Radio Nacional de España*, the state broadcasting authority, airs certain programmes in Galician on the two stations they operate (Euromosaic, 2005: 6).[21]

Another official media network introduced in the 1980s is the regional television channel, TVG (*Televisión Galega*), which now broadcasts 24 hours a day, seven days a week in Galician and is also currently setting up joint agreements with the television channels of other self-governing regions regarding the possibility of satellite transmission. [22] The commercial channels do not offer programmes in Galician, but an additional 20 hours is provided by the regional centre of the state television channel, *Televisión Española* (Eurolang.net, 2005). The PNL advocates that this number of hours be increased substantially in the future.

One of the best ways to connect with the younger members of a community and to provoke a change in their attitude or behaviour is via the media. In the afternoons, TVG (and TVE) broadcasts a successful animated show entitled *Shin Chan*, aimed at promoting the use of Galician amongst their younger viewers, although the much vaunted television club for children, the *Clube Xabarín*, is broadcast no longer. The PNL would like TVG to extend their programming aimed at pre-school children so that they can be initiated into the Galician language environment (Eiré & Valverde, 2005).

As far as the print media is concerned, until 1994 and the launch of the Galician language paper *O Correo Galego* by the Castilian-speaking *Correo Gallego* group, there was no daily newspaper published entirely in Galician. In 2003, *Correo Gallego* was replaced by *Galicia Hoxe*, with estimates regarding its particular circulation varying from under 4,000 to nearly 10,000 copies daily. However, by far the most widely read news paper is still the Spanish language La Voz de Galicia, with more than 500,000 readers daily, followed by *El Correo Gallego*, with some 95,000 readers daily. Very few articles in either newspaper are written in Galician, although the PNL want these main daily newspapers to be encouraged to increase the use of Galician in their pages to a minimum of 30% in the future (Eiré & Valverde, 2005). A number of other, specialist periodicals and magazines on culture, economics, the environment and so on, are published in Galician, such as the weekly *A Nosa Terra*. However, the nature of their content dictates that circulation figures are extremely limited.[23]

A huge effort to promote and disseminate literature and other books written in Galician has been ongoing since the mid 1980s, aided by the funding initiatives and subsidies offered by the *Xunta*, particularly for the publication of educational materials. As a result, their number saw a huge increase in the 80s and 90s, from 354 in 1987 to 760 in 1992 (Euromosaic, 2005: 6). So too, has the number of publishing houses advocating the use of Galician in the work they publish and who are endorsing the translation into Galician of many famous books from other countries, such as J.K. Rowling's 'Harry Potter' series. As I discussed in Chapter 3, *Editorial Galaxia* still leads the way, closely followed by *Xerais, Sotelo Blanco, Ir Indo, Edicións do Castro*, and so on.

As far as the performing arts and public entertainment industry are concerned, progress has been somewhat slow but consistent. The *Xunta* has made funding available and has even completely financed some of the eight full-length Galician language feature films produced since 1987 (Euromosaic, 2005: 6), although they are not generally widely distributed. Many foreign films have also been dubbed, and the PNL encourages more of this in the future (Eiré & Valverde, 2005). In addition, the theatre is the sector of cultural production where the greatest progress has been made as far as introducing normalisation policies are concerned. The *Centro Dramático Galego* [Galician Drama Centre] was created in the 1980s and receives a certain amount of public funds to finance festivals and shows in Galician and primarily, about the Galician culture. Indeed, 99% of theatrical endeavours are now in Galician (www.galego. org). Museums, libraries and cultural centres, especially in the larger towns and cities, often promote and display exhibitions of works of art pertaining to Galician culture, and almost always offer explanations and descriptions in both Galician and Castilian. Finally, although the extremely popular band *Os Resentidos* has now disbanded, groups such as *Milladoiro*, *Heredeiros da Crus* and *Dios que te crew*, all of whom enjoy a substantial local following, generally sing in Galician. Their music ranges from traditional folk music and ballads to more contemporary rock and pop and rap, and their lyrics often centre around what has been dubbed the 'Galician situation'; that is, regionalist, cultural, and even linguistic issues. Again, the PNL encourages more of the same in the future (Eiré & Valverde, 2005).

It is certainly true that these measures appear to be a step in the right direction. However, it remains questionable as to how far the use of Galician as the communicative medium is able to exert any kind of influence on the population in general. Television and radio channels that broadcast exclusively in Galician continuously fail to capture the public's attention and allegiance, and this may help explain the rather limited viewing figures noted earlier. Furthermore, the increase in coverage of satellite and digital television has introduced a far greater selection of channels, both in Castilian and in other languages to the region, except for the most outlying reaches. Hence, even if such modes of communication were able to encourage more people to speak Galician on a daily basis, it is extremely debatable whether this would persuade them to adopt the standard written form as well.

As far as the press is concerned, the major publishing houses *Galaxia* and *Xerais* employ the officially sanctioned standard, but the readership of Galician language publications is still limited. Consequently, the vast majority of the older population at the very least, rarely read a standardised form – or indeed, any form of Galician. At one time, many secondary school teachers and certain other sectors of the press (depending on political allegiance) employed the unofficial but now defunct AS-PG version of the written standard, despite legislation advocating the use of the *Normas*. However, this is no longer the case. The demise of the AS-PG standard has meant that there is no longer any viable alternative to the recently revised official written norm, which, as we have seen (see my comments, pp. 129–134), *has* taken into consideration a number of the demands advocated by the less radical *reintegracionistas*.

Once again, one of the main issues regarding the use of Galician in the public domain is that of the largely Castilian model of pronunciation currently dominating the media and entertainment industry. Santamarina (1995: 81) makes the important point that pronunciation is learnt by imitation. Fishman's GIDS scale (p. 48) suggests that formal educational practices are not necessarily the best place to promote a written standard, a point I will return to later. However, I would add in this context that this might also be the case for the model of pronunciation.

As we saw in the case of teachers, when Galician television and radio programmes were initially aired, there were no centres where broadcasters could train in the language. Although linguistic assessors from the University of Santiago were employed from the beginning, they had little impact on the pronunciation of Galician, focusing instead on the veracity of written texts (Kabatek, 2000: 112–113). Indeed, many broadcasters are still either not from the region itself or are Castilian L[1] speakers from the urban areas. Like actors and dubbing artists, they are required to learn the standard form of Galician in order to become presenters, newsreaders, or reporters. However, some find it difficult not to employ an ostensibly Castilian phonetic system, intonation pattern as well as other prosodic features, and once the camera is switched off, they may revert once again to speaking in Castilian. This simply exacerbates the problem of the oral form of the language since instances of underdifferentiation (pp. 100–101) are rife on the television and on the radio, as are non-Galician word and sentence stress patterns. Moreover, even if a prestige model of pronunciation based on Galician forms were implemented, as is advocated by SSRAG (2003: 186), it does not necessarily mean that broadcasters, actors, and even teachers would adopt it.[24]

The use of such a model of pronunciation has also far-reaching implications for the viewers and listeners themselves, particularly those who are still relatively isolated from the urban conurbations and who still have strong dialectal accents. Such speakers are likely to view the use of such a form as somewhat conflictual and even discriminatory. It is not their language – it is the language of others, those who live in the towns and cities. Hence, it is clear that the diffusion of a model of pronunciation through television and radio does not necessarily mean that viewers and listeners will adapt their linguistic practices, even if it is feted as the prestige model, as Saladino has found in Italy (1990).

We have seen earlier that the local government is ultimately responsible for normalisation and normativisation practices in the region, but until now it has been largely unclear whether they themselves employ Galician on a regular basis. In order to evaluate the impact of linguistic policies on the policy-makers themselves, I now take a review briefly at the use of the Galician standard by local authorities and public services.

Local authorities and public services

Lei 5/1988, passed on the 23rd of June of the same year, was intended to reinforce the stipulations set down by the *Lei de Normalización Lingüística* in 1983 regarding Galician as the official language of use by local government and other local authorities. Indeed, it is apparent that within the central offices of the *Xunta*, Galician is employed almost exclusively for both oral and written purposes, and the majority of politicians and local representatives employ Galician in debates of the regional parliament (Euromosaic, 2005: 5). Moreover, as I have seen earlier, legislation also states that as Galician is an official language of the region, members of the public have the right to employ the language in their dealings with local authorities and administrative bodies, such as the local judicial system should they wish to do so.[25] Consequently, it follows that regional public officials and civil servants should have a sound knowledge of Galician in order to be able to carry out their public duties. This is often cited as a criterion for employment within the region's institutions, and to this end, such employees are offered specialised language training (Euromosaic, 2005: 5). However, although many municipal authorities appear to employ Galician for their local administrative functions, most regional offices dealing with collective state administration employ Galician only sporadically.

Many official documents tend to be written in both languages. Written notices are generally in either Castilian or both languages, as are public hoardings and billboards. However, the *Lei de Normalización Lingüística* stipulates that the official language of place names should be Galician (Euromosaic, 2005: 5). Although it this is indeed the practice, in some areas place names have been vandalised, the Galician name being spray painted over and replaced by the Castilian version.

The recent PNL adds that businesses and commerce should be encouraged to promote the use of Galician within their workforce. Finally, the use of Galician should also be promoted in the Church, in tourism, in social services, and associated institutions (Eiré & Valverde, 2005). Although this does appear to be occurring, it is not yet as widespread as was originally intended, mainly because the authorities have not yet insisted on compliance, particularly by the Church.

Concluding Remarks

This chapter is somewhat a counterpart to Chapter 3, in that its main thrust has been to examine the implications of linguistic policy-making and planning in Galicia. Based upon my earlier contentions that education may be of prime importance to the survival of a minoritised language in such a context, I have focussed on legislation pertaining to such and specifically regarding its potential impact on L^1 variation and the acquisition of language skills. In addition, I have tried to evaluate the potential repercussions on the way people perceive their language and formulate notions of prestige and status. These central themes form the basis of my hypothesis that linguistic policies and planning impact on the behavioural practices of language users, and that these practices are in turn reflected in their attitudes towards the language. What is specifically important to point out is that the data examined comes from both governmental and non-governmental studies. In this way, I would hope that my account offers a balanced view, rather than one potentially influenced by other considerations.

My account of legislation and its impact on language use by the media and local authorities and institutions, has offered evidence that Galician is being increasingly used in such scenario, and based on these findings, I am generally optimistic that the efforts that have been made so far have been worthwhile. However, I would still question whether the media in particular can play any significant role in the diffusion of the language, and for this reason, I would contend that a more detailed analysis is warranted. Nonetheless, the implications of the findings in this chapter for language choice within bilingual settings should not be underestimated. What I do maintain is that the model of pronunciation currently heard on many television and radio programmes, based to a certain extent on Castilan forms, does influence the perceptions and attitudes of certain sectors of society viewers and listeners, for they will retain dialectal forms and may feel discriminated against. The next chapter takes these investigations one step further, by evaluating the attitudinal and functional features of language choice in the bilingual setting.

Chapter 8
Societal and Individual Roles of Galician

Introductory Remarks

In the previous chapter, I outlined Galician policy and planning strategies delineated by local government legislation over the last 30 years, by offering a general overview of the ways in which various laws and decrees have been integrated into the daily procedures and practices of institutions and organisations such as the education system, local authorities and the media. I also considered L^1 variation and language competencies, and I briefly looked at generic language choice patterns as evidenced by contemporary investigations.

I now return to the issue of language choice. The two hypotheses pertinent here concern how linguistic policies and planning impact on the behavioural practices of language users, and how these practices are reflected in attitudes towards the language, and how despite potential changes, the sociolinguistic relationship between Galician and Castilian has not been resolved.

The present chapter is divided into two parts. In the first, I continue to examine governmental and non-governmental empirical research carried out since devolution. I consider the influence of first language acquisition on habitual language use, taking into account geographical, age and class differentiation factors. My main focus is on urban spaces and age variation, based to a large extent on the fact that the towns and cities are the hubbub of linguistic normalisation activity. As I pointed out in the Introduction (p. 2), one of this book's more original contributions is the use of an apparent time analysis to examine the use of different languages at different life stages, in order to determine whether one language is generally used more at one stage in life than another, or whether a shift in language use is actually taking place. Thus, the aim throughout is to evaluate the viability, if any, of functional demarcation, based on the premise that due to the changes that have occurred over the last few decades, there may be more than two overriding scenario now in play. The notion of bilingual communicative competence is important to this analysis, and to this end, I examine spoken proficiencies in more detail.

The second part of this chapter details my own research into the relationship between language use and attitudes therein, and the question of whether language loyalty can secure linguistic confidence. My study was principally carried out in the 1990s in the city of Santiago de Compostela and focused on the linguistic behaviour of different age groups. Once again, the issue of apparent time data becomes pertinent, as does the notion of using language change methodologies to plot language shift in Galicia.

My examination of the uses of and attitudes towards, different languages at different life stages attempts to determine whether one language is generally used more at one stage in life than another, or whether a shift in language use is taking place. My general conclusions are somewhat tentative, although I maintain an essentially optimistic view of the current sociolinguistic situation in Galicia and in particular, of the reassignment of uses and prestige values to Galician.

Language Selection and Domains of Usage

First language acquisition

One of the most striking findings unearthed by studies carried out in the 1990s (see Chapter 7, pp. 165–166) concerns first language selection. Even when the parents' L^1 is Galician, many currently appear to be making a conscious decision to raise their children in Castilian. As an example, Fernández Rodríguez and Rodríguez Neira's survey (see Figure 7.1, p. 166) demonstrates that over 73% of the 46 to 65 year old age bracket were raised speaking Galician. More than 43% of the youngest age group interviewed (16 to 25 age group) learnt Castilian in the home environment, whilst only 39% were raised exclusively in Galician (1994: 39–41). This appears to be a general pattern within minoritised groups who are about to undergo, or have just started to undergo, linguistic revitalisation, and is discussed in more detail below.[1]

Despite these findings, it would be rather naïve to believe that this situation is comparable throughout the region. Many of the earlier studies demonstrated a degree of variation in first language selection and acquisition according to the place of residence. Indeed, demarcation between the prevalent mother tongue in urban and rural areas appears to follow a distinct pattern. Once again, Fernández Rodríguez and Rodríguez Neira (1994) found that the percentage of Galician L^1 speakers was inversely related to the size of the community in question. In the larger, urban conurbations, Castilian started to predominate when parents employed it with their children, whereas in remote, rural areas, Galician was widely used as the L^1 and passed to the children as such, as demonstrated by Figure 8.1.

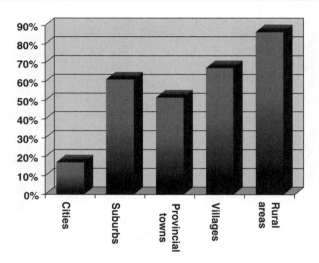

Figure 8.1. Galician as the L^1, by place of residence (Source: Fernández Rodríguez and Rodríguez Neira, 1994: 43)

This is not a new phenomenon, for historically, as I discussed in Chapter 2, the isolated rural areas had little contact with Castilian and, as a result, Galician tended to predominate in all walks of life. However, in towns and cities, the enforcement of Franco's stringent language censorship policies was pervasive. Consequently, in the largest conurbations, Castilian predominated as the L^1. However, the isolated rural areas and smaller villages were mostly cut off from the authoritarian activities of the dictatorship. Monitoring of language use within small, isolated communities and outlying districts presented a serious challenge to the authorities. As a result, Galician survived as the language of village and local community life and was passed down from generation to generation.

Although somewhat stark, the geographical demarcation of mother tongue use I have presented above is illustrative of the overall situation in the region during the 20th century, as it is generally consistent with the findings presented in Figure 8.1 above. I concede however, that this clear-cut split in L^1 acquisition did not apply to all families in all areas, a point that will be taken up now in my discussion of recent IGE data.

Most of the research cited so far in this section was carried out in the early 1990s, a time when the future of the language was still considered uncertain by many Galicians, and before any influence, albeit minor, of the *Xunta's* normalisation policies was in evidence. More recent data, such as that of IGE (2004), should be able to provide a detailed and direct comparison with earlier data regarding L^1 acquisition throughout the region. However, this is not entirely possible, as the IGE does not demarcate geographical zones by community size and configuration. Nonetheless, the IGE data does shed light on certain trends in spatial demarcation, in that it compares and contrasts tendencies within the four provinces of Galicia taken as a differentiated whole. Let us firstly consider the IGE results on intrafamily language use (Figure 8.2) and first language acquisition (Figure 8.3).

Overall, over half of parents in all but one province (Pontevedra) claim to use only Galician with their children. These figures correspond well with the data on both first language acquisition and recollections made by respondents of the language in which their parents addressed them as children. Over 30% of the respondents throughout the region also employed Castilian to some extent with their children (Figure 8.2) or were raised predominantly in it (Figure 8.3). Indeed, over 25% of the parents state that they only use Castilian with their children at the present time (Figure 8.2).

Despite the lack of a clear urban/rural breakdown, the data allows some useful observations. For historical reasons, the interior eastern provinces of Lugo and Ourense are less developed and industrialised than the coastline western provinces of A Coruña and Pontevedra. The internal migrations discussed in Chapter 2 (p. 66) were from the interior provinces of Galicia towards the coast, since these areas were more industrialised

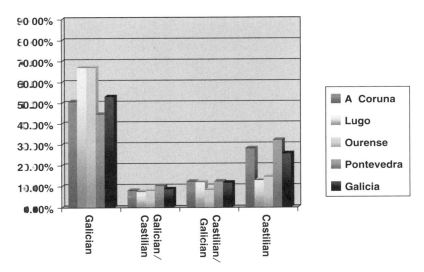

Figure 8.2. Parents and the Language they speak to their children in Galicia, by Province (Source: IGE, 2004)

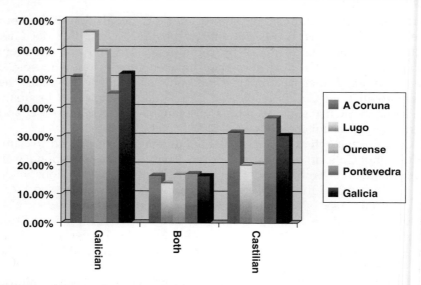

Figure 8.3. First language acquisition in Galicia, by province (Source: IGE, 2004)

and developed, and it was here that non-Galicians also tended to settle. In Lugo and Ourense, Galician predominates both as the language of home life (over 75% in both cases) and as the first language (65% and 60% respectively, compared to 20% for Castilian). In A Coruña and Ponteve-dra, by contrast, the figures for Galician drop substantially–59% and 55% respectively for the language of home life, 51% and 45% for first language acquisition.

Figures 8.2 and 8.3 consider recent first language acquisition and language use by parents to their children. In contrast, Figure 8.4 (p. 193) outlines older data on the language of childhood according to the present age of the respondent. The overall percentages for all ages indicate that some 58% were, or are, spoken to only in Galician by their parents. However, when the data is broken down, this percentage increases or decreases according to age: 77% of the over 50s, reducing to 38% of the youngest age group (5 to 29). The number of respondents raised solely in Castilian increases correspondingly (13% to 27%), but there is also a substantial increase in the number whose parents employ both languages with them.[2] Figures 8.2 and 8.3 show that throughout the provinces, bilingual language use in childhood and first language acquisition is fairly stable (17–22% and 14–17% respectively). However, the cross-age comparison in Figure 8.4 demonstrates that only 10% of the over 50 age group were raised in bilingual situations, compared to 36% of the youngest age group.

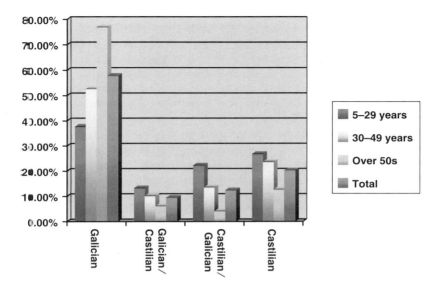

Figure 8.4. Language spoken by parents to respondents in childhood in Galicia, by age (Source: IGE, 2004)

In order to examine these trends further, I will now consider habitual spoken language and language preferences, taking into particular account any potential association between the former and the language of childhood.

Habitual language use

The research team that compiled the third volume of investigations based upon the *Mapa Sociolingüística de Galicia*, focussed upon the linguistic and sociolinguistic history of Galicia, the self-reported linguistic competence of the population and their attitudes towards language use in particular settings (Fernández Rodríguez & Rodríguez Neira, 1996). Their findings confirm the 1991 census data (see p. 168) and further IGE data (Figure 8.5, p. 194) in which the habitual language of use throughout the region was confirmed as Galician. Some 75% of the population in Fernández Rodríguez and Rodríguez Neira's study (1996) also expressed a preference for Galician in their spoken interactions.

The IGE data in Figure 8.5 also reveals a potential association between habitual language use, first language acquisition, and language use in childhood. The majority of respondents for whom Galician is their habitual language of use are concentrated in the provinces of Lugo (58%) and Ourense (52%) and throughout Galicia, habitual

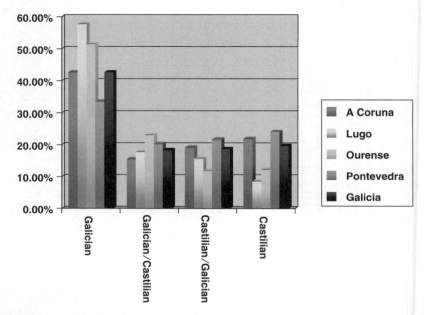

Figure 8.5. Spoken language of habitual use in Galicia, by province (Source: IGE, 2004)

bilingual language use is more prevalent (37%) than sole use of Castilian (20%).

One variable that has so far not been considered in any detail is that of class differentiation. Galician is still the majority language of use in all but the upper middle class, as demonstrated in Figure 8.6 (p. 195).

Regueira Fernández's comments (2006: 75–77) regarding the intergenerational transmission of Galician are important in this context. In the last few years, Galicia has undergone a process of accelerated urbanisation, with a consequent loss of much of the rural population. The poorer working classes, typically in the outlying areas, continue to be isolated from the social implications attached to the use of Castilian, and continue, mainly through necessity, to employ Galician in their everyday lives. However, relatives who are now located in the towns and cities are starting to be conscious of the social implications and possibilities for advancement attached to the use of Castilian, for although the social prestige of Galician has improved, the difficulties associated with a change habitual language of use should not be underestimated (SSRAG, 2003: 187–189). Hence, just as happened historically with the social elites, aspiring lower and middle class individuals and families are also beginning to relinquish the use of Galician in certain intragroup spheres of activity, paralleling to a large extent the historical situation discussed

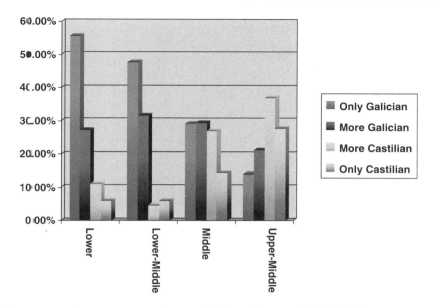

Figure 8.6. Language use, by social class (Source: IGE, 2004)

earlier in Chapter 5.[3] In other words, these speakers now have a choice of language that their families in the rural areas do not generally have, and the transmission of Galician from generation to generation may once again be lost, as we saw was the case above.

The data presented in Figure 8.6 is not directly comparable with that of Fernández Rodríguez *et al.* (1994: 43) in Figure 8.1 regarding L^1 distribution (p. 190). Nonetheless, what is interesting is that in the 1980s, Castilan predominated as the L^1 in the towns and cities, and predominates now as the habitual language of use in the same conurbations. This would suggest a correlation between L^1 acquisition and habitual language use in this group, but without further data, this may be tenuous.

Language proficiencies

I now turn to the issue of whether there is a direct correlation between language proficiencies and habitual language of use in the major cities. Table 8.1 (p. 196) indicates no major disparities between the cities regarding language proficiency in Galician, although I discuss the figures pertaining to Santiago de Compostela in more detail later in this chapter. One pertinent example from Table 8.1 demonstrates a similar potential for understanding and speaking Galician in the capital cities of Pontevedra and Ourense, even though 46% of Pontevedra respondents

Table 8.1 Galician users in the main cities of Galicia, by linguistic proficiency

	Understand	*Speak*	*Read*	*Write*
A Coruña	86.00%	69.02%	51.2%	33.42%
Ferrol	87.88%	70.55%	48.36%	29.87%
Santiago	78.37%	71.86%	52.28%	37.48%
Lugo	83.91%	76.43%	49.79%	38.46%
Ourense	89.68%	78.52%	47.79%	33.62%
Pontevedra	87.44%	78.62%	46.19%	29.46%
Vigo	89.55%	73.94%	49.10%	31.30%

Source: Vieiros.

in the IGE data employ Castilian totally or chiefly on a day-to-day basis and 24% of Ourense respondents claim the same.

Differences regarding the use of Castilian as habitual language of use have less to do with class and more to do with historical context and geographical situation, as we saw above. However, the consistency in language competencies underlines the sociolinguistic aspects of language selection in Galicia. These figures demonstrate that there is no strong link between habitual language selection and proficiency in linguistic skills. Furthermore, they appear to demonstrate that in the cities at least, there is much work to be done regarding reading and writing skills. However, age differences are patently not taken into consideration in these data, which means that the figures may be somewhat skewed. As we discuss below, age appears to play a significant role in competencies regarding such linguistic skills. Therefore, although these figures highlight that there are no huge disparities between the cities themselves, despite differences in habitual language use, they offer us little explanation as to why this should occur.

Bilingual language use

Taking age tendencies into consideration complicates the situation even further, but does at least offer likely explanations regarding language use. Unlike other studies I have examined, Monteagudo and Santamarina's 1993 study does not take into account the habitual use of both languages. Thus, the data in Figure 8.7 once again indicate that in the 1990s Galician was the first language of the vast majority of the people, and that the process of degaleguisation was rife. However, it also indicates that Castilian alone, rather than any bilingual language use, was replacing Galician as the spoken language of the younger generations.

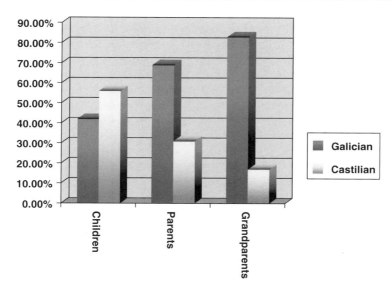

Figure 8.7. Spoken language variation, by age group (Source: Monteagudo and Santamarina, 1993: 133)

Research carried out since that time has considered habitual use of both languages. The second volume of the *Mapa Sociolingüística de Galicia* details the findings pertaining to what they term the functional uses of Galician and Castilian. Their conclusions indicate that nearly 51% of the respondents considered bilingual usage to be the norm, nearly 39% considered monolingual Galician use to be the norm, and nearly 11% claimed monolingual Castilian use to be the norm (Fernández Rodriguez & Rodriguez Neira, 1995: 27–28).

Yet even these figures may appear somewhat unclear and incomplete when compared with the later IGE data displayed in Figure 8.8 below, as they do not break down bilingual use into 'more or less' Galician or Castilian. The IGE data demonstrate clearly that the younger the respondent, the more likely that Galician is *not* the sole language of habitual use and that the use of both Galician and Castilian, or Castilian alone, is much more prevalent. Whereas nearly 60% of the over 50 age group predominantly use Galician, there is a sharp decrease in Galician speakers in the 30 to 49 age group (37%), and another, albeit less severe, in the 5 to 29 age group (28%). This decrease in Galician speakers appears to be offset by an increase in the number of young people always, or predominantly, using Castilian on a day-to-day basis: 56% of the 5 to 29 year olds, compared to 42% and 22% of the 30 to 49 and over 50 age groups respectively. This figure takes into account those speakers who employ

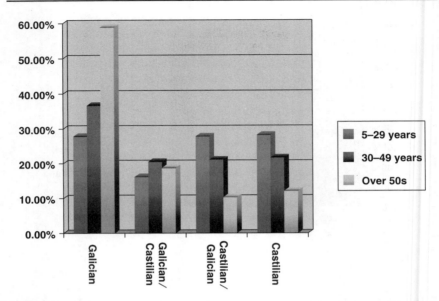

Figure 8.8. Spoken language of habitual use in Galicia, by age (Source: IGE, 2004)

both languages habitually, even if Castilian does tend to prevail. However, the number of bilingual speakers who predominantly use Galician is fairly static across the age groups; from just under 19% in the over 50s to just over 16% in the 5 to 29 year old group.

Rodríguez-Neira's latest study in Galicia (2003: 75–112) also aims to evaluate the extent to which languages are retained or abandoned. Once again, his sample is from the *Mapa Sociolingüístico de Galicia* [Sociolinguistic Map of Galicia] (Fernández Rodríguez & Rodríguez Neira, 1994, 1995), so it must be appreciated that the present situation may have changed somewhat. Rodríguez-Neira was concerned with the 16,273 individuals (41.8% of the total) who, in response to question 28, stated that they have modified their normal language usage. He avers that this was more common in respondents born in an urban environment and living in town, who were under 46 years of age at the time, were employed in non-manual work, had completed secondary or university education, were from the middle or upper middle class, displayed bilingual usage or whose original language of habitual use was Castilian (Rodríguez Neira, 2003: 81). Rodríguez-Neira concluded that language retention was generally high, especially among bilinguals and initial Galician speakers, but that there was a general low-scale shift towards bilingualism, where the original language of habitual use predominates.

This change in use is consolidated usually before 30 years of age. Rodríguez Neira offers a varied range of reasons for such changes: adaptation from the rural to the urban environment, work reasons, the influence of the educational system, or personal reasons (2003: 111–112).

The above sections make it clear that the pervading sociolinguistic situation in Galicia regarding language choice is in a state of flux. Generally, it is unsurprising given that devolution only occurred 20 or so years ago, and that normalisation processes were fully implemented only fairly recently. The increase in bilingual users, particularly in the urban areas and particularly among the younger respondents, would indicate that both languages might be starting to acquire new spheres of activity. It is to this latter question that I now turn.

Functional demarcation

The data presented in Figures 7.6 (p. 181) and 8.1 to 8.7 (pp. 190–195, 197) are eminently valid, and my explanations regarding historical and class factors illustrate the relevance of the urban/rural demarcation. Yet, as we have seen, the issue of functional demarcation in Galicia is in no way clear-cut.

In her early work, Skutnabb-Kangas (1981: 90) considered the assignment of positive prestige values to two or more languages and their accepted uses within a multilingual and sociocultural environment. Ideally, all languages implicated in a situation of community bilingualism or multilingualism should enjoy equal status and prestige value, and overarching linguistic policies should work to ensure this. In Chapter 7, I examined the idea of *bilingüismo limpo e harmónico* [clean, harmonious bilingualism] (pp. 176–182) that has been incorporated into Galician linguistic policy since the 1980s. Based on Regueiro Tenreiro's assertion that both Galician and Castilian are community languages and as such, representative of the collective identity (1999: 56), *bilingüismo harmónico* appears to adhere to this vision by advocating linguistic and social harmony and the avoidance of competition and conflict scenario. Thus, it is an intrinsic feature of the PNL.

In order to fulfil this vision, individual speakers do not need to be aware of any social norms and rules pertaining to contextual use, for ostensibly at least, there are none. This underlines my earlier comment in the Introduction regarding diglossic functions. I concede that Fishman's earlier contention (pp. 14–15) that the social structure of a bilingual community in a society tends to be reflected in a diglossic, hierarchical use of their languages was perhaps valid before devolution, but I do not think that this is the case now such as Galicia. In line with Martin-Jones (1989: 108–112), I would suggest that many bilingual individuals in contemporary Galicia select a language in a given context in accordance with their own competencies, preferences, allegiances, and other extra-linguistic factors, rather than with any superimposed norms pertaining to diglossic use. Thus, languages tend to overlap in their uses: language choice occurs in the context of a social network, and as such, reflects sociolinguistic realities rather than abstract constructs.

In theory, if a traditional, diglossic bilingual scenario *were* to exist throughout present-day Galicia, then simply based upon a state/region language distribution, I would expect the following functional distribution to emerge:

- Galician – generally informal, intragroup functions, such as within the family, within the community, and with friends and acquaintances: for group identity purposes.
- Castilian – generally more formal, intergroup functions, such as within institutions, within society outside the immediate neighbourhood, and with strangers.
- Either or both languages – an occupational function within the workplace, depending upon context.[4]

In practice, the situation is not so clear-cut. Even though the policy of *bilingüismo harmónico* was not implemented long ago, language demarcation according to spheres of activity is already not categorical. Despite political intervention and in particular, the actions of the state government in Galicia over the last century, the data I have examined so far indicates that this schema does not really apply to any particular community or zone in the region. Before the linguistic repression instigated by Franco's regime and the consequent imposition of Castilian onto Galician society, Galician was still retained as the L^1 of many rural and (lower class) urban inhabitants. However, by the end of the last century, even the most isolated of rural communities (and these are increasingly rare) had a receptive knowledge of spoken Castilian. In the urban areas, Castilian had already become well established as an alternative form to Galician in informal contexts in all classes, as well as being the generic written language.

Galicia is undergoing what the detractors of *bilingüismo harmónico*, in line with Fishman (1989), would consider a transition period, where competition and even conflict is occurring between Castilian and Galician for contextual uses, and which may ultimately lead to Galician losing out to the State language. However, proponents of *bilingüismo harmónico* would perhaps point out that this scenario is a logical step to full societal bilingualism and linguistic harmony, although once again, pronouncements regarding its viability and successes are rare. Moreover, this policy allows the substantial number of monolingual speakers in the region to override any potential norms of usage and apply their autochthonous language in all contexts. This brings me back to issues regarding the implication of historical factors on contemporary language use in Galicia.

In Chapter 2, and as discussed above, we saw that in the Middle Ages, alongside the small bilingual Galician nobility, two monolingual, class-differentiated communities appear to have existed in Galicia; the dominant Castilian-speaking aristocracy and the autochthonous, Galician-speaking inhabitants. At this time, functional demarcation does appear to have been strictly adhered to by the bilingual group, and the adoption of Castilian for formal functions by the Galician nobility, and, ultimately, other inhabitants of the towns and cities, paved the way for what has indeed traditionally been considered a bilingual/diglossic situation, at least within this sector of the urban community. According to this analysis, the use of Castilian corresponded to the traditional diglossic definitions of a super-posed variety (see p. 14 for definitions) whilst Galician corresponded to the definition of a day-to-day community variety.

This scenario echoes to a large extent my earlier delineation (pp. 16–17) of the ways in which minoritised languages forego functions to the dominant or majoritised language in such cases. Indeed, this approximation of uses engendered competition for functional domains between Galician and Castilian, and the bilingual nobility gave up the diglossic norms and began to use Castilian in many contexts.

However, even then, functional demarcation was by no means wide-spread and language use became associated more with social class and geographical location. We have seen that Galician continued to dominate in the lower classes of the chiefly rural areas and that Castilian dominated in the upper echelons of society who had come to the urban conurbations from outside the region. It is not an easy task to deconstruct this long-standing and somewhat traditional demarcation of language, and the present-day situation, with its inherent problems and issues, demonstrates this to some extent.

From a political perspective, functional assignment would not fully empower the Galician language, for as was discussed earlier (p. 178), the strict compartmentalisation of language through domain segregation can affect a society's perceptions regarding the value and prestige of a language (Romaine, 1995: 37). Thus, a linguistic policy other than *bilingüísmo harmónico* may simply reinforce certain prejudices regarding the use of Galician in certain spheres of activity. However, as Regueira Fernández has pointed out (2006: 85), Galician may now be a protected language under the auspices of this policy, but as ever, it is still subordinate in many ways to the State sponsored language of Castilian.

In this respect, the case of Catalan we saw earlier (pp. 80–81) is somewhat unusual and does not lend itself well to a comparison with Galician. Even though the language of the State is still Castilian, Catalan is the language associated with economic power. It has been able to adopt those functions associated with command, influence, and control, and has been able to enhance its already high prestige value. For a long time, it has enjoyed the loyalty and support of its autochthonous speakers. This is patently not the case of Galicia. Once again, its subordination to Castilian, tacit or not, would suggest that it is far from achieving such positive notions of status and importance amongst its speakers.

The languages of childhood

In my preceding discussions, I have pointed out the potential impact that both place of residence and social class may have on the distribution of Galician. I have also looked at apparent-time cross-sectional data from different age groups on language acquisition and language use, and I commented on the role of age in the manifestation of linguistic competencies. Of course, cross-sectional data from different age groups at a given point in time, and particularly regarding habitual language use, may merely indicate patterns of age differentiation similar to age-preferential patterns of linguistic variability (Cheshire, 1987: 764–765) (see pp. 18–29 for a discussion of this issue). In this case, language distribution in the population as a whole would not be affected over time. However, I contend that the same cannot be said for the data on the languages used and acquired in childhood. Here, some form of pattern of change in use seems to be apparent, similar once again to what Cheshire has defined as generation-specific differences.

The supposition that these are synchronic demonstrations of a diachronic change in progress is reinforced by extra-linguistic data having had an impact on linguistic behaviour, at least within urban homes. For example, the reading and writing skills in Galician of those people who were children during the Franco era, and were raised in Galician in the home but taught in Castilian at school, are either absent or largely inadequate. However, many younger people were raised speaking Castilian in childhood. Their reading and writing skills in both languages have been honed due to the (partial, at least) introduction of Galician into the school curriculum and into other public domains, even when the same cannot be said for their speaking skills. Therefore, the socio-political setting may have facilitated these changes.

It is certainly true that Galicia has undergone upheaval since the 1980s. As I have tried to emphasise throughout this discussion, the language planners do not accord clearly defined functions to Castilian and Galician. Hence, language use is in no way consistent with the predicted schema outlined above, in that the languages overlap in their distribution. Individual language use may differ according to disparate experiences and circumstances and according to geographical distribution, class or age, as we have seen, and societal bilingualism does not imply that individual linguistic repertoires have to be analogous to that of the community as a whole. Even when certain sectors of the language community in Galicia claim monolingual status, still they can be fully paid up members of that community without necessarily sharing all linguistic resources. Bearing in mind the comments made in this section, I will examine my fieldwork carried out in the mid 1990s in Santiago de Compostela in the following section.

Fieldwork: Santiago de Compostela

As one of the main cites in Galicia and dominated by its huge cathedral and medieval epicentre, Santiago de Compostela is the final destination for Christian pilgrims who have travelled *O Camino de Santiago*, [the Way of Saint James], to pray at his supposed resting place. As the regional capital, it is also the home of the *Xunta* as well as the academic centre of normalisation policy-making and institutional planning. In the 20th century, its population increased greatly: from 20,120, in 1900 to 82,404 in 1981 and finally, to 92,298 in 2004 (IGE, 2004; INE, 2005), primarily due to mass migration from the surrounding rural areas where dialectal Galician was the norm. This huge increase in the population of Santiago brought with it its own set of linguistic problems. As I have pointed out in the preceding section, mutual comprehension between oral Galician and Castilian at the very least is relatively straightforward. As a result, lexical transference phenomena became rife, primarily amongst the incoming rural, working class and the older populations.

Fernández Rodríguez and Rodríguez Neira cite the distribution of L^1 speakers in Santiago de Compostela in the 1990s (see Figure 8.9).

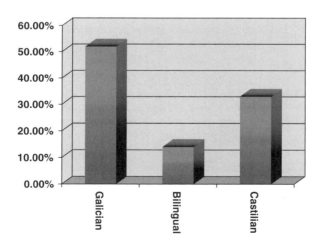

Figure 8.9. L^1 distribution in Santiago de Compostela (Source: Fernández Rodríguez and Rodríguez Neira, 1994: 56)

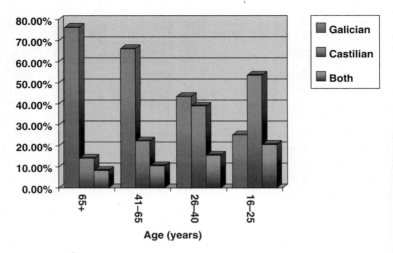

Figure 8.10. L^1 distribution in Santiago de Compostela, by age (Source: Dubert García, 1999: 17)

At this time, Santiago was the only city where the total percentage of mother tongue Galician speakers was higher than for Castilian. Dubert García adds that Galician predominated as the mother tongue only amongst the older age groups. However there are both Galician and Castilian L^1 speakers in the younger age groups (see Figure 8.10). Habitual language use is presented in Figure 8.11 for the same period.

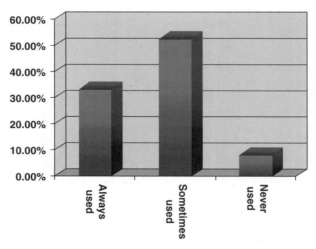

Figure 8.11. Galician as the language of habitual use in Santiago de Compostela (Source: Dubert García, 1995: 72)

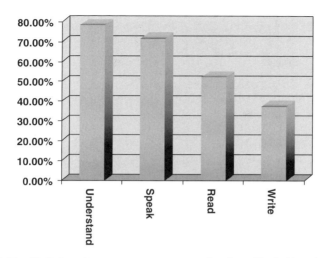

Figure 8.12. Galician language competencies by discipline in Santiago de Compostela (Source: www.galego.org./english/today/general/census. html, 2005)

Dubert García (1999: 17) also states that there is a difference in spoken use according to age. Whereas over 47% of the over 65s claim to always use Galician, this figure drops to under 15% in the 16 to 25 age group. At the same time, the figure for those using only, or mostly, Castilian appears to be on the increase; from just over 19% in the over 65 group to 65% in the 16 to 25 age group. Moreover, as I found for the region overall, there is a marked increase in bilingual use.

Figure 8.12 is a summary of data relevant to Santiago de Compostela regarding language skills (found in Table 8.1, see p. 196).

Santiago in the 21st century is an extremely vibrant and cosmopolitan capital city with a larger than average number of non-Galician residents, which may explain why the percentage of respondents who understand Galician is lower than in any other of the cities studied, and why the number who speak the language is also lower than for the majority of the other cities. However, Santiago is also the focus of many of the pro-Galician language activities, in particular *autonomismo*, and many schools in the city have already implemented Galician immersion programmes. These factors may go some way to explaining why conversely, Santiago has the highest number of respondents who claim to be able to read and write the language.

Empirical research

Firstly, I would like to reiterate the general comment I made in the Introduction (pp. 9–10) regarding my own status as a researcher of

Galician. I employ fieldwork, along with other data I have outlined in Chapter 6, in the full knowledge that my analysis will not be from the perspective of a constituent member of Galician society, since I am in no way personally involved in the pervading sociolinguistic situation. However, my repeated trips to the region, together with sustained contact by phone and letter with all of the respondents initially over a period of five, and ultimately over eight years, created a level of trust I had only previously dreamed of gaining. Although initially I may have been considered somewhat of an outsider to my research group, by the time I carried out my fieldwork, all of the respondents felt able to converse with me in both Castilian and Galician. They trusted me enough to discuss – and complain about – local issues, and all treated me like a member of their families. This way, I gained access to data, perspectives, and opinions that more politically or ideologically involved insider researchers may not have. My evaluation is therefore from an academic perspective, but with 'insider' experience and information to hand, acknowledging both the benefits and drawbacks that this position implies.

A comment regarding methodology is also warranted. Some years ago, Labov (1972: 107) made an important observation regarding the use of questionnaires to elicit information about language use. He stated that 'self-reporting language use' may differ from actual use. Although this must be borne in mind when an interpretation is made of the present data, I would add that the very nature of any contradictory results arising from the use of direct and indirect methodological processes, offers invaluable information regarding individual's perceptions and attitudes regarding language status.

My initial studies were carried out in the summers of 1995 and 1996 in Santiago de Compostela. The aim was to examine possible changes in the employment of languages between people who had, and who had not, received some form of formal education in Galician.[5] The hypothesis was that mother tongue, intragroup speakers were likely to learn the intergroup language because of the prestige associated with its use, but that this variety would also be increasingly employed in informal settings between speakers. The implication of this is that Galician speakers will learn Castilian and apply it in formal settings, but that Castilian speakers will not learn Galician and will apply Castilian in all settings.

Linguistic surveys of this nature sometimes require that the respondents satisfy certain sociolinguistic and extra-linguistic criteria. For example, if it is imperative that all respondents are bilingual from birth, it becomes necessary to reject those who do not conform to this criterion. Williamson and Williamson's early paper on Galician (1984) was centred primarily upon the notion of a bilingual community. They insisted that each respondent was socialised to some extent in the minority language and therefore ensured that over two-thirds of the respondents had acquired Galician before Castilian and that the majority acquired Castilian as late as during their first year of school. It could be argued that restrictions such as these may limit to a certain extent the validity of the results, in that they cannot be said to apply legitimately to the whole sector of the population being investigated. The alternative method, involving a random selection of a sample from an electoral roll or register, would ensure that there were no limitations regarding such factors. This latter type of investigation tends to collect and collate many different types of information from a huge sample of respondents; see in this vein the region-wide sociolinguistic surveys carried out by Fernández Rodríguez and Rodríguez Neira (1994, 1995, 1996) discussed earlier.

The decision regarding how to select the informants of a linguistic survey is, therefore, linked to the number of informants to be consulted. In some cases, such as that of Williamson and Williamson cited above (1984), it may be that a completely random choice of respondent is not always possible or even required. These investigators elected 104 respondents for their regional-wide study. Trudgill (1974) elected to interview 60 respondents from a total of 118,610 inhabitants (that is, 0.05% of the total population) for his dialectal investigation of Norwich English.

In a similar way, the selection of suitable respondents for my studies was defined by sociolinguistic and extra-linguistic criteria. Given that I wanted to evaluate any possible changes in attitude and behaviour between different age groups, age was an important variable, with the restrictions I highlight below. Place of residence and social and educational background are also important criteria (see Rodríguez Neira's study and results regarding language change in urban environments (2003: 199). Hence, irrespective of their place of birth, my respondents must have lived within the city or immediate suburbs of Santiago de Compostela from childhood in order to ensure the notion of an urban setting; must have a middle class background and must have completed, or be completing, the compulsory education system, in order to control the social grouping. Gender however, was not a delimiting factor.

In order to find appropriate informants, a brief questionnaire was circulated (see Appendix 4, p. 281) in May 1993 and June 1994 requesting information and help from people. It was deposited in the Faculty of Arts at the University of Santiago de Compostela, in a bread shop and café in the centre of the city, and in a primary and a secondary school near the centre. The form aimed to establish the background details of the respondents and was loosely based upon the methodology behind the questionnaire used by Martínez Martín in his study of the phonetic and sociolinguistic traits of Burgos (1983: 60–61).

Seventy-one people expressed an interest in participating in the survey and believed that they conformed to the specified criteria. Fifty-one of the questionnaires (see Appendix 5, p. 282) subsequently distributed were duly completed. Of these, five were considered unsuitable candidates for a bilingual study, their answers indicating that they were probably monolingual speakers. Four did not satisfy the criteria of having lived in Santiago de Compostela for most of their lives and four were rejected on the grounds of educational background. Six were outside the age range selected for the study. Participants under the age of 10 were excluded, given that deviations in their linguistic patterns are more likely to be developmental differences and as such, examples of true age-grading. I also chose not to interview or observe anyone over the age of 70, because of the inherent difficulties in getting them to speak to me or in front of me or a tape recorder in Galician. The selected 32 subjects were categorised according to age and circumstances and their personal details can be found in Appendix 6 (p. 283):[6]

- 10 to 21 years of age at the time of the initial study (1996). All were born after 1975 and entered the Galician primary education system in the 1980s and early 1990s, when the teaching of and in Galician should have been fairly well established and implemented within the schools of Santiago de Compostela.
- 21 to 40 years of age at the time of the initial study. Either university or college graduates; they had entered the Galician primary education system before the implementation of the *Normas*, hence, they were predominantly educated in Castilian. However, the younger members may have experienced a limited amount of teaching of and in the Galician language in the mid to late 1980s whilst at secondary school.
- 40 to 70 years of age at the time of the initial study. Educated solely in Castilian, they attended school during the era of Franco's dictatorship and so were educated in Castilian. All also went either to university or further education college.

The findings of this research are summarised in Tables A7.1 to 7.7 of Appendix 7 (p. 285). Where feasible, my observational data generally corresponded with the findings of the self-reporting sessions. Therefore, in accordance with my earlier comments regarding the viability of these two methodologies (see above), I highlight inconsistencies between the admissions of the respondents themselves regarding language use and observed practices only where they occur. In the following section, I summarise the findings pertaining to language preference and language use for each of the age groups in turn.

Language preference and language use

The 40 to 70 age group report that their language of preference is either Galician or Castilian; no respondent states that they have no preference. Those who choose primarily to use Galician (50%) state that it is the language of childhood. All these respondents use Galician, or both Galician, and Castilian, with their children, receiving replies in Castilian or in both languages. These respondents also use Galician, with the rest of their families, in shops, bars and restaurants, and with friends. With work colleagues, the language used depends on the interlocutor: with strangers, nearly all would use Castilian unless they were addressed in Galician. These respondents are generally rather unsure of their mastery of written forms of both Galician and Castilian. However, one respondent states that, despite being prohibited, Galician was sometimes employed at school as the language of instruction, and it is he who claims written competence in both languages.

The respondents who prefer to use Castilian as their primary means of communication (50%) used Galician, or Galician and Castilian, at home in childhood. All now use Castilian with their living relations, but both languages are employed with their offspring. I observed that this depended less on the topic than the location of the conversation: generally, Galician is not used outside the home. Castilian predominates in shops, bars and restaurants, although either Galician or Castilian may be used in conversations with friends and work colleagues, or when meeting a stranger. All are confident that their reading and writing skills in Castilian are good but that those in Galician are not; Galician was neither taught nor used as the language of instruction at school.

In sum, there appears to be a relationship between Galician as the language of preference and of the home, yet those respondents who prefer to use Castilian also used Galician, or both languages, in childhood. This latter use of Galician is in itself unsurprising because, as I commented earlier (pp. 69–70, 190), despite the linguistic repression during Franco's dictatorship, in many homes, Galician continued to be employed within the immediate family. The switch from Galician to Castilian appears to be a conscious decision, and may be linked to issues of identity. As I pointed out in Chapter 2, for many centuries Castilian has been considered the language of social prestige and power, with clearly marked high domains of usage. The enforced implementation as the language of education and social advancement under Franco coincided with the childhood of those respondents who were under 60 years of age at the time of this study. These measures were in practice in Galicia by the time 50% of this group (those under 50 years of age) were in primary school, and it is these respondents who state a preference for spoken Castilian over Galician.

Language preference in the 21 to 40 age group is highly variable. Those respondents who express no preference for using one or another of the languages (25%) state that in their childhood, both Galician and Castilian were used at home. Both languages are used with family members and acquaintances, generally depending on context, but only Castilian is employed with strangers. All had Galician language classes for some of their school years, and state that a few of their other subjects were taught in Galician. All claim good reading and writing skills in both languages.

Where a respondent expresses a preference for using Castilian (33%), it is confirmed also as the language used at home in childhood. Nowadays, these respondents employ both Galician and Castilian with family members, including their children, who all reply in both languages. Castilian predominates with friends, in work and study settings or with strangers, but Galician is used in neighbourhood shops and bars. None of these respondents had Galician language classes or had subjects taught in Galician at school: all claim good reading and writing skills only in Castilian.

Of the respondents who express a preference for using Galician (42%), only one states that it was the language of his childhood, and only he solely employs Galician with family (although I did observe him using Castilian with a cousin who was visiting from Lugo). The remaining respondents use both Galician and Castilian with family, including their children, who respond in the same way. Both languages are used also with friends and acquaintances, but Galician is used with strangers. All received some Galician language classes at school but Castilian predominated as the language of instruction. Only one respondent claims reading and writing skills in both languages.

In sum, the respondents from the 21 to 40 age group who do not express a preference for either language (25%) appear to be fluent in both and were exposed to both during their childhood, both at home and at school. A similar association is found also for those who prefer to use Castilian.

Although the teaching of and in the Galician language was still prohibited during the primary and secondary schooling of the oldest members of this age group, it would have been initiated during the 1980s, at a time when the younger members of this age group were attending school. We have seen that 42% cite Galician as their preferred language of use, yet only one was raised speaking Galician at home. All the respondents of this group were under 26 years of age at the time of this study and state that they did learn a little Galician in school, and do claim reading and writing skills in both languages. However, Galician was rarely if ever used as the medium of instruction.

Finally, in the 10 to 21 age group no one uses Galician solely and preferentially. Where the respondents indicate a preference for spoken Castilian (30%), it was, and still is, the dominant language at home, with friends and with acquaintances, although Galician is employed with grandparents.

The remaining respondents in this age group (70%) were raised predominantly in Galician but state that they are happy to use either Castilian or

Galician in most contexts. For example, most will use both languages with parents, friends, and acquaintances, although Castilian predominates with siblings.

All respondents use Castilian in formal contexts unless they are addressed in Galician. 30% state that Galician is the main language of instruction, with the remaining 70% stating that both languages are used depending on subject. All respondents in this age group have received language classes in Galician. All respondents are confident in their reading and writing skills in both languages.

There appears to be an association between language preference and language of childhood for this group. There also seems to have been a substantial increase in the use of Galician as the language of instruction, but those respondents who were raised solely in Castilian continue to use it preferentially.

One of the most noteworthy findings here concerns reading and writing skills. The 10 to 21 age group is the only one to fully claim these skills in both languages and the only one in which all respondents received Galician languages classes and were taught further subjects in the same. These results suggest that for these respondents, linguistic normalisation processes within the educational sector have enjoyed some success.

In a similar vein, 70% of the youngest respondents express no preference between the two languages. This is in stark contrast to the 40 to 70 age group, all of whom would choose *either* Castilian *or* Galician. Again, any kind of far-reaching prognosis based upon these data would be rather hasty, but it would appear that the youngest respondents are equally confident in using both languages.

Regarding L^1 use, half of the 40 to 70 age group were raised speaking both languages and half speaking Galician. Childhood Castilian predominates in the 21 to 40 age group, and the bilingual mother tongue figure drops to 25%, but rises again to 60% of the 10 to 21 age group, with Castilian being the L^1 of the remaining respondents. These results would seem to indicate that Galician has undergone a revival as a language used within the home, but that Castilian is still used in this context. Therefore, bilingual language use within the home would appear to be the norm for the youngest respondents.[7]

Finally, for the majority of respondents in each group (78% of the total), the question pertaining to speech and counting acts (what I have designated as intra language) corresponds either wholly or partially with preferred language use. In no case are the intra and preferred language completely different.

Functional distribution

I will now reconsider issues pertaining to functional distribution briefly discussed earlier (pp. 17, 199–202).

In the 40 to 70 age group, most of the respondents employ their language of preference, or both languages, for nearly all functions, either formal and informal. When meeting someone for the first time, they state that the language employed is determined by the interlocutor rather than by the respondent, and this would appear to override the norm that dictates the use of the intergroup language with strangers, or the use of a lingua franca. Moreover, they do not seem to find their interlocutor's choice of Galician peculiar in a formal context, nor do those who use Castilian in informal contexts.

In the 21 to 40 age group, it is somewhat difficult to establish any type of pattern pertaining to functional use. Again, if either Castilian or Galician is cited as the preferred language, then it tends to dominate in most or all contexts. Similarly, those respondents who express no preference for either language (25%) do not demonstrate a clear-cut use of the two languages corresponding to the traditionally cited diglossic pattern, where Galician is restricted to non-official and private use, and Castilian is the prestigious, superposed variety. In this group, once again Galician may be used with acquaintances and strangers, and Castilian with friends and close relatives. The only conclusion that can be drawn at this stage for these respondents is that functional distinctions are extremely blurred. Even where certain respondents attempt to differentiate particular domains, there seems to be no consensus as to which language is used.

The 10 to 21 age group respondents who express no preference for either language tend to contradict the assertion that only Castilian is the predominant language of home life, for both languages are used with families, friends, and acquaintances. When Castilian is preferred, then it tends to be used exclusively in such contexts. However, although these younger respondents have increasingly learnt Castilian in the home, some, who nonetheless claim to prefer using Castilian, admit of late to 'trying out' Galician on their parents. This broader application of a language that is learnt almost exclusively within the confines of the school gates may indicate a certain acknowledgement on the part of these respondents that it can re-assume functions within home and family life. Interestingly, all respondents use Castilian exclusively with strangers, in shops, and so on This may have to do with the tendency to use Castilian as some form of lingua franca, whereby the respondents assume 'stranger and non-Galician speaker' in the first instance.

Most of the behaviour patterns I have found appear to counter any potential assertions that a predictable diglossic framework prevails in urban Galician society. Respondents either tend to favour the use of one language or the other in all settings (with the notable exception of the youngest respondents and formal contexts discussed above), or they use both languages rather indiscriminately. The former situation concurs well with the results of the RAG survey described earlier in this Chapter (pp. 165–166), since although it examined the linguistic habits of the entire region, it is relevant to my analysis that some 63.7% of L^1 Galician speakers claimed to use Galician exclusively for all their communications (Fernández Rodríguez and Rodríguez Neira, 1994: 49). In a similar way, 36.9% of respondents whose L^1 was Castilian used it exclusively, 45.9% used it most of the time, and only 14.9% affirmed that Galician had taken over as their primary means of communication (1994: 50).

Transference

In Chapter 5, I discussed the long-term effects of acculturation processes between Castilian and Galician. Penny's discussion of the bilingual situation in Galicia also considers these issues. He states (Penny, 2000: 33–34) that the facility for transference between the two languages is why the term diglossia has never really truly applied to their overall coexistence in Galicia. As Galician and Castilian share a large number of linguistic items, they should be considered overlapping varieties of language. That is, exclusively Galician items belong to typical intragroup uses and exclusively Castilian items are reserved for intergroup uses, but there is a broad intermediate set available for both environments.

Along similar lines to Penny, in the 1980s García González (1985: 115) had already distinguished four language varieties prevalent in Galicia. He too, believed that these formed a kind of linguistic continuum. As well as the usual terminology for Galician and Castilian in their respective standardised forms of the language, García González used the term *chapurrao* to refer to dialects of Galician or 'popular Galician', strongly influenced, especially in the lexis, by Castilian. He uses the term *castellano agalegado* to refer to a transitional, colloquial form of Castilian prevalent in semi-urban areas around Santiago de Compostela and displaying both phonetic and morphological transference from Galician.

Monteagudo and Santamarina (1993: 145–147, 167) described speakers' attitudes towards such forms. They limited García González's use of the term *chapurrao* to an extremely unstable transitional variety between Galician and Castilian used in sectors that were undergoing degaleguisation, when the speaker considered their speech forms to be in some way corrupt or impure. They also claimed that the term *castrapo* was used pejoratively to describe a variety of Castilian strongly influenced by Galician linguistic items and used mainly by Galician speakers, and added that its speakers were typically members of the Galician-speaking community who had abandoned their use of Galician, and, hence, retained no loyalty to the language. These authors added that the predominant form employed by the increasing number of monolingual

Castilian speakers in the 1990s, tended to conform to such colloquial varieties of Castilian, what they term 'regionalised Castilian', standard Castilian being rare except among the younger upper classes.

Other more recent language contact studies in Galicia have revealed that such varietal differentiation may coincide with a type of geographical continuum, in which traditional Galician features predominate in rural areas, but gradually diminish in intensity in favour of typical Castilian features in more urban zones, such as towns and cities.[8]

These discussions highlight the linguistic similarities between standard and colloquial or dialectal forms of Castilian and Galician. They also indicate that a two-way differentiation in terms of language use in Galicia does not describe the contemporary situation. My earlier discussions indicate that there is a continuum of use, with tendencies towards Galician and Castilian at each extreme. Thus, the clear-cut differentiation between the two is more a social-perceptual one, rather than a linguistically describable one. This is reinforced to a large extent by my earlier discussion regarding linguistically similar languages (pp. 109–112), since here, it may well be that in focusing their speech towards one or another variety, speakers are demonstrating an 'act of identity' (Le Page & Tabouret-Keller, 1985) (see p. 104). Consequently, one of the aims of the research presently under examination was to determine whether the languages found in Galicia were sufficiently distinguishable from a linguistic perspective. In other words: were speakers able to avoid transference phenomena, such as code-switching and lexical borrowing? Was there only partial knowledge of one or the other of the languages in question? Or, was there any confusion in their minds as to the provenance of a particular linguistic form? Once again, I will discuss each of the age groups in turn.

Almost all the respondents in the 40 to 70 group using Castilian as their primary means of communication believe that they always employ dialectal or non-standard forms of Galician. However, marginally fewer admissions of non-standard language use are made by those respondents in this age group who prefer to use Galician. Reports and, indeed, my own observations of consciously selected code-switching samples and intra-sentential code-switching samples (what was originally termed code-mixing) are also uncommon, although one respondent states that she borrows a term from Galician when she is unaware of its cognate in Castilian, *anque sei que non é ben facelo* [even though I know it is wrong to do so].

When asked further about non-standard and dialectal forms, all the respondents who prefer to use Castilian in the 21 to 40 age group state that they use the transitional, colloquial form they designate as *castellano agalegado* when speaking Castilian, as well as non-standard varieties of Galician. My observations did not confirm that these varieties were always employed, but that there was a tendency for these respondents to intrasententially code-switch, particularly into Galician. Respondents who claim no preference of use, state that they use non-standard forms in both languages and also deny any intrasentential switching. Similarly, where Galician is the preferred language, no respondents claim any use of dialectal or non-standard varieties of the same, although *castellano agalegado* does appear to be prevalent. Again, instances of intrasentential switching are totally denied, and admissions of selective code-switching are uncommon. However, I did observe the use of selective switching techniques when Castilian words were inserted into Galician speech as an attempt at humour or irony.

Finally, no one in the 10 to 21 age group admits to using a non-standard or dialectal form of either Castilian or Galician, nor do they admit to any type of switching between the languages in any way. This confidence was generally borne out by my observations, although some instances of intrasentential switching were in evidence, particularly with the first person singular of the verb *ser* (*son* [I am]).

Attitude and language status

I now turn to the respondents' replies regarding language prestige values. Knowledge about the relative status and worth of languages to a community is invaluable to an analysis of their societal treatment. In the above sections, the respondents' assertions regarding language use and so on. generally coincide with my own observations of their behaviour. However, in order to determine if, and how, notions of prestige and status can be applied to the languages in question, the final part of this study is concerned less with usage and more with respondent attitudes towards Castilian and Galician, and whether these attitudes can be correlated in any way with behavioural practices.

The final three questions of the questionnaire used in this study (Appendix 5) pertain to issues of loyalty towards Galician and its chances for survival, in order to evaluate language attitudes towards the use of Galician and Castilian, and to determine whether any association can be established between responses, perceptions of other people's attitudes, and personal behaviour. The responses varied greatly in their content and length, and are thus not included within the charts in Appendix 7, but instead, are discussed here in more detail.

No consensus could be reached in the 40 to 70 age group regarding general attitudes towards Galician and whether or not it will survive, although the majority tend to think that it might. Some claim that it is not held in high esteem and that it tends to be the language of the lower classes, with the middle classes preferring to employ Castilian. Others take a more positive view, advocating its protection as a symbol of Galician identity, claiming that the standardised form will survive and that there has been increased interest in learning it. Nearly all think that language use should be dictated by context, with Galician being the natural language for use in informal situations such as the home.

In the 21 to 40 age group, a minority of respondents vehemently doubt that Galician will survive, claiming that it undergoes heavy transference from Castilian, that most people prefer to use Castilian, that its nationalistic connotations are problematic, and that many are ashamed of it as their vernacular. However, the overriding conviction is that many of the younger population, and in particular students, totally accept Galician as their own language and use it regularly, although some do not use it often but feel that they should be doing so, and also feel a need to preserve the language at all costs. The majority contend that the setting must dictate the choice of language in a bilingual society, but only advocate the standard as the 'correct' form of Galician to be used. One respondent states that those who only use Castilian cannot be Galician, whereas those who only use Galician must be from the rural areas.

The majority of the 10 to 21 age group are convinced that Galician will survive, but opinions regarding general attitudes to the language differ substantially. The consensus of this group is that people generally accept Galician as a national-regional identity marker, and that many want to learn it. However, some respondents comment that some people may consider Galician a dialect of Castilian and for this reason, not want to use it. Again, the majority of these respondents advocate the use of both languages, depending on context.

These results highlight some valuable points regarding language behaviour and attitudes in the urban, bilingual community in Galicia, but it must be constantly borne in mind that this is a small-scale study. Although I do not claim any far-reaching conclusions based upon these findings, they offer a worthwhile account of the role of prestige and attitudes towards language in the enhancement of a Galician ethnic identity and are discussed further below. I now turn to the issue of perceived linguistic competence.

Linguistic competence

As I have highlighted above, nearly everyone in the 40 to 70 age group who prefers to use Castilian states that they use non-standard forms in Galician. Whether they are aware what actually constitutes these forms, and whether this admission is simply a way of displaying preconceived prejudices about a language that has tolerated negative connotations for the majority of their lives, is not totally clear, however. The respondent who voiced the earlier comment regarding borrowing (p. 215) offers an interesting perspective in that she displays a clear lack of confidence in her use of both languages. She believes that she uses non-standard

Castilian and dialectal Galician, sometimes without being entirely aware of it, and she states that, at other times, she introduces Castilian words into her spoken Galician and makes mistakes in her written forms. In an earlier paper (Beswick, 1999a) both her son and her daughter attest separately that their mother is rather ashamed of the variety of Galician she employs, as she has stated on numerous occasions that they employ *unha forma mais correcta* [a more correct form] than she does (1999a: 65). Yet, despite this insecurity, her loyalty to Galician is manifest in her consideration of it as her native language and her preference for its use over Castilian in both informal and formal situations. She has even switched from Castilian to Galician when she writes notes to herself, indicating an increased confidence in both her written ability to use the variety and in the fact that she no longer views it in pejorative terms.

Members of the 21 to 40 age group who display a positive attitude towards the survival of Galician and its role as a national-regional identity marker, also tend to claim it as their preferred language of use. This may imply that their perceptions regarding a general acceptance of the language has encouraged their own use of Galician as their primary means of communication, or that, by accepting themselves that Galician fulfils this role, they then perceive that this is the general attitude throughout the region. Indeed, in some cases it is unclear where a preference for using Galician stems from, although it is noteworthy that these respondents tend to consider their use of Castilian to be non-standard.[9] Moreover, even though the respondents who prefer to use Castilian state that they speak *castellano agalegado*, they clearly demonstrate through their other responses that Castilian is their dominant language throughout. Examples of intrasentential code-switching in both languages do happen, with the respondents claiming that this occurs because they are unaware whether certain forms of a word are Galician or Castilian – given that Galician has been borrowing lexis from Castilian for centuries, this is not surprising. As I pointed out earlier, some speakers may not have a clear idea of the linguistic boundaries they are crossing when they code-switch, particularly if they have not been formally educated in one, either or both of the languages in question. Hence, such speakers may not actually be aware that certain words they consider Castilian are actually integrated into the Galician lexical system.[10]

Indeed, perceptions regarding lexical items and their provenance are rife with confusion. The middle and older age groups considered words such as *agradable* [pleasant] and *desde* [since] as forms that corrupted and devalued their spoken language, in contrast to what they perceived as the more traditional Galician forms of *agradabel* and *dende*. They also stated that unless they really thought about it, they found it difficult to avoid using them. However, even though these words are identical in Castilian, they conform to the standardised relexification processes and are integrated into Galician dictionaries.[11] In other instances, the respondents did display instances of intrasentential code-switching by inserting Castilianisms such as *acera* [pavement], *calle* [street] and *entonces* [then] when speaking Galician, instead of the cognate Galician forms *beirarrúa*, *rúa*, and *entón*. Instances where speakers would correct this usage and revert to the Galician form were not common, but when they did so they were fully aware that they were employing a form charged with connotative meaning.

Other respondents display a sufficiently high level of bilingual confidence to be able consciously to insert lexis from one language into the other to add a note of irony or humour. This recalls my earlier discussion of code-switching mechanisms in Chapter 4 (pp. 102–104). In this case, the switch is consciously used to draw on specific associations inherent within the languages in order to provoke a particular reaction in the interlocutor and for identity – negotiating purposes – what Le Page and Tabouret-Keller (1985) have termed 'focussing'. The situations I witnessed involved inserted switched items from the L^2 into the L^1, I contend that these respondents are employing a rhetorical use for their amusement or to create some form of dramatic effect.[12]

No one in the 10 to 21 age group admits to any use of dialectal or non-standard forms of either language, or of any transference phenomena between them, despite the observation regarding verb forms flagged earlier (p. 215). It is highly debatable whether language selection can be linked in any way to normalisation processes initiated within the education system. However, given that 75% of this age group confidently use both Galician and Castilian, it would appear that some form of shift in use for these respondents is occurring, even though this data cannot confirm the same for the society as a whole. Nonetheless, it is worth reiterating that when a language is standardised and institutionalised, schoolchildren may start to acquire an understanding of what constitutes the standard form and what does not, and become aware of the intricacies of the language they use.

Language loyalty versus linguistic insecurity

I now return to issues surrounding whether Galician is upheld due to language loyalty, or discriminated against due to linguistic insecurity. In Chapter 4, I commented that within a bilingual or multilingual community, a language may acquire status as a symbol of ethnic identity if it is viewed as advantageous to that community's political aspirations regarding autonomy or self-government. Thus, it is envisaged that positive attitudes towards the revitalisation or revival of the language and the expansion of its functional use outside home life will help it acquire new prestige value. Efforts will also be made to secure functional rights for the language and to maintain it in its 'purest' form through standardisation processes.

One of the intentions of the *Xunta's* recent normalisation policies concerning the dissemination of spoken and written Galician through institutional practices, discussed in Chapter 7, is to instil a sense of loyalty to the Galician language and to expunge the stigma attached to its use. To this end, in a previous section of that chapter (pp. 176–182), I appraised the policy of *bilingüísmo limpo e harmónico*. My conclusions as to whether it impedes or supports the functional expansion of Galician were somewhat tenuous. In order to clarify the situation further, I now consider whether it has any effect on loyalty factors.

In general, respondents who proffer rather pessimistic opinions regarding the survival of Galician may still claim it as their preferred means of communication. Conversely, for others habitual language use appears to determine their belief in its survival. Vehement convictions that Galician must survive and assertions regarding its role as an identity marker would appear to highlight a strong sense of loyalty to and solidarity with the language, particularly within the 10 to 21 age group, even by those who claim Castilian as their preferred language of use.

Positive attitudes towards Galician reflect its general use for some of the 40 to 70 age group respondents, whereas negative comments regarding either its status or its survival tend to be reflected in its rejection as habitual language of use. However, these respondents also manifest little confidence in their linguistic abilities in Galician. The vast majority of replies manifest an awareness of bilingual status and an acceptance that both varieties are valid for societal use. Yet, any awareness of potential diglossic differentiation is rather unclear from this survey, although there is a general acceptance that Galician can encompass intragroup functions, especially within the home. In intergroup situations, Castilian tends to function as a type of *lingua franca*, in that initially, it is nearly always employed with people from outside the immediate neighbourhood or district. If this person replies in Galician or makes it known that they would prefer to communicate in Galician, then the switch is made.

General observations on language use and language attitude

As I have already pointed out, clear conclusions based upon these findings are rather difficult to draw because of the small-scale nature of this study. As a result, they can only serve as an indicator of change that may, or may not, be occurring within the wider context of the Santiago de Compostela community. Likewise, I must reiterate that this is a study in apparent rather than real time, in accordance with my outline of such in the Introduction (pp. 18–21). Real-time examinations of successive generations of speakers who represent stages in the evolution of a speech community are rarely practical. In apparent time studies, some form of cross-sectional variation can be examined in different age groups at the same time.

One of the more original contributions of this book is to consider whether language change phenomena and methodologies can be employed to plot language shift in Galicia though such apparent time analyses. My examination of the uses of and attitudes towards, different languages at different life stages attempts to determine whether one language is generally used more at one stage in life than another, or whether a shift in language use is taking place.

Distinguishing between patterns of true change and patterns of variation that occur only in specific age groups is often difficult. For instance, the predominant tendency of the 10 to 21 age group in this study is to use both languages, the 40 to 70 age group use either one or the other language most of the time, whereas in the middle age group, some respondents favour one language and others use either language. If compared to the results of the more wide-ranging studies examined in the first part of this chapter, it would appear that a general shift in language use is taking place here. However, given that these differences may well be tendencies associated with a particular age group, which change as individuals grow older, I cannot categorically infer that language shift is in evidence, even though the extra-linguistic and sociolinguistic evidence present would appear to reinforce this claim.

In light of this predicament, in 2001 I decided to return to Santiago and talk to the same respondents, if at all possible, in order to determine whether they had maintained the same linguistic practices and attitudes demonstrated five years previously. I managed to contact all the respondents, who agreed unanimously to talk to me once again. I asked them the same questions as before, without telling them their previous replies, and all confirmed the earlier data, both for language use and attitudes therein. The tendencies inherent to each age group outlined above are not categorical. However, each respondent maintains the same configuration of use some five years later, which is indicative of an age-differentiation pattern.

Notwithstanding the differences in language use and concomitant attitudes towards such use, my results also indicate that this group are predominantly bilingual. However, my analysis of functional demarcation reveals that a diglossic scenario, where each of the languages is functionally distinguishable, is not in evidence, once again confirming the results of the studies examined in part one of this chapter. Consistent with the aims of *bilingüísmo harmónico* and with the theories of language shift delineated earlier (pp. 15–18), any diglossic demarcation would not be expected to be a straightforward replacement of one language for the other in a given context, which is demonstrated to a certain extent by the overlapping in contextual use of Castilian and Galician.

However, if Galician starts to assume inter- as well as intragroup functions, then it will enter into competition with Castilian. From a historical perspective, loyalty to the autochthonous language of Galician was a general prerequisite to avoid shifts of values and domains to Castilian, the language of power and prestige. Despite attempts by some sectors of Galician society to safeguard their linguistic identity, Castilian still retains the title of intergroup language throughout the region. However, there also appears to be an overriding optimism regarding the survival of Galician displayed by a cross-section of all ages but in particular, by the youngest age group. This would also explain the display of confidence manifested by these respondents in their self-reported use of the standard, together with their denials of the use of any dialectal variation. This attitude contrasts well with the sense of embarrassment manifested by certain older respondents to their use of such non-standard or dialectal forms.

These findings highlight Regueira's earlier claims (pp. 134–137) regarding the customary model for pronunciation. The younger respondents' confidence in using the standard could be enhanced by the similarities between the oral forms they are taught in school and Castilian. However, the older respondents view the introduction of Castilian words and sounds into their spoken Galician as 'mistakes' and demonstrate a degree of insecurity about their knowledge of how to use the standard form of the language or the oral forms they hear on the television and radio, and that their children are starting to adopt. Thus, consistent with Le Page and Tabouret-Keller's (1985) acts of identity, these speakers are aware of often crossing linguistic boundaries and the potential social implications therein.[13]

Yet even respondents claiming to dislike using Galician or who are not confident in its use seem aware that to lose that language would mean a loss of their collective identity. I suggest that the general awareness of linguistic forms and uses, together with the general enthusiasm surrounding the survival of Galician are linked to a change in attitude towards the role of the language in the formation of a Galician ethnicity. Although I cannot emphatically claim that this is a direct result of normalisation processes for all the respondents, the marked increase in such activities since devolution has at the very least, raised the profile of Galician.

Opinions regarding the prestige and Galician do offer an important insight into how the institutionalisation of Galician is making the younger respondents reappraise their attitudes. We appear to be witnessing some type of adjustment in the status assigned to Galician by these respondents, underpinned by their partial immersion in the language, particularly at school. Indeed, given that Castilian often fulfils an informal function in their home lives, the younger age group may be in the incipient stages of a reassignment of values and tokens to both languages.

However, although standard Galician may have been introduced into the compulsory education system, there have been quite a few initial problems regarding its uptake, leading to the implementation of a number of review procedures discussed earlier. Fishman's (1991) GIDS scale indicates that formalised educational programmes are not necessarily the only, or even the best, option for reversing language shift (pp. 48, 185). He states that before this can have any effect, a positive sense of identity associated with the use of the autochthonous language, particularly among the younger generations, must be initiated, followed by the re-establishment of the language's oral sociofunction as the intragroup language and the acquisition of literacy skills. Based on the results of my investigations, as well as those of the other studies expounded in this book, I would contend that at least in urban Galicia, these initial stages are being achieved, but that there is still some way to go before all the population can accept Galician on a par with Castilian. Furthermore, the revitalisation of a language does not happen overnight, so it may be too soon to make far-reaching predictions about overall attitudes and uses of Galician.

Once again, a hypothesis such as this, garnered from such a small sample, is extremely limited in its import. I reiterate that the progression witnessed in this study, despite confirmation some years later, may still reflect age-differentiated linguistic variables. Moreover, given that all the respondents are from the middle classes of Santiago de Compostela, then the examples I have found may simply be class-differentiated variables. Nonetheless, it seems likely that, just as it became quite common in urban communities to use Castilian in the home under the dictatorship, some form of shift towards the acceptance and use of Galician in contexts formerly reserved solely for Castilian is now occurring. Moreover, the concomitant re-emergence of bilingual behaviour as opposed to use of one language for all functions appears to be on the increase.

Concluding Remarks

Two of the principal hypotheses of this book were the following: that linguistic policies and planning impact on the behavioural practices of language users, and these practices may be reflected in their attitudes towards the language; and that whilst a reversal in traditional perceptions and attitudes is resulting in a reaffirmation of Galician as the autochthonous language, its sociolinguistic relationship with Castilian has not been resolved.

This chapter has been eminently comparative and somewhat experimental. By reconsidering bilingual language practice from the perspective of choice and attitude and taking into consideration other extralinguistic factors, I have had to re-evaluate the successes and failures of current linguistic policies and planning strategies. By examining the functional demarcation of Galician and Castilian over the last few decades, together with issues pertaining to bilingual competencies, I have tried to evaluate their societal relationship. By asking whether language loyalty can secure linguistic confidence and, conversely, enhance linguistic use, my empirical research in particular has posed the question of complex and multifaceted notions of identity.

I have attempted throughout to integrate current theories and concepts clarified in the Introduction, Chapter 1 and Chapter 4, and largely, the analysis has proven to be useful. In the second part of this chapter, I have adopted an intergenerational analysis to determine whether any differences in attitude and language use can be plotted across different age groups, and whether the latter is indicative of a change in progress or is an age-graded phenomenon. Again, this has been valuable, and my conclusions regarding differences in language use and attitudinal factors between different age groups are particularly enlightening.

The remaining hypothesis to be examined pertains to the characterisation of language within the notion of Galician ethnic identity, together with the issue of multiple identities. To this end, although as the final chapter, Chapter 9 is a synthesis of this book's findings, the assimilation of language and identit(ies) – inherent to the title – will be the focus.

Chapter 9

The Future of Galicia, its People, and its Language

Introductory Remarks

This final chapter reviews the main issues of the book by means of a general analysis and synthesis of the arguments and discussions I have put forward in my previous chapters. To this end, I begin by summarising the role of language in ethnic identity, for these are the two main issues this book addresses. I then divide the chapter into two and analyse firstly the language dynamic: I review the role and uses of Galician in general urban settings, and I examine the relationship between behavioural practices and attitudes towards these. In particular, I revisit once again the issues surrounding normalisation policies and planning, and discuss in some detail the role of the written standard and the bearing it may have on ethnic identity issues. We have already seen that the government's policy of *bilingüismo harmónico* is somewhat controversial, but that the overall objective of eliminating overt functional demarcation at the very least, does appear to be in its incipient stages. I will now voice my opinions and reservations regarding how this is to be achieved in the long run, taking into consideration the existence of a largely Castilianised model of pronunciation, as well as the issue of code-switching practices and linguistic differentiation, and the use of characteristic features to under or overplay allegiance to a sense of 'Galicianness'.

Fundamental to the success or otherwise of planning and policy strategies in minoritised communities around the world, is the bond between the language and ethnic identity. The second part of this chapter considers this in some detail. The manifestation of a Galician ethnic identity has also far-reaching consequences for its relationship not only with the rest of Spain, but also with Portugal. Moreover, the acceptance of such an ethnic identity does not negate the validity of other identities. I therefore discuss in some detail the notion of multiple identities within Galicia, and bearing in mind contemporary notions of belonging, throughout this discussion I also take into consideration the more global perspective. My considerations regarding whether language is a necessary requirement of Galician identity, and whether it may fulfil a more symbolic role, underline the multifaceted nature of our everyday identities. Language may not be the only way we can articulate our identities, and we may wish to enhance different identities at different times. Nonetheless, language is a valuable tool to reinforce the relevance of ethnic identity to a community as diverse as Galicia.

In my final comments, I make some tentative proposals regarding the future of Galicia and its autochthonous language, which may help to maintain the language as a viable means of communication and a positive ethnic identity marker. I take into consideration the issue of dialectal variation, and address concerns regarding the written standard and a proposal for a model of pronunciation. However, I do not want to undermine what has already been achieved; largely through the endeavours of the government, Galicia and its people are slowly coming to terms with their unique language and unique sense of ethnic identity, overlaid as it is by their membership of the Spanish State.

Ethnicity and Identity

In previous chapters, I observed that loyalty factors play an important role in efforts designed to secure linguistic confidence, by the reassignment of forms, function and values to language, and, ultimately, by its relevance as a viable symbol of ethnic identity. As was pointed out in Chapter 1 (p. 32), identity is not just a simple form of self (or other) awareness; it is also a socially constructed phenomenon, subject to change (Holt & Gubbins, 2002: 1).

Language affords meaning to a group because it connects the present with the past as a carrier of its oral traditions, literary forms, music, history, and customs. However, in itself, language is also a viable symbol of a group's ethnic identity. Gudykunst and Schmidt (1988: 1) observe that 'language and ethnic identity are reciprocally related, that is, language [...] influences the formation of ethnic identity, but ethnic identity also influences language attitudes and language usage'. Thus, the reciprocal relationship between language and identity is reflected in societal and individual attitudes towards the use of the language, which, in turn, determine notions of language prestige, solidarity and status. Although language is not fundamental to the construction of ethnic identity, it is often an extremely important identifier of a minoritised group's dynamism, status and distinctiveness.

However, ethnicity may represent the intrinsic, fixed, enduring, and largely symbolic perceptions of a sense of belonging, as well as the socially constructed, fluid, and dynamic manifestations of daily life. Thus, language can be considered an expression of primordial group traits, or can be selected from among other characteristics to mark a constructed boundary: the line between essentialist and constructivist notions of identity is not totally evident, for language operates as a boundary marker in both cases. Allied to the constructivist perspective are circumstances where groups will emphasise language as part of a 'situational' response, even though it may not be one of their core values (see pp. 41–43 for definitions).

These principles become particularly relevant when a language is the autochthonous language of a community more or less stigmatised because of its indigent state, its lack of formal education or its (perceived) unsophisticated culture, customs and traditions. We have seen that in many bi- and multilingual situations, the state encourages assimilation to the majoritised language as a way of minimising linguistic, social and cultural differences. In such cases, the minoritised community may come to view the use of the autochthonous language as representative of a lower social status, but conversely, language solidarity may be regarded as a viable, politically charged tool and prominent symbol of the collective identity, even when not all members use it.

Let us consider the case of Galician. In Chapter 3 and elsewhere, we saw how historical factors strongly influenced the destiny of Galician. Once it had lost the vestiges of its former status and prestige as a literary language, it also lost some of the loyalty of its people. It acquired a reputation as a corrupt and degraded dialect of Castilian, its use perceived as indicative of the low social status of Galicia within the nation-state of Spain. The regional nationalist movement attempted to turn this negativity around by emphasising that linguistic differentiation was an important and valuable idiosyncratic trait, one that identified Galicia and its societal and cultural differentiation from the rest of Spain in a positive light. Indeed, both *reintegración* and *autonomismo* highlight the value of a collective linguistic identity, albeit with different emphases.

At the time of the *Rexurdimento*, within intellectual, urban circles at least, the use of Galician began to be seriously considered as a valid indicator of regional and ethnic identity and, potentially, of social and cultural progress. The re-association of such positive traits with the language had, as a result, substantial implications for more contemporary movements, culminating in the creation of the *comunidad autónoma* of Galicia in the post-Franco era and the subsequent standardisation of its autochthonous language. This chapter then, will assess the contemporary situation and the implications for the future of Galicia, its autochthonous language and its people.

Language Use in Urban Settings

Throughout my discussion of the roles and values associated with the Galician language, it has been clear that over the course of the last century, Galician lost speakers in traditional strongholds such as the home, whereas Castilian experienced a widening of its use in this type of communal, intragroup domain. However, as much of the data examined in Chapters 7 and 8 indicate, this situation may now be changing. Once again, I stress that the results of my empirical study in Santiago de Compostela are not necessarily indicative of far-reaching changes within the wider community, but broader studies do appear to support my findings, at least in part. Even in the late 1980s, Fernández Rei (1988: 88) claimed that the younger members of Galician urban society were adopting Galician once again in certain circumstances, despite the fact that their parents had been forced to reject it in favour of Castilian. More recently, Regueira Fernández (1994: 38) also claimed that since devolution, Galician has started to encroach on contextual uses in which Castilian used to dominate. SSRAG's findings, whilst somewhat discouraging regarding the practical implementation of Galician in new contexts, does nonetheless acknowledge that in theory, the language can and should be used more widely (SSRAG, 2003: 189). Given the extralinguistic, societal influences I have outlined, it does not seem totally ridiculous to speculate whether some form of move towards the acceptance and use of a form of Galician for at least some intergroup functions formerly reserved solely for Castilian, may be starting to occur, at least in some urban areas and especially with the younger age groups.

Additionally, Portas (1999) found that older members of urban society were beginning to employ Galician for informal uses, suggesting change at both ends of the age range. Moreover, the concomitant re-emergence of bilingual behaviour as opposed to the use of one variety for most or all functions also appears to be on the increase. All these features may well be indicative of a potential change in progress.[1] Although it is too soon to posit with some confidence that the initial stages of an urban bilingual scenario are taking place, I could argue that at least in some of the cities and based largely on this increase in bilingual use, there has been a slowdown in the rate of decline regarding the use of Galician in recent years.

This, of course, raises questions as to whether these changes imply an ongoing breakdown of or at least modification in the functional differentiation of the languages in question, in which diglossic functions will not be maintained to the extent that they have been in the past. Before discussing this, however, I turn my attention to the role of policy and planning initiatives in the enhancement of the status and to the ultimate survival of the Galician language.

Language Status and Survival

In Chapter 2, we saw that throughout the history of Spain, the alternation between centralisation and decentralisation processes often correlates with more or less authoritarian and dictatorial rule. The importance of such processes to linguistic and regional nationalist identity issues is paramount, since this process can either repress local identities and languages, or provide spaces within which they can flourish. Language policy and planning initiatives adopted in the democratic, post-Franco era were the first concerted effort to formalise the revitalisation and revival of the Galician language, despite the attempts at creating a standard written form of the language in the last two centuries. However, these initiatives may not have been carried out quite as rigorously as was perhaps anticipated. Even though the political and social status of Galician as a language in its own right is generally accepted, much of the data I have reviewed in earlier sections regarding language application and promotion in Galicia is rather negative in its outlook. Indeed, Green (1994: 168) has even complained that the involvement of the *Xunta* in such normalisation processes has been 'well intentioned but misguided' and in no way guarantees the survival of the language.

However, I would counter these rather pessimistic assertions about the situation in Galicia. Firstly, the current legislation outlined in Chapters 2, 7 and 8 *does* encompass the concept of both individual and collective rights delineated by the Draft Universal Declaration of Linguistic Rights. Although this declaration is in no way legally binding, its main principles have become constitutional in all of Spain and are realised in detailed legislation. For Galicia, these principles are implicit within Galician language policy making and planning strategies outlined earlier (see, in particular, pp. 71–73). *Decreto* 247/1995 is a good example of the former, making explicit reference to the role of language as part of the distinctiveness strategies of Galician society.[2]

The evidence supplied in this book demonstrates that these rights have largely also been enforced. Thus, at an individual level, Galicians have the right to be recognised as members of a (distinct) linguistic community; they have the right to use their language(s) in private and in public; and have the right to maintain and develop their own culture. Similarly, at a collective level, they have the right to education in their own language; and have the right to cultural and media services in their own language; and have the right to use their own language in official and administrative domains. It could be argued that these collective rights, and in particular, those pertaining to education, are not fully or thoroughly implemented throughout the region, as is suggested by much of the data in Chapter 7 and discussed in more detail below. One of the main difficulties is Galician is somewhat of a 'transition' zone, and enforcing a generic set of legislative procedures on an amalgam of different linguistic and sociolinguistic configurations throughout the region is highly problematical. The example of Santiago de Compostela serves as a good illustration of this point. Generally, the use of Galician as the language of instruction and institutional practice has been implemented throughout. In the established middle classes of the city, the new legislation and its implementation appear to be having a positive effect on linguistic practices, but there are still substantial areas where the social implications and possibilities for advancement attached to the use of Castilian appear to be of paramount importance to the population.

The Galician Standard

In Spain, normalisation procedures are generally carried out through the education system, and through the use of the language in the media and other institutions. In the case of Galician, they include the pre-scription of a written standard; they are designed to offer the language a way of enhancing a positive self-image and the competencies of its users, as well as acquiring further users through social or territorial expansion of its range (pp. 77–78). To an extent, they also affect the way in which a language is pronounced even when no model for pronunciation is advocated. In other words, the use of the language should become a 'normal', everyday occurrence.

Bearing this in mind, what part has the development of a written standard language played in normalisation practices in Galicia? In Chapter 1, we saw how the establishment of a written form of a language through corpus planning activities is but one of the stages of language planning that can serve to enhance and consolidate the status of the language as a community marker. The shared set of linguistic norms that ensues underpins the structure and form of the language and at the same time, serves as a means of written communication between disparate groups. Thus, the written language becomes fundamental to the group's ethnicity and acquires prestige as an important identifier of the group's dynamism, status and distinctiveness (pp. 34, 47–48).

Until very recently, one of the biggest problems facing the *Xunta* regarding the general acceptance of the standard has been that, primarily for historical reasons, only a small minority of the Galician population would consider employing a written form of the language, even for the most informal and casual note taking. A switch to the use of Galician in such contexts has been attempted with some difficulty. Even well edu-cated people would nearly always use Castilian as the written form (Pérez-Barreiro Nolla, 1990: 197–198), because for a long time, it was the only language of instruction. The result of this is that at least at the present time, for many people, and particularly in the more rural zones of the region, the prescribed written standards may be a largely irrelevant feature of normalisation.

However, I would counter that an over-zealous and, patronising crusade to 'convert the masses' cannot and should not be advocated. The GIDS scale (Fishman, 1991; p. 48) highlights that there are inherent problems in trying to reverse language losses through the education system before a sense of allegiance and identity with the language has been instilled and it has become the intragroup form of spoken communication. Yet, the coherent and consistent presence of Galician in all facets of everyday life is vital to the revival of positive associations with the language, and the presence of an official, written standard differentiated as far as possible from Castilian, reinforces the idea among its users that Galician is a language in its own right.

This issue of differentiation from Castilian brings me back to a further issue pertaining to normalisation. In a lengthy debate on the Galician Studies email discussion list (November 2004: galician-studies@jiscmail.ac.uk), David Mackenzie states that many people do not understand why a formal written code, together with concomitant normalisation and normativisation procedures, are even needed in the first place. They do not appreciate that a standard orthography, available for use in all local institutions, procedures and practices, has not been set up to stigmatise or even discredit their (predominantly spoken) regional or non-standard varieties, but to reinforce the role played by the language as a whole in the consolidation of an idiosyncratic Galician ethnicity.

What is important here is the perception that apart from a written standard, a spoken standard is being imposed, compared to which the speakers' variety of Galician is viewed as inferior. Furthermore, Mackenzie's comment also raises an important point regarding the beliefs and opinion of the autochthonous population and the problems therein for normalisation. Traditionally, the main thrust of a stereotypical Galician ethnicity has been entrenched in the maintenance of a collective, deeply embedded and highly complex sense of inferiority and subservience regarding its status and its long-term value and import within Spain. Until recently, the hierarchical structure of the social order implicit within Galicia sanctioned both the political and linguistic domination of the overriding state. In accordance with nationalistic practices discussed in Chapter 1, the assimilation of the populace under the banner of the Spanish 'nation' ignored diverse ethnicities and languages. Through their demarcation of linguistic practices, social and cultural characteristics of the majoritised group, the authorities in Madrid enforced the notion of one sovereign entity throughout the country, hence the associations of 'national' language stated above.

Without doubt, this has had a concomitant effect on group and individual identification strategies in Galicia, as I discussed briefly in Chapter 8. Monteagudo avers that many people still tend to consider Galician as a dialect of Castilian (1995: 9–10). This may or may not be the case, but to argue that it is a reflection of their lack of social, cultural and political aspiration, as Wardhaugh does (2002: 98), is rather disparaging. It has probably more to do with the fact that a strong, prestigious idiosyncratic linguistic identity is still some way off from recognition by all the community, despite Galician being recognised as a language in its own right on political grounds. Negative attitudes towards the use of Galician still exist in the region, and they may well manifest themselves overtly in many spoken language behavioural patterns. An example from my own research is the use of Castilian in the home. Time and time again, I have experienced instances in which older Galicians throughout the region, irrespective of whether they claim to be sympathetic or disdainful as to the survival of the language, simply refuse to speak Galician even though there is ample evidence that they can, and indeed, do so, on many intragroup occasions.[3]

Mackenzie's comment brings me back to my earlier discussion of a model for pronunciation based upon Castilian, or a 'castilianised' form of Galician (pp. 134–137). Many people appear to consider their spoken variety of Galician inferior to what they perceive an oral standard to be and, hence, consider it largely inadequate for many interactions. Rather than make a mistake and utilise what they deem to be an inappropriate dialectal pronunciation, word or grammatical form, many appear to prefer consciously replacing the whole utterance with Castilian forms and structures.

This is rather disheartening. Before normalisation practices started to take effect, people perceived their autochthonous language as inferior to Castilian. Through normalisation, people have become more receptive to the idea of using Galician. However, the initial positive sense of identification with the language appears to have been replaced in certain quarters by a sense that their accent is not good enough and that a specific, spoken standard has been imposed. The written standard and its model of pronunciation based on the Castilian phonetic system, may be perceived as the creation of new urban varieties of Galician by traditional speakers. In this way, it is an obstacle to their use of the language and a further step towards assimilation with Castilian (Regueira Fernández, 2006: 80). Hence, it is not so much that they regard the written standard as an imposition, more that they now associate a sense of inferiority with the use of spoken Galician _and_ a Galician accent. Because of this, many may revert back to the default solution, that it, to use Castilian, since even overlaid by a Galician accent, it is considered more acceptable universally and indicative of social advancement.

In light of this latter comment, it is somewhat ironical that the spoken model perceived in such cases is based primarily on Castilian. Indeed, this is why Regueira Fernández's comments (2004) regarding the creation of a model of pronunciation based upon Galician linguistic traits are eminently valid, and the development of such a model may even prevent such speakers from reverting to Castilian.

Nonetheless, social prestige in the Galicia milieu *does* depend on which spoken form of Galician is employed. Class discrimination may occur between those who speak Galician with a dialectal accent and those, typically young and professional urbanites, who identify with a more prestigious form of the spoken language that separates them symbolically from the lower classes. In this sense, the use of a Castilian model of pronunciation does facilitate the acceptance and employment of Galician in contexts where Castilian formerly dominated. Furthermore, it is to be wondered whether such aspirants would accept a model based on Galician traits. The extensive, in-depth, innovative, qualitative and quantitative study of the linguistic attitudes of young people in Galicia recently carried out by SSRAG highlighted the vitality of traditional prejudices and perceptions of inferiority associated with the Galician accent, and the positive attributes of innovation and social competence associated with a Castilian accent (2003: 185–186).[4]

I do not believe that the *Xunta* intends normalisation processes to discredit local, non-standard spoken varieties of Galician, but this is a somewhat contentious issue that needs to be resolved, particularly as the dialectal variation prevalent in the region in the middle of the 20th Century is being reduced severely (see pp. 131–134). Over the last 30 or so years, the efforts of the *Xunta* and their institutions have not all been in vain; the general findings of SSRAG vindicate the efforts that have been made in recent years to improve at least attitudes towards the use of Galician (2003). I too, still uphold my earlier optimism regarding a slow-down in the rate of decline in the use of Galician in recent years, together with a potential re-evaluation of the role and status of the language in some urban sectors of society. Even minor encouraging shifts in the behaviour of some communities towards the use of Galician may be starting to provoke a practical and highly beneficial modification in how the language is valued within the society as a whole. This, in turn, may provoke a more positive attitude towards the notion that a Galician ethnic identity is a valid and viable asset to the community and do away with negative perceptions of the Galician people as a beleaguered community, their self-esteem bruised and battered. Of course, this also raises questions as to whether these changes imply an ongoing breakdown of or at least modification in the functional differentiation of the languages in question, in which diglossic functions will not be maintained to the extent that they have been in the past.

Bilingüísmo Harmónico and Diglossia

Despite the fact that his comment was made over 25 years ago, Rodríguez Neira succinctly summarises the overall prevailing linguistic situation in Galicia by contrasting the regalicianisation scenario of many of the urban areas with that of degalicianisation in the more rural areas (Rodríguez Neira, 1988: 256–262).

My earlier comments reinforce this point. Both languages are still undergoing a substantial degree of upheaval, in that in many quarters, functional differentiation is rather blurred. As a result, some view the division of linguistic use in Galician as a case of accepted diglossia towards one of a diglossia in conflict (pp. 14–18), where the employment of both languages breaks traditional barriers against utilisation in given linguistic domains (Portas, 1999: 155). In this respect, I should recall my earlier conclusions regarding the *Xunta*'s current linguistic policy subsumed under the title of *bilingüismo harmónico* (pp. 176–179) since I have averred that supporters of the policy may view the lack of any clear functional demarcation of Galician and Castilian as something to be applauded. They may also view the notion of a transition period, and the concomitant upheaval as far as usage is concerned, as a logical step to full societal bilingualism and harmony and equality in contextual use.

Indeed, the acceptance of at least the standard form of Galician for certain urban intergroup communications and functions normally associated with Castilian is counterbalanced by the use of Castilian for certain intragroup communications in some rural situations. This exchange of linguistic domains is not entirely disastrous, because such a readjustment of values and functions associated with each language variety does not necessarily imply that assimilation procedures have been instigated. The fact that the standard Galician form does appear to be gaining some ground, however small, in some of the urban areas, or at the very least, is inciting interest in its use, cannot be deleterious to the overall prognosis for the survival of Galician, and the fact that there *has* been a slowdown in the rate of decline regarding the use of Galician, means that certain members of the urban middle classes at least are beginning to flout earlier norms regarding its use.[5]

The problem is not necessarily that there is now more competition for domains; rather, it is that any type of final scenario in which societal bilingual language use without defined contextual use is endorsed may have implications for the minoritised language in the relationship, in that it is the language that may lose out, especially if it does not enjoy the overall loyalty and support of the population. In a scenario where either language can be used in either context, what is to stop speakers from simply electing to use one for all functions and in all contexts, just as monolinguals do? *Bilingüismo harmónico* does not fully explain how it will avoid one of the languages taking over from the other in all contexts; rather it prefers that competition for functional use does not occur, but if it does, then the inference is that may the best language win.

Despite these reservations, I would contend that there are still no viable alternatives to *bilingüismo harmónico*, as I stated in Chapter 8. Regueira

Fernández (2006: 77–90) in particular, offers an excellent discussion of the proposals and their political implications. In my earlier account of the creation of the *Normas*, I have already discussed the (political) *independentista* proposals regarding monolingualism in Galician and the *reintegración* proposals regarding integration into the Portuguese-speaking world (pp. 125–131). In this section, I simply would highlight the claim advocated by the *Asociación Gallega por la Libertad de Idioma* (AGLI) [The Galician Association for the Freedom of the Language], that monolingualism in Castilian is the only logical outcome of the Galician situation. This however, is a rather idealistic and largely unpopular perspective, given its far-reaching implications for the political and social status of the region. Furthermore, any linguistic policy in Galicia has to be realistic regarding the sociolinguistic configuration of the region. Given that the measures already implemented have led to an increase in the number of bilingual speakers, a claim to monolingual status in favour of Castilian or indeed, in favour of Galician, would be largely untenable at the present time.

Code-Switching Practices

A very specific type of switching process is occurring in Galicia that has implications for *bilingüismo harmónico*. Although the aim of this model is to avoid competition and conflict between the languages in question, the switch delineated below involves a wholesale or almost wholesale situational switch between these languages, prompted by a change of context or type of interlocutor. Thus, it is associated with leaky or otherwise diglossia.

This type of switch may take place within the nucleus of the family (pp. 103–104). Research carried out in Galicia regarding switching code practices within a home environment, such as that of Argente Giralt and Lorenzo Suarez (1991) into the community of Coiro in Pontevedra, found that even when an adult's mother tongue and language habitually used with the rest of the family was Galician, Castilian was nearly always used with the children. This type of switch does not demonstrate any type of change in the relationship between the speakers, nor does it have anything to do with diglossic functions, for conversations with family members typically take place within informal scenario. This switch is simply to do with the fact that these parents have chosen to raise their children speaking Castilian, and as such, this is a type of language shift phenomenon.

This appears to be a very common situation in urban and semi-urban areas. The term a *xeración ponte* [the bridging generation] is often used to describe such parents, and refers to the fact that these parents are the link between older, Galician-speaking family members and the younger, Castilian-speaking members. Implicit within this term is the belief that the convergence with Castilian will lead ultimately to its adoption and the rejection of Galician within family settings. Portas' (1999: 149) Galician sample purports to highlight such intra-familial switching techniques. He demonstrates that the employment of both languages tends to be codified according to which family member is being addressed at the time. Portas (1999) concludes his study by stating that this could predict a more gradual, societal age and language transition., endnote: See for example, the online website of the *Consello da Cultura Galega* [the Council for Galician Culture] at http://www.consellodacultura.org/.

My investigation results also manifest cases of switching between languages that demonstrates a definite age-group variance in mother tongue application within a single family.[6] However, there is also evidence in my data of bilingual conversations taking place between some parents and children, whereby the latter are starting to reply not in Castilian, but in Galician. Taking these findings into consideration, I would agree that this *could*, potentially be viewed as the forerunner to a more gradual age and language transition within the community, in that there may be a switch in overall language use, certainly in informal contexts. I would contend however that, in this case, it is not at all clear which language would fulfil the majority of functions. In the cases of switching for joke telling purposes, the speakers may select the marked language in a given social setting, here, Galician, in order to accentuate their linguistic differences from their interlocutors. In general situations within the home, the use of Castilian by parents with their children does appear to be associated with notions of advancement and promotion. Yet, the use of Galician by the children in such contexts is highly significant, because it implies a revival of Galician in this context.

In my discussion of code-switching practices in Chapter 4, I examined the notion that a lack of full competence in both or all languages implied a degree of semilingualism. I countered this by quoting Milroy and Muysken's (1995: 3) statement that bilingual language use tends to correspond with different contextual use, and that generally, speakers do not select between the two in each and every context. However, these examples demonstrate that there is a substantial degree of overlapping in contextual use in Galicia, at least in informal, intragroup home contexts. As I have implied above, one of the reasons may be the increase in the number of people displaying confidence in their employment of both languages and, therefore, displaying a high level of individual bilingualism, as evidenced in Chapters 7 and 8. Age, rather than class differentiation, appears to be the determining factor as to whether someone employs one language predominantly or whether they switch between the two according to the given setting, theme, interlocutor, and so on. IGE data (2004) concluded that throughout the region at the turn of the millennium, 44% of 5 to 29 year olds used both Galician and Castilian this way, compared with only 29% of over 50 year olds. Moreover, in Santiago de Compostela, whereas the more senior age group tended to claim one dominant language, three quarters of the youngest age group demonstrated proficient bilingual language use and, on the whole, appeared happy to use either.

In Chapter 8, I discussed how the insertion of Castilian lexis into the Galician spoken by some of my study's younger respondents to add a note of irony or humour, is an excellent example of intersentential rhetorical code-switching from the L^2 into the L^1. In itself, this does not signify that some form of linguistic shift is in play, since the autonomy of linguistic structures is maintained, and switches from one language appear as foreign elements within the speech of the other. What it does demonstrate, however, is the high level of bilingual confidence held by these particular respondents in their own ability to manipulate language in this manner. Their motivation to display a particular viewpoint or position regarding language selection, rather than the semantic content of the utterance, is also significant, since as I contended, this practice is also employed as an identification strategy; what Le Page and Tabouret-Keller (1985) have termed 'focussing'. These factors may jointly reveal a degree of ethnic identification and even solidarity with Galician, and imply a symbolic distinction between the 'in-group', that is, the Galician speakers, and the 'out-group', that is, those who are not.[7]

Emblematic Features and Linguistic Transference

These issues of in-group and out-group solidarity and identification are also implicit in my earlier discussion of emblematic features in Chapter 6. The *gheada* is found in, but not restricted to, the western areas of the region; the velar nasal is found throughout, but their uses or otherwise, suggest different issues regarding identification strategies and transference phenomena. Firstly, in some cases, even Castilian words ending in $-n$ will often be resolved as the velar nasal; whether I can consider this to be an example of transference however, is extremely tenuous, given the restricted use of such forms. However, as I pointed out in Chapter 1, any change that is integrated 'from below' tends to simplify the articulation of a particular word (Mesthrie *et al.*, 2000: 118) – and, at least for the velar nasal, I have already rejected the weakening hypothesis regarding its diachronic evolution.

Patently, the use of the *gheada* does not simplify the articulation of *g*. Moreover, the extralinguistic connotations of the use of the *gheada* would appear to imply that once again speakers are aware that they are using it and consider it to be a mistake; hence, I would propose that its *avoidance* might well be an incipient sign of transference.

In the case of speakers code-switching for a rhetorical purpose, every Castilian word inserted into the Galician speech stream was overlaid by a strongly Galician pronunciation. Thus, both the velar nasal and the *gheada* occurred, even when a given speaker did not normally use the latter in their dialect (although this was not common). I have already postulated that in no way do these examples of code-switching imply that some form of linguistic change is in play. Rather, I have claimed that it may reveal a degree of ethnic identification and even solidarity with Galician. This reiterates to a large degree my earlier suggestions made in my conclusions of Chapter 6 regarding at least the *gheada* (pp. 159–160). Despite the traditional negative connotations surrounding its use, Alvarez-Cáccamo's and Celso (1990), my own studies, and to a degree, those of Kabatek (2000) reveal an association between the use of the *gheada* and local identity reinforcement strategies, functioning as solidarity mechanisms. Moreover, the use of the *gheada* appears to be deliberate for speakers who code-switch for a rhetorical purpose.

However, I will have to revise slightly my comments regarding the velar nasal. In Chapter 6, I stated that no prestige appears to be attached to the use of the velar nasal, that its use is generally unconscious, although the whole population recognise its significance as a linguistic trait of Galician. Yet, in my code-switching examples, there did appear to be a conscious effort to use the velar nasal as a Galician identity reinforcer, rather than as an unconscious example of overdifferentiation.

I tentatively hypothesise that the use of both characteristics in this instance reinforces the group's reasons for rhetorical code-switching. These attempts at a positive identification strategy highlight the notion of in-group solidarity through linguistic differentiation and demarcation even when Castilian is being used.[8]

My summarising comments highlight the somewhat confusing nature of these features in Galician. One the one hand, the *gheada* may be a dialectal feature consciously avoided by speakers, who claim that its presence in their speech is one of the reasons why they do not speak 'good Galician'. On the other hand, in some highly restricted quarters, it may be used as a solidarity reinforcer, a salient phonological feature that is adopted consciously by speakers. Similarly, on the one hand the velar nasal is a largely unconscious feature of all varieties of Galician. Its use is not deleterious to the prestige of Galician, and it may even be heard when the speaker articulates Castilian final nasal. On the other hand, in some cases, it may even demonstrate similar, consciously manipulated identity reinforcing characteristics as the *gheada*. Whether these could be sound changes, and therefore designated as 'off the shelf' or 'under the counter' (Milroy, in press) (pp. 20–21) is somewhat contentious due to the apparent-time nature of this research, as we have seen, but as such, they would be socially motivated. Nonetheless, further research would also be needed to confirm at least some of these findings, since the fact that some uses are highly significant to the speakers themselves means that what will occur in the future is extremely difficult to predict.

Linguistic Differentiation

The examples of intrasentential code-switching also raise an important point regarding the linguistic differentiation of the two languages in question. Williamson and Williamson have pointed out (1984: 403) that the proximity of Galician to Castilian may facilitate the acquisition and retention of Galician by its speakers, but that it also leads to linguistic transference. In bilingual situations, extremely high levels of transference and convergence to one language from another may imply a reallocation of many communicative functions and usages from one to the other language, and may also imply a loss of value and prestige.

Some Galician linguists, predominantly *reintegracionistas*, have been concerned from the beginning with what they consider to be official attempts to impose at the very least an orthographic standard language that is heavily based upon Castilian, to the exclusion of any Portuguese cognates, as I discussed earlier (pp. 125–131). Although the political ramifications of these assertions are clear, nonetheless until recently it has been true that in some cases of Galician relexification, the form selected is cognate in Castilian. It could be argued correctly that these forms are already well established within the Galician language, given that they were borrowed many years ago, but this may well serve to bring Galician closer to linguistic assimilation with Castilian in a way that, as I have already stated, a readjustment of values and functions associated with each language does not. In my example above, although my respondents considered the forms *agradable* and *desde* to be Castilianisms, the fact that they have become integrated into the standard form means that they have officially been accepted as part of the Galician language. The inference then, is that older people at least recognise lexical forms that are not 'traditionally' Galician, and continue to view them as alien to their own language. Thus, in some ways the emergence of a standard form reduces linguistic diversity.

Yet, if it was indeed the case, then would it not also be true for forms related to Portuguese? To date, there are no available data on speakers' perceptions of such forms, but the modifications made to the *Normas* and associated grammars and glossaries in 2003 *have* attempted to incorporate certain characteristics that are more in line with Portuguese cognates. Some of the recent orthographic innovations that approximate Portuguese include the use of the orthographic form *ao* instead of the earlier form *ó*, to represent the contraction of the preposition *a* [to] plus the masculine definite article *o* [the]. Lexical innovations include *estudar* [to study] and its derivatives to replace *estudiar*; reitor [rector] and its derivatives to replace *rector*; *ouvir* [to hear] are admitted as correct forms alongside *oír*; and *até* [until] is also admitted as a correct form alongside *ata*. With the exception of the latter form, all the replaced forms are Castilian cognates.

Portuguese/Spanish Issues

If Galicians started associating these forms with Portuguese cognates, there could be potential ramifications for their perceptions of their language are an expression of their idiosyncratic ethnic identity within the whole Portuguese/Spanish dynamic discussed earlier (pp. 89–90). An awareness of who we are as individuals often focuses upon the recognition and appreciation of where we come from and of what we share with the community as a whole – such as language, as we have already seen. In the debate regarding Galician identification strategies, it is tempting to discount proposed Celtic associations, for example, as somewhat whimsical and idealised notions of a far-away and highly stylised past that plays no real role in the everyday lives and consciousness of Galicians today. It is the case, nonetheless, that certain customs such as the *gaiteiro* or the *queimada* are relics of a Celtic past, and even if people are not aware of this, they may still identify with them in some way.[9] A similar statement could be made regarding Portuguese associations, were it not for the fact that Portugal is a geographical neighbour, and a sense of Portuguese involvement in Galician issues is still alive. Even if the ongoing debates surrounding the inherent structure and form of the Galician standard are not vented generally at a popular level, the media does afford them airtime. It is to be wondered what effect the *reintegracionista* perspective in particular, together with its socio-political implications, may have on the psyche of people who have already experienced a fair amount of upheaval in the last few decades. It is also to be wondered what response any vehement attempts to reinforce Galician's early historic connections with Portuguese would receive.

In the course of the empirical research discussed in Chapter 8, the respondents were happy to discuss such matters informally, and I found that the majority were fairly resolute about the issue. One of my respondents stated that where he worked, everyone was tired of listening to the 'same old rhetoric' regarding integration with Portugal. His work colleagues argued that the standard already implemented in newspapers, and so on approximated their own perceptions of form and structure, so why try and change it? Moreover, if changes did need to be made, why should Portuguese be involved? Another respondent was clearly incensed that this debate was still going on. She was happy to learn the standard, and happy to try and use it, but she complained that Portuguese had nothing to do with Galicia any more. A further respondent, this time of school age, wondered what the fuss was all about. She had often heard about the debate regarding standardisation, but argued that it was largely irrelevant to her and her friends. They all accepted the Galician standard on an equal footing to that of Castilian, even though some of the forms were different to the Galician spoken by grandparents and other older members of their families. The final respondent was clearly worried about the potential implications of a reinforced connection between the two languages. He found it extremely difficult at times to understand spoken Portuguese because its pronunciation was, in his eyes, more sophisticated than that of Galician, hence his concerns regarding the superimposition of Portuguese phonetic forms onto Galician.

Naturally, these are just a few of many potentially different perspectives, and as such, cannot be said in any way to be representative of the general opinion. Nonetheless, if the acceptance of Portuguese forms into the standard were to be perceived as a threat to the region's overriding national identity, what would be the general response? It must be remembered that Spain has been part of the societal, cultural, and linguistic configuration of Galicia for over 700 years, and the notion of a Spanish identity allied to a Galician one must not be overlooked, as I will discuss further below. Whilst it is true that the pro-Portuguese groups may be able to lay claim to strong historical links with Portugal, Galicia is part of Spain, and Galicians speak Castilian, not Portuguese, as well as Galician. Within the region itself, such strategies may simply lead to the population embracing the overriding, state-oriented national identity and underlining their inclusiveness within the Spanish nation as a way of rejecting and opposing any perceived threat from outside.[10] Moreover, as has already been demonstrated (pp. 89–90), Portugal itself is rather ambivalent regarding the reinforcement of any linguistic, social, historical, and cultural ties with Galicia, other than perhaps for economic gain. As I pointed out in Chapter 5, there is a long-standing tradition of hostility between the majority of Portuguese and Galicians, based upon linguistic, social, and cultural issues. Henderson's comments regarding this hostility (1996: 196–199) imply that the mistrust engendered between the two groups on the part of the Galicians may simply stem from deep-seated ignorance of the past, strongly influenced by centralising policies of the Madrid authorities. Although I find this statement rather divisive, overriding allegiance to Spain is in itself relevant, for once again it underlines the notion of in-group – Spain – versus out-group – Portugal.

Were it to occur, the potential espousal of 'Spanishness' would be understandable in the context of an introduction of Portuguese forms into the standard language. On the other hand, despite the fairly limited supplies of traditional written sources in Galician to which current lexicographers, grammarians, and so on have recourse, the use of Castilian forms in the language is not in any way accepted as an inevitable outcome of the pervading sociolinguistic scenario in Galicia. ILG, for example, still continues to carry out detailed field research into linguistic variation throughout the region, and the glossaries compiled of their findings are a valuable resource. Nonetheless, the *perception* still remains in many quarters that Castilianisms are rife within standard dictionaries and glossaries.

An obvious ramification of acculturation processes with Castilian is that linguistic differentiation would cease to be a marker of Galician ethnic identity, although its symbolic value may be preserved. Were this to happen, even if links to a common cultural tradition, historical memories, and other communal artefacts denoting 'Galicianness' were to be retained, the language itself would undergo assimilation.

Once again, Catalonia serves as a valuable comparison (see also pp. 80–81). In the discussion of language rights in Spain (23/11/04 galician- studies@jiscmail.ac.uk), Philip Davies points out that although issues such as comparative economic prosperity, political culture and demographics may vary, Catalan shares the same ethnolinguistic issues, such as linguistic proximity to Castilian, with Galician. Davies is extremely pessimistic regarding the future of Galician, claiming that the reason why Catalan will survive into the next century and Galician will not, is because the Catalans absolutely refuse, in every aspect, to allow their distinctive language and culture to be dominated by Castilian. To his mind, this is a linguistic position and not necessarily a political one, even though the Catalans may adopt an extremely confrontational stance and as a result, face a barrage of criticism from all sides.

Such negativity could be considered rather counterproductive, but it does highlight the importance of dynamic community support for and loyalty to the language, without which all formal, institutional attempts by the regional authorities to revive and promote Galician both as a means of communication and a viable political tool, may struggle to achieve their aims. Inherent to such practices is the community's desire to instil and maintain a positive sense of Galician ethnic identity, and the issue of other overarching and potentially competing identities.

Multiple Identity Strategies

The *Xunta* has taken some positive steps in the right direction. There has been a substantial amount of disparaging commentary, primarily politically motivated, levelled at the normalisation processes introduced by the regional authorities, as I have already commented. Nonetheless, the overall establishment and incipient implementation of language policies has been extremely important to the political and social aims of the region. Irrespective of the problems inherent within the configuration of the standard itself, and despite the reticence displayed by some towards what has been perceived as the Castilian bias, debates surrounding its use are nowadays often covered by the media, and may even be contributing to its employment in some new contexts. At the very least, the perceived standing of Galician has been improved since the region achieved self-governing rights, and the aims and conscious efforts of the government to reinforce the language as an expression of Galician identity and to afford it formal and legal status, have, to some extent, been carried out. Thus, within the dominant state of Spain, Galician is now considered a viable regional language, at least officially.

There also appears to be a strong correlation between the albeit tentative reassignment of Galician to domains by certain members of the urban younger age group whose parents used predominantly Castilian, and issues of status and identity.[11] As I commented in Chapter 1 (pp. 46–51), the values and prestige a given community affords a language will have some bearing on the language's attendant use, and it would certainly appear that certain sectors of society are beginning to view both their own status and that of their autochthonous language in a different light. The more they perceive the use of their group language as an indicator of status and as a reinforcer of their distinct identity, the more they will appreciate its prestige value and the more they will recognise that maintaining a sense of linguistic differentiation from Castilian is paramount. Once again, this underlines the discussion in Chapter 1 and above (pp. 36–37) regarding in-groups and out-groups and notions of kinship. It may be that, as a direct result in the increased use of their idiosyncratic language, certain sectors of the urban Galician community at least, are beginning to create a form of social boundary, one that is inclusive towards its members but exclusive towards non-members. Thus, through such overt self-identification strategies, they may be seen to be reinforcing their collective sense of and identification with a Galician ethnicity, and, ultimately, their desire to be considered part of the Galician ethnic group.[12]

However, this potential correlation between language use and identification strategies is not manifest throughout the region. MSG data for example, (Fernández Rodríguez *et al.*, 1996) demonstrates that the majority of the population (55.4%) view Galician as the language of the future.[13] Yet, although this is an extremely positive insight into how people feel about the language, it is largely unclear at this stage whether a common redefinition and alliance with an idiosyncratic Galician ethnic identity is also occurring both in urban and rural areas, and both in younger and older age groups. The region-wide data presented in Chapters 7 and 8 indicates that a substantial proportion of young people do not use Galician as a spoken form. If Galician is to undergo social recuperation, then as we have seen, it needs to be accepted by the community as a viable and useful manifestation of their collective allegiance and aspirations, and used as such.

This raises an extremely important point regarding identity. If a person self-identifies with a particular ethnic group, then they demonstrate a willingness to be perceived and treated as part of that group. Although such allegiances to Galician and to the notion of a Galician ethnic identity are crucial, minoritised cultures and communities cannot ignore other layers of their multifaceted identity. As Dauenhauer and Dauenhauer (1998: 77) observe '[...] ethnicity, by definition, implies a relationship to other groups in the total society'. My discussions of identity throughout Chapter 1 highlighted some pertinent factors that are inherent to the notion of fluid, dynamic and multiple social identities, which I summarise here for convenience. Almost everyone simultaneously belongs to different social, cultural, and even linguistic groups and bilingual, bicultural groups are the general outcome of contact situations between two disparate societies. One, single ethnic self-identification strategy is extremely unlikely, because existing identities are not necessarily discarded when others are assumed. Even though people may perceive themselves as belonging more to one particular group than to another at a given point in time, this may be due to manipulation and negotiation strategies according to what identity best suits a situation at a given point in time and in a given context (Liebkind, 1999: 145–147; Hidalgo, 2001: 61–62). This also recalls my earlier discussion of the construction of ethnicity.

As far as the concept of nation is concerned, Galicians have at the very least bilingual and bicultural identities, and it may well be the case that many people are starting to overtly redefine and ally themselves with their Galician as well with their overarching Spanish sense of belonging.[14] However, to posit that they must emphasise their 'Galicianness' over their 'Castilianness' would imply, as does Llobera (1994: 131–132) amongst others, a situation of conflict. This is somewhat counterproductive and simply does not reflect the reality of the situation. The implementation of *bilingüismo harmónico* has meant that Galician and Castilian now overlap in their contextual use, and despite its avowed aim to avoid linguistic conflict, the languages are to an extent in competition for such uses. What Galicians themselves do harmoniously share are complementary, multifaceted identities pertaining to issues of belonging, and any calls to ignore, reject, or even fight against their Castilian identity are simply missing the implications of the socio-political-historical configuration of the region, as well as the whole ethos and rationale behind the premise of multifaceted identities.

The Language-Identity Dynamic

Let me now reconsider the role of language within the concept of identity. When a given community wants to revive and promote its language, it has to engage in positive self-identification strategies.

However, the opposite is not strictly true; the reinforcement of a viable ethnic identity is not always reliant upon the maintenance of an autochthonous language. Even when not actively used, the outmoded language commonly remains in place as an underlying and key reference point of ethnic identity. Iglesias-Alvarez and Ramallo have recently carried out a valuable and interesting study into the relationship between language and identity in Galicia (2003: 255–287). By adopting what they considered a non-essentialist concept of identity (see pp. 43–45), they looked at the use of language in processes of identity construction within nine discussion groups from both rural and urban environments in and around Vigo. Their main hypothesis was that the autochthonous language was conceived as the cohesive element of the multiple dimensions of the Galician identity (2003: 257). They concluded that in response to globalisation, Galicia is undergoing the construction of a symbolic, rural localist identity, and that language is its main, but not sole, characteristic.

Regueira Fernández (2006: 90–91) also states that the links between notions of Galician nationalism and language now mean that even people who do not speak or even read the language, are still identifying with it as a symbol of their ethnic origins. This echoes SSRAG's findings that the practical use of Galician is not always essential to sentiments of Galician ethnic identity (2003: 187–188). Le Page and Tabouret-Keller's comments that it does not make any difference whether people know, speak, or just claim an ethnically related language as long as one is available for them to associate with, reinforces these points (1985: 237). In this way, language does not stop being a core value (Smolicz, 1997: 67), even if it is not overtly accepted or not as a means of communication, because its symbolic and emotional values may still serve to reinforce a sense of identity within the community.[15] Some members of the community may have rejected the language for reasons of prestige, but they have not necessarily also rejected their sense of Galicianness.

I illustrate the above points with a recent study carried out on the island of Jersey into the role of language in the construction of ethnic identity amongst young people who were born in Madeira or the Portuguese mainland, or who were first generation migrants to Jersey (Beswick, 2005). The older members of the families of these migrants have been able to maintain a sense of their own, idiosyncratic ethnicity by establishing tight-knit communities in which they are able to maintain their autochthonous language, social norms, and customs, generally to the exclusion of cognates within the host community. Unlike their parents, many of the younger members are fluent in English. Here, as an interesting contrast to my earlier example of code-switching in Galician, it is these younger respondents who tend to underplay and undervalue their linguistic abilities in Portuguese. They describe how they have to switch to English in certain situations and often borrow English terms, and they view these switches and mixing strategies negatively, as a sign of laziness or as a mistake made when they cannot immediately think of the appropriate Portuguese word. Despite this, their self-identification strategies indicate that the majority still regard themselves as Portuguese or specifically, Madeiran Portuguese, as well as English. The Portuguese language is still employed as an emblematic, reinforcing, and unifying symbol of group identity by the community as a whole, even though the younger generations are acquiring a notion of 'Englishness' at school and learn the host community's language.[16] This study demonstrates that the younger respondents' perception of their group membership at least, is not totally reliant on the regular use of Portuguese.

Le Page and Tabouret-Keller's (1985) earlier research into 'acts of identity' (see pp. 32–33, 103) in Belize and the Creole-speaking Caribbean came to similar conclusions. These authors found that although ethnic choice had to coincide with language choice for the parent's generation, members of the younger generation seemed to be able to establish their ethnic identity separately from their language identity, which allowed them to have respect for their parents and their Spanish loyalty while giving voice to the social linguistic evolution towards Creole. This 'mixed' identity allowed them to retain a sense of Spanish identity (le Page & Tabouret-Keller, 1985: 221).

Regarding Galicia, Pérez-Barreiro Nolla (1990: 205–6) has also stated that making extravagant claims for the language as the decisive and virtually sole element of a Galician identification strategy would be a mistake, because few people manifest any strong allegiance to it. Hence, they are unlikely to manifest any allegiance to the notion of a Galician ethnic identity based upon it. I agree that focussing entirely on Galician as the one and only representation of Galician ethnicity would be somewhat limiting and may have rather poor consequences. Yet, this issue of language loyalty warrants further consideration. Although my assertions are based upon small-scale empirical data, my research often reveals a marked lack of linguistic confidence among the older age groups, with some members making rather disparaging remarks about the language itself and its use in anything other than extremely informal, in-group and above all, private, interactions. In contrast, even in interactions with other sectors of society, many of the younger age group are starting to explore the sociolinguistic possibilities of employing Galician in domains where Castilian used to prevail. However, in the case of the older respondents, the traditional and general inferiority complex regarding the language does not translate as a rejection of Galician ethnic identity. For the younger respondents, the use of Galician where Castilian was the norm also expresses their feelings of 'Galicianness'. In this sense, I would agree with Andersen's earlier statement (1991; p. 78) that the use of a language (nearly) always implies (a degree of) solidarity with its inherent ethnic group.

Therefore, whilst I agree that few Galicians have any *strong* allegiance to the language at the moment, a tentative reassertion of loyalty to its use may be starting to appear, at least within some of the younger age group, thus upholding my earlier observations in Chapter 1 regarding the reciprocal nature of language and ethnicity. As well as my own findings, there is other evidence of a steady reassertion and reappraisal of the role and significance of Galician, helping to define the region's idiosyncratic identity. Thus, when a Galician-speaking individual chooses to call himself or herself *español/española* or use Castilian in a given situation, they are *not* overtly deciding to put their ethnic identity to one side in order to manifest their allegiance to their state identity. They are simply negotiating their language and identity choices according to context; they are exercising their right to be integrated into the Castilian milieu. In other circumstances, the same individuals may choose to reinforce their Galician origins by using the terms *galego/galega* to describe themselves, or by using Galician.[17]

Of course, the multilayered nature of identity also includes those from a local, regional, national, and global perspective, so the manipulation of other identities, such as 'European' is also possible and indeed, probable, as I will discuss below. What my discussion implies is that a Galician sense of ethnic identity is as important as that associated with Spain as the overarching state. However, the problem facing many of the current attempts to foster a forward-thinking attitude towards a positive Galician ethnic identity is that many of the traditional images employed do not inspire in any way the younger generations to want to associate with them. As in many European countries, older people in Galicia may cling to their traditional past and struggle to come to terms with their global future, but the same cannot always be said of their children. Teachers may enthusiastically describe the notion of a Galician ethnicity, as well as the effects of Galicia's historical, cultural, and social roots on the establishment of a distinctive and deeply embedded identity, but this in itself may not always incite allegiance. Similarly, visions of rural life, of farming and the countryside, of fishing and the sea may portray life for their grandparents, but to a 14-year-old girl living in Santiago, such images are simply old-fashioned symbols of a bygone era. Even calls to embrace a Galician literary tradition, whilst extremely laudable, may not capture the imagination of a teenager. I have stated above (p. 242) that both political and cultural nationalist doctrines may require the conscious selection and promotion of such idiosyncratic characteristics with a view to fostering a sense of community identity. However, the maintenance and protection of cultural differences and the reinforcement of essentialist 'inner core' (Iglesias-Alvarez & Ramallo, 2003: 258) links to a far-off historic past built on myths and shared memories has to compete with other, more cosmopolitan, futuristic, and exciting notions of identity.

This is, I believe, one of the main issues that any attempts at promoting the notion of a Galician ethnolinguistic and socio, cultural and historical distinctiveness have to contend with. Throughout the western world, we all have to manipulate and negotiate increasingly multiple identities. Young people in particular demand to embrace and be part of a global culture. Identification with the English-speaking world, and in particular, the United States, or with the macro Spanish-speaking world within Latin America and the United States, is becoming an everyday feature of many young people's lives, because with it comes the perception of prestige, status, and the feeling that you are connected to something bigger than that dictated by your place of birth. In mainland Europe, all ages are now trying to embrace the concept of 'being European', of being part of, and identifying with, a conglomerate larger than one's region, nation, or country, and comprising many different histories, societies, cultures, and languages. In Spain, members of the ethnic minoritised communities may view the concept of a Spanish identity as fashionable, a trait of extreme importance in today's image-conscious climate, and its language one of self-promotion. To the 14-year-old Galician girl, the Spanish pop singers Enrique Iglesias and Alejandro Sanz are the height of cool. She sings along in Castilian, and probably also talks about them with her friends not in Galician, but in Castilian. Moreover, as Rodríguez Neira's latest study reveals (2003; see also p. 199), the recent rural exodus from Galicia of people in search of work has meant that on a daily basis, more and more people are witnessing the domination of Castilian Spanish within many influential areas of everyday life affected by the Castilian Spanish-speaking world, such as television, music and film. Indeed, the popularity of the Latin American film industry in Spain is a case in point.

Of course, whether or not the specifics of such a scenario occur in reality is largely immaterial. The important point is that Galicians, like other minoritised communities, develop strategies in order to deal with the configuration of identities central to their situation.[18] My earlier overview of thriving Galician social and cultural mores and customs is a fair indicator of how the notion of a Galician identity distinct from a Spanish identity is maintained, for they reflect a sense of ethnic distinctiveness but are reinforced by the pervading presence of Galician. Galician affords credence and depth to the historical relevance of these traditions, and in doing so, establishes their viability as markers of ethnic identity. Language use may not always be an overt prerequisite for ethnicity, but its presence at a non-functional level firmly enhances it.

If I *were* to reject the notion that language is important to a sense of Galician ethnic identity, I should also reject any efforts made by the *Xunta* to maintain, preserve and even enhance it, and I am not prepared to do. Although in Galicia, incontrovertible evidence of a strong, dynamic link between loyalty and prestige issues and calls for the preservation and elaboration of the Galician language is not entirely forthcoming, normalisation and normativisation policies and practices are, from many cultural, social and political perspectives, for the most part well-founded, as we have seen in the course of this book. From a political viewpoint, the region's calls for self-governing status were based in the first place upon claims to an idiosyncratic ethnicity and language. In line with the Basque Country, it may well be that the choice of language as the representation of all things Galician, was influenced by the fact that such issues were highly topical at the time, due in no small part to similar assertions being strongly made by the Catalans. Yet, irrespective of the initial motivations behind the government's actions, in line with Catalonia, the Basque Country, and many other autochthonous peoples, the *Xunta* of Galicia has implemented educational policies centred around the language rather than around other issues of Galicianness, precisely because it believes that this is the way to revive the Galician sense of ethnic identity. Whilst I concede that the role of formal education in the maintenance and support of a minoritised language is not entirely clear-cut, what is pertinent is the idea, proposed by Skutnabb-Kangas, that perceptions and attitudes towards such a language may also be altered by educational practices (2000: 570–571). Once the community recognises the far-reaching implications and increased potential of their own linguistic practices, it will also recognise its relevance to collective identity issues. This way, the enhancement of the status of the language becomes the focus of community solidarity.

The Future of Galician

If the changes I have discussed above are to have any far-reaching effects, then of course, they have to be implemented throughout Galicia. The population as a whole needs to be involved, so that a collective sense of solidarity is able to permeate throughout the region – and once again, this is where the government and its associated institution have to play an essential role. Galicia is made of a series of social groups and speech communities with different needs and different linguistic behaviours, that are simultaneously undergoing a highly transitional period in their region's history. As Del Valle points out, all these different linguistic behaviours are a viable manifestation of Galician ethnic identity (Del Valle, 2000: 127); they are what make Galicia fairly unique in the configuration of Spanish *comunidades autónomas*.

On the surface, it would appear that institutional practices have not been entirely successful in reinforcing the status of Galician throughout the region. However, some younger urban speakers in particular, *have* started to consider Galician functionally interchangeable with Castilian. Nonetheless, the implicit sense of inferiority associated with Galician and that has prevailed for centuries cannot be eradicated overnight. Political, social and cultural repression has resulted in a somewhat denigrated, intractable, and highly subjective perspective on life in general and on this issue of being Galician in particular. Whilst many people appear to be quite prepared to accept Galician as their rightful mode of communication in some contexts, it is not in any way the language of advancement, prestige and 'cool' at the present time. This situation is being exacerbated at the present time by internal, urban, econ-omic migration and the concomitant displacement in some quarters of Galician by Castilian as the language of habitual use.[19] The *Xunta*, in col-laboration with academia and the media, needs to have the means at its disposal to elevate the status of Galician, so that its use can be further pro-moted throughout institutional and community practices. The promotion of Galician as the main core value of an ethnic community is extremely laudable, but this may not be enough to guarantee its continued existence in today's fast-moving, global culture. In order to survive, Galician also has to be linked universally to the overt signs of social and cultural pro-gression and trend in the 21st century, such as areas of technology, the media, and the arts, instead of quaint and sentimental depictions of rural and provincial life. If Galician is marketed correctly, then a positive sense of language awareness may obtain, one that will persuade the 14-year-old Galician girl, and many others like her, that it is okay, or even rather prestigious, to talk about pop idols in Galician. In other words, the younger age groups at the very least have to be persuaded that they can still 'have it all' by using Galician. Of course, Castilian still has a valu-able role to play, but in accordance with the stated aims of *bilingüismo har-mónico*, the increased use of Galician should complement rather than conflict with the use of Castilian, and in doing so, enhance a sense of ethnic viability alongside the pervading sense of 'Spanishness'. The main-tenance and use of both languages *does* reflect the political, social, cultural, and linguistic reality of the region. Attempts to establish monolingualism in Castilian or in Galician would not.

Some activists view the government's somewhat 'softly softly' approach as irresponsible *laissez-faire*, since it combines intervention in the form of legislation, the creation of a writing system, educational policies, and so on with a recognition that these sociolinguistic processes take their time, and with a willingness to allow them to take their own course. Whether the *Xunta*'s current linguistic policy is tenable in the long run remains to be seen. Nonetheless, the government and its linguistic institutions actively continue to address the issue of the orthographic standard. The recent amendments of 2003 have taken into account criticisms levelled at earlier drafts regarding the influence of Castilianised forms, but given the historical connotations, this issue remains somewhat of a moot point. Linguistic assimilation of Galician by Castilian is in no way inevitable, but even if the perception that recent transference phenomena from Castilian have been assimilated into the standard is not borne out in reality, many people have yet to be convinced. More importantly still, the way the various formats have been drafted and then introduced into public life has exacerbated the perception of pre-scriptiveness. The authorities *have* attempted to be descriptive rather than prescriptive regarding syntactical and morphological forms advocated by the standard (Santamarina, 1995: 80). As I have already discussed (pp. 238–239), recent concessions mirror a degree of variation still found regarding pronoun position, the use of the definite article with the possessive pronoun, contractions of the article with prepositions and conjunctions, all of which are also found in Portuguese. Moreover, the use of the *gheada* is referred to in the *Normas* despite the fact that its use tends to have no prestigious status attached to it. However, these amendments do little to placate the more vociferous *reintegracionistas*. Hence, their effect on the perception that the standard does not represent the autochthonous language remains to be seen.

I fully accept that the situation regarding the *Normas* is extremely complex and I also accept that the governmental and non-governmental bodies involved in their formation and implementation still have a daunting task ahead of them. However, the situation regarding the model for pronunciation is similarly fraught with difficulties. As I have already pointed out (pp. 131–137), not all of the dialectal and stylistic variation that was present in Galician throughout the 20th century has survived, but older people in particular still continue to employ lexical forms distinct from the standard and pronunciation traits that are distinct from those found on the television and radio. Younger members generally do not since they are taught the written standard at school, and even if their teachers utilise a predominately Galician pronunciation, the Galician disseminated by the media is overlaid by a characteristically Castilian phonetic system.

Variation in itself is not problematic: a degree of variability is inherent to any language and if treated with respect, may even inspire allegiance to the language as a reinforcer of ethnic identity. Indeed, for this reason, it may well be more prudent to advocate an even more descriptive set of comprehensive yet provisional written norms that encompass and allow for such dialectal variation, with the aim over time of amalgamating the most prevalent into an orthographic and morphological standard that reflects the linguistic reality of the region. Moreover, this may facilitate the acceptance and utilisation of spoken dialectal variation in wider spheres of activity, and may facilitate the substitution of the current, albeit unofficial, model of pronunciation for something that approximates a Galician pronunciation system, with at least some of its characteristic phonetic traits intact.

Once again, however, issues of perception and time are allied to these tentative suggestions. Castilian, not Galician, is still the written language of the region for much of the population, and until everyone is used to writing, reading and speaking Galician, there may be a general sense that its use is somewhat of an imposition, a reflection of government intervention into their lives. The same could be said if a standardised oral form of the language were to be introduced. As I have pointed out above, there are two languages in Galicia. It remains to be seen whether a balance can be struck between the use of one without it being to the detriment of the other, and whether a positive sense of Galician ethnicity can be fully attained in such circumstances. It is not an easy task.

I wholeheartedly believe that in the spirit of optimism, no-one, Galician or otherwise, should subscribe to the catastrophic visions that are often propounded and highly exaggerated regarding the imminent death of the Galician language – that unless people start to use it right now, it will be defunct by the time their children are adults. On the one hand, as Craig Patterson has stated on the Galician Studies email discussion list (November 2004: galician-studies@jiscmail.ac.uk), impressions of doom and gloom will simply send a loud and clear message to the Galician youth that there is no point learning and using the language, and to their parents that there is no point transmitting it. Patterson goes on to point out that Galician has already survived high-literary and low-cultural ridicule – and this would seem to imply that it is not quite ready to roll over and die. Instead, I believe that the *Xunta*, its institutions, and indeed, everyone even slightly involved with Galicia, should proclaim the advantages of the revival of the language and the development of a modern ethnic identity to the region as a whole. By emphasising strong Galician community solidarity and a viable Galician collective identification, efforts to improve the status and use of Galician will no longer be linked to particular political groups and ideologies, that merely serve to alienate many potential sympathisers to the overall cause.

However, it must not be forgotten that Galicians are also Spanish, and any attempts at eradicating a sense of Spanish identity – and the language – would meet with much resistance both within the region itself and from the overarching Spanish authorities. The inherent complementary nature of multiple identities means that people can choose to emphasise or underplay a given group membership, and this choice is paramount to the Galician situation. The sooner these issues are understood, the sooner the region can get more on track: the sooner the language can be safeguarded, the sooner a positive and proactive sense of ethnic identity can start to work for the people themselves.

In the Introduction to this book, I outlined my principal hypothesis as fourfold. Firstly, I contended that the Galician language, whether used or not, was an intrinsic characteristic of Galician ethnic identity. Secondly, that linguistic policies and planning impact on the behavioural practices of language users, and that these practices in turn, may be reflected in their attitudes towards the language. Thirdly, that whilst a reversal in traditional perceptions and attitudes is resulting in a reaffirmation of Galician as the autochthonous language, as yet, its sociolinguistic relationship with Castilian has not been resolved. Fourthly, that Galicians have to negotiate multiple identities, but that these are subject to change and adjustment.

In general, my findings and discussions have confirmed these assertions. What I have not been able to do, however, is to state categorically that any of the prevailing trends I have encountered will continue in the future. This book is an overview, a chance to look at the issue of Galician ethnicity and language use from the perspective of an onlooker, rather than a participant. Nonetheless, as a 'galegophile', I am fully committed to the enhancement and survival of its autochthonous language and ethnic identity. Long live Galicia, its language(s) and its people.

Notes to Chapters

Introduction

1. All translations of citations in this book are the author's own.
2. Reproduced with the kind permission of the European Commission – Press and Communication Publications, and can be located online at http://europa.eu.int/abc/maps/members/spain_en.htm.
3. Reproduced with the kind permission of *Galicia Espallada*, and can be located online at http://www.galespa.com.ar/MAPA.htm.
4. As both a native and a researcher of the area, Vaidehi Ramanathan encounters slightly different problems in her work on beliefs and uses of autochthonous language and English in Gujarat, India. She comments 'I am attempting to understand some pro-vernacular sentiments when I am seen as a product of the very ideologies they are trying to resist' (2005: 3).
5. These comments, by the editor John Thompson, are taken from the introduction to Bourdieu's (1994) book.
6. Throughout the world, monolingual societies are atypical. The 15th edition of *Ethnologue* (Gordon, 2005) puts the number of known, living languages in the world at 6912 in 2005, surpassing the number of politically defined states (228) by as much as 30 to 1. Probably half the world's population, and the majority of states, are either bilingual or multilingual, even when all the languages spoken within their boundaries are not officially recognised or, at best, have restricted status in one way or another. However, see my discussion in Chapter 5 regarding what constitutes a language, for a definition based upon linguistic criteria is somewhat difficult.
7. This example of societal bilingualism in Wales is discussed in more detail in Chapter 1 (pp. 49–50).
8. Barbour (2002: 11) and Cheshire (2002: 33) both argue that the term 'native speaker' is part of the nationalistic and monolingual discourse and, therefore, should be avoided. For this reason, I prefer to use the term 'autochthonous speaker' in my own evaluation of the Galician/Castilian situation.
9. Mackey revisits his early definition in his later work; see, for example Mackey (2000: 26–54; 2002: 328–344) and Mackey, Bastardas and Boix (1994: 25–54). The early work of Haugen (1966b, 1976) and Weinreich (1966) also emphasises the relevance of bilingualism to sociolinguistic research.
10. Gumperz and Fishman and others since, then took the application of the term one step further. They included any society in which two or more varieties, registers or even dialects are employed with a high degree of functional demarcation (see Fishman 1971: 74; Gumperz 1975: 27–49). This implies that every society is diglossic, as even slight differences employed in, say, a journalistic text and a humorous anecdote, would be considered indicative of some form of functional demarcation. Hudson (2001: 50–51) voices general concerns about this. He is somewhat sceptical of expanding the use of diglossia to encompass such variation and prefers to employ the term 'social-dialectia' in order to delineate between this type of variation and that of more highly differentiated diglossic sociolinguistic patterns.

11. According to the traditional, stable notion of diglossia, non-bilingual/ diglossic situations typically occur when two or more groups become united religiously, politically or economically, yet continue to retain their socio-cultural differences and languages in isolation. Hence, the situation may be relatively stable and long-term, such as in parts of Canada, where the French- and English-speaking communities maintain their idiosyncratic linguistic repertoires side by side. However, some form of *lingua franca* is generally required for intergroup communication purposes. In some communities, this may ultimately lead to the predominately monolingual speakers learning the other language; hence, the situation may be temporary.
      Non-bilingual/non-diglossic situations are rare nowadays. Although Fishman characterised countries such as Portugal, Cuba and Norway as such in the 1980s (1980: 9), immigration processes have augmented their overall linguistic configuration in the last 30 or so years. The only such societies left are generally small and cut off from contact with other communities, as in parts of Papua New Guinea and the Amazon rainforest. However, even these communities appear to have ceremonies and pastimes that involve a specific set of linguistic terms from which certain members are excluded.

12. Ferguson looked at Arabic, Modern Greek, Swiss German and Haitian Creole (Ferguson, 1959). In the Arabic case, he found that popular or colloquial Arabic comprised the many local varieties employed in the home and local community, whereas modern standard Arabic, based as it is on the classical form, was used for all educational and religious purposes. He also found that the speakers of the defining languages regarded H as superior to L, to the extent that the existence of L was even denied. Even when the feeling of superiority of H was not so strong there was usually a belief that H was somehow more beautiful, more logical, and better able to express important thoughts. Such attitudinal issues will prove important in my own discussion of language use in Galicia (see Part 3 of this book).

13. In his early work on micro-interactionist perspectives, Gumperz (1982a) focused less on stable patterns of choice and more on variation and change over time.

14. For further examples, see also Chambers (2003: 216–291) and Chambers and Trudgill (1998: 149–153).

15. See, for example the dialect surveys carried out by the National Language Institute in Tokyo at 20-year intervals (1950, 1971, 1991), which is discussed in Chambers (2003: 213–216), and Marjut Aikio's doctoral thesis work (1991), in which she documented the language mainly spoken by every single person with every other person in the village during every decade in the village of Vuotso, Finland.

16. Although subject to certain limitations, early studies carried out by Trudgill (1974), Martinez Martín (1983) and Williamson and Williamson (1984) indicate that the age of the respondent is a major influence as to whether a minoritised language is generally employed. Dorian's illustration of the situation of the Tiwi language spoken on Melville and Bathurst Islands off the north coast of Australia (1994: 479–494) is a typical example of an autochthonous language overtaken by the rapid expansion of a wide-currency language, in this case English. In the 1990s, an older, largely bilingual age group who used a conservative, traditional form of the language co-existed with a younger and wholly bilingual age group, who used a modified form of the same language.

17. However, this analysis does not account for the marked use of covert prestige forms exemplified in Chapter 6.
18. See Sankoff *et al.* (1989: 107–118) for a more recent account of these issues in Montreal French. See Kalmar *et al.* (1987) for an interesting account of language attitude in Canton Province, China.
19. See also Cheshire (1997: 185–198).
20. For further discussions of the implications of social networks, see Milroy and Milroy (1997: 199–211) and Milroy (2002: 549–572; in press). See also Gordon (1997: 47–64) and Kiesling (1998: 69–100) for interesting investigations into gender-influenced speech variability.
21. See for example, Brown and Gilman's (1960) early investigation into second-person pronoun usage in French, German, Italian and Spanish, where they proposed that usage was governed by power and solidarity semantics.

Chapter 1

1. A point regarding terminology. I accept that when referring to communities or languages, the terms 'majority' and 'minority' often carry ideological connotations, as do 'majoritised' and 'minoritised'. I employ the latter throughout my discussion in order to establish a distinction from political and social perspective, rather than from any desire to extend any philosophical beliefs or aspirations, but the reader should be aware of these potential implications.
2. Further excellent accounts of the role of language in nationalist discourse are found in Barbour (2002: 11–18) and Mar-Molinero (2000b: 3–17).
3. Whilst the United States and the western world need to secure continued access to the Arab oil-producers, it is averred that religious extremists in the Arab world wants to oust anyone who trades with the west and put in their place strict Islamic fundamentalist regimes. For an informative view, see the article *Huntington's spectre* by Sayeed Hasan Khan and Kurt Jacobsen at http://www.globalissues.org/Geopolitics/MiddleEast/TerrorInUSA/Clash.asp.
4. Like May, I take the middle line: the entity is both a political and an ethnocultural/ethnolinguistic community. However, I will examine in more detail the two perspectives and their relevance to identity on pp. 43–45.
5. Even the term 'nation' is not completely endorsed. International law for example, opts for the term 'people' as the entity that is claimed to have the right to self-determination, and communities themselves may consider the term highly subjective. However, implicit therein are connotations of power and autonomy from others, and it is for this reason that it is still often used to encompass aspirations of self-determination. These points are borne in mind in my use of the term throughout this book.
6. May argues that all groups incorporate an ethnic dimension, and the failure of majoritised ones to recognise this is to do with differential power relations (2001: 26) rather than with their constituent components.
7. Bugarski for example, highlights the pressures 'to homegenise within, and heterogenise outwardly' (2001: 73) in the establishment of Yugoslavia the nation.
8. May points out (2001: 6) that this is why Gellner's definition of nationalism as a 'theory of political legitimacy which requires that ethnic boundaries should not cut across political ones' (1983: 1) is somewhat simplistic, since the boundaries of political and national identity do not necessarily coincide, and ethnically exclusive linguistic and cultural homogeneity is untenable in such situations.

9. See Barbour (2000: 18–43) for an excellent account of the role of national language varieties in Britain and Ireland.
10. See also May (2001: 20).
11. However, Galicia is still a region, albeit autochthonous, of Spain, and in my more generic historical and social discussions, I consider 'region', 'regional' and equivalent terms to be pertinent, given that no particular political ideology is in play.
12. As Fishman (1999a: 155) puts it, ethnic identity may be called into consciousness by historical and cultural 'saliency raising experiences'. These ideas are discussed further in the section on essentialism versus constructivism (pp. 43–45).
13. Gellner (1983) emphasises the role of literary works and the shared history he examines in the construction of a nation and its national identity. I return to this point regarding Galicia in Chapter 2.
14. Barth later revisits these issues (Barth, 1994).
15. Liebkind (1999: 145) comments that the success, or otherwise, of these strategies, is dependent on three sets of factors: status (economic, political and linguistic prestige), demographic strength (numbers, concentration, birth rates and migration) and institutional support and control factors (the representation of one's own language in the media, government and education). See also my recent research on the Portuguese diaspora in Jersey (Beswick, 2005).
16. In *An Other Tongue*, Arteaga (1994) has assembled a series of articles that examine issues surrounding the nation and the use of national and other languages to reinforce ethnic identity in the United States. He himself was born in the United States, hence has North American nationality. Ethnically, he considers himself, and others consider him, to be Mexican: racially, he is *mestizo*. Importantly, the language he employs as his autochthonous tongue, Spanish, reflects and determines his position in relation to the United States and to Mexico (1994: 3–4).
17. Demarcation on linguistic grounds is discussed in Chapter 5.
18. Skutnabb-Kangas believes that the term 'mother tongue' is conceptual; it is an identity signifier that exists in people's consciousness. See her discussions (1981: 12–20; 2000: 465–468).
19. To this end, Andersen (1991: 123) states that 'in a world in which the nation state is the overwhelming norm, all of this means that nations can now be imagined without linguistic commonality'. The notion of imagined communities is discussed below.
20. See May (2001: 5). For an overview of language policy in the former Yugoslavia, see Franolic (1988), and for a more recent article on how language differences are being emphasised, see Ivic (2001).
21. In Croatia for example, 'an artificial administrative Newspeak is being promoted there, with strong echoes in the public use of language generally, saturated with Croatian archaisms, regionalisms, and neologisms, the terminologies of various scholarly disciplines are likewise being croatised, and spelling reforms are advocated [...] Croatia, while in a hurry to join Europe and the advanced world, is ruthlessly purging its public language of internationalisms ... widespread among all the other countries' (Bugarski, 2001: 84).
22. See my discussion in Chapter 9 for a criticism of this use of 'compete'.
23. For an interesting account of counter-nationalism in Catalonia, see Mar-Molinero (2000b: 41–47).

24. See The European Charter for Regional or Minority Languages: Initial Periodical Report from the United Kingdom (no year www.fco.gov.uk/ Files/kfile/minoritylanguages,0.pdf). It is estimated that some 30% of respondents to the 1991 and 2001 censuses could speak Scots, although its status is highly contested, because it consists primarily of lexical items that are switched when English is being spoken.

25. See in particular, Llobera (1994: 124–125). The objective of the European Charter for Regional or Minority Languages (ECRML) is to protect and promote autochthonous European regional and minoritised languages that differ significantly from the majoritised language. Adopted in 1992 under the auspices of the Council of Europe, the Charter also applies to languages that have official status within regions or provinces, such as Galician, but which are not official at state level. The UK has ratified the Charter and devolved power was formally handed over to the new Scottish Parliament and the new National Assembly for Wales in 1999. Article 8 of the Charter stipulates the obligations the UK has regarding the use of Welsh (27), Scottish Gaelic (43) and Irish (54) in education. However, as occurred in earlier legislation, which was aimed at promoting and facilitating the Welsh language and Scots Gaelic (see, for example the 1993 Welsh Language Act and the Education (Scotland) Act 1980), there is no mention of Scots (The European Charter for Regional or Minority Languages: Initial Periodical Report from the United Kingdom).

26. National and ethnic identities may result in ethnocentric nationalism to the exclusion of others, or in constructive forms of patriotism to the inclusion of others. In the former case, core values are used to differentiate between 'them' and 'us', typically to the detriment of the others. In the latter case, core values are used as self-identification factors but are enjoyed, protected and shared with others (Smolicz, 1997: 67).

27. The following discussion is based on comments in Chapters 1 and 2 of May (2001).

28. Stuart Hall's four-way expression of identity, published in an edited book dedicated to his work on cultural studies (1996) is eminently non-essentialist and demonstrates the complexity of the issues at stake. He states that identity may be expressed:

Through difference; through the notion of 'otherness' and binary opposition or dualism between different cultures or ethnicities, such as the Irish in Northern Ireland and British rule.

Through multiplicity; through the notion of having more than one ethnic identity, such as the Irish Americans.

Through fluidity and change, such as that experienced by certain African communities in the UK.

Through hybridity, when new self-identification strategies arise from the union of differing cultural identities, such as that of white people in the United Kingdom who adopt cultural and social norms of their black neighbours, and vice-versa (1996: 441–449, 465–475).

29. This is discussed in greater detail in Chapters 8 and, in particular, Chapter 9.

30. In a recent study, Penelope Eckert (2000) examined linguistic variation as a social practice in Detroit. Her term 'community of practice' allowed her to focus on social categories, in order to highlight how language is used to construct different identities in different social interactions.

31. Moreover, as has already been pointed out, the manipulation of identity and linguistic practices often occurs because of pressure from the dominant society itself. For example, social and economic opportunities nearly always go to speakers of the state-sponsored language (Dorian, 1999: 26), one reason why a community may choose to distance itself from its autochthonous language.

32. Again, I refer the reader back to the discussion of endo- and exo- notions of ethnicity on pp. 37 and 44.

33. This is another area where 'state-nationalist' and ethnonationalist policies begin to resemble each other, as we saw earlier.

34. For excellent accounts of language policy and planning, I direct the reader in particular to Cooper (1989), especially Chapter 2, Williams (1992), Turi (1994), Blommaert (1996), Schiffman (1996), Kaplan and Baldauf (1997), especially Chapters 5, 10 and 11, and Paulston (1997). My brief discussion of language planning follows Cooper (1989). See also Skutnabb-Kangas (2000: 570–638) regarding the role of education in language planning and bilingual educational practices.

35. See earlier discussion of status and solidarity in the Introduction (pp. 21–23).

36. However, Farrell *et al.* counter that in South East Wales there have been 'net gains in the percentages of younger Welsh speakers' (1998: 489). Williams (2003: 3) emphasises once again that overall gains throughout the younger population of Wales are mainly to do with educational initiatives, and that in fact, the pervading statistics refer to bilingual speakers only.

37. See (Woolard, 1989a) for an excellent account of bilingualism in Catalonia. Green (1994: 167) warns however, that full equality with Castilian is still some way off. He claims that it is proving difficult to persuade the monolingual Castilian-speaking migrants, even long-established workers, to learn and use Catalan. In addition, certain key areas of 'power' still function in Castilian, as seen with the example of political dominance. I will return to the issue of Catalonia in Chapter 3.

38. See for example, Williams (1982, 1988, 1991).

39. Accordingly, all laws are written in both languages; the local government and the houses of representatives are allowed to employ either language in their business and can be addressed in either by the general population as well (Badia i Capdevila, 2004: 4).

40. Badia i Capdevila adds (2004) that the creation of the National Council of the Maltese Language, the aim of which is to create a sustainable language policy in order to promote the use of Maltese within all educational, media, political, administrative, economic, social, and cultural institutions and to take on the responsibility for orthographic reform, is also under debate. The draft proposal states clearly that the Maltese language is a key element of the national identity of the Maltese people, and that the State has the duty to protect it from decline.

Chapter 2

1. See for example, Trotsky's pronouncements on the political situation in early 1930s Spain (1931).

2. Should the reader wish to become further acquainted with the historical context of the Galician language, I would recommend Mariño Paz (1998) as a extremely detailed and analytical synthesis of the major works in the field.

Other accounts contributing to the following chapter are Livermore (1966), De Oliveira Marques (1972), Saraiva (1978), Álvarez Cáccamo (1983), Azevedo Maia (1986), Monteagudo and Santamarina (1993), Nogueira (1996), Cano Aguilar (1999), and Penny (2000, 2002). For overviews of the pre-Roman linguistic composition of the whole Iberian Peninsula, see in particular De Oliveira Marques (1972: 5–9), Freixeiro Mato (1997), Cano Aguilar (1999: 16–26) and Penny (2002: 74–82, 90–94). Livermore (1966: 14–40) and Saraiva (1978: 13–31) offer excellent accounts of the Roman, Swabian, Visigothic and Arabic occupations and they discuss in some detail the rise of Afonso Henríquez (Livermore, 1996: 40–54; Saraiva, 1978: 33–46). For an extremely detailed account of the political and social history of Galician until the 20th century, see González López (1980). For detailed accounts of the history of the Galician language, see Ferreiro (1996), Freixeiro Mato (1997), Gómez Sánchez and Freixeiro Mato (1998), and Alvarez Blanco, Fernández Rei and A. Santamarina (2004).

Álvarez Cáccamo (1983: 23–42), Monteagudo and Santamarina (1993: 121–123), and Penny (2002: 16–22) also offer brief accounts of the historical emergence of Castilian as the dominant language within Spain. See also Freixeiro Mato (1997: 53–112) for a very detailed and interesting, if slightly biased account (and also his comments at p. 174) of the influence of Castilian on the evolution of Galician from the Middle Ages until the present day. For a good overall historical account of the history of the Portuguese language, see Silva Neto (1979). Finally, Vásquez Corredoira (1998) offers a detailed, if somewhat subjective, diachronic and synchronic account of the evolution of the Portuguese language, using Galician as a point of reference.

3. A form of Galician is also spoken in what has been termed the *Franxa Exterior*, the border areas of Asturias, Castile-León and Zamora. There are also various communities in other parts of Spain, in other Western European countries and in the Americas.

4. Lipski (1994: 45) contests the claim that from the 15th century onwards, almost all regions of Spain were totally diglossic, with residents possessing some Castilian common denominator in addition to any regional languages or dialects. He maintains that even well into the 20th century, large numbers of rural residents in Galicia, amongst other areas, spoke little or no Castilian. We will examine this point further in Part 3 of this book.

5. The *Academia* has developed and refined its role throughout the centuries. Its Statute defines the prevailing situation: *tiene como misión principal velar porque los cambios que experimente la Lengua Española en su constante adaptación a las necesidades de sus hablantes no quiebren la esencial unidad que mantiene en todo el ámbito hispánico* [this vigil is its main mission, because the changes that the Spanish Language undergoes as it constantly adapts to the needs of its speakers must not damage the fundamental unity that it maintains throughout the Spanish-speaking world]. For further information, see their official online website at www.rae.es.

6. See Chapter 5 (pp. 116–117) regarding the problems that these authors encountered in their endeavours.

7. Lipski cites documentary evidence of the influence of Portuguese and Galician in the Canary Islands and, due to historical factors, in certain parts of Spanish-speaking Latin America, particularly in the Caribbean from the 16th century onwards (1994: 55, 60–61). Penny (2000: 155–157) attests that the velarisation of word-final – n, which predominates in Latin America, may either have Andalusian origins or may be indicative of

varieties spoken in the northwest of the Peninsula for example, Galicia, Asturias, Leon and Cantabrica.

8. In 1971, it was estimated that 400,000 descendants of autochthonous Galicians lived in Buenos Aires, making it the largest Galician immigrant community in the world (Martínez-Barbeito, 1971: 37).

9. Nowhere is this more apparent than in the presentation of the constitution of the _Real Academia Galega_ RAG [the Royal Galician Academy] in 1906 (see p. 116), in which the President, Manuel Murguía, makes his inaugural speech in Castilian.

10. As I will discuss later, in the 1960s and 1970s, Galician nationalist discourse advocated monolingualism in Galician, but this was not upheld in the years of the IF since not all members were able to converse fully in Galician.

11. For an excellent summary of the denial of language rights throughout Spain under Franco and the subsequent struggles to have them implemented during the transition to democracy, see Mar-Molinero (2000b: 83–96).

12. Some of the books published during the Franco era, for example Rodríguez-González's _Diccionario Enciclopédico gallego-castellano_ [The Encyclopedic Dictionary of Galician-Castilian] in 1958–62, were financed externally by the _Casa de Galicia_ in Caracas, Venezuela, whilst the _Historia de Galicia_ [a History of Galicia] compiled by Otero Pedrayo, was edited in Buenos Aires.

13. See Chapter 5 (pp. 131–134) for a succinct discussion.

Chapter 3

1. Similar schema had also been proposed by Garvin and Mathiot (1956). See Cooper (1983), Haugen (1987), and Muljačić (1997: 387–393) for further reading.

2. Sometimes, a standard enables speakers of mutually unintelligible varieties to communicate. For example, a speaker of Cantonese cannot converse with a speaker of Mandarin. However, a shared writing system means that literate Cantonese and Mandarin speakers have a way of communicating. Moreover, both speakers may even consider that they speak dialects of Chinese rather than two different languages (Henderson, 1996: 23).

3. Cooper (1989: 154) devised a three-way process of corpus planning that takes these stages into account:

    Graphisation – the development and provision of writing systems for unwritten or little written languages;
    Modernisation – lexical elaboration for the purpose of new communicative functions;
    Renovation – 'an effort to change an already developed code' (Cooper, 1989: 154).
    For a more detailed account of codification, see Mesthrie _et al._ (2000: 388–394).

4. There has been some debate as to whether certain aspects are necessary or even desirable. For example, whether pronunciation norms should be prescribed, or whether dialectal variation should be totally excluded.

These issues play a role in my discussion of the Galician model and are discussed in more detail in Chapter 5, pp. 125–137.

5. The existence of a standardised form can be used to deliberately slow down or prevent changes seen as corruptions of a language. For example, a main function of the *Académie Française* is to prevent the French language being corrupted by words borrowed from other languages, and in particular, from English. It has ruled as incorrect anglicisms such as *le weekend* and *le shopping* for *la fin de semaine* and *les courses*. Castilian anglicisms include *fútbol* [football], *gol* [goal], *mitin* [meeting], *gánster* [gangster], *nailon* [nylon], *beicon* [bacon].

6. The transfer of political power in Spain from centre to periphery is currently at an advanced stage. Madrid has relinquished partial control to some 17 regions, but although they are all considered self-governing, in reality they enjoy different levels of autonomy. Seven, including Galicia, Catalonia and the Basque Region, have more control over certain areas of local administration and services than do others.

7. See Colomer (1986) for a good account of the concepts of Catalan nationalism under Franco.

8. See online at http://www6.gencat.net/llengcat/legis/lleipl.htm.

9. Mar-Molinero (2000b: 92–95) presents a brief but worthwhile account of language planning in Catalonia. See also Branchadell (1996).

10. Mercator Education: European Network for Regional or Minority Languages and Education is one of three research and documentation centres within the EU that deals with regional and minority community issues, such as language protection rights and the promotion of linguistic diversity. For further information, see their website at www.mercator-education.org.

11. Hoffman wonders (2000: 439) just how far a region such as Catalonia, a constituent of a multilingual member state of the EU, can go in promoting such monolingual language policies. This, of course, would also have implications for Galicia.

12. The distinctive archeological and architectural relics found throughout the region include the *castros*, settlements dating back to the Iron Age, dolmens and cave paintings from the same period, Roman, Swabian and Visigoth monuments, Romanesque, Renaissance and Baroque architectural masterpieces, and the highly traditional *hórreos* [raised granaries] and *pazos* [Galician manor-houses]. For further information on the cultural background of Galicia, see the extremely informative tourist guide at http://www.galinor.es/galeria/arte-e.html and *Galicia Espallada* at http://www.galespa.com.ar.htm.

13. See Regueira Fernández (2006) for an excellent account of socio-political issues surrounding normalisation policies in Galicia.

14. In order to do so, the *Eje Atlántico del Noroeste Peninsular* serves as a regional lobby in relations with the two state governments and with the EU, principally to secure funding and investment. See in particular my earlier paper (Beswick, 2005a) and online at http://www.eixoatlantico.com/.

15. All primary and secondary school attendance, be it private or public, is compulsory from 6 to 16 years throughout Spain and is disseminated by the Spanish Government through the *Ley de Ordenación General del Sistema Educativo* (LOGSE) [Education System General Planning Law] (Mercator Education: European Network for Regional or Minority Languages and Education, 2001: 6).

Chapter 4

1.   Hence, it is rare to find any linguistic variable the variants of which corre-
     spond exactly with any social variable, although it is common to find vari-
     ables that match each other sufficiently closely to imply at least some kind
     of casual connection.
2.   I would add that in the latter case, if the speakers select a particular form for
     its connotations of solidarity, then it is not an unconscious action. I will return
     to this point in Chapter 8. See also Labov (1994: 542–543).
3.   Other contact phenomena, such as code mixing, incomplete language acqui-
     sition, and incompetent knowledge of the borrowed language, have been
     researched extensively over the past few decades, and are subsumed
     under these labels.
4.   Non-basic vocabulary appears to be borrowed before basic items. Minor pho-
     nological and syntactic features such as the temporary appearance of new
     phonemes or a non-disruptive change in word order may follow if the
     level of contact is increased. See Thomason and Kaufmann (1988: 74–76)
     for a succinct description of borrowing stages.
5.   Haugen (1950: 217), and others, has claimed that people who grow up from
     childhood as bilinguals tend to retain L^2 'foreign' phonemic sequences in the
     lexis they borrow and transfer into their L^1. Rather, even though the word or
     morpheme concerned is then assimilated into the lexicon of the L^1, it will still
     be pronounced in a phonetic form that mirrors closely that of the L^2. This was
     certainly true when the L^2 enjoyed great cultural or social prestige within the
     L^1 language community, for example, French in 19th-century England. In the
     case of the French loan words *restaurant*, *café* and *impasse*, a pseudo L^2 pro-
     nunciation is often still heard in certain sectors of English society.
     However, non-bilinguals tend to reproduce such words according to the pho-
     netic rules of the L^1. See Weinreich (1966: 7–18) and Lehiste (1988: 2–13) for
     more detailed discussions.
6.   Thomason and Kaufman propose a borrowing probability scale, covering
     various parts of the linguistic subsystems such as the lexicon, morphosyntax,
     and phonology, with the aim of predicting what types of contact-induced
     changes may occur in what circumstances (1988: 73–95).
7.   Other languages manage to retain their idiosyncratic phonemic distinctions,
     despite the consistent influence of another without the same distinctions.
     Hamp (1989: 205–207) offers us many examples amongst which is the tena-
     ciously resolute phonetic and phonological conservatism of West Kintyre, at
     the limits of the Gaelic-speaking area of the Highlands of Scotland. Here, a
     dialect of Islay precariously survived as the local language of a handful of
     the older population in 1989, and two fluent speakers from the village of
     Muasdale were still able to demonstrate certain phonological distinctions
     completely at odds to those found in English. So in both the lateral and
     nasal systems, each retained no less than six distinctive phonemes.
8.   Bilinguals tend to avoid inter-language difficulties such as word-order differ-
     ences and ungrammatical fragments by the use of intra-sentential equival-
     ence sites found in both languages – easier if they share a common root.
     For a relevant discussion, see in particular, Clyne (2003: 70–76).
     Certain literature has proposed that there is some form of relationship
     between code-switching and borrowing. Myers-Scotton in particular (see
     especially, 1992), argues that although there are some important differences

between the forms of the material that appears in such discourse, they generally arise from related or similar processes. She concludes, therefore, that both code-switching and borrowing forms are located along a process continuum (1992: 37). However, Poplack strongly maintains the borrowing/switching distinction (see for example, Poplack, 1980; Poplack & Sankoff, 1988; Poplack & Meechan, 1998). In borrowing, there tends to be phonological or morphological integration that does not occur in code-switching, and for this reason, I too prefer to maintain the distinction.

9. See also Holmes (2001: 34–42) and Wardhaugh (2002: 99–112) for examples of the main types of code-switching. Appel and Muysken (1987: 118–121) also define the following functions: referential, directive, expressive, phatic, metalinguistic, and poetic.

10. See in particular, Myers-Scotton (1993), Auer (1998: 259–60) and Rampton (1995, 1998). See also Auer (1984) regarding the use of Conversational Analysis (CA) as a potential framework within which to interpret code-switching.

11. There are a lot of language-specific studies available for comparison, such as English/Spanish data (Sankoff & Poplack, 1981; Silva-Corvalán, 1983), English/Swahili, English/Kikuyu data (Myers Scotton, 1993), Dutch/French and Turkish/German data (Treffers-Daller, 1994, 1998), to name but a few.

12. In his comparison of the Neogrammarian and Lexical Diffusion hypotheses, Labov, like Yaeger-Dror (1988: 1593) and Hajek (1992: 30–32) previously, concluded that both could occur in complementary distribution with each other. In recent times, the Neogrammarian hypothesis has been considered at best an extremely naïve theory, focussing solely upon the end result of linguistic change rather than the processes involved.

13. For further examples of lexical diffusion, see also Holmes (2001: 203–204); Hudson (2001: 182–184); Mesthrie *et al.* (2000: 118–120).

14. See also the earlier discussions of Weinreich (1953) and Appel and Muysken (1987) for example.

Chapter 5

1. Other varieties of a language can be social, gender-based, age-based, situational, stylistic or subcultural (Skutnabb-Kangas, 2000: 7), and are significant insofar as they may characterise the linguistic behaviour of both society and of the individual, as I will highlight in later chapters.

2. This is what Lorenzo (1975: 155–157) refers to when he states that the Portuguese standard acquired a centre-meridional tone.

3. For an enlightening discussion regarding the definitive split of Galician from Latin, see Mariño Paz (1998: 74–85).

4. Azevedo Maia's tome (1986) offers an extremely detailed analysis of Galician-Portuguese texts from the 13th, 14th and 15th centuries in order to try and establish the point at which the two varieties we now designate Galician and Portuguese diverged. In his consideration of the question, Lorenzo (1975) asserts that although minimal, there was evidence of differentiation even at the beginning of this period, which was accentuated in the 14th century and became definitive from the 15th century onwards. Both authors discuss the diverse opinions put forward by other eminent linguists such as Lindley Cintra, Leite de Vasconcelos, Carolina Michaëlis and Menéndez Pidal (Lorenzo, 1975: 155–158; Azevedo Maia, 1986: 5–6;

889–890). For example, Leite de Vasconcelos (1970: 52–53) claims that the *Crónica General* by Alfonso X has a Galician provenance, whereas others state that it is more likely to be Galician-Portuguese. Rübecamp (1933) also carried out a detailed study of potential Galician and Portuguese traits in the *Cantigas de Santa Maria*, and Morais Barbosa (1961) utilised his results to establish later on that the *Crónica General* was indeed Galician. Mariño Paz's account (1998: 92–129) comprehensively highlights many of the linguistic differences that resulted from the scission.

5. For a comprehensive list of transference phenomena at this time, see Mariño Paz (1998: 437–446).

6. See as an example, my later quote from Cotarelo Valledor (1927) regarding the use of the gheada (p. 144).

7. Fernández Salgado and Monteagudo (1993: 204–205; 211) offer examples of both processes, such as the rejection of my earlier example *lágrima* [tear] synonymous with the Castilian form, for the Galician *bágoa*, and of *contento* [happy] for *ledo*.

8. For an excellent synthesis of 19th and 20th century written tendencies, see Mariño Paz, 1998: 446–488.

9. The following have been consulted: for Portuguese; Lorenzo (1975), Willis (1984), Teyssier (1990). For Galician; Alvarez Blanco (1983), Alvarez Blanco *et al.* (1986), Fernández Rei (1990). For Castilian; Penny (2000; 2002) Pountain (2003). The categorisation and comparison of Galician and Portuguese as linguistic varieties of the same source can also be found in works carried out in the 70s by Portuguese writers such as Leite de Vasconcelos (1970) and Cuesta and Da Luz (1971: 53–127). A version of this list is also found in Beswick (2005a).

10. Given the magnitude of examining lexical items and the fact that their provenance is not necessarily a standardisation issue, these are not considered here. For further information, see Azevedo Maia's tome (1986).

11. There appears to be no short/long vowel distinction, for although tonic vowels tend to be longer in Romance than atonic ones, durational differences heard between tonic and atonic vowels are not generally considered distinctive (Porto Dapena, 1991: 24).

12. See Chapter 6 (pp. 153–155) for a more detailed explanation of where nasal vowels arose from.

13. See Regueira Fernández (2004: 81) for an interesting account of the reasons behind the selection of this standard form.

14. See in particular Lorenzo (1975: 165).

15. A selection of the more relevant AGAL conference papers are Montero Santalha (1980; 1988: 327–37), López Eire (1989: 811–17), and Santamarina (1991: 289–307). See also Rodrigues Lapa (1973), Piñeiro (1973), and Azevedo Filho (1986). For further discussion of the *Normas Ortográficas*, see Alonso Estravis (1987: 69–78), López Valcárcel (1990; 1991), Fernández Rei (1991;1992), Cidrás Escáneo (1994) and Regueira Fernández (1994).

16. Freixeiro Mato (1997: 127–360) carries out an excellent discussion of the standardisation debate from a *reintegracionista* perspective.

17. It must be stressed that this comparative analysis is in no way intended to be comprehensive, but merely serves as an example of some of the differences found between the different standards. For a more comprehensive account of the *reintegracionista* perspective, see in particular http://membres.lycos.fr/questione/documentos/cuadro_comparativo.html.

18. In an email to the Linguist List in October 1995 (http://linguistlist.org/), Alvarez-Cáccamo states 'As it stands, anything that passes as Spanish may also pass as 'Galician', while anything that sounds 'too Portuguese' is, literally, banned from officially sanctioned written and oral texts'.

19. *Le concept de langue 'ausbau' est d'abord sociologique...il se rapporte à des langues qui ont été délibérément refaites jusqu'à devenir des moyens variés d'expression littéraire. Plusieurs des grandes langues du monde, parmi lesquelles l'anglais, le français et l'allemand, sont à la fois des langues abstand et ausbau, c'est-à-dire qu'on les appelle langues à la fois parce qu'on les a refaites dans un sens littéraire et à cause de la distance interne qui les sépare de toutes les autres langues.*

   [The concept of an *Ausbau* language is predominately a sociolinguistic one...it refers to languages which have been deliberately recreated in order to become the varied means of literary expression. Several of the major world languages, such as English, French and German, are both *Abstand* and *Ausbau* languages, that is, they are termed both because they have been recreated in a literary sense and because of the internal distance which separates them from all other languages].

   Le concept de langue 'abstand' est à prédominance linguistique...Une langue abstand est une entité linguistique qu'on devrait appeler langue même si aucun de ses mots n'avait jamais été écrit, et que par conséquent la plupart des sociologues n'hésiteraient pas à classer parmi les dialects.

   [The concept of an *Abstand* language is predominately a linguistic one... an *Abstand* language is a linguistic entity which should be termed a language even if it has never been written down, and which, consequently, the majority of sociologists would not hesitate to class as a dialect] (Kloss and Mc'Connell, 1974: 32–33).

20. Other dialectal works carried out before the introduction of the standard include De la Torre's thesis on the dialect spoken in Orense (1962) and Muñiz's examination of the Valledor dialect and the linguistic continuum between Galicia and Asturias (1978). Research published by *Verba* and *Cadernos da Lingua*, official publications of the *Instituto da Lingua Galega* [The Galician Language Institute] (ILG), as well as other Galician publishing houses, includes the dialects of the following areas: Feas, A Coruña (Couceiro, 1976), O Grove, Pontevedra (Enríquez, 1976), El Ferrol (Porto Dapena, 1991), Ancares, Asturias (Fernandez González, 1978), Valley of Verín (Taboada, 1979) and Somiedo (Cano González, 1981). More recently, Frías Conde's work (1999) also examines Galician outside the region itself.

   Some dialectal surveys continued to be carried out after the introduction of the *Normas*, including (Silva Valdivia, 1991), Terra Cha (Regueira Fernández, 1989), Val do río Ellas (Costas González, 2002), Valley of Verín (Fernández Rei, 1993), Navia, Villallón, Allande and Ibias (Babarro González, 1994), O Bierzo, As Portelas and the Valley of Asturias (Fernández Rei, 1994), Santiago de Compostela (Dubert García, 1995).

21. López Eire (1989: 811) also employed the term *koiné* back in the 1980s to refer to the Galician standard. The original definition was based upon the Greek word meaning 'common', which was then applied to the variety that became the *lingua franca* or trade language of the Mediterranean region.

22. This map is reproduced with kind permission of PROEL: *Promotora Española de Lingüística* [the Spanish Linguistics Promoter] and can be located online at http://www.proel.org/direccion.htm.

23. Vowel timbre, the velar nasal and the *gheada* are discussed in detail in Chapter 6.

Certain structural forms cognating with Castilian ones are also present in the linguistic repertoires of some speakers, although they are often L[1] Castilian speakers with a lack of proficiency in Galician. For example, in Galician the definite article is used with the possessive pronoun, but such speakers may omit it in line with the Castilian form:

Std.Gal. o meu gato
  (masc.def. art. + 1[st]pers. masc. sing. poss. pron. + noun)
Var.   Ø meu gato   } 'my cat'
Cast.   mi gato

24. For an interesting discussion of written and oral forms of Galician used by the same speakers, see Kabatek (2000: 227–239).

Chapter 6

1. See, for example, Porto Dapena (1991: 34–5), Pensado (1983: 98–103), Fernández Rei (1990: 12), Green (1994: 162), Freixeiro Mato (1998: 142–159; 162–175), Dubert García (1999: 137), Regueira Fernández (1999: 82–85), Alvarez Blanco and Xove (2002) and Recalde (2003: 44). The latter also alludes to laryngeal articulations.
2. In order of occurrence, Labraña-Barrero and van Oosterzee (2003: 2) found the following articulations: voiceless pharyngeal fricatives, voiceless velar fricatives, voiceless glottal fricatives, voiced uvular fricatives, voiceless uvular fricatives, voiced glottal fricatives, voiceless palatal fricatives and voiced pharyngeal fricatives.
3. Another linguistic trait traditionally employed by dialectologists such as Carballo Calero (1968) and Fernández Rei (1990) in order to define a specific area of Galicia is the *seseo* pronunciation of orthographic *c* in certain contexts. Carballo Calero (1968: 38–43) also identified as defining characteristics:

    (a) Derivations of Lat. –ANUM
    (b) Derivations of Lat. –ANAM
    (c) Plural of nouns in –*n*
    (d) Plural of nouns in –*l*
    (e) Diminutive suffix –*iño*
    (f) Types of *s*
    (g) Distinction or neutralisation of implosive (word final) *s* and *z*

4. Frías Conde (1999: 249) points out that the *gheada* also occurs in the Galician of Ancares (Asturias), albeit sporadically.
5. *Ghicho* or *guicho* without the *gheada*, always carries the connotation of 'small' and can refer to a small piece of land, for example. In the western coastal areas, it is a colloquial and somewhat vulgar term to refer to a boy or kid, and is comparable with the Castilian *un tío* (Regueira, personal communication).
6. See also Santamarina (1980), Fernández Rei (1990: 181–182; 186) and Regueira Fernández (1994).
7. Pensado (1983) and Pensado Ruiz (1983) devote an entire special issue to the subject. See also Freixeiro Mato (1998).
8. This substitution of /g/ and its allophones by [x] in Castilian tokens can be regarded as an example of hypercorrection. It is generally termed *gueada* – see Pensado (1983) for further discussion.
9. The orthographic symbol *x* is pronounced variously as [ʃ] *xícara* [cup]; [z] *exito* [success]; [ks] *fixar* [to fix]; [s] *próximo* [next] (Willis, 1984: 84–85).

10. This is particularly apparent in castilianisms such as *ejemplo* 'example' and *colegio* 'college'.

11. The superimposition of Castilian phonetic forms onto spoken Galician may be a clear example of a conscious 'change from above' (Mesthrie *et al.*, 2000: 118) and status enhancement, as discussed earlier (p. 98).

12. By way of comparison, consider the stigma attached, until quite recently, to the non release of /t/ at the end of words such as 'what', and the non articulation of /h/ at the beginning of words such as 'have', in certain dialects, including RP, of British English.

13. However, Tuttle (1991: 38) believes that VNV clusters may also evolve a syllable-final velar nasal in the Italian dialects of Turin and Genoa.

14. See, for example Canfield (1981) and Lipski (1994).

15. See Hajek (1992: 124) for a fuller account. See also Hyman (1985: 171–173) for a particularly lucid account of the phonetic and phonological distinction between nasalised and nasal vowels.

16. See Porto Dapena (1991), Veiga Arias (1976), Perez Pascual (1982), Alonso Estravis (1987), and Beswick (1994) for fuller accounts and examples of this diachronic evolution.

17. See also Parkinson (1983, 1987).

18. Veiga Arias (1976), Alvarez Blanco *et al.* (1986: 107), and González and González (1994: 17) posit that the intervocalic velar nasal arose from its appearance word-finally in the masculine form *un*, to which was added the gender morpheme /a/, a theory not entirely incompatible with Sampson's explanation.

19. Std.Gal.   /m/: bilabial nasal   man 'hand'
               /n/: alveolar nasal   nada 'nothing'
               /ɲ/: palatal nasal ñu   'gnu'
    See for example, Veiga Arias (1976: 121), González and González (1994: 2) and the most recent edition of the *Normas* (RAG/ILG, 2004: 20). There does exist a restricted set of non-standard words beginning with /ɲ/. Veiga Arias (1976: 103–105) states that /ɲ/ occurs in 18 words of the *Diccionario de Franco Grande* but he does not clarify whether these are autochthonous or loanwords. González and González (1994: 3) cite examples such as *ñu, ñapa, ñato* and so on.

    Although I have stated in the course of my discussion that the velar nasal occupies syllable-final position, there is actually a degree of debate as to whether this is indeed the case and whether the velar nasal can indeed be considered a phoneme. However, this falls outside the scope of this book and will not be considered further. For a recent analysis of the phenomenon, see Beswick (1999b) and Dubert García's online document at http://web.usc.es/~fgdubert/artigos/nvelar1.pdf.

20. For further descriptions, see Veiga Arias (1976: 121–123), Muñiz (1978: 190), Alvarez Blanco *et al.* (1986: 20, 33), Montero Santalha (1988: 333), González and González (1994: 3) and RAG/ILG (2004: 20).

21. *irmao* and *irmá* are also found in the eastern regions.

22. The following explanations and many of the examples may be found in Carballo Calero (1968: 124), Alvarez Blanco (1983: 171–173), Alvarez Blanco *et al.* (1986: 34, 136–137, 163, 179) and RAG/ILG (2004).

23. When the preceding word ends in -*r* or -*s*, then the use of the *lo* form is triggered and allows the final /r/ or /s/ to drop, and in order to differentiate the article from the pronoun, the former is attached to the verb by a dash:
    Std.Gal. *tes que leva-las gafas ben postas* [you have to wear the glasses correctly]
                    tes que leválas ben postas [you have to wear them correctly]

24. A similar assertion is made regarding third person plural verb forms, for which it is contended that historically, assimilation of the *l-* of the definite article with the *-n* verb form ending resulted in a cognate form, /nn/, which in turn, underwent reduction to /n/:
    Std. Gal. fan-lo > fan-no > fa-no 'they, you (pol.) do/make it'
25. Alonso's account of dialectal Galician also cites the case of *engalar* [ẽɲgalar] 'to fly' < Lat. IN-AL-ARE (Alonso, 1972: 458), and draws the same conclusion with respect to the appearance of *g*.
26. The researchers also repeated a sample of the target words in isolation and in phrases in order to corroborate the syllable division and hence, the phonetic realisation of the nasal segment. Examples of tokens include:

u $ nha/unh $ a	'one' (fem.sing)
ma $ ne $ xar/man $ ex $ ar*	'to handle'
alg $ u $ nha/al $ gunh $ a	'some' (fem.sing)
co $ mi $ no/com $ in $ o	'I ate it'
ni $ n o $ ho $ me/nin $ o $ ho $ me	'not even the man'
ta $ mén $ o fa $ go/ta $ mé $ no $ fa $ go	'I also do it'
nin $ guén $ a fa $ lou/nin $ gué $ na fa $ lou	'no one talked to her'
sen $ a su $ a $ a $ xu $ da/se $ na su $ a $ a $ xu $ da	'without his, her your help' (pol.sing.)

27. In the first edition of their influential grammar book, Alvarez Blanco *et al.* confirm:
    Con todo, existe unha tendencia na fala a pronunciar sempre como velar esa consoante [. . .] nun registro estándar coidado esta tendencia debe evitarse.
    [However, in speech there is a tendency to always pronounce this consonant as a velar [. . .]. In the standard register, this tendency should be avoided] (Alvarez Blanco *et al.*, 1986: 138).
28. In accordance with Lehiste's (1988: 5) earlier definitions (pp. 100–101), a form of overdifferentiation occurs for nearly 70% of the total respondents in my study, in which Galician phonetic distinctions are imposed onto their spoken Castilian tokens. This is discussed in more detail in Chapter 8.
29. In this respect, compare Kabatek's thesis (2000: 150–151), which finds that word final orthographic *n* is mostly pronounced as a velar nasal, but instances of the alveolar nasal are considered interference phenomena. Once again, the influence of Castilian on Galician intonation patterns and phonetic output can be cited as other evidence. See my earlier discussion at pp. 134–137 and later at p. 185.
30. Of course, the contrary applies in the case of respondents who use only [n]. I will revisit this issue in Chapter 9.

Chapter 7

1. See for example González Fernández (1978), García Pérez (1985), Varela Barreiro (1991), Fernández Salgado (1991), García Cancela and Díaz Abraira (1994), Ferro Ruibal and Casares (1996), Gómez Clemente *et al.* (1997), and Rivas Quintas (1997).
2. Some of Wardhaugh's comments regarding the historical use of Galician are sparse and partially factually inaccurate. For example, he states that historically, Galician was only ever a spoken language, lacking a literature and a written form, a claim that clearly does not take into account the *cancioneiros*, or Galician medieval prose (Wardhaugh, 1987: 127).
3. Although the Spanish education system underwent an overhaul in the late 1990s, with changes being made to the terminology, the categories have

remained essentially the same. Pre-school education is voluntary, from 0 to 6 years of age. Primary education (what used to be termed EXB) lasts from 6 to 12 years of age and is divided into three cycles: from 6 to 8 years of age, from 8 to 10 years of age and from 10 to 12 years of age. Compulsory secondary education is from 12 to 16 years of age.

4. Monteagudo and Santamarina attempt a similar review, but conclude that their quantitative data is based upon random samples that are difficult to subject to a comparative analysis, in that they come from different sources and sections of society (1993: 126–127).

5. The definition of what constitutes 'normal' usage is still the subject of some debate, and is discussed in some detail below (pp. 176–182).

6. Even in the 1980s, knowledge of and linguistic competence in Galician was, in theory, a pre-requisite for all primary and secondary school teachers, and to this end, the *Dirección Xeral de Política Lingüística* (DXPL) [General Directorate of Linguistic Policy] promoted Galician language courses. See López Valcárcel (1991) and Rábade Paredes (1993) for further early studies on the influence of language in schools.

7. Moreover, of the 90,000 people living in the Asturias/Galicia and Castille-Leon/Galicia border regions, about 45% claim that they normally express themselves in their own variety of Galician. For further information, see also www.eurolang.net/ State/spain.htm#Galician.

8. But see (pp. 176–182), where this notion of harmony between languages will be seen to be one of the main aims of the *Xunta's* linguistic policy.

9. This group is part of the *Nova Escola Galega* [the New Galician School] (NEG), an association founded in 1983 with the aim of bringing together various academic professionals to promote the use of Galician. As well as playing a fundamental role in training and development, many of the members of NEG produce books, handbooks and teaching resources written in Galician. One notable publication is the *Revista Galega de Educación* [the Galician Journal of Education]. Further information on the Linguistic Normalisation Models recommended by this association can be found at http://www.nova-escola-galega.org/Normalizacion/Situacion_actual.htm.

10. Further information regarding the Census and statistical evidence are located on the *Xunta* website at http://www.ige.xunta.es/ga/home.htm.

11. See Figure 7.2.

12. Other recommendations include: the greater involvement of nongovernmental institutions, improvements in the university training of academic providers and specialists, an increase in the promotion of the language socially through the consolidation, reorganisation and management of existing linguistic services (Domínguez Salgado *et al.*, 1999: 265), and further promotion of the language via the World Wide Web and other modern means of communication (1999: 328–329).

13. *Galicia Hoxe*: http://www.galicia-hoxe.com/, October 2004. See also various articles discussed by the *Mesa da Normalización Lingüística* at http://clientes.vianetworks.es/colectivo/amesanl/.

14. The PNL is available as an online document at: http://www.consellodacultura.org/arquivos/cdsg/docs/plandenormalizacionlinguagalega.pdf

15. Article 6 stipulates that there are plans to teach even more courses in Galician, such as philosophy, biology, history, technical drawing, geography and so on, at *bacharelato* level, which is roughly equivalent to 'A' level standard in the UK (*Decreto* 247/1995).

16. The PNL reiterates the aims of these earlier policies regarding teaching strategies in primary and secondary education, but adds that content courses taught in Galician should now include mathematics and technology.

17. Ironically, Regueira Fernández points out (2006: 70) that the BNG virtually abandoned its *reintegracionista* stance after it had been involved in the reform of the *Normas* in 2003. When it became part of the government in 2005, it was largely due to the votes of the the young, urban middle classes.

18. A case in point is Haiti, where the standardisation of Creole began in the 1980s. Speakers already demonstrated a strong attachment to their language in the face of unwelcome competition from French (Valdman, 1988) and it is eminently possible that competition for functional uses between the two languages has already started to arise (Lefebvre, 1998). The same is occurring in Mauritius with Creole and the official languages of English and French. See the Ethnologue section (Gordon, 2005) online at http://www.ethnologue.com/, and also Eriksen (1992). See also Ninyoles regarding the Valencian linguistic situation (1969, 1975).

19. See once again, the highly charged comments of Eiré and Valverde (2005: 3).

20. *The Dirección Xeral de Política Lingüística* also carried out an exhaustive survey of language use in education (1998). For an excellent synthesis of its results, see Bouzada Fernández *et al.* (2002: 85–95).

21. Euromosaic country and language reports are located at: http://europa.eu.int/comm/education/policies/lang/languages/langmin/euromosaic/index_en.html.

22. TVG is also currently setting up joint agreements with the television channels of other self-governing regions regarding the possibility of satellite transmission.

23. For a more detailed analysis of the use of Galician within the media, see López Dobao (1993, 1994) and Alonso (1994).

24. See also the excellent account in Kabatek (2000) regarding a potential model of pronunciation in Galicia.

25. However, it would appear that in practice, formal use of Galician in the judicial system is rare even though most of its employees regularly employ it in oral interactions (Euromosaic, 2005: 5).

Chapter 8

1. See for example, the many cases cited in Huss *et al.* (2003).

2. Similar results were found when the respondents were asked about the language generally employed with their mothers in childhood. Once again, the younger the age group, the more likely that the language used is predominantly Castilian: 60% of the 5 to 14 year old age group, compared to just under 23% of the over 50's age group claim to speak (or have spoken) Castilian to their parents. In the 15 to 29 age group, the number is just over 50% (IGE: 2003).

3. This point is taken up later in this chapter (pp. 203–223) when I discuss my own research carried out in the 1990s in Santiago de Compostela.

4. This scenario is loosely based upon the Basque sociolinguist Sánchez Carrión's intra- and intergroup functions of a language as a means of communication (1987), also summarised in Portas (1999: 13).

5. See Beswick (1999a) for further detail.

6. Six of the questionnaires were excluded from the original analysis (Beswick, 1999b) because the respondents did not want their details included in the

survey. However, in 2001 all the respondents who took part in this study were contacted once again (see my comments, pp. 219–220) and all gave their consent for their details now to be included.

7. Beswick (1999a) examines code-switching and mixing phenomena in bilingual conversations between members of the same families, and finds that with parents, some younger people are starting to use Galician rather than Castilian. This is discussed in more detail in Chapter 9.

8. See, for example, Rojo (1981).

9. The assertion by one respondent that his written Castilian is not fully competent does not fully accord with the fact that he received his education in Castilian until the age of 16. Accordingly, he must have some other reason for always using Galician, such as wanting to display his identity as such. However, this respondent refused to comment further on this point.

10. Compare Williamson and Williamson's claim (1984: 411) that it is common to find a sense of awkwardness about which language to use in a given context. Their respondents feared making mistakes and they were particularly worried that their Castilian could be contaminated by Galician.

11. The earlier example of *agradable* is pertinent (p. 217). An online dictionary of Galician is maintained by the University of Vigo's Computational Linguistics Group at http://sli.uvigo.es/CLIG/clig_en.html.

12. See Beswick (1999a) for examples. Further research is needed, however, to confirm this hypothesis.

13. In his own investigations, Kabatek (2000) also found that his informants were extremely aware of issues regarding the form of spoken Galician. See also SSRAG's findings (2003: 187), in which they cite lack of confidence as a reason for some respondents avoiding the use of Galician.

Chapter 9

1. Rodríguez–Neira's study (2003: 75–112), discussed earlier (p. 199) cannot be used as a direct comparison to my investigation, given the different sample size and hypothesis. Nonetheless, one of its relevant findings pertains to the increase in habitual bilingual use in those under 30 years of age, with education being cited as one of the primary reasons for the change.

2. To whit, *A língua constitue unha das bases esenciais da identidade do pobo e o máis forte vencello de unión entre as suas xentes* [...] [Language is one of the fundamental underpinnings of the identity of a community and the strongest bond of the commonality that exists between its people] (*Decreto* 247/1995).

3. Pérez-Barreiro Nolla (1990: 197) details his similar experiences.

4. The stigma attached to the use of the Castilian pronunciation tends to be manifest by mother tongue Galician speakers only and is overlaid with political connotations (SSRAG, 2003: 187).

5. This belief is also held by Monteagudo and Santamarina (1993: 146). They state that in certain sectors of society within Santiago de Compostela at least, this increase in the use of Galician is spurred on by 'an ideological consciousness', especially amongst the middle classes.

6. For a more detailed account and examples, see also Beswick (1999a). In this respect, consider Fuentes and Vilariño's (in Portas, 1999: 150) study, which reveals some interesting perceptions regarding habitual language use in urban areas in the late 1980s. They found that 25% of those parents who employed Castilian with their children did so because they considered it a

more universal language than Galician: 1% because it was the national language; 13% because it was more refined and cultured; 11% because of habit; 11% simply because they preferred it as a medium of communication, and 2% because they were ashamed of using Galician. There also appears to have been a strong association between the conscious selection of Castilian by parents in urban areas as the language of habitual use with their children, and issues of status, prestige, and identity, as evidenced by my earlier data in Chapter 8.

7.   Other respondents demonstrated intrasentential code-switching based on their confusion between the provenence of certain lexical items. This is somewhat to be expected given the transitory phase Galicia and its language are going through, and the linguistic similarities between the two languages (see Chapter 5).

8.   However, I am not claiming here that these examples are indicative of far-reaching changes in the relationship between Galician and Castilian.

9.   The *gaiteiro* is the traditional bagpipe player; the *queimada* is a typical Galician ritual involving the reciting of a Galician *conxuro* 'spell' over a pot of potent alcoholic brew that is set alight.

10. In a recent paper on language use in the borderland regions of Galicia and Portugal (Beswick, 2005a), briefly summarised in Chapter 5, I commented that the linguistic configuration and distribution of varieties in context does not entirely mirror that experienced elsewhere in the region. Here, there appears to be a specific identity emerging, reinforced perhaps by the degree of mutual intelligibility transcending the national boundary. What I claimed may be developing is a communal borderland identity that exists along with regional and national identities. I tentatively concluded that the emergence of a borderland identity that transcends political, cultural, historical, and geographical borders appears to be reinforced in this instance by a degree of convergence with respect to the phonology of the dialects in question, which, in turn, has been facilitated by the degree of contact witnessed on a weekly, if not daily, basis.

11. Of course, the phenomenon of new speakers, members of the younger age group who have received some education in Galician and have chosen to use it as their habitual language at a given point in their lives, is not exclusive to Galician, and is also found in other self-governing regions of Spain.

12. As a comparison, it should be mentioned that in their 1980s study, Williamson and Williamson (1984: 401) assert that the younger subjects interviewed in their bilingual survey were acutely aware of the need to protect Galician. Moreover, some 58% of the people interviewed in Rodríguez Neira's early study (1988) believed that Galician would continue to survive; they appeared extremely conscious of the fact that to lose their language could imply a loss of their collective identity.

13. The MSG findings regarding the language of the future in Galicia were the following: only Galician: 3.3%; mostly Galician: 55.4%; both languages: 28.9%; mostly Castilian: 11.9%; only Castilian: 0.6% (Fernández Rodríguez *et al.*, 1996).

14. Erik Allardt's studies in Finland show a similar scenario (1981). There are many similar studies; see as a small example, the articles in the The Journal of Linguistic Anthropology (2000: 10, 2); the Journal of Language, Identity and Education (2003: 2, 3); and especially Pavlenko and Blackledge (2003).

15. Le Page and Tabouret-Keller (1985: 239–40) address this point by claiming that when feelings of ethnic identity are institutionally buttressed, then they may be able to survive such total language loss.

16. Santarita and Martin-Jones' research into the Portuguese-speaking community in London (1991) unearthed similar results, however López Trigal (2001) has found that in Portuguese-speaking communities in Spain, the use of mixed codes tended to devalue self-identification strategies.
17. According to Giles and Johnson's (1987) theory of ethnolinguistic identity, discussed earlier in Chapter 1 (pp. 36–37), this switch to the in-group language of Galician implies that some younger people at least may be starting to adopt strategies of psycholinguistic distinctiveness, partially to reinforce solidarity with their community and partially because they are questioning their feelings of self-identification.
18. See in this vein Bouzada Fernández (2003: 334).
19. See, for example, Iglesias Alvarez and Ramallo (2003: 257, 262).

Appendix 1

Major Orthographic Differences between the Galician Standard, Castilian and Portuguese

Symbol in Galician	Galician Standard	Castilian	Portuguese	Gloss
x	xeral	general	geral	'general'
	xema	yema	gema	'yolk'
	xaneiro	enero	janeiro	'January'
	peixe	pez	peixe	'fish'
nh	unha	una	uma	'one' (fem.sing.)
	algunha	alguna	alguma	'some' (fem.sing.)
ll	ollo	ojo	olho	'eye'
	tella	teja	telha	'material, cloth'
ñ	teño	tengo	tenho	'I have'
l	castelo	castillo	castelo	'castle'
ch	chama	llama	chama	'flame'
m	home	hombre	homem	'man'

Use of the Gheada, Santiago de Compostela, 1995, 1996

Questions:

1. Do you use the *gheada* in everyday conversation?
2. Are you aware that you are doing so?
3. What does the use of the *gheada* signify to you?
4. Could you avoid using it?
5. Would you ever try to? Where?

Table A2.1 10 to 21 age group use of the *gheada*

Respondent/ Question	DB	ECL	LCV	MCG	DRL	MACL	PFCR	CRS	TRMC	LGD
Daily use	Yes	Yes	Yes	Yes	Yes	Yes	Yes	Yes	Yes	Yes
Awareness	Mostly	Always	Always	Always	Always	Always	Always	Mostly	Always	Always
Significance	Community speech	Community speech	Community speech	Informal speech	Community speech	Community speech	Community speech	Unsure	Informal speech	Informal speech
Avoidance	Probably	No	No	Yes	No	No	No	No	No	No
When/ where	No/n/a	No/n/a	Never/n/a	Unsure/ school?	No/n/a	Never/n/a	No/n/a	No/n/a	Unsure/ school?	Unsure/ school?

Table A2.2 21 to 40 Age group use of the *gheada*

Respondent/Question	JCG	MGL	XMPS	NMV	ACG	PBG
Daily use	Yes	Yes	Yes	Yes	Yes	Yes
Awareness	Always	Mostly	Always	Always	Always	Always
Significance	Informal speech	Informal speech	Community speech	Inferior speech	Informal speech	Informal speech
Avoidance	With difficulty	Probably	No	With difficulty	No	No
Attempt/where	Yes/work	Yes/with strangers	Never/n/a	Yes/all contexts	Unsure/with children?	Yes/work

Table A2.3 21 to 40 age group use of the *gheada*

Respondent/ Question	MCR	BGB	PLA	CMR	RMQS	ADL
Daily use	Yes	Yes	Yes	Yes	Yes	Yes
Awareness	Always	Mostly	Rarely	Mostly	Always	Mostly
Significance	Informal speech	Inferior speech	Informal speech	Community speech	Inferior speech	Geographical location
Avoidance	No	With difficulty	No	With difficulty	With difficulty	No
Attempt/where	Yes/work	Yes/all contexts	No/n/a	No/n/a	Yes/all contexts	Yes/work

Table A2.4 40 to 70 age group use of the *gheada*

Respondent/ Question	JCF	SCF	MDGQ	MPG	ASG	ISS	ECM	MGS	SIFF	XPR
Daily use	Yes	Yes	Yes	Yes	Yes	Yes	Yes	Yes	Yes	Yes
Awareness	Always	Mostly	Always	Mostly	Always	Always	Always	Mostly	Always	Always
Significance	Inferior speech	Geographical location	Community speech	Informal speech	Informal speech	Community speech	Inferior speech	Inferior speech	Informal speech	Informal speech
Avoidance	Yes	No	No	Probably	No	No	Yes	No	No	No
When/ where	Yes/all contexts	No/n/a	Never/n/a	Unsure/ with younger family	Yes/with younger family	Never/n/a	Yes/all contexts	Yes/all contexts	Yes/with younger family	Yes/all contexts

Appendix 3

Written and Spoken Tokens, Santiago de Compostela, 1995, 1996

Galician Token	English Translation
unha	'one' (fem.sing)
algunha	'some' (fem.sing)
inhabilidade	'inability'
comeuna	'he, she, you (pol.sing.) ate it'
fixéronos	'they (pl.) did it'
chámannos	'they, you (pol.pl.) call us'
connosco	'with us'
man útil	'useful, good hand'
comen	'they, you (pol.pl.) eat'
comen às tres	'they, you (pol.pl.) eat at three o'clock'
comen o pan	'they, you (pol.pl.) eat the bread'
comeno	'they, you (pol.pl.) eat it'

Castilian Token	English Translation
perenne	'everlasting, constant'
me gustan el pan y el agua	'I like bread and water'
era un amor eterno	'it was a never-ending love'
lo hago en un instante	'I will do it in an instant'
entró Sebastián	'Sebastian came in'
era una indiscreción	'it was an indiscretion'

Appendix 4
Petición de axuda (Appeal for Help)

Poderás axudarme? Son inglesa e estou aquí en Santiago para facer unha investigación sobre as actitudes e os comportamentos da comunidade bilingüe. A miña intención é a de atopar persoas que falen ámbo-lo galego como o castelán, e que estén dispostas a responder a algunhas preguntas sinxelas sobre o emprego das duas linguas na vida cotiá.
   Os requerimentos son:

- capacidade para conversar nas duas linguas atá un bo nível
- residencia na cidade de Santiago ou arredores
- ser estudiante da EXB ou ben ter terminado o ensino superior

Non é preciso saber escribir nin ler nas duas linguas, nin ter cursado a asignatura de lingua galega. Gardarás o anonimato dos participantes e empregaranse as respostas unicamente na investigación que levo a cabo neste momento.
   Se che interesa axudarme, responde às seguintes preguntas e entrega ou manda o cuestionario a:

ILG
r/. Hórreo, 31-2°
15702 Santiago de Compostela
Atención: Jaine Beswick
Moitas gracias pola sua atención.

Nome: _____   Idade: _____

Enderezo: _____   Nacido/a en: _____

_____   _____

_____

Lingua materna: _____   Nivel de ensino: _____

Profesión: _____

Nivel de coñocemento do castelán: _____   dogalego: _____

Sociolinguistic Questionnaire – Santiago de Compostela 1995, 1996, 2001

1. Which language did you normally use at home before you started school?
2. Did you learn any Galician/Catalan at school?
3. Which language do you normally use with your children?
4. Which language do you normally use with your brothers and sisters?
5. Which language do/did you now normally use with your parents and which with your grandparents?
6. Which language do your children normally reply in?
7. Which language do/did your parents normally reply in?
8. Which language do you normally use with friends?
9. Which language do you normally use with work colleagues, teachers or other pupils?
10. Which language do you normally use when you enter a shop, bar or a restaurant?
11. Which language do you normally use when you meet someone for the first time?
12. Which language do you prefer to speak in?
13. Can you read and write in Galician/Catalan? And in Castilian?
14. Which language do you normally use if you are counting or talking out loud to yourself?
15. Which language do you normally use to write yourself a note?
16. Do you think you ever use a non-standard form?
17. Do you ever insert words of the other language, either by mistake or on purpose?
18. In your opinion, what is the general attitude to the Galician/Catalan language?
19. Do you think it will survive?
20. What do you think of people who always use either Galician/Catalan or Castilian, irrespective of the situation?

Appendix 6
Respondent Details

Table A6.1 10 to 21 age group

Respondent	Age	Gender	Place of Birth	Residence	Profession
DB	10	M	Santiago–city	Santiago–city	Schoolboy
ECL	12	F	Santiago–outskirts	Santiago–city	Schoolgirl
LCV	12	F	Zurich, Switzerland	Santiago–city	Schoolgirl
MCG	17	F	Santiago–city	Santiago–city	Schoolgirl
DRL	13	M	Vigo, Pontevedra	Santiago–outskirts	Schoolboy
MACL	18	M	Santiago–outskirts	Santiago–city	Student
PFCR	20	M	Santiago–outskirts	Santiago–city	Student
CRS	19	M	Santiago–outskirts	Santiago–city	Student
TMRC	15	F	Santiago–city	Santiago–city	Schoolgirl
LGD	14	F	Boiro, A Coruña	Santiago–outskirts	Schoolgirl

Table A6.2 21 to 40 age group

Respondent	Age	Gender	Place of Birth	Residence	Profession
JCG	23	M	Santiago–city	Santiago–city	Army cadet
MGL	36	F	Ourense, Ourense	Santiago–outskirts	PA
XMPS	27	M	Ferrol, A Coruña	Santiago–outskirts	Researcher
NMV	27	F	O Saviñao, Coruña	Santiago–outskirts	Secretary
ACG	25	F	Santiago–city	Santiago–city	Researcher
PBG	30	F	Ourense, Ourense	Santiago–city	Teacher
MCR	26	F	Negreira, A Coruña	Santiago–city	Law postgrad
BGB	25	F	Santiago–city	Santiago–city	Law PA
PLA	25	F	Santiago–city	Santiago–city	Lawyer
CMR	30	F	Outes, A Coruña	Santiago–city	Cartographer
RMQS	33	F	Santiago–outskirts	Santiago–city	Dental asst.
ADL	38	M	Santiago–outskirts	Santiago–outskirts	Lecturer

Table A6.3 40 to 70 age group

Respondent	Age	Gender	Place of Birth	Residence	Profession
JCF	40	M	Santiago–outskirts	Santiago–outskirts	Vet
SCF	50	F	Santiago–outskirts	Santiago–city	Teacher
MDGQ	56	F	Santiago–outskirts	Santiago–city	Teacher
MPG	54	M	Santiago–outskirts	Santiago–city	Lecturer
ASG	58	F	Santiago–outskirts	Santiago–outskirts	Doctor
ISS	61	M	Laracha, A Coruña	Santiago–outskirts	Teacher
ECM	48	M	Vigo, Pontevedra	Santiago–city	Engineer
MGS	42	M	Santiago–city	Santiago–city	Accountant
SIFF	44	F	Santiago–outskirts	Santiago–city	Solicitor
XPR	44	M	Ferrol, A Coruña	Santiago–city	Teacher

Appendix 7

Language Preference and Language Use, Santiago de Compostela 1995, 1996, 2001

Table A7.1 Breakdown of preferred language by age group

Language Choice/Age Group	Galician	Castilian	Both Galician and Castilian
40 to 70 years old	5 (50%)	5 (50%)	– (0%)
21 to 40 years old	5 (42%)	4 (33%)	3 (25%)
10 to 21 years old	– (0%)	3 (30%)	7 (70%)

Table A7.2 10 to 21 age group language use and language choice

Respondent/Question	DB	ECL	LCV	MCG	DRL
1. Home	Castilian	Both	Both	Castilian	Both
2. School: Language classes Language of instruction	Yes Both	Yes Galician	Yes Galician	Yes Both	Yes Galician
3. Children	n/a	n/a	n/a	n/a	n/a
4. Siblings	Castilian	Both	Both	Castilian	Both
5. Other family	Both	Both	Both	Both	Both
6. Childrens' replies	n/a	n/a	n/a	n/a	n/a
7. Parents' replies	Both	Both	Both	Castilian	Both
8. Friends	Castilian	Both	Both	Castilian	Both
9. Work/ teachers/peers	Castilian	Both	Both	Castilian	Both
10. Shops/bars/ restaurants	Castilian	Both	Both	Castilian	Both

Continued

Table A7.2 *Continued*

Respondent/Question	DB	ECL	LCV	MCG	DRL
11. First meetings	Castilian	Castilian	Castilian	Castilian	Castilian
12. Preference	Both	Both	Both	Castilian	Both
13. Total reading/ writing skills	Both	Both	Both	Both	Both
14. Intra language	Both	Both	Both	Castilian	Both
15. Notes	Castilian	Both	Both	Castilian	Both
16. Non-standard/ dialectal forms	No	No	No	No	No
17. Word insertion: by mistake/on purpose	No	No	No	No	No

Table A7.3 10 to 21 age group language use and language choice

Respondent/Question	MACL	PFCR	CRS	TMRC	LGD
1. Home	Both	Both	Both	Castilian	Castilian
2. School: Language classes	Yes	Yes	Yes	Yes	Yes
Language of instruction	Both	Both	Both	Both	Both
3. Children	n/a	n/a	n/a	n/a	n/a
4. Siblings	Both	Both	Castilian	Castilian	Castilian
5. Other family	Both	Both	Both	Both	Both
6. Childrens' replies	n/a	n/a	n/a	n/a	n/a
7. Parents' replies	Both	Both	Both	Castilian	Castilian
8. Friends	Both	Both	Castilian	Castilian	Castilian
9. Work/teachers/peers	Both	Both	Castilian	Both	Both
10. Shops/bars/restaurants	Castilian	Castilian	Castilian	Castilian	Castilian
11. First meetings	Castilian	Castilian	Castilian	Castilian	Castilian
12. Preference	Both	Both	Both	Castilian	Castilian
13. Total reading/ writing skills	Both	Both	Both	Both	Both
14. Intra language	Both	Both	Castilian	Both	Both
15. Notes	Both	Both	Castilian	Both	Both
16. Non-standard/ dialectal forms	No	No	No	No	No
17. Word insertion: by mistake/on purpose	No	No	No	No	No

Table A7.4 21 to 40 age group language use and language choice

Respondent/ Question	JCG	MGL	XMPS	NMV	ACG	PBG
1. Home	Castilian	Both	Galician	Castilian	Castilian	Both
2. School: Language classes	Yes	Yes	Yes	No	Yes	Yes
Language of instruction	Castilian	Both		Castilian	Both	Both
3. Children	Both	n/a	n/a	Both	Both	n/a
4. Siblings	Both	Both	Galician	Both	Both	Both
5. Other family	Both	Both	Galician	Both	Galician	Both
6. Childrens' replies	Both	n/a	n/a	Both	Both	n/a
7. Parents' replies	Galician	Both	Galician	Both	Galician	Both
8. Friends	Both	Both	Galician	Castilian	Both	Both
9. Work/ teachers/ peers	Both	Both	Galician	Castilian	Both	Both
10. Shops/ bars/ restaurants	Galician	Both	Galician	Both	Galician	Both
11. First meetings	Galician	Castilian	Galician	Castilian	Galician	Castilian
12. Preference	Galician	Both	Galician	Castilian	Galician	Both
13. Total reading/ writing skills	Castilian	Both	Galician	Castilian	Castilian	Both
14. Intra language	Both	Both	Galician	Castilian	Both	Both
15. Notes	Castilian	Both	Galician	Castilian	Castilian	Both
16. Non-standard/ dialectal forms	Castilian	No	No	Both	Castilian	No
17. Word insertion: by mistake/ on purpose	No/No	No/No	No/No	Maybe/ No	No/Into Galician	No/ No

Table A7.5 21 to 40 age group language use and language choice

Respondent/Question	MCR	BGB	PLA	CMR	RMQS	ADL
1. Home	Both	Castilian	Castilian	Castilian	Castilian	Castilian
2. School: Language classes Language of instruction	Yes Both	No Castilian	Yes Castilian	Yes Castilian	No Castilian	No Castilian
3. Children	n/a	Castilian	Both	Galician	Both	Both
4. Siblings	Both	Castilian	Both	Both	Both	Both
5. Other family	Castilian	Castilian	Galician	Both	Both	Both
6. Childrens' replies	n/a	Both	Both	Both	Both	Both
7. Parents' replies	Galician	Castilian	Galician	Both	Both	Both
8. Friends	Galician	Castilian	Galician	Both	Castilian	Castilian
9. Work/teachers/peers	Both	Castilian	Galician	Both	Castilian	Castilian
10. Shops/bars/restaurant	Galician	Both	Galician	Galician	Both	Both
11. First meetings	Castilian	Castilian	Galician	Galician	Castilian	Castilian
12. Preference	Both	Castilian	Galician	Galician	Castilian	Castilian
13. Total reading/writing skills	Both	Castilian	Castilian	Castilian	Castilian	Castilian
14. Intra language	Both	Castilian	Both	Galician	Castilian	Castilian
15. Notes	Both	Castilian	Castilian	Castilian	Castilian	Castilian
16. Non-standard/dialectal forms	No	Both	Castilian	No	Both	Both
17. Word insertion: by mistake/on purpose	No/Into Castilian	Both/No	No/ Into Galician	No/Into Castilian	Into Galician /No	Into Galician /No

Table A7.6 40 to 70 age group language use and language choice

Respondent/Question	JCF	SCF	MDGQ	MPG	ASG
1. Home	Both	Galician	Galician	Galician	Galician
2. School: Language classes Language of instruction	No Castilian	No Castilian	No Castilian	No Castilian	No Castilian
3. Children	Castilian	Both	Galician	Both	Both
4. Siblings	Castilian	Galician	Galician	Galician	Galician
5. Other family	Both	Galician	n/a	Galician	Galician
6. Childrens' replies	Castilian	Both	Both	Castilian	Castilian
7. Parents' replies	Castilian	Galician	Galician	Galician	Galician
8. Friends	Castilian	Galician	Galician	Both	Both
9. Work/teachers/peers	Castilian	Both	Both	Both	Both
10. Shops/bars/restaurants	Castilian	Galician	Galician	Galician	Galician
11. First meetings	Castilian	Both	Castilian	Galician	Galician
12. Preference	Castilian	Galician	Galician	Galician	Galician
13. Total reading/writing skills	Castilian	Neither	Neither	Neither	Neither
14. Intra language	Castilian	Galician	Galician	Both	Galician
15. Notes	Castilian	Galician	Galician	Castilian	Castilian
16. Non-standard/dialectal forms	Galician	Both	No	No	No
17. Word insertion: by mistake/ on purpose	No/No	Into Galician/No	Maybe/No	No/Into Galician	No/Into Galician

Table A7.7 40 to 70 age group language use and language choice

Respondent/ Question	ISS	ECM	MGS	SIFF	XPR
1. Home	Galician	Galician	Galician	Both	Both
2. School: Language classes	No	No	No	No	No
Language of instruction	Both	Castilian	Castilian	Castilian	Castilian
3. Children	Galician	Castilian	Both	Both	Both
4. Siblings	Galician	Castilian	Castilian	Castilian	Castilian
5. Other family	n/a	Castilian	Castilian	Castilian	Castilian
6. Childrens' replies	Both	Castilian	Both	Both	Both
7. Parents' replies	n/a	Castilian	Castilian	Castilian	Castilian
8. Friends	Galician	Castilian	Both	Both	Both
9. Work/teachers/ peers	Galician	Castilian	Both	Castilian	Castilian
10. Shops/bars/ restaurants	Galician	Castilian	Galician	Galician	Galician
11. First meetings	Galician	Castilian	Castilian	Castilian	Castilian
12. Preference	Galician	Castilian	Castilian	Castilian	Castilian
13. Total reading/ writing skills	Both	Castilian	Castilian	Castilian	Castilian
14. Intra language	Galician	Castilian	Castilian	Castilian	Castilian
15. Notes	Galician	Castilian	Castilian	Castilian	Castilian
16. Non-standard/ dialectal forms	No	Galician	No	Galician	Galician
17. Word Insertion: by mistake/ on purpose	No/No	No/No	No/No	Maybe/No	No/No

Glossary

This glossary is intended as a very general guide to the linguistic terms covered and used in several parts of the book. An asterisk (*) indicates the use of a term that is explained further in the glossary. The International Phonetic Alphabet can be found at: http://www2.arts.gla.ac. uk/IPA/IPA_chart_(C)2005.pdf.

Allophones The phonetic realisations of a phoneme* that are determined by the overall phonetic environment. They are variants found in complementary distribution to each other: that is, one is pronounced to the exclusion of all the others. For example, the various articulations of the voiced* alveolar phoneme /n/ in RP English: as a dental allophone before dental consonants 'bend' [bɛn̪d]; as a labiodental before /f, v/ 'confuse' [ˈkɔɱfuz] and [n] elsewhere 'nine' [naɪn].

Anti-hiatic device In change processes, a consonant inserted between two vowels for articulation purposes. See the diachronic processes regarding nasal consonants (pp. 153–155).

Assimilation The frequent process in speech by which a sound becomes similar to an adjacent sound through linguistic influence. For example, in certain speech styles, the /d/ of 'good' in English 'good boy' is pronounced as /b/ due to the influence of the adjacent /b/ in 'boy'.

Atonic vowel Any non-stressed vowel in a word. For example, bold /i/ in English 'linguistics'.

Clitic An unstressed, typically grammatical morpheme that shares the syntactic characteristics of a word but is bound to another. For example, the contraction of 'is' in English 'what's happening?'

Consonant clusters A grouping of two or more consonants together in a word. For example, English 'linguistics', 'amplitude'.

Diphthong A vowel sound comprising two separate vowels. For example, /oi/ in English 'boy', in contrast to monophthongs, which comprise a single vowel sound, such as /ɔ/ English 'cot'.

Generative phonology The component of generative grammar that through a series of rules, allocates a phonetic representation to a speaker's utterances in order to represent their innate and underlying knowledge of the phonological system.

Long vowel   The length or duration of a vowel sound. Long vowels create a phonemic distinction with short vowels in some languages, such as Finnish and Japanese, but in many languages, they are simply an intrinsic feature of particular vowels, such as open vowels*.

Morpheme   The smallest unit of meaning in the grammar of a language. For example, English 'cats' has two morphemes; 'cat' is the lexical morpheme that conveys the basic meaning of the word, and -s is a grammatical morpheme indicating plurality.

Morphology   The study of the structure and form of words and the ways in which morphemes* are combined together. A morphological system pertains to a particular language.

Nasal attrition   The loss of a nasal consonant or nasality of a vowel through linguistic change processes.

Nasalised vowel   A vowel produced with a lowered velum so that the airstream can escape through the nose as well as through the mouth, but which does not produce a phonemic contrast with an oral vowel*.

Nasal vowel   A vowel produced with a lowered velum so that the airflow can escape through the nose as well as through the mouth, and which contrasts phonemically with an oral vowel*. For example, /õ/ versus /o/.

Open and close vowels   The distinction made between vowels according to the degree of tongue elevation that occurs within the mouth. The vowels of a given language are plotted on a two-dimensional vowel quadrilateral to locate their phonetic qualities relative to a set of standard reference points and in accordance with tongue height and tongue fronting.

Oral vowel   A vowel produced with a raised velum. For example, English /e/.

Palatalisation   To pronounce as or alter to a palatal sound.

Paragogic   A sound or syllable added to the end of a word to lengthen it.

Phonemes   An abstract concept, phonemes are the minimal unit of sound in speech that permit distinction in the meaning of words. For example, /h/ and /k/ in the English words 'hot' and 'cot' are both phonemes.

Phonetics   The study of the production, transmission, and reception of the sounds of spoken language. These speech sounds are termed phonemes*.

Phonological systems   An inventory of sounds that are used distinctively in a language, as well as their features and a set of rules that detail how such sounds can combine with each other.

Phonology   The branch of linguistics that studies the sound systems of languages and how sounds pattern in language.

Pretonic vowel   A non-stressed vowel that occurs before the tonic vowel* in a word. For example, bold /i/ in English 'linguistics'.

Syntax   The study of the rules that govern the way in which different words categorised as nouns, adjectives, verbs, and so on are arranged and combined into clauses and sentences. A syntactic system pertains to a particular language.

Tonic vowel   The vowel that takes the stress in a word. For example, bold /i/ in English in 'little'.

Voiced sound   The presence of vocal fold vibration in the larynx slightly impedes the movement of air through the glottis and results in a voiced articulation of a sound. For example, English /g/ is voiced; /k/ is not.

Voiceless sound   The absence of vocal fold vibration in the larynx, meaning that the airflow through the glottis is not impeded so a voiceless sound is produced. For example, English /t/ is voiceless; /d/ is voiced.

Tautosyllabic   The relationship between two or more phonemes that occur in the same syllable.

References

Abbreviations

AGAL   *Associaçom Galega da Língua*
Agália   *Revista da Associaçom Galega da Língua*
AS-PG   *Asociación Sócio-Pedagóxica Galega*
CSIC   *Consejo Superior de Investigaciones Científicas*
IGE   *Instituto Galego de Estatística*
INE   *Instituto Nacional de Estatística*
ILG   *Instituto de Lingua Galega*
INIC   *Instituto Nacional de Investigação Científica*
RAG   *Real Academia Galega*
SSRAG   *Seminario de Sociolingüística da Real Academia Galega*

Aikio, M. (1991) The Sami language: Pressure of change and reification. *Journal of Multilingual and Multicultural Development* 12 (1 and 2), 93–103.

Allardt, E. and Miemois K.J. (1981) *The Swedish-Speaking Minority in Finland*. Helsinki: University of Helsinki.

Alonso, D. (1972) Galego-asturiano engalar, 'volar' [Galician-Asturian *engalar*, 'to fly']. In D. Alonso (ed.) *Obras Completas* (Vol. 1) (pp. 457–464). Madrid: Gredos.

Alonso, F. (1994) 1993: Situación do galego na prensa [1993: The situation of Galician in the press]. *Xornadas de Formación en Lingua Galega*, 257–267.

Alonso Estravis, I. (1987) *Estudios filológicos galego-portugueses* [Galician-Portuguese Philological Studies]. Madrid: Ediciones Alhena.

Alonso Montero, X. (1990) *Informe(s) Sobre a Lingua Galega (presente e parsado)* [Account(s) of the Galician language (past and present). Vilaboa: Edicións do Cumio].

Alvarez Blanco, R. (1983) O artigo en galego. Morfoloxía [The article in Galician: Morphology]. *Verba* 10, 169–182.

Alvarez Blanco, R., Fernández Rei, F. and Santamarina, A. (eds) (2004) *A Lingua Galega: Historia e Actualidade* [The Galician Language: Past and Present]. Actas do I Congreso Internacional 16–20 de setembro de 1996, Santiago de Compostela.

Alvarez Blanco, R., Regueira, X.L. and Monteagudo, H. (1986) *Gramática Galega* [Galician Grammar]. Vigo: Ed. Galaxia.

Alvarez Blanco, R. and Xove, X. (2002) *Gramática da Lingua Galega* [A Grammar of the Galician Language]. Vigo: Ed. Galaxia.

Álvarez Cáccamo, C. (1983) Cara unha caracterización da diglósia galega: História e presente dunha dominación lingüística [Towards a characterisation of the Galician diglossia: The past and present situation of linguistic dominance]. *Grial* 79, 23–42.

Álvarez Cáccamo, C. (1990) Rethinking conversational code-switching: Codes, speech varieties, and contextualization. *Proceedings of the Sixteenth Annual*

Meeting of the Berkeley Linguistics Society, February 16–19, 1990. General Session and Parasession on the Legacy of Grice. Berkeley: Berkeley Linguistics Society, pp. 3–16.

Amodia, J. (ed.) (1998) *The Resurgence of Nationalistic Movements in Europe*. London: Longman.

Andersen, B. (1991) *Imagined Communities: Reflections on the Origin and Spread of Nationalism*. London: Verso.

Andrews, E. (1990) *Markedness Theory: The Union of Asymmetry and Semiosis in Language*. Durham [N.C.]: Duke University Press.

Appel, R. and Muysken, P. (1987) *Language Contact and Bilingualism*. London: Edward Arnold.

Argente, G., Joan, A., Lorenzo, S., and Anxo, M. (1991) A relevancia social da alternanica lingüística [The Social Relevance of Linguistic Alternation]. *Cadernos de Lingua* 3, 91–109.

Arteaga, A. (ed.) (1994) *An Other Tongue*. London: Duke University Press.

Associaçom Galega da Língua (AGAL) (1983) *Estudo Crítico das Normas Ortográficas e Morfolóxicas do Idioma Galego* [A Critical Study of the Orthographic and Morphological Standards of the Galician Language]. A Coruña: AGAL.

Associaçom Galega da Língua (AGAL) (1985) *Prontuário Ortográfico Galego* [A Handbook of Galician Orthography]. A Coruña: AGAL.

Asociación Sócio-Pedagóxica Galega (AS-PG) (1980) *Orientacións Para a Escrita do Noso Idioma* [Guidelines Regarding the Written Form of our Language]. Santiago de Compostela: Xistral.

Auer, P. (1984) *Bilingual Conversation*. Amsterdam: Benjamins.

Auer, P. (1995) The pragmatics of code-switching: A sequential approach. In L. Milroy and P. Muysken (eds) *One Speaker, Two Languages: Cross-Disciplinary Perspectives on Code-Switching* (pp. 115–135). Cambridge: Cambridge University Press.

Auer, P. (1998) Introduction: Bilingual conversation revisited. In P. Auer (ed.) *Code-Switching in Conversation: Language, Interaction and Identity* (pp. 1–24). London: Routledge.

Azevedo Maia, C. de (1986) *História do Galego-Português: Estado Linguístico da Galiza e do Noroeste de Portugal Desde o Século XIII ao Século XVI* [The History of Galician-Portuguese: The Linguistic Situation of Galicia and of the Northwest of Portugal from the Thirteenth to the Sixteenth Century]. Coimbra: INIC.

Azevedo F. and Leodegário A. de (1986) Fonologia de lingua Galega [Phonology of the Galician language]. *Agália* 8, 411–416.

Babarro González, X. (1994) A fronteira lingüística do galego co asturiano. Delimitación e caracterización das falas de transición dos concellos de Navia, Villallón, Allande e Ibias [The linguistic frontier of Galician and Asturian. Demarcation and characterisation of the transitional speech forms of the provinces of Navia, Villalón, Allande and Ibias]. *Lingua e Cultura Galega de Asturias*, 81–148.

Badia i Capdevila, I. (2004) A view of the linguistic situation in malta. *Revista de Sociolingüística*. On WWW at http://www6.gencat.net/llengcat/noves/hm04primavera-estiu/docs/a_badia.pdf.

Barbour, S. (2000) Language, nationalism, europe. In S. Barbour and C. Carmichael (eds) *Language and Nationalism in Europe* (pp. 1–17). Oxford: Oxford University Press.

Barbour, S. (2002) Language, nationalism and globalism: Educational consequences of changing patterns of language use. In P. Gubbins and M. Holt (eds) *Beyond Boundaries Language and Identity in Contemporary Europe* (pp. 11–18). Clevedon: Multilingual Matters.

Barth, F. (ed.) (1969) *Ethnic Groups and Boundaries: The Social Organisation of Cultural Difference*. Oslo: Universiteforlaget.

Barth, F. (1994) Enduring and emerging issues in the analysis of ethnicity. In H. Vermeulen and C. Govers (eds) *The Anthropology of Ethnicity: Beyond 'Groups and Boundaries'* (pp. 11–32). Amsterdam: Het Spinhuis.

BBC News (2005) Gaelic bill secures MSPs' support. On WWW at http://news.bbc.co.uk/1/hi/scotland/4227947.stm.

Berruto, G. (1997) Code-switching and code-mixing. In M. Parry and M. Maiden (eds) *The Dialects of Italy* (pp. 394–400). London: Routledge.

Beswick, J.E. (1994) The nasalisation of vowels in Galician: A case study. Unpublished master's dissertation, University of Manchester.

Beswick, J.E. (1999a) Observacións sobre as actitudes e os comportamentos relativos ós cambios de código en Santiago de Compostela [Attitudinal and behavioural observations on lexical code-switching in Santiago de Compostela]. *Cadernos de Lingua* 18, 53–78.

Beswick, J.E. (1999b) The velar nasal in Galicia: Case-study of a linguistic variable in a bilingual community. Unpublished PhD thesis, University of Bristol.

Beswick, J.E. (2002) Galician language planning and implications for regional identity: Restoration or elimination? *National Identities* 4 (3), 257–271.

Beswick, J.E. (2005a) Linguistic homogeneity in Galician and Portuguese borderland communities. *Estudios de Sociolingüística* 6 (1), 39–64.

Beswick, J.E. (2005b) The Portuguese diaspora in Jersey. In B. Preisler, A. Fabricius, H. Haberland, S. Kjaerbeck and K. Risager (eds) *The Consequences of Mobility Linguistic and Sociocultural Contact Zones*. Roskilde, Denmark: Roskilde University. On WWW at http://www.ruc.dk/isok/skriftserier/mobility/.

Blom, J.P. and Gumperz, J.J. (1972) Social meaning in linguistic structure. In J.J. Gumperz and D. Hymes (eds) *Directions in Sociolinguistics* (pp. 407–434). London: Holt, Reinhart and Winston.

Blommaert, J. (1996) Language planning as a discourse on language and society. The linguistic ideology of a scholarly tradition. *Language Problems and Language Planning* (20) 3, 99–223.

Bourdieu, P. (1994) *Language and Symbolic Power*. Cambridge: Polity Press.

Bouzada Fernández, X. (2003) Change of values and the future of the Galician language. *Estudios de Sociolingüística*, 3 & 4 (1), 321–341.

Bouzada Fernández, X. and Lorenzo Suárez, A. (1997) *O Futuro da Lingua. Elementos Sociolingüísticos Para un Achegamento Prospectivo da Lingua Galega* [The Future of the Language. Sociolinguistic Elements towards a Potential Unification of the Galician Language]. Santiago de Compostela: Consello da Cultura Galega.

Bouzada Fernández, X., Fernández Paz, L. and Suárez, A. (2002) *O Proceso de Normalización do Idioma Galego (1980–2000). Volume II: Educación* [The Process of Normalisation of the Galician Language (1980–2000). Volume II: Education]. Santiago de Compostela: Consello da Cultura Galega, Sección de Lingua.

Branchadell, A. (1996) *La Normalitat Improbable* [The Improbable Normality]. Barcelona: Empúries.

Brandão de Carvalho, J. (1988) Nasalité et structure syllabique en portugais et en galicien: Approche non lineaire et panchronique dun problème phonologique [Nasality and syllabic structure in Portuguese and in Galician: A non-linear and panchronic approach to a phonological problem]. *Verba* 15, 237–263.

Brown, R. and Gilman, A. (1960) The pronouns of power and solidarity. In T.A. Sebeok (ed.) *Style in Language* (pp. 253–276). Cambridge, MA: Massachusetts Institute of Technology.

Bugarski, R. (2001) Language, nationalism and war in Yugoslavia. *International Journal of the Sociology of Language* 151, 69–87.

Campbell, L. and Muntzel, M.C. (1989) The structural consequences of language death. In N.C. Dorian (ed.) *Investigating Obsolescence: Studies in Language Contact and Death* (pp. 182–191). Cambridge: University Press.

Canfield, D.L. (1981) *Spanish Pronunciation in the Americas*. Chicago: Chicago University Press.

Cano Aguilar, R. (1999) *El Español a Través de los Tiempos* [Spanish Across the Ages]. (4th edn). Madrid: Arco/Libros.

Cano González, A.M. (1981) El habla de Somiedo (Occidente de Asturias) [The speech of Somiedo (West Asturias)]. *Verba*, Anejo 21.

Carballeira Anllo, X.M. and Cid Cabido, X. (2000) *Gran Diccionario Xerais da Lingua* [The *Xerais* Dictionary of the Galician Language]. Vigo: Xerais de Galicia.

Carballo Calero, R. (1968) *Gramatica Elemental del Gallego Común* [A Basic Grammar of Common Galician]. (2nd edn). Vigo: Ed. Galaxia.

Carballo Calero, R. (1980) *A Fortuna Histórica do Galego. Problemática das Línguas sen Normalizar. Situación do Galego e Alternativas* [The Historical Fortune of Galician. The Challenge for Non-Standardised Languages. The Situation of Galician and Alternatives]. Ourense: Asociación Socio-Pedagóxica Galega/Edicións Xistral.

Carballo Calero, R. (1981) *Problemas de Lingua Galega* [Problems with the Galician Language]. Lisbon: Sá da Costa.

Castelao, A.R. (1961) [1944] *Sempre en Galiza* [Forever in Galicia]. Buenos Aires: As Burgas.

Chambers, J.K. (2003) *Sociolinguistic Theory* (2nd edn). Oxford: Blackwell.

Chambers, J.K. and Trudgill, P. (1998) *Dialectology* (2nd edn). Cambridge: Cambridge University Press.

Chen, M. (1973) Nasals and Nasalisation in Chinese: Explorations in Phonological Universals. Ph.D. dissertation, University of California.

Cheshire, J. (1978) Present tense verbs in reading English. In P. Trudgill (ed.) *Sociolinguistic Patterns in British English* (pp. 52–68). London: Edward Arnold.

Cheshire, J. (1987) Age and generation-specific use of language. In U. Ammon, N. Ditmar and K.J. Mattheier (eds) *Sociolinguistics: An International Handbook of the Sciences of Language and Society* (Vol. 1) (pp. 760–767). Berlin: Walter de Gruyter.

Cheshire, J. (1997) Linguistic variation and social function. In N. Coupland and A. Jaworski (eds) *Sociolinguistics: A Reader and Coursebook* (pp. 185–198). Basingstoke: MacMillan (reprinted from S. Romaine (ed.) (1982) *Sociolinguistic Variation in Speech Communities* (pp. 153–166). London: Edward Arnold.)

Cheshire, J. (2002) Who we are and where were going: Language and identities in the new Europe. In P. Gubbins and M. Holt (eds) *Beyond Boundaries. Language and Identity in Contemporary Europe* (pp. 19–34). Clevedon: Multilingual Matters.

Chomsky, N. (1965) *Aspects of the Theory of Syntax*. Cambridge: MIT Press.

Chomsky, N. (1980) *Rules and Representation*. Oxford: Blackwell.

Chomsky, N. and Halle, M. (1968) *The Sound Pattern of English*. New York: Harper and Row.

Cidrás Escáneo, F.A. (1994) Modelos de lingua e variación sintáctica [Linguistic models and syntactic variation]. *Cadernos da Lingua* 10, 103–118.

Clyne, M. (2003) *Dynamics of Language Contact: English and Immigrant Languages*. Cambridge: Cambridge University Press.

Cobarrubias, J. (1987) Models of language planning for minority languages. *Bulletin of the Council for Advancement of Adult Literacy* (CAAL) 9, 47–70.

Cohen, A.P. (1982) *Belonging: Identity and Social Organisation in British Rural Cultures*. Manchester: Manchester University Press.

Cohen, A.P. (1986) Of symbols and boundaries, or, does erties greatcoat hold the key? In A.P. Cohen (ed.) *Symbolising Boundaries: Identity and Diversity in British Cultures* (pp. 1–19). Manchester: Manchester University Press.

Colomer, J.M. (1986) *Cataluña Como Cuestión de Estado: La Idea de la Nación en el Pensamiento Político Catalan (1939–1979)* [Catalonia as the State Question: The Idea of the Nation in Catalan Political Thought]. Madrid: Tecnos.

Constitución Española (1978) Boletín Oficial del Estado: 29/12/78 [The Spanish Constitution: The Official Bulletin of the State]. Editora Nacional. On WWW at http://www.constitucion.es/.

Cooper, R.L. (1983) Language planning, language spread and language change. In C.U. Kennedy (ed.) *Language Planning and Language Education* (pp. 17–36). London: George Allen & Unwin.

Cooper, R. (1989) *Language Planning and Social Change*. Cambridge: Cambridge University Press.

Corredoira, F.V. (1998) *A Construção da Lingua Portuguesa Frente ao Castelhano (o Galego Como Exemplo a Contrario)* [The Formation of the Portuguese Language in Comparison with Castilian Spanish (with Galician as a Counterexample)]. Santiago de Compostela: Edicións Laiovento.

Costas González, X.H. (2002) *Tipoloxia das Falas do Val do Río Ellas* [A Typology of the Speech of Val do río Ellas]. Cáceres: Associación Cultural Alén do Val.

Cotarelo Valledor, A. (1927) El castellano en Galicia [Castilian Spanish in Galicia]. *Boletín da la Real Academia Española* 14, 83–136.

Couceiro, J.L. (1976) El habla de Feas [The speech of Feas]. Santiago de Compostela. *Verba*, Anejo 5.

Couceiro Freijomil, A. (1935) *El Idioma Gallego: Historia, Gramática, Literature* [The Galician Language: History, Grammar, Literature]. Madrid: Martín.

Coulmas, F. (2005) *Sociolinguistics: The Study of Speaker's Choices*. Cambridge: Cambridge University Press.

Crespo Pozo, J.S. (1963) *Contribución a un vocabulario Castellano-Gallego: Con Indicación de Fuentes* [Contribution to the Castilian-Galician Lexicon: With Sources]. Madrid: Estudios.

Crystal, D. (1988) *The English Language*. Harmondsworth: Penguin.

Cuesta, P.V. and Da Luz, M.A.M. (1971) *Gramatica Portuguesa* [Portuguese Grammar] (3rd edn). Madrid: Gredos.

D'Anglejan, A. and Tucker, R.G. (1973) Sociolinguistic correlates of speech style in Quebec. In R.W. Shuy and R.W. Fasold (eds) *Language Attitudes: Current Trends and Prospects* (pp. 1–27). Washington: Georgetown University Press.

Dauenhauer, N.M. and Dauenhauer, R. (1998) Technical, emotional, and ideological issues in reversing language shift: Examples from southeast Alaska. In L.A. Grenoble and L.J. Whaley (eds) *Endangered Languages: Language Loss and Community Response* (pp. 57–98). Cambridge: Cambridge University Press.

Decreto 173 Sobre a Normativización da Lingua Galega [Decree 173 Pertaining to the Normativisation of the Galician Language] (1982) 17/11/1982. On WWW at www.fa.knaw.nl/mercator/ regionale_dossiers/PDFs/galicia-def.pdf.

Decreto 247 do Emprego do Galego no Ensino [Decree 247 Pertaining to the use of Galician in Education] (1995) 15/09/1995. On WWW at http://www.cig-ensino.com/descargas/00455.pdf.

De la Torre, J.M.G. (1962) Estudios Sobre el Gallego de Orense [A Study of the Galician of Orense]. Ph.D. thesis, University of Madrid.

De Oliveira Marques, A.H.R. (1972) *History of Portugal. Volume I: From Lusitania to Empire*. London: Columbia University Press.

Del Valle, J. (2000) Monoglossic policies for a heteroglossic culture: Misinterpreted multilingualism in modern Galicia. *Language and Communication* 20, 105–132.

Dirección Xeral de Política Lingüística (1998) *Estudio Sobre o Uso do Idioma Galego* [A Study on the Use of the Galician Language]. Santiago de Compostela, DXPL, CEOU, Xunta de Galicia.

Domínguez Salgado, A., Mayo Redondo, S. and Romero Rodríguez, D. (1999) *Actas II Encontros Para a Normalización Lingüística* [Proceedings of the Second Conference on Linguistic Normalisation]. Santiago de Compostela: Consello da Cultura Galega.

Donnan, H. and Wilson, T.M. (1999) Linguistic and ethnographic fieldwork. In J.A. Fishman (ed.) *Handbook of Language and Ethnic Identity* (pp. 25–41). Oxford: Oxford University Press.

Donnan, H. and Wilson, T.M. (2001) *Borders, Frontiers of Identity, Nation and State* (2nd edn). Oxford: Berg.

Dorian, N.C. (1994) Purism versus compromise in language revitalization and language revival. *Language in Society* 23, 479–494.

Dubert García, F. (1995) Algúns fenómenos morfolóxicos do galego de Santiago [Some morphological phenomena of the Galician of Santiago de Compostela]. *Cadernos de Lingua* 11, 71–101.

Dubert García, F. (1996) Algúns fenómenos fonéticos e fonolóxicos da fala de Santiago de Compostela [Some phonetic and phonological phenomena of the speech of Santiago de Compostela]. In R. Lorenzo and R. Alvarez (eds) *Homenaxe á profesora Pilar Vázquez Cuesta* [Feitschrift to Professor Pilar Vásquez Cuesta]. (pp. 133–155) Santiago de Compostela: Universidade de Santiago de Compostela.

Dubert García, F. (1999) Aspectos do galego de Santiago de Compostela [Aspects of the Galician of Santiago de Compostela]. *Verba* 44, 1–249.

Dubert García, F. (no date) Reflections on the Syllabification of *Unha, Algunha* and *Ningunha*. On WWW at http://web.usc.es/ ~ fgdubert/artigos/nvelar1.pdf.

Durand, J. (1990) *Generative and Nonlinear Phonology.* London: Longman.

Eckert, P. (1980) Diglossia: Separate and unequal. *Linguistics* 18, 1053–1064.

Eckert, P. (2000) Linguistic variation as social practice: The linguistic construction of identity in Belten High. *Language in Society*, 27.

Edwards, J. (1985) *Language, Society and Identity.* Oxford: Blackwell.

Eiré, A., Valverde, R. (2005) Preséntase o Plano de Normalización da Lingua sen saber que apoio terá do Goberno [The Linguistic Normalisation Plan is presented without the unequivocal support of the Government]. On WWW at anosaterra.com. Accessed 5.6.05.

Ellul, S. (1978) *A Case Study in Bilingualism: Code-Switching between Parents and their Pre-School Children in Malta.* Cambridge: Huntington.

Enríquez, M. de C. (1976) Fonética y fonología del gallego de o Grove [The phonetics and phonology of the Galician of O Grove]. *Verba* 3, 128–160.

Eriksen, T.H. (1992) *Us and Them in Modern Societies: Ethnicity and Nationalism in Mauritius, Trinidad and Beyond.* Oslo: Scandinavian University Press.

Eurolang.net (2005) Country profile of Galicia. On WWW at http://www.eurolang.net/State/spain.htm#Galician.

Euromosaic (2005) Language policies – Galicia. On WWW at http://europa.eu.int/comm/education/policies/lang/languages/langmin/euromosaic/index_en.html.

European Charter for Regional or Minority Languages: Initial Periodical Report from the United Kingdom (no year). On WWW at www.fco.gov.uk/Files/kfile/minoritylanguages,0.pdf.

Farrell, S., Bellin, W., Higgs, G. and White, S. (1998) The distribution of younger Welsh speakers in anglicised areas of south east Wales. *Journal of Multilingual and Multicultural Development* 18 (6), 489–495.

Fasold, R. (1984) *Introduction to Sociolinguistics* (Vol. 1): *The Sociolinguistics of Society.* Oxford: Blackwell.

Fasold, R. (1988) Phonetics/Phonology. In U. Ammon, N. Ditmar and K.J. Mattheier (eds) *Sociolinguistics: An International Handbook of the Sciences of Language and Society* (Vol. 2) (pp. 1126–1134). Berlin: Walter de Gruyter.

Fasold, R. (1990) *Introduction to Sociolinguistics* (Vol. 2): *The Sociolinguistics of Language*. Oxford: Blackwell.

Ferguson, C.A. (1959) Diglossia. *Word* 15, 325–340.

Fernández, G. and José, R. (1978) Etnografia del Valle de Ancares. Estudio lingüístico según el método palabras y cosas [Ethnography of the Valle de Ancares. Linguistic study using the word-object model]. *Verba*, Anejo 10.

Fernández, M. (2004) O uso do galego nos espacios urbanos [The use of Galician in urban spaces]. In R. Alvarez Blanco, F. Fernández Rei and A. Santamarina (eds) *A Lingua Galega: Historia e Actualidade* [The Galician Language: Past and Present]. *Actas do I Congreso Internacional, 16–20 de Setembro de 1996*: Santiago de Compostela (Vol. I), (pp. 245–256).

Fernández Rei, F. (1982) Bloques e áreas lingüísticas do galego moderno [Linguistic blocs and zones of modern Galician]. *Grial* 77, 257–296.

Fernández Rei, F. (1988) Posición do galego entre as linguas románicas [The status of Galician among the Romance Languages]. *Verba* 15, 79–107.

Fernández Rei, F. (1990) *Dialectoloxia da Língua Galega* [Dialectology of the Galician Language]. Vigo: Ediclións Xerais de Galicia.

Fernández Rei, F. (1991) A normalización da franxa exterior de Lingua galega [Normalisation of the Galician language spoken outside the region]. *Cadernos da Lingua* 4, 5–25.

Fernández Rei, F. (1992) A normalización da franxa exterior de Lingua galega [Normalisation of the Galician language spoken outside the region]. *Cadernos da Lingua* 5, 47–73.

Fernández Rei, F. (1993) Galego oriental: O Bierzo, As Portelas e O Val de Verín [Eastern Galician: O Bierzo, As Portelas and O Val de Verín]. *Lindeiros da Galeguidade* II, 97–108.

Fernández Rei, F. (1994) Delimitación xeográfica e características lingüísticas do Galego de Asturias [Geographical demarcation and linguistic characteristics of the Galician of Asturias]. *Britonia* 1, 123–138.

Fernández Rodríguez, M. and Rodríguez Neira, M. (coords) (1994) *Lingua Inicial e Competencia Lingüística en Galicia. Compendio do I Volume do Mapa Sociolingüístico de Galicia* [Mother Tongue and Linguistic Competence in Galicia. A Compendium of the First Volume of the Sociolinguistic Map of Galicia]. A Coruña: Real Academia Galega.

Fernández Rodríguez, M. and Rodríguez Neira, M. (coords) (1995) *Usos Lingüísticos en Galicia. Compendio do II Volume do Mapa Sociolingüístico de Galicia* [Linguistic Uses in Galicia. A Compendium of the Second Volume of the Sociolinguistic Map of Galicia]. A Coruña: Real Academia Galega.

Fernández Rodríguez, M. and Rodríguez Neira, M. (coords) (1996) *Actitudes Lingüísticas en Galicia, Compendio do III Volume do Mapa Sociolingüístico de Galicia* [Linguistic Attitudes in Galicia. A Compendium of the Third Volume of the Sociolinguistic Map of Galicia]. A Coruña: Real Academia Galega.

Fernández Salgado, B. (1991) *Diccionario de Dúbidas da Lingua Galega* [A Dictionary of Conundrums of the Galician Language]. Vigo: Galaxia.

Fernández Salgado, B. (2000) Os rudimentos da lingüística galega: un estudio de textos lingüísticos galegos de principios do século XX (1913–1936) [The origins of Galician linguistics: A study of Galician linguistic texts from the beginning of the twentieth century (1913–1936)]. *Verba*: Anexo 47.

Fernández Salgado, B. and Monteagudo, H. (1993) The standardization of Galician: The state of the art. *Portuguese Studies* 9, 200–213.

Ferreiro, M. (1996) *Gramática Histórica Galega: Manual* [Galician Historical Grammar: A Guide]. Santiago de Compostela: Laiovento.

Ferro Ruibal, X. and Casares, C. (1996) *Cadaquén Fala Coma Quen é: Reflexións Verbo da Fraseoloxía Enxebre* [Everyone Speaks in their Own Way: Verbal Reflections on Authentic Phraseology]. A Coruña: Real Academia Galega.

Fishman, J. (1964) Language maintenance and language shift as a field of inquiry. *Linguistics* 9, 32–70.

Fishman, J. (1967) Bilingualism with and without Diglossia: Diglossia with and without Bilingualism. *Journal of Social Issues* 23 (2), 29–38.

Fishman, J. (1971) *Sociolinguistics: A Brief Introduction.* Massachusetts: Newbury House.

Fishman, J. (1972) The impact of nationalism on language planning. In J. Fishman (ed.) *Language in Sociocultural Change* (pp. 224–243). Stanford, California: California University Press.

Fishman, J. (1974) Language modernisation and planning in comparison with other types of modernisation and planning. In J. Fishman (ed.) *Advances in Language Planning* (pp. 79–102). The Hague: Mouton.

Fishman, J. (1980) Bilingualism and biculturalism as individual and societal phenomena. *Journal of Multilingual and Multicultural Development* 1, 3–17.

Fishman, J. (1989) *Language and Ethnicity in Minority Sociolinguistic Perspective.* Clevedon: Multilingual Matters.

Fishman, J. (1991) *Reversing Language Shift. Theoretical and Empirical Foundations of Assistance to Threatened Languages.* Clevedon: Multilingual Matters.

Fishman, J. (1999a) Sociolinguistics. In J. Fishman (ed.) *Handbook of Language and Ethnic Identity* (pp. 152–163). Oxford: Oxford University Press.

Fishman, J. (1999b) Concluding comments. In J. Fishman (ed.) *Handbook of Language and Ethnic Identity* (pp. 444–454). Oxford: Oxford University Press.

Franco Grande, X.L. (1984) *Vocabulario galego-castelán* [Galician-Castilian Lexis]. (4th edn). Vigo: Galaxia.

Franolic, B. (1988) *Language Policy in Yugoslavia with Special Reference to Croatian.* Paris: Nouvelles Editions Latines.

Freeland, J. (2003) Intercultural-bilingual education for an interethnic-plurilingual society? The case of Nicaragua's Caribbean Coast. *Comparative Education* 39 (2), 239–260.

Freeland, J. and Patrick, D. (2004) Language rights and language survival: Sociolinguistic and sociocultural perspectives. In J. Freeland and D. Patrick (eds) *Language Rights and Language Survival: Sociolinguistic and Sociocultural Perspectives* (pp. 1–33). Manchester: St. Jerome Publishing.

Freixeiro Mato, X.R. (1997) *Lingua Galega: Normalidade e Conflito* [The Galician Language: Standardisation and Conflict]. Santiago de Compostela: Edicións Laiovento.

Freixeiro Mato, X.R. (1998) *Gramatica da Lingua Galega I. Fonetica e Fonoloxia* [A Grammar of the Galician Language. I. Phonetics and Phonology]. Vigo: A Nosa Terra.

Frías Conde, X. (1999) *O Galego Exterior às Fronteiras Administrativas* [Galician Beyond the Region]. Gijón: VTP.

Frías Conde, X. (2001) *Resumo de Gramática Eonaviega* [A summary of 'eonaviega' Grammar]. CCV. On WWW at http://www.terra.es/personal/cvalledor.

Fundación Galicia-Europa [The Galicia-Europe Foundation] (2005) On WWW at http://www.fundaciongaliciaeuropa.org.

Gal, S. (1979) *Language Shift: Social Determinants of Linguistic Change in Bilingual Austria*. New York: Academic Press.

Gal, S. (1987) Linguistic repertoires. In U. Ammon, N. Ditmar and K.J. Mattheier (eds) *Sociolinguistics: An International Handbook of the Sciences of Language and Society* (Vol. 1) (pp. 286–292). Berlin: Walter de Gruyter.

Gamkrelidze, T.V. (1989) Markedness, sound change and linguistic reconstruction. In O.M. Tomic (ed.) *Markedness in Synchrony and Diachrony* (pp. 87–102). Berlin: Mouton de Gruyter.

García Cancela, X. and Díaz Abraira, C. (1994) *Manual de Linguaxe Administrative* [A Guide to Administrative Language] (3rd edn). Santiago de Compostela: Escola Galega de Adminstración Pública.

García de Diego, V. (1984) [1909] Elementos de gramática histórica gallega (fonética-morfología) [Elements of Galician historical grammar (phonetics and morphology)]. [Burgos.] Repr. *Verba* Anejo 23, 1–201.

García González, C. (1985) [1976] Interferencias lingüísticas entre gallego y castellano [Linguistic interference between Galician and Castilian]. In C. García González (ed.) *Temas de Lingüística Galega* (pp. 109–140). A Coruña: La Voz de Galicia.

García González, C. (1986a) El castellano en Galicia [Castilian in Galicia]. In M. Alvar (ed.) *El Castellano Actual en Las Comunidades Bilingües en España* [Modern Castilian in the Bilingual Communities of Spain] (pp. 49–64). Salamanca: Junta de Castilla y León.

García González, C. (1986b) Vicisitudes históricas del desarrollo del gallego [Historical transformations in the development of Galician]. In M. Alvar (ed.) *Lenguas Peninsulares y Proyección Hispánica* [Peninsular Languages and Hispanic Projections]. Madrid: Fundación Friedrich Ebert.

García Negro, M.P. (1991) *O Galego e as Leis. Aproximación Sociolingüística* [Galician and the Law: a Sociolinguistic Assessment]. Madrid: Edicións do Cumio.

García Negro, M.P. (2000) *Direitos Lingüísticos e Control Político* [Linguistic Rights and Political Control]. Santiago de Compostela: Laiovento.

García Pérez, C. (1985) Glosario de voces galegas de hoxe [A glossary of present-day Galician terms]. *Verba*, Anejo 27.

Gardner-Chloros, P. (1995) Code-switching in community, regional and national repertoires: the myth of the discreteness of linguistic systems. In L. Milroy and P. Muysken (eds) *One Speaker, Two Languages: Cross-Disciplinary Perspectives on Code-Switching* (pp. 68–90). Cambridge: Cambridge University Press.

Galicia Espallada (2005) Mapa de Galicia [Map of Galicia]. On WWW at http://www.galespa.com.ar/MAPA.htm.

Galician Studies email discussion list (2004) On WWW at Galicia-Studies@jiscmail.ac.uk.

Garvin, P. and Mathiot, M. (1956) The urbanization of the Guarani language – A problem in language and culture. In *Men and Cultures. Selected Papers of the Fifth International Congress of Anthropological and Ethnological Sciences* (pp. 783–790). Philadelphia: Pennsylvania Press.

Geerts, G. (1987) Research on language contact. In U. Ammon, N. Ditmar and K.J. Mattheier (eds) *Sociolinguistics: An International Handbook of the Sciences of Languages and Society* (Vol. 1) (pp. 580–606). Berlin: Walter de Gruyter.

Gellner, E. (1983) *Nations and Nationalism*. Oxford: Blackwell.

Giles, H. (1973) Accent mobility; a model and some data. *Anthropological Linguistics* 15, 247–252.

Giles, H. and Johnson, P. (1987) Ethnolinguistic identity theory: A social psychological approach to language maintenance. *International Journal of the Sociology of Language* 68, 256–269.

Gómez Clemente, X.M., Noia Campos, M.C. and Benavente Jareno, P. (1997) *Diccionario de Sinónimos da Lingua Galega* [A Dictionary of Synonyms of the Galician Language]. Vigo: Galaxia.

Gómez Sánchez, A. and Freixeiro Mato, X.R. (1998) *Historia da Lingua Galega* [The History of the Galician Language] (2nd edn). Vigo: A Nosa Terra.

González Fernandez, I. (1978) Sufijos nominales en el gallego actual [Nominal suffixes in modern Galician]. *Verba*, Anejo 11.

González González, M. and González González, M. (1994) *Algunhas Consideracións ó Redor do /η/ en Galego* [Some Thoughts about the Galician Velar Nasal]. Paper presented at IV Congreso da Asociación Internacional de Estudios Galegos, University of Oxford, Sept. 1994.

González López, E. (1980) *História de Galicia* [The History of Galicia]. A Cor: La Voz de Galicia, Serie Nova.

Gordon, E. (1997) Sex, speech, and stereotypes: Why women use prestige speech forms more than men. *Language in Society* 26, 47–64.

Gordon, R.G. Jr. (ed.) (2005) *Ethnologue: Languages of the World* (15th edn). Dallas, Texas: SIL International. On WWW at www.ethnologue.com/.

Green, J. (1993) Representations of Romance: Contact, bilingualism and diglossia. In R. Posner and J. Green (eds) *Trends in Romance Linguistics and Philology Vol. 5: Bilingualism and Linguistic Conflict in Romance* (pp. 4–21). The Hague: Mouton.

Green, J. (1994) Language status and political aspirations: The case of northern Spain. In M. Mair Parry, W.V. Davies and R.A.M. Temple (eds) *The Changing Voice of Europe* (pp. 155–172). Cardiff: University of Wales Press.

Grin, F. (2000) *Evaluating Policy Measures for Minority Languages in Europe: Towards Effective, Cost-effective and Democratic Implementation*. ECMI Report 6, October 2000. Flensburg: ECMI.

Gudykunst, W.B. and Schmidt, K.L. (eds) (1988) *Language and Ethnic Identity*. Clevedon: Multilingual Matters.

Gumperz, J.J. (1968) The Speech Community. *International Encyclopedia of the Social Sciences*. London: Macmillan, pp. 381–386.

Gumperz, J.J. (1975) On the ethnology of linguistic change. In W. Bright (ed.) *Sociolinguistics. Proceedings of the UCLA Sociolinguistic Conference 1964* (pp. 27–49). The Hague: Mouton.

Gumperz, J.J. (1982a) *Discourse Strategies*. Cambridge: Cambridge University Press.

Gumperz, J.J. (1982b) (ed.) *Language and Social Identity*. Cambridge: Cambridge University Press.

Guy, G.R. (1997) Competence, performance, and the generative grammar of variation. In F. Hinskens, R. van Hout and L. Wetzels (eds) *Variation, Change and Phonological Theory* (pp. 125–144). Amsterdam: John Benjamins.

Hajek, J. (1992) The Interrelationship Between Vowels and Nasal Consonants: A Case Study in Northern Italian. Unpublished Ph.D. thesis: University of Oxford.

Hall, S. (1996) New ethnicities. In D. Morley and K.-H. Chen (eds) *Stuart Hall: Critical Dialogues in Cultural Studies* (pp. 441–449). London: Routledge.

Hall, S. (1996) What is this black in black popular culture? In D. Morley and K.-H. Chen (eds) *Stuart Hall: Critical Dialogues in Cultural Studies* (pp. 465–475). London: Routledge.

Hamp, E.P. (1989) On signs of health and death. In N.C. Dorian (ed.) *Investigating Obsolescence: Studies in Language Contact and Death* (pp. 197–210). Cambridge: University Press.

Harris, J. (1969) *Spanish Phonology.* Cambridge, Mass: MIT Press.

Harris, J. (1983) *Syllable Structure and Stress in Spanish – A Nonlinear Analysis.* Cambridge, Mass: MIT Press.

Harvie, C. (1994) *The Rise of Regional Europe.* London: Routledge.

Haugen, E. (1950) The analysis of linguistic borrowing. *Language* 26, 210–231.

Haugen, E. (1966a) Dialect, language, nation. *American Anthropologist* 68, 922–935.

Haugen, E. (1966b) *Language Conflict and Language Planning: The Case of Modern Norwegian.* Cambridge, Mass: MIT Press.

Haugen, E. (1976) *The Scandinavian Languages: An Introduction to their History.* London: Faber.

Haugen, E. (1987) *Blessings of Babel.* Amsterdam: Mouton de Gruyter.

Heller, M. (2004) Analysis and stance regarding language and social Justice. In J. Freeland and D. Patrick (eds) *Language Rights and Language Survival: Sociolinguistic and Sociocultural Perspectives* (pp. 283–286). Manchester: St. Jerome Publishing.

Henderson, T.K. (1996) Language and Identity in Galicia: The Current Orthographic Debate. Unpublished PhD thesis, University of Southampton.

Hermida Gulías, C. (1995) Sociolingüística do galego. Historia e actualidade [Galician sociolinguistics; past and present]. Paper presented at the *VIII Curso de lingua e cultura galegas para extranxeiros*, Santiago de Compostela, July 1995.

Herrero Valeiro, M.J. (1993) Identidade e espaço nacional no discurso sobre a(s) língua(s) na Galiza (mínimas reflexões glotopolíticas e político-linguísticas) [Identity and national space in discussion of language or languages in Galicia (minimum glottopolitic and politico-linguistics deliberations]. *Actas do Congresso Internacional A Língua Portuguesa no Mundo, Terceira Língua de Comunicação Internacional, 200 Milhões de Lusófonos* (pp. 139–145).

Herreiro Valeiro, M.J. (2003) The discourse of language in Galiza: Normalisation, diglossia and conflict. *Estudios de Sociolingüística*, 3, 2 and 4 (1), 289–320.

Hidalgo, M. (1988) Perceptions of Spanish-English code-switching in Juárez, Mexico. *Latin American Institute Research Paper.* University of New Mexico, Alburquerque.

Hidalgo, M. (2001) (ed.) Between koineization and standardization: New World Spanish revisited. *International Journal of the Sociology of Language*, 149. Berlin, New York: Mouton de Gruyter.

Hoare, R. (2000) Language attitudes and identity in Brittany. *Journal of Multilingual and Multicultural Development* 21 (4), 324–347.

Hockett, C.F. (1950) Age-Grading and Linguistic Continuity. *Language* 26, 449–459.

Hoffmann, C. (2000) Balancing Language Planning and Language Rights: Catalonia's Uneasy Juggling Act. *Journal of Multilingual and Multicultural Development* 21 (5), 425–441.

Holmes, J. (2001) *An Introduction to Sociolinguistics* (2nd edn). London: Longman.

Holt, M. and Gubbins, P. (eds) (2002) Beyond Boundaries: Language and Identity in Contemporary Europe. Clevedon: Multilingual Matters.

Hooper, J.B. (1976) *An Introduction to Natural Generative Phonology.* New York: Academic Press.

Hudson, R. (2001) *Sociolinguistics* (2nd edn). Cambridge: University Press.

Huntington, S.P. (1996) *The Clash of Civilizations and the Remaking of a New World Order.* New York: Simon & Schuster.

Huss, L., Camilleri Grima, A. and King, K.A. (eds) (2003) *Transcending Monolingualism: Linguistic Revitalisation in Education*. Multilingualism and Linguistic Diversity Series, Tove Skutnabb-Kangas (ed.) Lisse, the Netherlands: Swets and Zeitlinger.

Hyman, L.M. (1985) *A Theory of Phonological Weight*. Dordrecht: Foris Publications.

Hymes, D. (1971) Competence and performance in linguistic theory. In R. Huxley and E. Ingram (eds) *Language Acquisition: Models and Methods* (pp. 3–28). London: Academic Press.

Hymes, D. (1987) Communicative competence. In U. Ammon, N. Ditmar and K.J. Mattheier (eds) *Sociolinguistics: An International Handbook of the Sciences of Languages and Society*. (Vol. 1) (pp. 219–229). Berlin: Walter de Gruyter.

Iglesias-Alvarez, A. and Ramallo, F. (2003) Language as a diacritical in terms of cultural and resistance identities in Galicia. *Estudios de Sociolingüística* 3, 2 and 4 (1) 255–287.

Instituto de Estudios de Administracion Local (1981) *Estatuto de Autonomia de Galicia* [The Galician Statute of Autonomy]. Madrid: Closas-Orcoyen.

Instituto de Língua Galega (ILG) (1990) *Atlas Lingüístico Galego Vol 1: Morfoloxía verbal* [The Galician Linguistic Atlas Vol. 1: Verbal Morphology]. A Coruña: Fundación Barrié de la Maza.

Instituto de Língua Galega (ILG) (1995) *Atlas Lingüístico Galego Vol 2: Morfoloxía non verbal* [The Galician Linguistic Atlas Vol. 2: Non-verbal Morphology]. A Coruña: Fundación Barrié de la Maza.

Instituto de Língua Galega (ILG) (1999) *Atlas Lingüístico Galego Vol. 3: Fonética* [The Galician Linguistic Atlas Vol. 3: Phonetics]. A Coruña: Fundación Barrié de la Maza.

Instituto de Língua Galega (ILG) (2003) *Atlas Lingüístico Galego Vol 4: Léxico. Tempo Atmosférico e Cronolóxico*. [The Galician Linguistic Atlas Vol. 4: Lexicon of Time and Weather]. A Coruña: Fundación Barrié de la Maza.

Instituto de Língua Galega (ILG) (2005) *Atlas Lingüístico Galego Vol 5: Léxico.O Ser Humano. I*. [The Galician Linguistic Atlas Vol. 5: Lexicon of the Human Being. I]. A Coruña: Fundación Barrié de la Maza.

Instituto Galego de Estatística (IGE) (2004) *Enquisa de Condicións de Vida das Familias. Coñecemento e Uso do Galego, Ano 2003* [Survey into Family Life. Knowledge and Use of Galician, 2003]. Santiago de Compostela: IGE - Xunta de Galicia servicio central. On WWW at http://www.ige.xunta.es/ga/sociais/benestar/cvida/indice_2003.htm.

Instituto Nacional de Estatística (INE) (2005). On WWW at http://www.ine.es/en/welcome_en.htm.

Iribarne, M.F. (1991) *De Galicia a Europa* [From Galicia to Europe]. Barcelona: Planeta.

Ivic, P. (2001) Language planning in Serbia today: Serbian sociolinguistics. *International Journal of the Sociology of Language* 151, 7–17.

Joseph, J.E. (1987) *Eloquence and Power. The Rise of Language Standards and Standard Languages*. London: Frances Pinter.

Kabatek, J. (1991) Interferencias entre galego e castelán: problemas do galego estándar [Interference between Galician and Castilian: Problems with the Galician standard]. *Cadernos de Lingua* 4, 39–48.

Kabatek, J. (2000) *Os Falantes Como Lingüistas: Tradición, Innovación e Interferencias no Galego Actual* [Speakers as Linguists. Interference and Language Change in Contemporary Galician]. Tübingen: Max Niemeyer.

Kalmar, I., Zhong, Y. and Xiao, H. (1987) Language attitudes in Guangzhou, China. *Language in Society* 16, 499–508.

Kaplan, R.B. and Baldauf, R.B. (1997) *Language Planning: from Practice to Theory.* Clevedon: Multilingual Matters.

Kiesling, S. (1998) Men's identities and sociolinguistic variation: The case of fraternity men. *Journal of Sociolinguistics* 2, 69–100.

Kloss, H. (1967) *Abstand* Languages and *Ausbau* Languages. *Anthropological Linguistics* IX vii, 29–41.

Kloss, H. and McConnell, G.D. (1974) *Linguistic Composition of the Nations of the World. 1. Central and Western South Asia.* Centre International de Recherche sur le Bilinguisme. Quebec: Presses de l'Université Laval.

Labov, W. (1966) *The Social Stratification of English in New York City.* Washington, D.C.: Center for Applied Linguistics.

Labov, W. (1967) The effect of social mobility on linguistic behaviour. In S. Lieberson (ed.) *Explorations in Sociolinguistics* (pp. 58–75). The Hague: Mouton.

Labov, W. (1972) *Sociolinguistic Patterns.* Philadelphia, Pennsylvania University Press.

Labov, W. (1977) *Language in the Inner City: Studies in the Black English Vernacular* (5th edn). Oxford: Blackwell.

Labov, W. (1994) *Principles of Linguistic Change: Internal Factors.* Oxford: Blackwell.

Labraña-Barrero, S. and van Oosterzee, C. (2003) An acoustic approach to Galician *Gheada*. In M.J. Solé, D. Recasens and J. Romero (eds) *Proceedings of the 15th International Congress of Phonetic Sciences* (pp. 945–948). Barcelona: Universitat Autònoma de Barcelona. CD-Rom.

Lane, J.E. and Ersson, S. (1987) *Politics and Society in Western Europe.* London: Sage Publications.

Laver, J. (1994) *Principles of Phonetics.* Cambridge: Cambridge University Press.

Lefebvre, C. (1998) *Creole Genesis and the Acquisition of Grammar: The Case of Haitian Creole.* Cambridge: Cambridge University Press.

Lehiste, I. (1988) *Lectures on Language Contact.* Cambridge: MIT Press.

Lei de Normalización Lingüística de Galicia [The Linguistic Normalisation Law of Galicia] (1983) 15/06/1983. On WWW at http://galego.org/lexislacion/xbasica/lei3–83.html, and http://www.ciberirmandade.org/cirman/arquivo/lexislac/normaliz.htm.

Leite de Vasconcelos, J. (1970) [(190)1] *Esquisse Dune Dialectologie Portugaise* [An Outline of Portuguese Dialectology]. (2nd edn). Lisbon: Centro de Estudos Filológicos.

Le Page, R.B. and Tabouret-Keller, A. (1985) *Acts of Identity. Creole-Based Approaches to Language and Ethnicity.* Cambridge: University Press.

Liebkind, K. (1999) Social psychology. In J. Fishman (ed.) *Handbook of Language and Ethnic Identity* (pp. 140–151). Oxford: Oxford University Press.

Lipski, J. (1975) On the Velarization of *n* in Galician. *Neuphilologische Mitteilungen* 76, 182–191.

Lipski, J. (1994) *Latin American Spanish.* London: Longman.

Livermore, H.V. (1966) *A New History of Portugal.* Cambridge: Cambridge University Press.

Llobera, J.R. (1994) *The God of Modernity: The Development of Nationalism in Western Europe.* Oxford: Berg.

Lodge, R.A. (1993) *French: From Dialect to Standard.* London: Routledge.

López Dobao, A. (1993) A lingua galega e a TVG: situación actual e propostas para unha nova política lingüística [The Galician language and the Galician television company: Present-day situation and proposals for a new linguistic policy]. *Cadernos de Lingua* 7, 27–44.

López Dobao, A. (1994) A lingua galega e a TVG: situación actual e propostas para unha nova política lingüística [The Galician language and the Galician television company: Present-day situation and proposals for a new linguistic policy]. *Cadernos de Lingua* 9, 27–53.

López Eire, A. (1989) Dialectología, sociolingüística e historia de la lengua: nuevas perspectivas para el idioma galego [Dialectology, sociolinguistics and history of language: New perspectives for Galician]. *Actas do II Congreso Internacional da Lingua Galego-Portuguesa na Galiza (1987)* (pp. 811–817). Santiago de Compostela: AGAL.

López Trigal, L. (2001) The Portuguese community. In M.T. Turell (ed.) *Multilingualism in Spain: Sociolinguistic and Psycholinguistic Aspects of Linguistic Minority Groups* (pp. 344–354). Clevedon: Multilingual Matters.

López Valcárcel, X. (1990) Normalización afectiva [Sentimental normalisation]. *Cadernos de Lingua* 2, 93–104.

López Valcárcel, X. (1991) Normalización e didáctica de lingua [The normalisation and didactics of language]. *Cadernos de Lingua* 4, 113–130.

Lorenzo, R. (1975) Gallego y português. Algunas semejanzas y diferencias [Galician and Portuguese: some similarities and differences]. In M. Studemund, H. Joseph Niedereche and H. Haarmann (eds) *Filología y Didáctica Hispánica. Homenaje al Profesor Hans-Karl Schneider* (pp. 155–171). Hamburg: Helmut Buske Verlag.

Mackey, W. (1970) The description of bilingualism. In J. Fishman (ed.) *Readings in the Sociology of Language* (pp. 554–584). The Hague: Mouton & Co.

Mackey, W. (2000). The description of bilingualism. In Li Wei (ed.) *The Bilingualism Reader* (pp. 26–54). London: Routledge.

Mackey, W. (2002). Changing paradigms in the study of bilingualism. In Li Wei, J.M. Dewaele and A. Housen (eds) *Opportunities and Challenges in Bilingualism* (pp. 328–344). Berlin: Mouton de Gruyter.

Mackey, W., Bastardas, A. and Boix, E. (1994) ¿Un Estado Una Lengua? La Organización Política de la Diversidad Lingüística [One State, One Language? The Political Organisation of Linguistic Diversity]. Barcelona: Octaedro.

Maíz, R. (1986) El nacionalismo gallego: apuntes para la historia de una hegemonía imposible [Galician nationalism: Notes concerning the history of an impossible hegemony]. In F. Hernández and F. Mercadé (eds) *Estructuras Sociales y Cuestión Nacional en España* (pp. 186–243). Barcelona: Editorial Ariel.

Mariño Paz, R. (1998) *Historia da Lingua Galega* [The History of the Galician Language]. Santiago de Compostela: Sotelo Blanco.

Mar-Molinero, F.C. (1997) *The Spanish-Speaking World: A Practical Introduction to Sociolinguistic Issues*. London: Routledge.

Mar-Molinero, F.C. (2000a) The Iberian Peninsula: Conflicting linguistic nationalisms. In S. Barbour and C. Carmichael (eds) *Language and Nationalism in Europe* (pp. 83–104). Oxford: Oxford University Press.

Mar-Molinero, F.C. (2000b) *The Politics of Language in the Spanish-Speaking World*. London: Routledge.

Martin-Jones, M. (1989) Language, power and linguistic minorities: The need for an alternative approach to bilingualism, language maintenance and shift. In R. Grillo (ed.) *Social Anthropology and the Politics of Language* (pp. 106–125). London: Routledge.

Martinez-Barbeito, C. (1971) *Galicia* (3rd edn). Barcelona: Destino.

Martinez Martín, F.M. (1983) *Fonética y Sociolinguística en la Ciudad de Burgos* [The Phonetics and Sociolinguistics of the City of Burgos] (pp. 30–124). CSIC: Madrid.

May, S. (2001) *Language and Minority Rights. Ethnicity, Nationalism and the Politics of Language*. London: Longman.

May, S. (2003) Misconceiving minority language rights: Implications for liberal political theory. In W. Kymlicka and A. Patten (eds) *Language Rights and Political Theory* (pp. 123–152). Oxford: Oxford University Press.

McMahon, A. (1994) *Understanding Language Change*. Cambridge: University Press.

Mercator Education: European Network for Regional or Minority Languages and Education (2001) *Galician. The Galician Language in Education in Spain*. On WWW at www.mercator-education.org.

Mesa pola Normalización Lingüística (2004). On WWW at http://clientes.vianetworks.es/colectivo/amesanl/.

Mesthrie, R., Swann, J., Deumert, A. and Leap, W.L. (2000) *Introducing Sociolinguistics*. Philadelphia: John Benjamins.

Mey, J. (1989) Saying it don't make it so: The 'Una Grande Libre' of language politics. *Multilingua* 8 (4), 333–355.

Milroy, J. and Milroy, L. (1997) Network structure and linguistic change. In N. Coupland and A. Jaworski (eds) *Sociolinguistics: A Reader and Coursebook* (pp. 199–211). Basingstoke: MacMillan.

Milroy, L. (1987) *Language and Social Networks* (2nd edn). Oxford: Blackwell.

Milroy, L. (2002) Social networks. In J.K. Chambers, P. Trudgill and N. Schilling-Estes (eds) *Handbook of Language Variation and Change* (pp. 549–572). Oxford: Blackwell.

Milroy, L. (in press) Off the shelf or under the counter? On the social dynamics of sound changes. In C. Cain and G. Russom (eds) *Shaking the Tree: Fresh Perspectives on the Genealogy of English*. Berlin: Mouton de Gruyter.

Milroy, L. and Gordon, M. (2003). Sociolinguistics: Method and Interpretation. Oxford: Blackwell.

Milroy, L. and Muysken, P. (1995) Introduction: Code-switching and bilingualism research. In L. Milroy and P. Muysken (eds) *One Speaker, Two Languages: Cross-Disciplinary Perspectives on Code-Switching* (pp. 1–14). Cambridge: Cambridge University Press.

Mioni, A.M. (1987) Domain. In U. Ammon, N. Ditmar and K.J. Mattheier (eds) *Sociolinguistics: An International Handbook of the Sciences of Language and Society* (Vol. 1) (pp. 170–177). Berlin: Walter de Gruyter.

Mira Mateus, M.H. (1987) *Fonologia do Galego e do Português. Actas do I Congreso Internacional da Lingua Galego-Portuguesa na Galiza* [The Phonology of Galician and of Portuguese. Proceedings of the First International Conference on the Galician-Portuguese Language in Galicia] (pp. 295–304). Corunha, Galicia: AGAL.

Monteagudo, H. (1995) Limiar [Introduction]. In H. Monteagudo (ed.) *Estudios de Sociolingüística Galega. Sobre a Norma do Galego Culto* (pp. 9–18). Vigo: Galaxia.

Monteagudo, H. (1999) *Historia Social da Lingua Galega. Idioma, Sociedade e Cultura a Través do Tempo* [The Social History of Galician. Language, Society and Culture across the Ages]. Vigo: Galaxia.

Monteagudo, H. (2000) *Castelao: Defensa e Ilustración do Idioma Galego* [Castelao: A Defence and Presentation of the Galician Language]. Vigo: Galaxia.

Monteagudo, H. and Santamarina, A. (1993) Galician and Castilian in contact: Historical, social and linguistic aspects. In R. Posner and J.N. Green (eds) *Trends in Romance Linguistics and Philology. Vol. 5: Bilingualism and Linguistic Conflict in Romance* (pp. 117–173). The Hague: Mouton.

Montero Santalha, X.M. (1980) *Directrices Para a Reintegración Lingüística Galego-Portuguesa* [Directives for the Linguistic Reintegration of Galician-Portuguese]. A Coruña: AS-PG/A Nosa Terra.

Montero Santalha, X.M. (1988) A pronúncia padrón galega: tentativa de formula-çom [The Galician pronunciation model: An attempt at its creation]. *ACTAS do I Congresso Internacional de Lingua galego-portuguesa na Galiza* (pp. 327–337). Santiago de Compostela: AGAL.

Morais Barbosa, J. (1961) Les voyelles nasales portugaises: interprétation pho-nologique [Portuguese nasal vowels: a phonological interpretation]. *Proceedings of the Fourth International Congress of Phonetic Sciences* (pp. 691–708). Helsinki.

Muljačic, Ž. (1986) L'enseignement de Heinz Kloss (Modifications, implications, perspectives) [The teachings of Heinz Kloss: Amendments, consequences, viewpoints]. In J.-B. Marcellesi (ed.) *Languages. Glottopolitique* (pp. 53–63). Paris: Larousse.

Muljačic, Ž. (1993) Standardization in Romance. In R. Posner and J.N. Green (eds) *Trends in Romance Linguistics and Philology* (Vol. 5) *Bilingualism and Linguistic Conflict in Romance* (pp. 77–116). The Hague: Mouton.

Muljačic, Ž. (1997) The Relationship between the dialects and the standard language. In M. Parry and M. Maiden (eds) *The Dialects of Italy* (pp. 387–393). London: Routledge.

Muñiz, C. (1978) *El Hable de Valledor: Estudio Descritivo del Gallego Asturiano de Allande* [The Speech of Valledor: A Descriptive Study of Allande Asturo-Galician]. Vigo: Galaxia.

Murphy, B., Diaz-Varela, C. and Coluccello, S. (2002) Transformation of the state in western Europe; regionalism in Catalonia and northern Italy. In P. Gubbins and M. Holt (eds) *Beyond Boundaries. Language and Identity in Contemporary Europe* (pp. 73–90). Clevedon: Multilingual Matters.

Myers-Scotton, C. (1992) Comparing code-switching and borrowing. *Journal of Multilingual and Multicultural Development* 13, 19–39.

Myers-Scotton, C. (1993) *Social Motivations for Code-Switching: Evidence from Africa.* Oxford: Oxford University Press.

Nelde, P.H. (1987) Research on language contact. In U. Ammon, N. Ditmar and K.J. Mattheier (eds) *Sociolinguistics: An International Handbook of the Sciences of Languages and Society* (Vol. 1) (pp. 598–612). Berlin: Walter de Gruyter.

Ninyoles, R.L. (1969) *Conflicte Lingüístic Valencià* [The Valencian Linguistic Conflict]. València: Tres i Quatre.

Ninyoles, R. (1975) *Estructura Social i Política Lingüistica* [Social Structure and Linguistic Policy]. Alzira: Bromera.

Nogueira, C. (1996) Sobre as orixes da cuestión nacional galega: a división de Gallaecia e a creación do Estado Portugués [On the origins of the Galician national question: the division of Gallaecia and the creation of the Portuguese nation-state]. *A Trabe de Ouro* 25, 11–79.

Noia Campos, M.C. (1988) Usos e actitudes lingüísticas na "Epoca Nós" [Linguistic uses and attitudes in the *Nós* Era]. *Grial* 100, 174–182.

Nova Escola Galega (2004) *Normalización en Galicia* [Normalisation in Galicia]. On WWW at http://www.nova-escola-galega.org/Normalizacion/Situacion_actual.htm.

Nunes de Leão, D. (1983) [1606] *Origem: Ortografia e Origem da Língua Portuguesa* [Origins: Orthography and the Origins of the Portuguese Language]. (5th edn). Lisboa: Imprense Nacional Casa da Moeda.

Oliveira, P. (2004) *Sobre Galicia* [On Galicia]. On WWW at http://www.galicia-hoxe.com/periodico20041020/Mare/N45860).asp. Accessed October 2004.

Padilla, A.M. (1999) Psychology. In J.A. Fishman (ed.) *Handbook of Language and Ethnic Identity* (pp. 109–121). Oxford: Oxford University Press.

Parkinson, S. (1983) Portuguese nasal vowels as phonological diphthongs. *Lingua* 61, 157–177.

Parkinson, S. (1987) Portuguese nasal vowels: Phonology and morphology. Paper presented at the *Congresso Sobre a Situação Actual da Língua Portuguesa no Mundo* (pp. 11–15). Lisbon.

Paulston, C. (1997) Epilogue: Some concluding thoughts on linguistic human rights. *International Journal of the Sociology of Language* 127, 187–197.

Pavlenko, A. and Blackledge, A. (eds) (2003) *Negotiation of Identities in Multilingual Contexts*. Clevedon: Multilingual Matters.

Penny, R. (2000) *Variation and Change in Spanish*. Cambridge: Cambridge University Press.

Penny, R. (2002) *A History of the Spanish Language* (2nd edn). Cambridge: Cambridge University Press.

Pensado, J.L. (1982) La lexicología gallega en el siglo XVIII [Galician lexicology in the 18th Century]. In D. Kremer and R. Lorenzo (eds) *Tradición, Actualidade e Futuro do Galego. Actas do Coloquio de Tréveris*. Xunta de Galicia.

Pensado, J.L. (1983) De nuevo sobre la gueada y geada gallegas [The Galician *gueada* and *geada* Revisited]. In J.L. Pensado and C. Pensado Ruiz (eds) *Gueada y Geada Gallegas*. Verba, Anexo 21, 9–92.

Pensado Ruiz, C. (1983) La geada, un cambio natural? [Is the *geada* a natural phonetic change?] In J.L. Pensado and C. Pensado Ruiz (eds) *Gueada y geada gallegas*. Verba, Anexo 21, 95–128.

Pérez-Barreiro Nolla, F. (1990) Which language for Galicia? The status of Galician as an official language and the prospects for its reintegration with Portuguese. *Portuguese Studies*, 6 (pp. 91–210). Dept. of Portuguese, Kings College, London.

Pérez Pascual, J.I. (1982) Observaciones en torno a la desaparición de la -N-intervocálica en gallego [Observations on the Disappearance of Intervocalic -N- in Galician]. *Verba* 9, 201–213.

Piñeiro, R. (1973) Carta a D. Manuel Rodrigues Lapa [Letter to D. Manuel Rodrigues Lapa]. *Grial* 42, 389–402.

Pittau, M. (1975) *Problemi di Lingua Sarda* [The Problem with the Sardinian Language]. Sassari: Libreria Dessi Editrice.

Poplack, S. (1980) Sometimes I'll start a sentence in Spanish Y TERMINO EN ESPANOL: Toward a typology of code-switching. *Linguistics* 18, 581–618.

Poplack, S. (1984) Variable concord and sentential plural marking in Puerto Rican Spanish. *Hispanic Review* 52 (2), 205–222.

Poplack, S. and Meechan, M. (1998) Introduction: How languages fit together in codemixing. *International Journal of Bilingualism* 2, 127–138.

Poplack, S. and Sankoff, D. (1988) Code-switching. In U. Ammon, N. Ditmar and K.J. Mattheier (eds) *Sociolinguistics: An International Handbook of the Sciences of Languages and Society* (Vol. 2) (pp. 1174–1180). Berlin: Walter de Gruyter.

Portas, M. (1999) *Lingua e Sociedade na Galiza* [Language and Society in Galicia]. Bahia: A Coruña.

Porto Dapena, J.A. (1991) El gallego hablado en la comarca ferrolana [The Galician spoken in the administrative district of El Ferrol]. *Verba*, Anejo 9. Santiago de Compostela: Universidad de Santiago de Compostela.

Pountain, C. (2003) *Exploring the Spanish Language*. London: Arnold.

Pride, J.B. and Holmes, J. (1972) *Sociolinguistics*. Middlesex: Penguin.

Prieto Alonso, D. (1980) Algunhas hipóteses sobre a geada [Some hypotheses on the *geada*]. *Verba* 7, 223–241.

Promotora Española de Lingüística (PROEL) (2005) *El Mundo Gallego* [The Galician World]. On WWW at http://www.proel.org/mundo/gallego.htm.

Puig i Pla (1997) La declaració de drets lingüistics. *Llengua i Us*, 8: 4–7.

Rabade Castinheira, C. and Alonso Estravis, I. (1985) *Prontuário Ortográfico Galego* [A Handbook of Galician Orthography]. Vigo: Universália.

Rábade Paredes, X. (1993) Situación e perspectivas da normalización no ensino [Situation and perspectives of normalisation in teaching]. *Cadernos de Lingua* 7, 45–52.

Ramanathan, V. (2005) Ambiguities about English: Ideologies and critical practice in vernacular-medium college classrooms in Gujarat, India. *Journal of Language, Identity and Education* 4 (1), 45–65.

Rampton, B. (1995) *Crossing: Language and Ethnicity Among Adolescents*. London: Longman.

Rampton, B. (1998) Language crossing and the redefinition of reality. In P. Auer (ed.) *Code-switching in Conversation: Language, Interaction and Identity* (pp. 290–320). London: Routledge.

Ray, P.S. (1963) *Language Standardization*. The Hague: Mouton.

Real Academia Galega (RAG) (1998) *Diccionario da Real Academia Galega* [Dictionary of the Royal Galician Academy]. (2nd edn). A Coruña: Galaxia.

Real Academia Galega (RAG) and Instituto de Língua Galega (ILG) (2004) *Normas Ortográficas e Morfolóxicas do Idioma Galego* [Orthographic and Morphological Standards of the Galician Language]. (19th edn). Santiago de Compostela.

Real Academia Española (RAE) (2005) Official Website. On WWW at www.rae.es.

Rebollo, E.O. (1981) *Estatuto de Autonomía de Galicia: Estudio Preliminar, Notas e Índice* [The Galician Statute of Independence: a Preliminary Study, with Notes and Index]. Madrid: Instituto de Estudios de Administracion Local.

Recalde, M. (1995) Unha aproximación ás actitudes e prexuízos cara á gheada [An estimate of the attitudes and prejudices towards the *gheada*]. *Cadernos de Lingua* 11, 5–31.

Recalde, M. (2003) [The Castilianist theory of the origin of the *gheada* revisted]. *Estudios de Sociolingüística* 3, 2 and 4 (1), 43–74.

Recasens, I. and Vives, D. (1986) *Estudis de Fonètica Experimental del Català Oriental Central* [An Instrumental Phonetics Study of Central Eastern Catalan]. Barcelona: Abadia.

Regueira Fernández, X.L. (1989) *A Fala do Norte da Terra Cha: Estudio Descritivo* [The Speech of the Northern Parts of *Terra Cha*: A Descriptive Study]. Santiago de Compostela: Santiago de Compostela University Press.

Regueira Fernández, X.L. (1994) Modelos fonéticos e autenticidade lingüística [Phonetic models and linguistic authenticity]. *Cadernos de Lingua* 10, 37–60.

Regueira Fernández, X.L. (1999) Galician. In *Handbook of the International Phonetic Association* (IPA) (pp. 82–85). Cambridge: Cambridge University Press.

Regueira Fernández, X.L. (2004) Estándar oral [The oral standard]. In R. Álvarez and H. Monteagudo (eds) *Norma Lingüística e Variación. Unha Perspectiva Desde o Idioma Galego* [Linguistic Norms and Variation. A Perspective of the Galician Language] (pp. 69–96). Santiago de Compostela: Consello da Cultura Galega/Instituto da Lingua Galega.

Regueira Fernández, X.L. (2006) Política y lengua en Galicia: La 'normalización' de la lengua gallega [Language and politics in Galicia: The 'normalisation' of the Galician language]. In J. Kabatek and M. Castillo-Lluch (eds) *Las Lenguas de*

Silva Neto, S. da (1979) *História da Língua Portuguesa* [History of the Portuguese Language]. Rio de Janeiro, Ed. Presença.

Silva Valdivia, B. (1991) Tipoloxía das Manifestacións de Contacto Lingüístico en Galicia. Algunhas Consideracións [A Typology of Linguistic Contact Scenario in Galicia. Some Considerations]. *Cadernos de Lingua* 4, 27–38.

Skutnabb-Kangas, T. (1981) *Bilingualism or not: The Education of Minorities*. (L. Malmberg and D. Crane, trans). Clevedon: Multilingual Matters.

Skutnabb-Kangas, T. (2000) *Linguistic Genocide in Education – or Worldwide Diversity and Human Rights?* London: Lawrence Erlbaum Associates.

Skutnabb-Kangas, T. (2003) *Can a "Linguistic Human Rights Approach" "Deliver"? Reflections on Complementarities, Tensions and Misconceptions in Attempts at Multidisciplinarities.* Keynote paper at the International conference on Language, Education and Diversity, University of Waikato, Hamilton, Aotearoa/New Zealand, 26–29 November 2003.

Smith, A.D. (1991) *National Identity*. Harmondsworth: Penguin.

Smolicz, J.J. (1981) Core values and cultural identity. *Ethnic and Racial Studies* 4 (1), 75–90.

Smolicz, J.J. (1991) Language core values in a multicultural setting. *International Review of Education* 37 (1), 35–52.

Smolicz, J.J. (1997) In search of a multicultural nation: The case of Australia from an international perspective. In R.J. Watts and J.J. Smolicz (eds) *Cultural Democracy and Ethnic Pluralism. Multicultural and Multilingual Policies in Education* (pp. 52–76). Frankfurt: Peter Lang.

Stein, D. (1989) Markedness and linguistic change. In O. Miseska Tomić (ed.) *Markedness in Synchrony and Diachrony* (pp. 67–86). Berlin: Mouton de Gruyter.

Strubell i Trueta, M. (1993) Catalan: Castilian. In R. Posner and J.N. Green (eds) *Trends in Romance Linguistics and Philology Vol. 5: Bilingualism and Linguistic Conflict in Romance* (pp. 175–207). The Hague: Mouton.

Strubell i Trueta, M. (1998) Language, democracy and devolution in Catalonia. *Current Issues in Language and Society* 5 (3), 146–180.

Taboada, C.M. (1979) El habla del Valle de Verín [The speech of the Valle de Verín]. Santiago de Compostela, *Verba*, Anejo 15.

Teyssier, P. (1990) *História da Língua Portuguesa* [History of the Portuguese Language]. (4th edn). Lisbon: Sá da Costa.

Thomason, S. and Kaufman, T. (1988) *Language Contact, Creolization, and Genetic Linguistics*. Berkeley: University of California Press.

Treffers-Daller, J. (1994) *Mixing Two Languages: French-Dutch Contact in a Comparative Perspective*. Berlin: Mouton de Gruyter.

Treffers-Daller, J. (1998) Variability in code-switching styles: Turkish-German code-switching patterns. In R. Jacobson (ed.) *Codeswitching Worldwide* (pp. 177–198). New York: Mouton de Gruyter.

Trotsky, L. (1931) *The Revolution in Spain*. Source pamphlet (1952). San Francisco: Bolerium Books.

Trudgill, P. (1974) *The Social Differentiation of English in Norwich*. Cambridge: Cambridge University Press.

Trudgill, P. (1983) *Sociolinguistics: An Introduction to Language and Society*. Harmondsworth: Penguin.

Trudgill, P. (1984) *Applied Sociolinguistics*. Middlesex: Penguin.

Trudgill, P. (1992) *Introducing Language and Society*. London: Penguin.

Turi, J. (1994) Typology of language legislation. In T. Skutnabb-Kangas and R. Phillipson (eds) *Linguistic Human Rights. Overcoming Linguistic Discrimination.*

Contributions to the Sociology of Language 67 (pp. 111–121). Berlin: Mouton de Gruyter.

Tuttle, E.F. (1991) Nasalization in northern Italy: Syllabic constraints and strength scales as developmental parameters. *Rivista di linguistica* 3, 23–55.

Valcárcel Riveiro, C. (2002) *Do Rural ó Urbano: Tentativa Dunha Análise Xeolingüística do Concello de Pontevedra* [From the Rural to the Urban: A Provisional Geolinguistic Analysis of the Administrative District of Pontevedra]. Vigo: Diputación Provincial de Pontevedra.

Valdman, A. (1988) Diglossia and language conflict in Haiti. *International Journal of the Sociology of Language* 71, 67–80.

Valladares Nuñez, M. (1970) [1892] *Elementos de Gramática Galega* [Elements of Galician Grammar]. Vigo: Editorial Galaxia.

Vallverdú, F. (1970) *Dues Ilengües: Dues Functions?* [Two Languages: Two Functions?] Barcelona: Edicions 62.

Varela Barreiro, F.X. (1991) *Vocabulario de Restaurants* [A Vocabulary of Restaurants]. Santiago de Compostela: Xunta de Galicia Consellería de Educación e Ordenación Universitaria.

Vásquez Corredoira, F. (1998) *A Construção da Lingua Portuguesa Frente ao Castelhano: o Galego Como Exemplo a Contrario* [The Construction of the Portuguese Language compared with that of Castilian, with Galician as a Contrast]. Santiago de Compostela: Edicións Laiovento.

Vázquez Cuesta, P. and Mendes da Luz, M.A. (1971) *Gramática da Língua Portuguesa* [A Grammar of the Portuguese Language]. Lisbon: Edições 70.

Veiga Arias, A. (1976) *Fonología Galega* [Galician Phonology]. Valencia: Bello.

Veiga Arias, A. (1998) *Estudios Lingüísticos: Galicia Medieval* [Linguistic Studies: Medieval Galicia]. A Coruña: Edicios do Castro.

Vieiros (2005) *Censo de 1991* [The 1991 Census]. On WWW at www.galego.org./hoxe/nivelxeral/censo.html.

Vikin, J. (2000) *Galician-English, English-Galician Concise Dictionary*. New York: Hippocrene.

Vilariño, J.P. (1987) Rasgos característicos de la identidad nacional galega [Characteristic traits of the Galician national identity]. *Comportamiento Electoral y Nacionalismo en Cataluña, Galicia y País Vasco*. Universidade de Santiago de Compostela, Servicio de Publicacións.

Villar, R. (2001) *CIG-Ensino e AS-PG Denúncian o Incumprimento do Decreto 247/95 de Normalización do Galego* [CIG-Ensino and the AS-PG denounce the non-implementation of Decree 247/95 on Galician linguistic normalisation]. On WWW at http://www.galizacig.com/index.html.

Villares, R. (1985) *História de Galicia* [History of Galicia]. Madrid: Alianza.

Wardhaugh, R. (1987) *Languages in Competition: Dominance, Diversity and Decline*. Oxford: Blackwell.

Wardhaugh, R. (2002) *An Introduction to Sociolinguistics* (4th edn). Malden, Massachusetts: Blackwell.

Watts, R.J. (1997) Introduction. In R.J. Watts and J.J. Smolicz (eds) *Cultural Democracy and Ethnic Pluralism. Multicultural and Multilingual Policies in Education* (pp. 9–21). Frankfurt: Peter Lang.

Weinreich, U. (1953) *Languages in Contact*. New York: Linguistic Circle of New York.

Weinreich, U. (1966) *Languages in Contact* (2nd edn). The Hague: Mouton.

Williams, C. (ed.) (1982) *National Separatism*. Cardiff: University of Wales Press.

Williams, C. (ed.) (1988) *Language in Geographic Context*. Clevedon: Multilingual Matters.

Williams, C.H. (1991) *Linguistic Minorities: Society and Territory.* Clevedon: Multilingual Matters.

Williams, C.H. (1994) *Called unto Liberty! On Language and Nationalism.* Clevedon: Multilingual Matters.

Williams, C.H. (1997) Territory, identity and language. In M. Keating and J. Loughlin (eds) *The Political Economy of Regionalism.* London: Frank Cass, pp. 112–138.

Williams, C.H. (2003) The revival of the Welsh language: Planning, economy and territory. Plaid Cymru discussion paper. On WWW at www.plaidcymru.org/plaid_policy_revival_of_the_welsh_language_ept.pdf.

Williams, G. (1979) Language group allegiance and ethnic interaction. In H. Giles and B. Saint-Jacques (eds) *Language and Ethnic Relations* (pp. 57–65). Oxford: Pergamon.

Williams, G. (1992) *Sociolinguistics: A Sociological Critique.* London: Routledge.

Williamson, R.C. and Williamson, V.L. (1984) Selected factors in bilingualism: the case of Galicia. *Journal of Multilingual and Multicultural Development* 5, 401–413.

Willis, C. (1984) *An Essential Course in Modern Portuguese*, Revised Edition. Surrey, UK: Thomas Nelson & Sons Ltd.

Woolard, K.A. (1989a) *Double Talk: Bilingualism and the Politics of Ethnicity in Catalonia.* Standford: Standford University Press.

Woolard, K.A. (1989b) Language convergence and language death as social processes. In N.C. Dorian (ed.) *Investigating Obsolescence: Studies in Language Contact and Death* (pp. 355–368). Cambridge: Cambridge University Press.

Xunta de Galicia (1989) *Lexislación Actualizada Sobre a Lingua Galega* [Present-day Legislation on the Galician Language]. Santiago de Compostela.

Xunta de Galicia (2005a) Official Website. On WWW at http://www.xunta.es/.

Xunta de Galicia, Consellería de Educación e Ordenación Universitaria and Dirección Xeral de Política Lingüísticas (2005b) *Plano Xeral de Normalización Lingüística* (PNL) [General Plan for the Linguistic Normalisation of the Galician Language]. On WWW at http://www.consellodacultura.org/arquivos/cdsg/docs/plandenormalizacionlinguagalega.pdf.

Yaeger-Dror, M. (1988) Sound change in progress. In U. Ammon, N. Ditmar and K.J. Mattheier (eds) *Sociolinguistics: An International Handbook of the Sciences of Languages and Society* (Vol. 2) (pp. 1591–1602). Berlin: Walter de Gruyter.

Zamora Munné, J.C. and Guitart, J.M. (1982) *Dialectologia Hispanoamericana* [Hispanic American Dialectology]. Salamanca: Ediciones Almar.

Zamora Vicente, A. (1953) De geografia dialectal: *-ao, -an* en gallego [Dialectal geography: *-ao, -an* in Galician]. *Nueva Revista de Filologia Hispánica* 7, 73–80.

Zamora Vicente, A. (1967) *Dialectología Española* [Spanish Dialectology]. (2nd edn). Madrid: Gredos.

Zamora Vicente, A. (1986) *Estudios de Dialectología Hispánica.* [Studies in Hispanic Dialectology]. Santiago de Compostela, Universidad de Santiago de Compostela.

Index

Passim indicates numerous mentions within page range; *ns* refers to endnotes; *a* refers to appendices.

317

A Discourse on Domination in Mandate Palestine

British discourse during the Mandate, with its unremitting convergence on the problematic of the 'native questions', and which rested on racial and cultural theories and presumptions, as well as on certain givens drawn from the British class system, has been taken for granted by historians. The validity of cultural representations as pronounced within official correspondence and colonial laws and regulations, as well as within the private papers of colonial officials, survives more or less intact. There are features of colonialism additional to economic and political power, which are glaring yet have escaped examination, which carried cultural weight and had cultural implications and which negatively transformed native society. This was inevitable. But what is less inevitable is the subsequent collusion of historians in this, a (neo-) colonial dynamic. The continued collusion of modern historians with racial and cultural notions concerning the rationale of European rule in Palestine has postcolonial implications. It drags these old notions into the present where their iniquitous barbarity continues to manifest. This study identifies the symbolism of British officials' discourse and intertwines it with the symbolism and imagery of the natives' own discourse (from oral interviews and private family papers). At all times, it remains allied to those writers, philosophers and chroniclers whose central preoccupation is to agitate and challenge author-ity. This, then, is a return to the Old School, a revisiting of the optimistic, vibrant rhetoric of those radicals who continue to inspire post- and anti-colonial thinking. In order to dismantle, and to undo and unwrite, *A Discourse on Domination in Mandate Palestine* holds a mirror up to the language of the Mandatory by counteracting it with its own integrally oppositional discourse and a provocative rhetoric.

Zeina B. Ghandour trained as a lawyer. She has since lived and worked in several of the world's 'troublespots'. Her first novel, *The Honey*, was published in 1999 and her short pieces have appeared in anthologies and magazines. She cu'   teaches Law.